Teacher's Edition

AUTHORS

Vesta A. H. Daniel

Lee Hanson

Kristen Pederson Marstaller

Susana R. Monteverde

Harcourt Brace & Company

Orlando   Atlanta   Austin   Boston   San Francisco   Chicago   Dallas   New York   Toronto   London

http://www.hbschool.com

Copyright © 1998 by Harcourt Brace & Company

All rights reserved. No part of this publication may be reproduced or transmitted in any form or by any means, electronic or mechanical, including photocopy, recording, or any information storage and retrieval system, without permission in writing from the publisher.

Teachers using ART EXPRESS may photocopy Copying Masters in complete pages in sufficient quantities for classroom use only and not for resale.

HARCOURT BRACE and Quill Design is a registered trademark of Harcourt Brace & Company. ART EXPRESS is a trademark of Harcourt Brace & Company.

Printed in the United States of America

ISBN 0-15-309078-2

6 7 8 9 10   059   2003 2002

Dear Educator,

Teaching the arts is an essential part of educating a child. The arts unlock children's creativity and open new pathways to learning. Research shows that the arts help students develop proficiency in critical thinking and aesthetic judgment.

Another compelling reason to teach the arts is *literacy*. Literacy in today's world no longer means simply reading and writing the language of written prose. Today, literacy must be multisensory—students must be able to make informed decisions in an environment teeming with sensory data.

Art Express **helps students see the world around them in new ways.** The core of *Art Express* is its collection of high-quality fine art reproductions representing a variety of artists, media, styles, and periods. The artworks serve as a springboard for the sequential, spiraling development of concepts and techniques.

Art Express **fosters appreciation of self and others.** Students view a wide variety of contemporary and classic artworks to help them better understand themselves and the world around them. Production activities encourage artistic expression of the student's own culture and heritage.

Art Express **promotes critical thinking.** Artworks organized into thematic units provide a framework in which students can relate the images to each other; to music, drama, and dance; to other content areas; and to their own experiences. Students exercise critical thinking skills through activities requiring visual discrimination, analysis, and evaluation.

Art Express **encourages creativity.** The program fosters creative thinking by offering a variety of options for imaginative expression and problem solving. Instruction develops behaviors that are essential not only to students' artistic development but also to their future careers and their contributions as citizens.

Art Express **meets the needs of teachers and students in a broad range of classroom environments.** To ensure that the arts are accessible to *all* students, the program provides a variety of strategies to help teachers adapt instruction to the needs of the heterogeneous classroom.

Whether your art curriculum is based on direct instruction of art elements and principles or is guided by related content-area lessons, *Art Express* will streamline your preparation and instruction and make your students' art experiences more lasting, meaningful, and fun.

Sincerely,

The Authors

AUTHORS

Dr. Vesta A. H. Daniel
Associate Professor of Art Education

**Department of Art Education
The Ohio State University
Columbus, Ohio**

The artworks selected for these texts represent art from across the country and around the world. Through these examples, students have the opportunity to consider the uniqueness of as well as the similarities among artists, including children and adults, women and men, and people who are culturally and ethnically varied.

As distant points on the globe become more accessible to us through technology, the need to explore increases. That exploration can begin with hometown artists and develop into a wonderful journey to new worlds of art that inform and enrich our lives.

"Art communicates powerful ideas in powerful ways."

Dr. Lee Hanson
Art Coordinator

**Palo Alto Unified School District
Palo Alto, California**

"Imagination is more important than information." —Albert Einstein

Art communicates powerful ideas in powerful ways. Quality art experiences—with all their potential for expression, creative problem solving, decision making, analysis, critical thinking, and imagination—provide meaningful opportunities to engage students with those ideas.

When a substantive art program is introduced as part of the core curriculum (alongside those other challenging subjects we call "the three Rs"), amazing things can happen. Classrooms are filled with a sense of adventure as students create and interpret artworks. Lively discussions about the purpose and value of art add to the feeling of excitement. Through examining art, history suddenly comes alive.

In the bright world of the twenty-first century, it is essential that all our young people have access to the arts so that they may gain a deeper understanding of themselves, their culture, and their civilization.

"The language of visual communication should be enjoyed by children of all ages."

Kristen Pederson Marstaller
Art Coordinator

Austin Independent School District
Austin, Texas

Creative activity is an expression of a child's mental growth in spatial and artistic awareness, sensing, and intuition; it is a natural outcome of children's experiences. Consistent experiences with art materials enable children to "practice" being creative and inventive and suggest that a creative approach to life is a significant and valued kind of human behavior. Through art activities, children can use their minds to build, invent, experiment, and find different answers to the same problems.

Visual images communicate qualities of experiences that often cannot easily be put into words. The language of visual communication should be enjoyed by children of all ages.

Susana R. Monteverde
Art Museum Education Consultant

Houston, Texas

When we ask students to imagine what they might hear or smell if they were in a landscape, or when we ask them to create a story that explains the relationship between people in a portrait, we are asking them to interact with works of art. Interaction, according to current research in educational theory, is key to the construction of knowledge. Moreover, when we invite students to re-create a sculpture with their bodies or to compose a piece of music for a painting, we are inviting them into art through different points of entry. These points of entry, or perspectives, enable students to learn by using the multiple intelligences they possess.

By providing students with many opportunities to interact with works of art and by allowing students to access their many intelligences, educators in the arts teach students how to make works of art come to life throughout their entire lives, whether in the museum or the art classroom, or through a chance encounter.

CONTENTS

Dear Educator iii
Authors iv
Looking at Art 10
Keeping a Sketchbook 12

UNIT 1  **Seeing Is Believing** • 14A

ART PRINTS	14B
UNIT PLANNER	14C
INTRODUCING THE UNIT	14

LESSON 1	Images of Nature	16
LESSON 2	Light and Shadow	18
CONNECTIONS	The Natural Art of Barbara Bash ART AND LITERATURE	20
LESSON 3	The Illusion of Distance	22
LESSON 4	Into the Scene	24
CONNECTIONS	Set Designer CAREERS IN ART	26
LESSON 5	Impressions of Light	28
LESSON 6	Showing Movement	30

REFLECTING AND REVIEWING 32

UNIT 2 Viewpoints. 34A

ART PRINTS	34B
UNIT PLANNER	34C
INTRODUCING THE UNIT	34

LESSON 7	Portraits	36
LESSON 8	Colors and Feelings	38
CONNECTIONS	Magazine Art ART AND CULTURE	40
LESSON 9	Mosaics	42
LESSON 10	Images that Inspire	44
CONNECTIONS	Heroic Statues COMMUNITY ART	46
LESSON 11	The Power of the Poster	48
LESSON 12	Pop Art	50

REFLECTING AND REVIEWING ... 52

CONTENTS vii

Unexpected Art. 54A

ART PRINTS 54B
UNIT PLANNER 54C
INTRODUCING THE UNIT 54

| LESSON 13 | Experimenting with Space 56
| LESSON 14 | The Art of Illusion 58

CONNECTIONS — Can You Believe Your Eyes?
EVERYDAY ART 60

| LESSON 15 | Imaginary Worlds 62
| LESSON 16 | Assembled Art 64

CONNECTIONS — The Power of Art
COMMUNITY ART 66

| LESSON 17 | Double Takes 68
| LESSON 18 | Outdoor Spectacles 70

REFLECTING AND REVIEWING 72

viii   ART EXPRESS

Harmony and Conflict • 74A

ART PRINTS 74B
UNIT PLANNER 74C
INTRODUCING THE UNIT 74

LESSON 19	Feelings of Harmony 76
LESSON 20	A Sense of Excitement 78
CONNECTIONS	The Lively Art of David Diaz ART AND LITERATURE 80
LESSON 21	In Balance 82
LESSON 22	Colors in Conflict 84
CONNECTIONS	Art on Parade CELEBRATION ART 86
LESSON 23	Visual Rhythms 88
LESSON 24	Lines of Expression 90

REFLECTING AND REVIEWING 92

CONTENTS   ix

UNIT 5 — New Ways to Create • 94A

ART PRINTS 94B
UNIT PLANNER 94C
INTRODUCING THE UNIT 94

LESSON 25	Book Art 96
LESSON 26	Is Photography Art? 98
CONNECTIONS	The Photographic Art of George Ancona — ART AND LITERATURE 100
LESSON 27	Sculptures Through Time 102
LESSON 28	The World of Animation 104
CONNECTIONS	Computer Animator — CAREERS IN ART 106
LESSON 29	Celebrations in Stone 108
LESSON 30	Unusual Architecture 110

REFLECTING AND REVIEWING 112

x ART EXPRESS

UNIT 6 Heritage and Change • 114A

ART PRINTS 114B
UNIT PLANNER 114C
INTRODUCING THE UNIT 114

LESSON 31	Stories on Walls 116
LESSON 32	Centuries in Clay 118
CONNECTIONS	African Adobe Architecture ART AND CULTURE 120
LESSON 33	A Timeless Art 122
LESSON 34	Patchwork Art 124
CONNECTIONS	The Artrain COMMUNITY ART 126
LESSON 35	Artwork to Wear 128
LESSON 36	Faces from Folk Art 130

REFLECTING AND REVIEWING 132

Art Safety 134

CONTENTS   xi

Resources

STUDENT RESOURCES 135A

TEACHER RESOURCES R16

MEDIA AND TECHNIQUES R17

ASSESSMENT R26

MEETING INDIVIDUAL NEEDS R32

SEASONAL ACTIVITIES R38

COPYING MASTERS
    Home Letters R44
    School-Home Connections R50
    Response Cards R56

MATERIALS R66

FOR YOUR INFORMATION R69
    Books, articles, technology, and videos

ACROSS THE CURRICULUM R74
    Charts and Correlations

SCOPE AND SEQUENCE R84

INDEX R88

ART Express

AUTHORS

Vesta A. H. Daniel

Lee Hanson

Kristen Pederson Marstaller

Susana R. Monteverde

Harcourt Brace & Company

Orlando Atlanta Austin Boston San Francisco Chicago Dallas New York Toronto London

http://www.hbschool.com

Copyright © 1998 by Harcourt Brace & Company

All rights reserved. No part of this publication may be reproduced or transmitted in any form or by any means, electronic or mechanical, including photocopy, recording, or any information storage and retrieval system, without permission in writing from the publisher.

Requests for permission to make copies of any part of the work should be mailed to: Permissions Department, Harcourt Brace & Company, 6277 Sea Harbor Drive, Orlando, Florida 32887-6777.

HARCOURT BRACE and Quill Design is a registered trademark of Harcourt Brace & Company.
ART EXPRESS is a trademark of Harcourt Brace & Company.

Printed in the United States of America

ISBN 0-15-309317-X

1 2 3 4 5 6 7 8 9 10 098 2000 99 98 97

Dear Students,

Why do people create art? Do they do it to share their thoughts and feelings? To show the beauty of the world? To explore the human imagination? Whatever the reason, it must be a very powerful one, because people have been creating art since the beginning of human history. In fact, archaeologists are finding earlier and earlier works of art, created thousands of years ago.

The artworks you will discover in this book come to us from across the centuries and from around the world. They vary in age from the earliest cave paintings to the latest computer animations. They vary in form from a twisted piece of wire to a carved block of marble to a soaring cathedral.

In this book you will view the masterpieces of artists from many cultures. You will also develop your own skills and stretch your own imagination. As you try your hand at painting, sculpting, weaving, and other art forms, you, like all artists before you, will create art.

Sincerely,

The Authors

CONTENTS

Dear Students • 3
Looking at Art • 10
Keeping a Sketchbook • 12

UNIT 1 Seeing Is Believing • 14

LESSON	1	Images of Nature 16
		DRAWING ORGANIC AND GEOMETRIC SHAPES
LESSON	2	Light and Shadow 18
		DRAWING EVERYDAY FORMS
CONNECTIONS		The Natural Art of Barbara Bash ... 20
		ART AND LITERATURE
LESSON	3	The Illusion of Distance 22
		SHOWING DEPTH
LESSON	4	Into the Scene 24
		USING LINEAR PERSPECTIVE
CONNECTIONS		Set Designer 26
		CAREERS IN ART
LESSON	5	Impressions of Light 28
		PAINTING A REFLECTION
LESSON	6	Showing Movement 30
		MAKING A WIRE SCULPTURE

REFLECTING AND REVIEWING 32

UNIT 2 Viewpoints • 34

LESSON	7	Portraits 36
		DRAWING A PORTRAIT
LESSON	8	Colors and Feelings 38
		PAINTING THE PAST
CONNECTIONS		Magazine Art 40
		ART AND CULTURE
LESSON	9	Mosaics 42
		MAKING A MOSAIC
LESSON	10	Images That Inspire 44
		MAKING A PHOTOMONTAGE
CONNECTIONS		Heroic Statues..................... 46
		COMMUNITY ART
LESSON	11	The Power of the Poster 48
		DESIGNING A PERSUASIVE POSTER
LESSON	12	Pop Art 50
		CREATING AN IMPASTO PAINTING

REFLECTING AND REVIEWING 52

UNIT 3 Unexpected Art • 54

LESSON	13	Experimenting with Space 56
		USING POSITIVE AND NEGATIVE SPACE
LESSON	14	The Art of Illusion 58
		EXPERIMENTING WITH COLORS
CONNECTIONS		Can You Believe Your Eyes? 60
		EVERYDAY ART
LESSON	15	Imaginary Worlds 62
		MAKING A DIORAMA
LESSON	16	Assembled Art 64
		CREATING AN ASSEMBLAGE
CONNECTIONS		The Power of Art.................. 66
		COMMUNITY ART
LESSON	17	Double Takes 68
		MAKING IMPOSSIBLE PAINTINGS
LESSON	18	Outdoor Spectacles 70
		MAKING A PAPIER-MÂCHÉ MODEL

REFLECTING AND REVIEWING 72

UNIT 4 Harmony and Conflict • 74

LESSON	19	Feelings of Harmony 76
		PAINTING WITH WATERCOLORS
LESSON	20	A Sense of Excitement 78
		SHOWING CONTRAST AND MOVEMENT
CONNECTIONS		The Lively Art of David Diaz 80
		ART AND LITERATURE
LESSON	21	In Balance 82
		CREATING A MOBILE
LESSON	22	Colors in Conflict 84
		MAKING A COLLAGE
CONNECTIONS		Art on Parade 86
		CELEBRATION ART
LESSON	23	Visual Rhythms 88
		MAKING A PRINT WITH VISUAL RHYTHM
LESSON	24	Lines of Expression 90
		PAINTING A LANDSCAPE

REFLECTING AND REVIEWING 92

UNIT 5 New Ways to Create • 94

LESSON	**25**	Book Art 96
		DESIGNING A BOOK COVER
LESSON	**26**	Is Photography Art? 98
		MAKING A PHOTOGRAM
CONNECTIONS		The Photographic Art of George Ancona 100
		ART AND LITERATURE
LESSON	**27**	Sculptures Through Time 102
		SCULPTING WITH TWO MATERIALS
LESSON	**28**	The World of Animation 104
		CREATING A FLIP BOOK
CONNECTIONS		Computer Animator 106
		CAREERS IN ART
LESSON	**29**	Celebrations in Stone 108
		MAKING A SCALE DRAWING
LESSON	**30**	Unusual Architecture 110
		MAKING A FOIL MODEL

REFLECTING AND REVIEWING 112

UNIT 6 Heritage and Change • 114

LESSON	**31**	Stories on Walls 116
		PAINTING A MURAL
LESSON	**32**	Centuries in Clay 118
		SCULPTING A SLAB POT
CONNECTIONS		African Adobe Architecture 120
		ART AND CULTURE
LESSON	**33**	A Timeless Art 122
		WEAVING A BOOKMARK
LESSON	**34**	Patchwork Art 124
		CREATING A PATCHWORK WALL HANGING
CONNECTIONS		The Artrain 126
		COMMUNITY ART
LESSON	**35**	Artwork to Wear 128
		MAKING JEWELRY
LESSON	**36**	Faces from Folk Art 130
		CREATING A MIXED-MEDIA MASK

REFLECTING AND REVIEWING 132

Art Safety • 134
Exploring Art Techniques • 136
Elements and Principles • 152
Gallery of Artists • 166
Glossary • 176
Index of Artists and Artworks • 186
Index • 188

LOOKING AT ART

Pages 10–11

Ask students about their experiences with fine art. Have students read the paragraphs on page 10 and look at the photograph. Ask them whether they have ever been to an art museum or looked through an art book. Discuss with those who have what details they remember from a piece of artwork they saw or what ideas they think it expressed.

Discuss ways to make viewing artwork more meaningful. Ask students what they could do the next time they view a piece of artwork. Discuss with students ideas such as taking the time to examine the artwork closely, looking for interesting details in it, or trying to relate it to something in their own experiences. Tell students that they may better appreciate a piece of art after they have learned something about the artist and about the way he or she created the artwork.

VIEWING/CREATING ART

Students' experience with art may be limited to projects they have made. They should not, however, think of art production as the only way to experience art. Art production should not be isolated from viewing and appreciating art. When students are given the opportunity to view fine art and begin to develop a critical understanding of it, they have a valuable context in which to create more meaningful art projects.

LOOKING AT ART

How do you make judgments about a work of art? Do you just say you like it or you don't?

To make a more meaningful judgment, take your time. For example, in a museum, don't try to see every artwork. Choose a few pieces, slow down, and really *look*.

1. **What do you see?** Think about the materials the artist used. Notice the main design elements, such as line, color, and shape. Take some time to describe the art.

2. **Ask yourself** how the artwork makes you feel. Does it remind you of anything? Think about how the art expresses thoughts and ideas.

3. **Focus on what is happening** in the art. What do you think the artist is trying to tell you?

4. **What do you think** of this work of art? Discuss your thoughts with others. You might also want to take notes in an art notebook.

10

FOSTERING VISUAL LITERACY

Just as students become conventionally literate by learning to read and interpret the written word, they become visually literate by learning observation and interpretive skills. Students must be encouraged to look longer, more thoroughly, and more intelligently in order to gather visual facts. In this way, they begin to view and think about art and other visual and sensory cues in their environment in an informed, organized way.

DISCUSS the steps.

Encourage students to read and discuss the steps on page 10. Reinforce that these steps provide suggestions for students to use as they view art.

You may wish to walk students through the four steps by using one of the artworks in this book or one of the *Art Prints*.

Model the thinking.

1 Tell what you see.
- Students begin by taking enough time to carefully observe the work.
- Students should resist the urge to offer interpretations at this stage. DESCRIPTION/INVENTORY

2 Explain what you see.
- Students look at the way the different parts are organized.
- Students may wish to view the artwork from different distances and angles and note how its parts work together. FORMAL ANALYSIS

3 Think about what it means.
- Students look for clues to the artist's message. What does the artist seem to be communicating?
- Each student's interpretation of an artwork is valid. However, to make the interpretation more meaningful, students should limit their interpretations to those ideas that can be visibly confirmed in the artwork. INTERPRETATION/EXPLANATION

4 Tell your opinion.
- Students discuss opinions about the artwork or a part of the artwork.
- As students become familiar with an ever-increasing body of artwork, they should begin to compare and contrast artworks. JUDGMENT/EVALUATION

▲ **Response cards 1–10** on pages R56–R65 provide questions for guiding students' thinking as they view specific kinds of artwork.

LOOKING AT ART 11

KEEPING A SKETCHBOOK

Pages 12–13

Reflect on the creative process. Ask students to name some steps writers can take when they begin an assignment. (sketch out their ideas quickly, make notes, fill in graphic organizers) Point out that artists can follow the same type of steps in the creative process.

Discuss the pages. Share with students the information about Jerry Pinkney below. Ask volunteers to tell about any books they have read that were illustrated by Jerry Pinkney. Then have them read pages 12 and 13.

Point out the similarities between Jerry Pinkney's use of a sketchbook and the student's use of one on page 13. Ask students to read some of the captions and describe the drawings in this sketchbook. Then encourage students to start and use sketchbooks themselves.

About the Artist

Jerry Pinkney was born in Philadelphia, Pennsylvania, in 1939. As far back as he can remember, he loved to draw. Jerry carried a sketchbook with him wherever he went, including to work! At age eleven, he was at work on the street corner, selling newspapers and sketching everything that he saw.

Jerry's ambition and hard work paid off. He is now one of the most honored illustrators in the United States, having won Caldecott Honors for *Mirandy and Brother Wind, The Talking Eggs,* and *John Henry.* He has also won a *New York Times* Best Illustrated Book award for *Turtle in July* and three Coretta Scott King Awards.

12 ART EXPRESS

The drawings and notes shown here are from a student's sketchbook.

Ideas for a school mural:
— The history of our school

Here are some ways to use your sketchbook:

- Plan your artworks.
- Record ideas for future projects.
- Write your thoughts about other people's art.
- Show what you see around you as an artist.

AS YOU can see, both professional artists and student artists keep ongoing sketchbooks. You can, too. Choose a notebook that is large enough and flexible enough to draw in. (Unlined paper works best.) Decorate the cover. Then start sketching! Fill the pages with your ideas, notes, and drawings.

IN THE STUDIO

Design a Sketchbook Cover

Students can add colorful and personalized covers to their sketchbooks.

- Tell students to choose a solid color of construction paper. Have them cut the paper to the exact size of the sketchbook cover and glue it down.
- Tell students to experiment with various forms of lettering—cut out letters, calligraphy, painted letters—in different styles, sizes, and colors. Have them use their favorite letter forms to spell out their names on the sketchbooks.

HOW TO START A SKETCHBOOK

Students may wish to purchase a sturdy notebook, preferably with unlined paper, or they may wish to create one using cardboard, a hole punch, yarn, and paper. See the In the Studio feature for one possible way to decorate the sketchbook cover.

HOW TO USE A SKETCHBOOK

Encourage students to use their sketchbooks every day as they observe the world around them. Encourage them to sketch scenes and objects as *they* see them rather than as other artists have portrayed them.

Stress that a sketch is not intended to be a final, perfect work of art. Students will value having a variety of sketches and ideas to choose from when it comes time to develop a finished product.

Seeing Is Believing

Artists can create images that appear very lifelike. They achieve this appearance through the use of illusion. For instance, an image on a flat surface can trick the viewer's eye simply by how the artist uses light and shadow. Or the artist can use line to create the illusion of movement.

In this unit, students will explore artists' uses of illusion to depict natural and human-made environments.

ART PRINT 1 *The Stampede* by Frederic Remington

Using the Art Prints

Display and introduce *Art Prints 1* and *2*. (Discussion suggestions appear on the back of each *Art Print*.) Have students discuss whether these images appear lifelike and in what ways.

RESPONSE CARD OPTION Have small groups of students use RESPONSE CARD 4, *Still Lifes and Objects in Nature*, on page R59 of this *Teacher's Edition* to guide a discussion of *Art Print 1*.

ART PRINT 2 *Whistling Jar*, Nazca Pottery

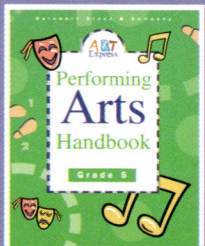

Performing Arts Handbook Dance, theater, and music activities to extend and enrich students' experiences with these *Art Prints* can be found in the *Performing Arts Handbook*.

UNIT 1: *Seeing Is Believing*

UNIT 1 SEEING IS BELIEVING

Introducing the Unit   pp. 14A–15

LESSON	VIEWING	CREATING	CURRICULUM CONNECTIONS
1 IMAGES OF NATURE PP. 16–17 • *Two Bison*, unknown artist • *Water Jar with Deer*, unknown artist	*Recognize that artists use shape and texture to record what is important to them.* **VOCABULARY:** organic, geometric, texture	*Draw a jar decorated with a familiar animal and geometric designs.* **MATERIALS:** large sheets of manila or black paper, glue, colored pencils, pastels (oil or chalk) or crayons	**Science** Shapes in Nature, p. 17 **Language Arts** Research, p. 17
2 LIGHT AND SHADOW PP. 18–19 • *A Spray of a Plant* by Leonardo da Vinci • *The Lighthouse at Two Lights* by Edward Hopper	*Understand how artists use value to create the illusion of three dimensions.* **VOCABULARY:** two-dimensional, three-dimensional form, hatching, highlighting, value	*Draw the contours of objects and add hatching to show three dimensions.* **MATERIALS:** manila or white paper, soft pencils	**Science** Drawing Like a Scientist, p. 19 **Performing Arts** Theater: Act in the dark, p. 19

CONNECTIONS: ART AND LITERATURE The Natural Art of Barbara Bash pp. 20–21

3 THE ILLUSION OF DISTANCE PP. 22–23 • *The Oxbow* by Thomas Cole • *Gould's Inlet* by Anna Belle Lee Washington	*Recognize how artists use perspective to suggest distance.* **VOCABULARY:** background, foreground, middle ground, overlaps, atmospheric perspective	*Make a collage showing background and foreground.* **MATERIALS:** wax paper, dark construction paper or other colored paper, white paper, scissors, glue, stapler	**Mathematics** Graphing Distance and Size, p. 23 **Performing Arts** Theater: Make a shoe box stage, p. 23
4 INTO THE SCENE PP. 24–25 • *Avenue of the Alyscamps* by Vincent van Gogh	*Recognize that artists use linear perspective to add depth and to draw viewers into a scene.* **VOCABULARY:** vanishing point, linear perspective	*Draw a scene using linear perspective.* **MATERIALS:** rulers, soft pencils, drawing paper	**Language Arts** Writing a Poem, p. 25 **Mathematics** Geometry in Painting, p. 25

CONNECTIONS: CAREERS IN ART Set Designer, Bob Phillips pp. 26–27

5 IMPRESSIONS OF LIGHT PP. 28–29 • *Summertime* by Mary Cassatt • *Harp of the Winds: View of the Seine* by Homer Dodge Martin	*Understand how the Impressionists tried to capture special moments in the natural world.* **VOCABULARY:** Impressionists, brushstrokes, horizontal symmetry	*Create a landscape in which an image is reflected.* **MATERIALS:** large sheets of tagboard or other white paper, tempera paints, watercolor paints, paintbrushes	**Science** Optics, p. 29 **Language Arts** Writing a Poem, p. 29
6 SHOWING MOVEMENT PP. 30–31 • *Horse and Rider* by Alexander Calder • *Skyward, My Friend* by Michael Naranjo	*Identify techniques artists use to create the illusion of movement.* **VOCABULARY:** sculpture, diagonal	*Make a wire sculpture of an animal and create the illusion that the animal is moving.* **MATERIALS:** flexible wire such as telephone or electrical wire, scissors or wire cutters, safety glasses	**Language Arts** Writing About Sculpture, p. 31 **Science** Motion in the Natural World, p. 31

Unit 1 Reflecting and Reviewing   pp. 32–33

Integrating Your Day

SUGGESTED READING	OPTIONAL VIDEOS/TECHNOLOGY
When Clay Sings by Byrd Baylor. Aladdin Books, 1987. EASY *Artists' Workshop: Animals* by Penny King and Clare Roundhill. Crabtree, 1996. EASY	Students can use Shapes in Art from *Look What I See!* to explore examples of shapes in nature.
How Artists See the Weather by Colleen Carroll. Abbeville Press, 1996. EASY *Edward Hopper* by Mike Venezia. Childrens Press, 1989. EASY 	Students can use 2-3D BLOX from *Thinkin' Things Collection 2* to explore 2-D shapes and 3-D forms.
Places in Art by Anthea Peppin. Millbrook, 1992. AVERAGE *My New York* by Kathy Jakobsen. Little, Brown, 1993. EASY	Students can use Snake BLOX from *Thinkin' Things Collection 2* to separate pictures into background and foreground layers.
A Weekend with Degas by Rosabianca Skira-Venturi. Rizzoli, 1991. AVERAGE *Come Look with Me: Exploring Landscape Art with Children* by Gladys S. Blizzard. Thomasson-Grant, 1992. AVERAGE	Small groups of students can work with *Imagination Express, Destination: Time Trip, USA* to create and write about their own scenes.
A Blue Butterfly: A Story about Claude Monet by Bijou Le Tord. Doubleday, 1995. EASY *A Weekend with Renoir* by Rosabianca Skira-Venturi. Rizzoli, 1990. AVERAGE	Have students view *Linnea in Monet's Garden* to learn about how one Impressionist artist depicted the natural world.
Drawing Life in Motion by Jim Arnosky. Lothrop, Lee & Shepard, 1987. AVERAGE *Alvin Ailey* by Andrea Davis Pinkney, illustrated by Brian Pinkney. Hyperion, 1993. AVERAGE 	Small groups of students can use BLOX-Flying Spheres from *Thinkin' Things Collection 1* to experiment with motion and the illusion of depth.

Art Minutes

Present one of these puzzles or activities for students to solve by the end of the week.

- ■ **Draw** something that seems to come right off the page. APPLICATION
- ■ **Play** statues with two classmates. Have them move and then stop when you say "freeze." Sketch one of their poses. APPLICATION
- ■ **Draw** an object on a rounded surface. Can you make the object appear flat? ANALYSIS
- ■ **Look** down a hallway. Then look down the same hallway using a magnifying glass. Write about the differences between each view. ANALYSIS
- ■ **Find** examples of illusions in advertisements. Identify and explain three of these illusions. SYNTHESIS
- ■ **Draw** a picture of your room, using shadows so that it appears to be nighttime. APPLICATION

After completing Lesson 1, distribute School-Home Connection 1, found on page R50. Students can enlist the help of family members to find a landscape scene to draw.

Activities and Resources CD-ROM provides additional teaching materials and interactive student activities for use with Unit 1.

UNIT 1: *Seeing Is Believing* **14D**

UNIT 1

INTRODUCING THE UNIT

The Fall of the Cowboy, Frederic Remington 1895.

14

Pages 14–15

Discuss *The Fall of the Cowboy*. Have students read pages 14 and 15. Invite students to study *The Fall of the Cowboy* and to discuss what is made by nature and what is made by humans in the painting.

Look at the artist's technique. Remington used techniques to make the scenes he painted seem almost real. He added the white highlights of snow on the fence rails. He added the dark shading of the horses' hoofprints on the ground. Such details help viewers believe in what they are seeing.

About the Art

The Fall of the Cowboy is one of many images of the American West that Remington painted. Inform students that Remington painted the West at a time of great changes. The open ranges, traveled for centuries by Native Americans and later by Europeans, were being fenced in. The end of this freer way of life is reflected in the postures of the cowboys and the horses. Even the sky seems sorrowful.

Another example of a Frederic Remington painting can be found in ***Art Print 1***.

TIME LINE

Have students choose one artwork from the unit and locate the period of its creation on the *Time Line*. Then have them use other sources to find out more about the period.

14   UNIT 1: *Seeing Is Believing*

UNIT 1

Seeing Is Believing

How does an artist make a viewer believe in a scene?

Frederic Remington's Old West was a world of great natural beauty. It was also a world in which animals and people struggled daily to survive.

Look at *The Fall of the Cowboy*. What is made by nature in this scene, and what is made by people? Why might Remington have chosen to set this scene on a dark and cold day?

ABOUT FREDERIC REMINGTON

Frederic Remington's subject matter was the American West. Through his many illustrations, paintings, and sculptures, he created a permanent record of life on the frontier.

Meet the Artist

Frederic Remington (1861–1909), although born to a middle-class New York family, was a rugged man who was well-suited to life on the Western frontier. Remington made many trips to the West, witnessing buffalo hunts, a Sioux uprising, and the day-to-day life of cowboys. His illustrations for magazines such as *Harper's Weekly* and *Collier's* made him a national figure. His careers included that of illustrator, reporter, novelist, painter, and sculptor.

LITERATURE CONNECTION

Mojave by Diane Siebert. HarperCollins, 1992. EASY

This book depicts the beauties and mysteries of the Mojave Desert through the use of poetry and unique paintings.

CLASSROOM MANAGEMENT

VIEWING: Response Cards If you prefer to have students work independently on one or more lessons in the unit, you may select appropriate Response Cards for them to use as they think about the artworks. For Lesson 4, Into the Scene, for example, you may provide students with Response Card 2, Everyday Life. The Response Cards begin on page R56 of this Teacher's Edition.

CREATING: Studio Activity Options If your classroom resources are limited, you may wish to have students complete the Quick Activity for one or more lessons. The Quick Activity in each lesson reinforces concepts and skills but usually requires fewer materials.

LESSON 1 Images of Nature

OBJECTIVES: Recognize that artists use shape and texture to record what is important to them. Draw a jar decorated with a familiar animal and geometric designs.
MATERIALS: feather, pinecone, apple, hairbrush, other objects with interesting textures

MOTIVATE

Explore natural and human-made objects. Invite students to close their eyes and identify objects by touch. Tell students that *texture* is the way a surface feels or seems to feel.

VIEWING ART

TEACH

Discuss organic and geometric shapes. Tell students to read about the artworks. Then discuss the two types of shapes on the jar. Point out that curved lines often produce organic shapes and that straight, angled lines often produce geometric shapes.

Discuss texture. Ask students what each artwork probably feels like. (Possible response: The bison probably feels rough; the jar probably feels smooth.) Explain that artists often use texture to make an image look more lifelike. Texture can be actual, as in a sculpture, or implied, as in a drawing or painting.

Critical Thinking Questions

- **How did the artist of A use texture to make the bison look realistic?** (Possible responses: scratching lines in the clay with a stick to show hair; showing muscles with lumps of clay) ART CRITICISM: ANALYSIS

- **Why do you think the artist mixed organic and geometric shapes on the pottery jar?** (Possible response: to give variety to the design) AESTHETICS: DRAW CONCLUSIONS

EXTRA SUPPORT To help students understand the terms *geometric* and *organic*, hold up simple geometric figures such as triangles, squares, and hexagons. Contrast them with the organic shapes of objects from nature such as leaves and pebbles.

LESSON 1 DRAWING ORGANIC AND GEOMETRIC SHAPES

Images of Nature

How do you think these artists felt about the animals in the pictures?

Artists make images of the things that matter most to them. Sometimes they show animals that they depend on for survival.

Use your finger to trace the outlines of the bison in sculpture **A** and the deer on the jar **B**. Feel their flowing, rounded shapes. Natural objects often have this **organic** shape. Now look at the sharp angles of the designs at the top of the jar. This type of shape is called **geometric**.

What do you think the bison sculpture feels like? What about the jar? **Texture** is the word for the way a surface

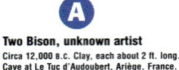
Two Bison, unknown artist
Circa 12,000 B.C. Clay, each about 2 ft. long.
Cave at Le Tuc d'Audoubert, Ariège, France.

16

SHARE ART HISTORY

A Stone Age artists are considered to be the world's first artists. The bison in this cave at Ariège, France, are the largest Stone Age sculptures ever found. These sculptures were created about 14,000 years ago. Stone Age artists also painted animals on cave walls, often using natural bulges in the walls to give texture and form to their paintings.

B The Zuñi [ZOON•yee] are a Native American people who settled in what is now northern New Mexico. Some Zuñis still live in stone and adobe houses in villages called *pueblos*. Many Zuñis farm the land, but in past times their ancestors hunted as well.

You may want to display *Art Print 2, Whistling Jar,* as an example of pottery from a different Native American culture.

16 UNIT 1: *Seeing Is Believing*

feels (A) or the way it appears to feel (B). An artist can use lines to show the texture of an object, even if it is painted on a smooth surface. Texture can make the object seem more lifelike or interesting.

 Water Jar with Deer, unknown artist of the Zuñi Native American people
Circa 1850. Clay, 10 3/4 in. high. Department of Anthropology, Smithsonian Institution, Washington, D.C.

IN THE STUDIO

MATERIALS
- manila paper
- black paper
- glue
- colored pencils
- pastels (oil or chalk) or crayons

Decorate a jar with a picture of an animal and geometric shapes. How can you use lines to show shape and texture?

1. On the manila paper, draw the outline of a pottery jar. Cut it out, and glue it to the black paper.

2. Draw an animal that matters to you. Think of what your animal would feel like if you touched it. Is it furry? Scaly? Feathery? Draw lines to show that texture.

3. Now decorate the rest of your pottery with geometric shapes.

17

ART ACROSS THE CURRICULUM

 SCIENCE: SHAPES IN NATURE Display specimens or photographs of snowflakes, crystals (including salt crystals), leaves, and other natural geometric forms. Point out that sometimes very small and very large things in nature (such as molecules and galaxies) have shapes that are different from the natural shapes we see every day. Then invite students to sketch one of these pictured geometric shapes from nature.

 **LANGUAGE ARTS: RESEARCH** Have pairs of students visit the local or school library and research the customs and beliefs of the Zuñi people. Partners may wish to retell a traditional Zuñi legend or demonstrate some steps of a traditional dance.

IN THE STUDIO

MATERIALS: large sheets of manila or black paper, glue, colored pencils, pastels (oil or chalk) or crayons

Drawing Organic and Geometric Shapes

CREATING ART

- If possible, display a ceramic jar or bowl so students can see its outline.

- Tell students to choose a shape and draw an outline for their jar on the manila paper.

- Have students cut out their outlines and glue them to the black paper.

- Ask students to draw their animal on the jar. Suggest that students choose a pet or another familiar animal to draw. If possible, have them refer to photographs. Ask them to keep in mind how their animal feels to the touch and to try to show this texture in their drawings.

- Now ask students to decorate other parts of their jar with geometric shapes. You may wish to point out examples of such patterns on students' clothing or in book illustrations or posters in the classroom.

OPTIONAL: Quick Activity Invite students to draw the organic shape of a familiar animal. Then have them use colored pencils to depict the texture of the animal by drawing fur, scales, or feathers.

WRAP-UP

INFORMAL ASSESSMENT

- **Why did the makers of the clay bison and the water jar use organic shapes?** (Possible response: They were showing things from nature, so they used the shapes found in nature.) ART CRITICISM: SUMMARIZE

- **How did you solve the problem of making the smooth paper look textured?** (Responses will vary.) PRODUCTION: PROBLEM SOLVING

LESSON 1: *Images of Nature* **17**

LESSON 2
Light and Shadow

OBJECTIVES: Understand how artists use value to create the illusion of three dimensions. Draw the contours of objects and add hatching to show three dimensions.

MATERIALS: three sports balls

MOTIVATE

Notice value in everyday objects. Place three sports balls on the floor at the front of the room. Invite students to examine them closely. Ask which parts of each ball seem darker or lighter and why.

VIEWING ART

TEACH

Compare two dimensions and three dimensions. Read pages 18 and 19. Ask students to examine the fruit and find the hatching lines. Point out that making parts of the fruit look darker makes the fruit seem rounded, or three-dimensional. The fruit seems to have form rather than just flat shape.

Discuss highlighting. Ask where the sun is shining from in B. (from the right) The artist showed shadows by adding black to his colors. The colors in the shadows have a darker value. Then ask students to find the shadows in C. (They are shown with hatching.) Ask whether the sneakers seem to have form. (yes)

Critical Thinking Questions

- **In B, on the square tower base, do the values change gradually or suddenly? Why?** (Possible response: The values change suddenly because the building turns a sharp corner.) ART CRITICISM: SYNTHESIZE

- **Why might you use hatching?** (Possible response: to make objects look three-dimensional) PRODUCTION: APPLICATION

EXTRA SUPPORT Help students find color values by examining the differences in light and shadow in the school classroom.

LESSON 2 DRAWING EVERYDAY FORMS

Light and Shadow

How do artists make objects in drawings look rounded?

A *A Spray of a Plant,* Leonardo da Vinci
The Royal Collection, Windsor Castle, England.

Paper is flat, or **two-dimensional**. But most of the objects artists draw are not flat. They have rounded **three-dimensional form** rather than flat shape. Look at how the artist showed the roundness of the fruit in picture **A**. He used tiny lines, or **hatching**. These lines also create shadows on the leaves and around the plant.

B *The Lighthouse at Two Lights,* Edward Hopper
1929. Oil on canvas, 29 1/2 X 43 1/2 in. Metropolitan Museum of Art, New York.

18

SHARE ART HISTORY

A **Leonardo da Vinci** [lay•oh•NAR•doh DAH VIN•chee] (1452–1519) was an Italian painter, scientist, and inventor. His Mona Lisa is one of the most famous paintings in the world. Leonardo was fascinated by what he saw in nature. He filled notebooks with detailed drawings of plants, animals, patterns he saw in rocks and water, and the human body.

B **Edward Hopper** (1882–1967) was an American painter who began painting seriously after the age of forty. His favorite subjects were scenes of ordinary American life. There are no people in most of his paintings, and the people he did paint seem lonely and isolated. Most of his paintings use simple, bold areas of light and dark to create a strong mood.

18 UNIT 1: *Seeing Is Believing*

IN THE STUDIO BIG BOOK p.2

Can you tell where the sun is in picture **B**? You can if you notice the <mark>highlighting</mark> along the right side of the tower and on the walls. Look at how the artist made some of the walls darker. The lightness or darkness of a color is its <mark>value</mark>. You can add a little black to any color to give it a darker value.

Can you find the shadows in picture **C**? How did the artist show the form of the sneakers?

C Student artwork

IN THE STUDIO

MATERIALS

Draw the edges of a group of everyday objects. Then make the objects look three-dimensional or rounded.

1. Choose objects with interesting forms. Place them in a group. Draw the objects' outside edge, using long lines. Then draw the inside edges.
2. Use hatching to show which parts of the objects are in shadow.

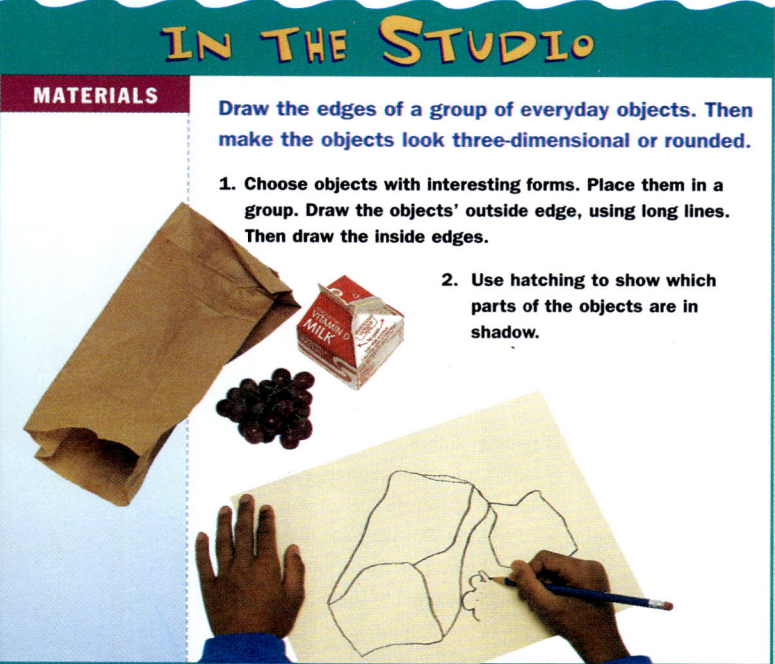

19

ART ACROSS THE CURRICULUM

SCIENCE: DRAWING LIKE A SCIENTIST Bring in an assortment of leaves and ask students to make detailed drawings of them. Then help students identify the leaves in a field guide. Discuss how drawing can help scientists observe a leaf's structure and shape. Invite students to write captions for their drawings.

PERFORMING ARTS: THEATER Help students discover how light can be used in theater. Ask groups to perform a scene from a familiar play or story. Explain that the room will be darkened; then students presenting the scene can use flashlights to light up objects and people at different times during the performance.

IN THE STUDIO

MATERIALS: manila or white paper, soft pencils

Drawing Everyday Forms

CREATING ART

- Invite students to choose everyday objects, such as staplers, books, or pieces of fruit, to draw.

- Read aloud the activity on page 19. Ask students to study their objects and trace the contours in the air, noting every curve in the outline.

- As students begin to draw, encourage them to imagine that their pencil is actually moving around the edges of the objects. They can then add any interior edges or corners.

- Ask students to add hatching to their contour drawings. First they should figure out where shadows fall on their objects. Explain that crossing layers of hatch lines (crosshatching) will create darker values. Short hatching lines that follow an object's curve will add depth and shape.

OPTIONAL: Quick Activity Shine a flashlight on a dark spherical object, such as a ball or an apple. Point out the different values that can be seen on the object, and let students quickly sketch the object, using hatching.

WRAP-UP

INFORMAL ASSESSMENT

- **Look at a classmate's drawing. How did he or she make the drawing look three-dimensional?** (Responses will vary.) ART CRITICISM: DESCRIPTION

- **Is your drawing more like Edward Hopper's or Leonardo da Vinci's? Explain.** (Accept reasonable responses: Students' drawings are similar to Leonardo's in that they show a common object, they are drawings rather than paintings, and they use hatching.) ART CRITICISM: COMPARE/CONTRAST

LESSON 2: *Light and Shadow* 19

ART AND LITERATURE

Identify favorite illustrated books. Ask students to think about their favorite illustrated books, and ask them what they liked about the illustrations. Have students read pages 20–21 to find out more about illustrating a book.

Discuss the illustrations. Share with students the information that Barbara Bash began her publishing career as a calligrapher [kuh•LI•gruh•fer] and a botanical artist. Calligraphers learn the art of stylized handwriting, and botanical artists draw plants realistically. Ask students to look at the baobab tree scene and talk about illusions reflected in the art. (Possible responses: three-dimensional depth, activity, softness)

 ART AND LITERATURE

The Natural Art of Barbara Bash

Nature illustrators use both their artistic talent and their scientific knowledge. They create images of nature that seem to come to life.

Long ago, most nature illustrators were also scientists. Before the camera was invented, these scientists roamed the world, looking for new plants and animals. They drew what they saw, clearly and carefully. These drawings were the only way other people could see many natural wonders. Today, of course, we have other ways to view nature. Still, nature illustrators like Barbara Bash can help us understand the world we live in.

▲ Barbara Bash

Barbara Bash is both an author and an illustrator. She creates books that combine information about nature with a love of creatures and plants. Before she set about writing and illustrating *Tree of Life: The World of the African Baobab,* she did careful research. She wanted her drawings to be accurate. She also wanted to share her love of nature.

20

SHARE ART HISTORY

Children's Book Art

Early children's books were illustrated with woodcuts. First, the artist drew an image on a piece of wood. Next, wood was cut from around the image, and ink was applied. Then, paper was placed over the woodcut, and the block and paper were run through the press, creating a printed image.

 ### SCIENCE

Botanical Sketch

Beatrix Potter is best known for her book *The Tale of Peter Rabbit*. Like Barbara Bash, she started her career as a botanical artist. She could not get her botanical prints published, so she turned to illustrating children's stories. Her art is filled with beautiful plants and settings. Have students create their own botanical illustrations. Remind them to use highlighting and shading to make the drawings realistic. (Students will need to refer to an actual plant or to a photograph of one.)

Look at the illustration of bushbabies on this page. How did Barbara Bash use color, texture, and line to bring these animals to life? What do you think a bushbaby would feel like if you could pet it?

◀ *Tree of Life: The World of the African Baobab,* by Barbara Bash

- What does this art communicate about the animals and their environment? (Possible responses: happiness; contentment; the animals appear to be at peace in their environment.) ART CRITICISM: INTERPRETATION

- What techniques did Barbara Bash use to make the bushbabies look soft? (Possible response: She used highlighting, shadows, fine lines, and hatching to create soft textures.) PRODUCTION: ANALYSIS

WHAT DO YOU THINK?
- What does this art communicate about the animals and their environment?
- What techniques did Barbara Bash use to make the bushbabies look soft?

21

 **LANGUAGE ARTS**

Nature Cards

Challenge students to imagine and sketch a greeting card with a nature theme. Have students write or choose a poem and illustrate it with appropriate images of nature. Remind them to make their illustrations lifelike.

IN THE STUDIO

Wonderful Trees

Have students design wonderful trees of their own. Provide these requirements:

- Each tree must have the appearance of a safe gathering place.
- The tree should have leaves, fruit, or flowers.
- The tree should be host to a bird, another animal, and an insect that could all live in it in harmony.

Encourage volunteers to share their wonderful trees.

CONNECTIONS: *Art and Literature* **21**

LESSON 3
The Illusion of Distance

OBJECTIVES: Recognize how artists use perspective to suggest distance. Make a collage showing background and foreground.

MOTIVATE

Discuss distance in landscapes. Ask students to look at a scene outside your classroom. Ask what objects seem far away and how they could tell even if they had never seen the scene before.

VIEWING ART

TEACH

Discuss perspective in art. Have students read pages 22 and 23 and study the paintings. Explain that faraway objects appear smaller and duller than those that are close to us. Close-up objects look more detailed. This change in detail and brightness is called *atmospheric perspective.*

Identify background, foreground, and middle ground. Help students identify the middle ground in A. (the oxbow, or U-shaped bend in the river, and the valley) Ask them to identify all three parts in B. (foreground–boardwalk, barrel, people; middle ground–rocks, boats, water; background–green horizon line, sky) Ask students to find overlapping in B. (Possible response: The rocks and the men overlap the water.)

Critical Thinking Questions

- **Which painting gives you a better sense of atmospheric perspective? Why?** (Responses will vary, but many students will choose A.)
  ART CRITICISM: MAKE JUDGMENTS

- **How do you think the artist felt about the landscape shown in picture A?** (Possible response: He thought it was impressive.)
  AESTHETICS: INTERPRETATION

EXTRA SUPPORT Place several items on a table. Ask students to view them at eye level and to point out overlapping, foreground, middle ground, and background.

LESSON 3 | SHOWING DEPTH

The Illusion of Distance

How do artists make some things look close and others look far away?

Put your finger on the part of the scene in picture **A** that looks farthest away. This is the **background** of the painting. Now point to the **foreground**, the part of the painting that looks closest to you. Where do you think the **middle ground** is in picture A? Can you point to the foreground, middle ground, and background in picture **B**?

In real life, moisture in the air makes things that are far away look pale and dull. That is why artists often use pale or dull colors to paint backgrounds. In this way, they show **atmospheric perspective**.

A View from Mount Holyoke, Northampton, Massachusetts, after a Thunderstorm—The Oxbow, Thomas Cole
1836. Oil on canvas, 51 1/2 X 76 in.
Metropolitan Museum of Art, New York.

22

SHARE ART HISTORY

A Thomas Cole (1801–1848) is known as the father of the Hudson River School of landscape painters. This group of American painters loved the grandeur of the New England wilderness. They created large paintings expressing the awe they felt when viewing grand vistas and wide horizons. Thomas Cole was fascinated by the oxbow, a shape made by the Connecticut River. Cole painted himself into the foreground.

B Anna Belle Lee Washington began painting as a child. After she retired from social service work in Detroit, she moved to St. Simons Island in Georgia. She admired the local landscapes and seascapes and began to paint them. Her ideas come from books, watching people, and visiting African American churches. She does not paint from models. She says, "The human shapes are in my mind."

22 UNIT 1: *Seeing Is Believing*

IN THE STUDIO BIG BOOK p.3

Look at how the hill in the foreground of picture A **overlaps** the river valley. When two objects in a picture overlap, the object that is blocked out is the one that is farther away. Can you find an example of overlapping in picture B?

B *Gould's Inlet*, Anna Belle Lee Washington
1993. Oil on canvas, 18 X 24 in.

IN THE STUDIO

MATERIALS
- wax paper
- construction paper or other colored paper
- white paper
- scissors
- glue
- stapler

Create a country or city scene. Use overlapping to show background and foreground.

1. Think of a scene in which some things are far away and some are closer. Choose two colors of paper. Cut out background objects and foreground objects from different colors.

2. Glue down the background objects first. Over that, place a sheet of wax paper. Next, glue down your foreground objects. Staple a paper frame around the edges of your artwork.

23

ART ACROSS THE CURRICULUM

 MATHEMATICS: GRAPHING DISTANCE AND SIZE Have students measure and mark 10-foot intervals up to 60 feet. Ask one partner to stand at the 10-foot marker; the other stands at zero and measures his or her partner's apparent height by holding a ruler at arm's length. Have students record the apparent height at each distance marker and make a bar graph showing the relationship between distance and size.

 PERFORMING ARTS: THEATER Have students use a shoe box to create a model for a stage set. Their set might show a scene from a favorite play or book. Encourage them to show a background and a foreground in their set. Ask them to explain how the actors will move around the set as they play the scene.

IN THE STUDIO

MATERIALS: wax paper, construction paper or other colored paper, white paper, scissors, glue, stapler

Showing Depth   CREATING ART

- Ask students to read the activity. From colored paper, students can cut out shapes for their foreground and background. Remind them that distant objects appear smaller and paler than closer ones.

- Have students experiment with overlapping their background shapes before gluing them onto the white paper.

- After students have glued down the background shapes, they should place a sheet of wax paper on top. This will help create atmospheric perspective.

- Next, students should arrange and glue down their foreground objects.

- Finally, students can staple a paper frame around the edges of their artwork to hold it together.

OPTIONAL: Quick Activity Have students cut out paper figures of varying heights up to 4 inches. They can move the figures around on a photograph or painting of a landscape, noting how the figures' sizes seem to change.

WRAP-UP   INFORMAL ASSESSMENT

- **Which painting do you think gives the greatest illusion of distance and depth?** (Responses will vary.) ART CRITICISM: COMPARE/CONTRAST

- **Look again at paintings A and B. Describe how you might make a painting of the scene you have shown in your collage.** (Possible response: by using the same shapes, and painting the foreground areas with brighter colors and the background areas with paler colors) PRODUCTION: GENERATE ALTERNATIVES

LESSON 3: *The Illusion of Distance*

LESSON 4

Into the Scene

OBJECTIVES: Recognize that artists use linear perspective to add depth and to draw viewers into a scene. Draw a scene using linear perspective.

MOTIVATE

Visualize a scene. Ask students to imagine they are looking down the middle of a flat, straight road into the distance. Ask several students to come to the board and sketch what they visualized.

VIEWING ART

TEACH

Review the problem of presenting three-dimensional scenes on a two-dimensional surface. Point out that artists who paint realistic landscapes must find ways to show depth on a flat surface. One method artists use is called linear perspective.

Discuss linear perspective. Invite students to view the art and read the text. Ask whether they can tell where the avenue in the painting ends. (Possible response: No; it may go on past the vanishing point.) If necessary, help students find the vanishing point. Use a straightedge to show students how the lines in the painting come together as they approach the vanishing point. Finally, point out that some figures on the avenue are shown as tiny specks. Ask why the painter did this. (to show that these people are far away)

Critical Thinking Questions

- **If you could walk down the road shown in this painting, would the vanishing point stay in the same place? Explain.** (No; as you walked, you would be able to see farther down the road.) ART CRITICISM: ANALYSIS

- **Do you feel as if you could "walk right into the scene"? Explain your answer.** (Responses will vary.) AESTHETICS: PERSONAL RESPONSE

EXTRA SUPPORT To help students understand *linear perspective,* point out that *linear* comes from *line.*

LESSON 4 USING LINEAR PERSPECTIVE

Into the Scene

How do artists "pull" viewers into their paintings?

Where does the road in this painting end? How can you tell? Put your finger on the part of the road that looks farthest away. You have just found the **vanishing point**. Notice how the sides of the road come closer together until they meet at the vanishing point.

Avenue of the Alyscamps, Vincent van Gogh
1888. Oil on canvas, 36 1/4 in. X 29 1/8 in. Collection of Mrs. A. Mettler-Weber, Zollikon, Switzerland.

24

SHARE ART HISTORY

Vincent van Gogh [VAN GOH] (1853–1890) was born in Holland but lived in France for the last part of his life. Although he sold only one painting when he was alive, van Gogh has become one of the most famous painters in the world. He often used bold colors and thick oil paint, making his brushstrokes easy to see. Van Gogh's paintings reveal his intense feelings about the beauty of nature as well as his own inner turmoil.

24 UNIT 1: *Seeing Is Believing*

IN THE STUDIO BIG BOOK p.4

When artists paint scenes this way, they are using **linear perspective**. Look at the top half of the picture. The tops of the trees form another pair of lines that come together at the vanishing point. What would happen if you could walk to this point?

Linear perspective is one way that artists show depth. Sometimes it can make you feel as if you could walk right *into* the scene.

IN THE STUDIO

MATERIALS
- ruler
- soft pencils
- drawing paper

Use linear perspective to draw a scene that pulls the viewer into it.

1. Think of a scene that includes pairs of lines, such as a road or railroad tracks.

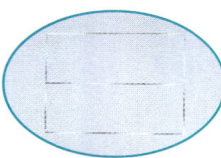

2. Draw a picture frame. Use your ruler to draw a horizontal line representing the farthest point you can see. This is the horizon line. In the middle of that line, mark a vanishing point.

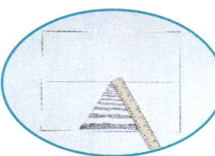

3. Now draw the lines for your road or railroad tracks. Line up your ruler with the horizon line so that your lines come together at the vanishing point. Then add objects, details, and color to the scene.

25

ART ACROSS THE CURRICULUM

LANGUAGE ARTS: WRITING A POEM Help students find a book of reproductions of van Gogh's paintings. Ask them each to choose one they especially like. Encourage students to write poems based on the paintings they chose. They may wish to read their poems aloud as classmates view the paintings described in the poems.

MATHEMATICS: GEOMETRY IN PAINTING Ask students to find two triangular shapes in van Gogh's painting: one formed by the sky and the other formed by the road. Ask where these two triangles come together. (at the vanishing point) Have students use tracing paper to copy these triangles. Then ask how each triangle in the painting would change if the horizon line were higher.

IN THE STUDIO

MATERIALS: rulers, soft pencils, drawing paper

Using Linear Perspective

CREATING ART

- If possible, take students outdoors where they can see for themselves that parallel lines such as the two sides of a road do indeed seem to come together toward a vanishing point.

- Ask students to read the activity on page 25. Help them think of scenes they might draw. Point out that parallel rows of trees or buildings can be shown with linear perspective, as can roads or railroad tracks.

- Model for students how to draw a horizon line and a vanishing point. Also show them how to use a ruler to make sure the lines in their scene come together as they approach the vanishing point.

- Encourage students to add items such as trees, buildings, cars, and figures to their scene. Remind them that objects in the distance should be smaller than objects in the foreground.

OPTIONAL: Quick Activity Students might quickly sketch the lines they see in van Gogh's painting. Encourage them to draw each pair of converging parallel lines that they notice. Have students compare their sketches.

WRAP-UP

INFORMAL ASSESSMENT

- **Find pairs of lines in a classmate's drawing. How does his or her drawing pull you into the scene?** (Responses will vary.)
ART CRITICISM: APPLICATION

- **If the road in van Gogh's painting were a winding road, would its sides still seem to get closer and closer in the distance?** (Yes, the road would narrow as it approached the vanishing point.) ART CRITICISM: SYNTHESIZE

LESSON 4: *Into the Scene* 25

CAREERS IN ART

Identify favorite shows. Point out to students that all shows have some form of scenery. The way that scenery is arranged, as a frame for the action, is called a *set*. Ask volunteers to identify the sets from some favorite plays, TV shows, or movies. (Responses will vary.) Have students read pages 26–27.

Discuss set design. Share with students that a set design is created with help from the director and other designers and technicians. Have students look at the sets. Discuss the techniques used to pull the audience into the scene. (Possible responses: backdrops, linear perspective, vanishing point, scale, colors)

 CAREERS IN ART

Set Designer

How do you make a 400-year-old play fun for today? How do you turn a house inside out in five seconds? How do you fit Elmo and Ruthie into Big Bird's nest with him for a sleep-over? For answers to these questions, you need to talk to Bob Phillips. As a set designer, Bob Phillips creates scenery for stage, television, and movies. Here he shares some of his designs and talks about his career.

▼ Design for *Two Gentlemen of Verona* at the Orlando Shakespeare Festival

"In my full-time job, I'm the art director for *Sesame Street*. In my spare time, I get to travel all over the United States to design scenery for regional theaters. For *Two Gentlemen of Verona*, the director moved up the time of Shakespeare's play from the 1500s to 1959 and added rock-and-roll music and radio deejays. I designed the signs on the poles to rotate to show different messages in different scenes.

26

SHARE CAREER INFORMATION

Set Designer

As part of a fine arts course in college, Bob Phillips was assigned to design a set for the college theater. He discovered that he was really good at solving the practical and artistic challenges of set design. Bob transferred to New York University and began to work his way up the professional ladder as a set designer in theater and television.

GEOGRAPHY

A Change of Climate

COOPERATIVE LEARNING Have students work in pairs to research play and movie settings. Have one student select any spot on the globe; then have the other select a spot with a very different climate. Students should develop fact sheets for their spots, including average temperatures, vegetation, weather, architecture, and clothing styles. Encourage pairs to share their fact sheets.

26 UNIT 1: *Seeing Is Believing*

▲ Design for Molière's *The School for Wives* at the Pennsylvania Shakespeare Festival

"In *The School for Wives*, two of the actors were also scene changers. They spun the walls around. Motors backstage rotated the ceiling and the benches, and the chandeliers flew in on wires. We were able to change the scene from outside to inside in less than five seconds.

"For *Sesame Street*'s twenty-fifth anniversary, we doubled the size of the set. The production designer and I used hundreds of photos of New York streets and buildings to create the design. That was a great project.

"Every day we make special things to help the puppeteers in their work. I love this job. I was thrilled when I found out that set design was actually a career. I can't imagine myself doing anything different."

▲ Bob Phillips on *Sesame Street* set

WHAT DO YOU THINK?
- What kinds of skills would be helpful to a set designer?
- What information do you think the director of a play would give to the set designer?

WHAT DO YOU THINK?
- What kinds of skills would be helpful to a set designer? (Possible responses: artistic skills, such as drawing; problem-solving skills; mechanical skills; listening skills) AESTHETICS: SYNTHESIZE
- What information do you think the director of a play would give to the set designer? (Possible responses: the time and place of the play, the look of the costumes, the number of scenes, the number of actors, any special effects) PRODUCTION: ANALYSIS

🎵 MUSIC
Sound Tracks
Encourage students to think about sound as part of a show's design. Call on volunteers to describe the music in the background of a favorite TV show or movie. Discuss how well the music fits with the show's look.

IN THE STUDIO
Set Puzzle
COOPERATIVE LEARNING Have students work in groups to design a backdrop for a play that meets these requirements:
- The scenery must include a sunset, birds, and clouds.
- The backdrop must have a horizon line.
- The clouds should be long streaks of color for linear perspective.
- The backdrop must have a vanishing point.

Have students compare their backdrops.

LESSON 5

Impressions of Light

OBJECTIVES: Understand how the Impressionists tried to capture special moments in the natural world. Create a landscape in which an image is reflected.

MOTIVATE

Describe natural scenes. Ask volunteers to think of a natural setting they have visited, such as a forest. Encourage each student to think of five words that could give someone a feeling for what that place is like. Then invite students to share their thoughts.

VIEWING ART

TEACH

Discuss Impressionism. Read page 28. Tell students that when the Impressionists first showed their work, most people thought it was sloppy, because it did not follow the "rules." Impressionists painted quickly, with visible brushstrokes, to capture special moments or the effects of light.

Discuss reflection and horizontal symmetry. Ask students to look at the paintings. Help students understand that the images and their reflections are symmetrical around a horizontal line. Point out that the reflections are distorted by the movements of the water.

Critical Thinking Questions

- **How would you describe the brushstrokes Mary Cassatt used?** (Possible responses: Cassatt's brushstrokes are thicker; they look as if she painted more quickly.) ART CRITICISM: DESCRIPTION

- **What feeling does each painting give you?** (Responses will vary.) AESTHETICS: PERSONAL RESPONSE

MEETING INDIVIDUAL NEEDS

STUDENTS ACQUIRING ENGLISH Tell students that an impression is a quick look or feeling. Ask students to share their first impressions of new foods, clothing styles, or customs.

LESSON 5 PAINTING A REFLECTION

Impressions of Light

How did one group of artists try to capture special moments?

A *Summertime*, Mary Cassatt
1894. Oil on canvas, 28 7/8 in. X 39 3/... Armand Hammer Museum of Art and Cultural Center, Los Angeles.

B *Harp of the Winds: A View on the Seine*, Homer Dodge Martin
1895. Oil on canvas, 28 3/4 in. X 40 3/4 in. Metropolitan Museum of Art, New York.

What season or time of day is shown in each of these paintings? How can you tell? The artists who painted pictures **A** and **B** tried to capture a quick, fleeting look, or impression. These painters were part of a group called the **Impressionists**. Impressionism started in France in the 1870s. Notice how the light hits the water in pictures A and B. With your finger, brush over each stroke in A as if you

28

SHARE ART HISTORY

A **Mary Cassatt (1844–1926)** was born in Pennsylvania but lived most of her life in France. She exhibited her paintings along with the Impressionists and followed the Impressionist style for most of her career. She is known for her portrayals of women and children in everyday situations.

B **Homer Dodge Martin (1836–1897)** had a lifelong love of nature. Despite (or perhaps because of) his impaired vision, he studied nature relentlessly, often staring at scenes with his eyes half-closed. He made mental images of natural scenes and painted them with a distinct and unusual sense of color that was not widely appreciated during his lifetime. In his final years, he painted while almost completely blind.

---

28 UNIT 1: *Seeing Is Believing*

IN THE STUDIO BIG BOOK p.5

were painting it yourself. These **brushstrokes** show the movement of the water.

Can you find where the top part of picture B is almost exactly like the bottom part? This is called **horizontal symmetry**. In this painting the water is like a mirror, reflecting everything above it.

C Student artwork

IN THE STUDIO

Make a painting that shows a reflection in water.

MATERIALS
- large sheets of tagboard or other white paper
- watercolors
- tempera paints
- paintbrushes

1. Fold a piece of paper the long way, and then open it. 
2. Using the watercolors, paint two backgrounds—a sky background above the fold, and a lake background below the fold. Let dry. Using the tempera paints, add objects above the fold, such as plants, trees, and buildings. These are the objects on the water's bank. 
3. After completing each object, fold the paper so that the tempera paint prints on the bottom half. This is the reflection in the lake.

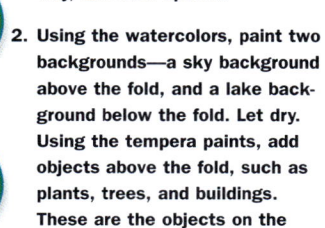

29

ART ACROSS THE CURRICULUM

SCIENCE: OPTICS
Explain that many Impressionists used a technique called *optical mixing*. Instead of blending colors, they placed dots or strokes of color next to each other. From a distance, the colors seemed to blend. The same principle is used in color printing—tiny dots of blue, red, yellow, and black create all the colors. You might have students look at printed colors through a magnifying glass.

LANGUAGE ARTS: WRITING A POEM
Invite students to write poems about their paintings. Encourage them to use descriptive words that help give an impression of the scene. You might provide this poem about Mary Cassatt's painting as a model:

Green and quiet   (2 adjectives)
leaves, river, boat   (3 nouns)
float and dream   (2 verbs)
in the still water.   (1 prepositional phrase)

IN THE STUDIO

MATERIALS: large sheets of tagboard or other white paper, tempera paints, watercolor paints, paintbrushes

Painting a Reflection   CREATING ART

- Demonstrate how to fold the paper to make a crease where the horizon belongs (not necessarily dead center).
- Students can use watercolors to paint the water below the fold and the sky above it. Allow to dry.
- Have students use tempera to paint a scene on the shore.
- Students should refold the paper while the tempera is still wet and press gently and evenly to print the image on the bottom half. They may need to do this several times while painting.
- Encourage students to give their painting a title.

OPTIONAL: Quick Activity Have students paint an object using quick, bold brushstrokes. Encourage them to show what they observe rather than their mental image of the object.

WRAP-UP   INFORMAL ASSESSMENT

- If you were to make this kind of painting again, would you do anything differently? Explain your answer. (Responses will vary.) PRODUCTION: EVALUATION
- Is your painting similar in any way to painting A or B? Explain why or why not. (Responses will vary.) ART CRITICISM: COMPARE/CONTRAST

LESSON 5: *Impressions of Light*   29

LESSON 6

Showing Movement

OBJECTIVES: Identify techniques artists use to create the illusion of movement. Make a wire sculpture of an animal and create the illusion that the animal is moving.

MOTIVATE

Identify dramatic movement. Ask students to mime simple everyday actions such as opening a refrigerator door or waving to a friend. Next, ask them to mime the same action dramatically by exaggerating their gestures.

VIEWING ART

TEACH

Discuss ways that artists create the illusion of movement. Point out that artists, too, may make their sculptures appear more dramatic by showing movement in them. Have students read about the artworks. Ask which parts of each sculpture seem to be moving. (the horse's legs in A; the figure's upraised arm and the bird's flapping wings in B)

Discuss how diagonal lines make viewers' eyes move. Tell students to trace the line of the figure's upraised arm in B. Point out the positions of the figure's head, its other arm, and the legs. Discuss how the lines of the sculpture suggest movement in the figures. You may wish to display *Art Print 1* and discuss the movement of its figures.

Critical Thinking Questions

- **What words would you use to describe the position and movement of the horse in A?** (Possible responses: proud, prancing, dramatic, upright) ART CRITICISM: DESCRIPTION

- **How do you think the person shown in B is feeling?** (Possible responses: happy to release the bird; wishing to be able to fly) AESTHETICS: INTERPRETATION

MEETING INDIVIDUAL NEEDS

CHALLENGE Have students imagine that the sculptures really are moving. Ask them to draw one of the sculptures as it might look a few seconds later.

LESSON 6 MAKING A WIRE SCULPTURE

Showing Movement

How do artists make objects seem to be moving?

Some artists create two-dimensional artwork such as paintings and drawings. Other artists create three-dimensional works of art called **sculptures**. Sculptures can be almost comically simple, such as **A**, or detailed and dramatic, such as **B**.

Sculptors often use long, slanting lines to make an object look as if it is moving. Find some slanting, or **diagonal**, lines in sculptures A and B. Which part of each sculpture seems to be moving? With your finger, trace some long, diagonal lines in sculpture B. Does this sculpture show a lot of movement or a little movement? Why do you think so?

Imagine that sculpture B could come to life. What might happen next?

A *Horse and Rider,* Alexander Calder
Circa 1950. Wire, 14 in. X 17 in. X 5 1/2 in.
Galerie Maeght, Paris.

SHARE ART HISTORY

A **Alexander Calder** (1898–1976) was one of the first American sculptors to become known around the world. He studied engineering and painting, but he is most famous for his sculptures. Calder created *mobiles*, or moving sculptures, as well as *stabiles*, which resemble mobiles but do not move. Calder's early artwork included miniature circuses.

B As a child, **Michael Naranjo** [nah•RAHN•hoh] (1944–) lived in Santa Clara Pueblo, New Mexico. There he hunted, fished, and celebrated feast days. His dream of becoming a sculptor was almost destroyed when he was twenty-four. While he was in the armed forces in Vietnam, he was blinded by an explosion. However, Naranjo drew on his extraordinary sense of touch to create evocative sculptures such as *Skyward, My Friend.*

UNIT 1: *Seeing Is Believing*

IN THE STUDIO BIG BOOK p.6

B detail from *Skyward, My Friend*, Michael Naranjo
1994. Bronze, 46 in. tall. Perna Gallery, Taos, NM.

IN THE STUDIO

MATERIALS
- wire or pipe cleaner

Make a wire sculpture of an animal. How can you show movement?

1. Use three pieces of wire for your basic "skeleton."
2. Twist the wires around each other to create an animal. 
3. Bend parts of your animal to show a movement such as running or leaping. 

31

ART ACROSS THE CURRICULUM

LANGUAGE ARTS: WRITING ABOUT SCULPTURE Point out that a sculpture can help to tell a story. Have students choose one sculpture to write about. They should include descriptions of what they think happened before and after the scene shown by the sculpture.

SCIENCE: MOTION IN THE NATURAL WORLD Have students research the fastest land and sea creatures. They might find out which animals run or swim the fastest, which bird flaps its wings the most times per minute, or which insect can devour a leaf the fastest. Discuss the challenges an artist might face in depicting a fast-moving animal.

IN THE STUDIO

MATERIALS: flexible wire such as telephone or electrical wire, scissors or wire cutter, safety glasses

Making a Wire Sculpture

CREATING ART

- Direct students to read the activity on page 31. Encourage them to plan their sculptures by drawing an animal in action. Remind them that they will use three pieces of wire for the basic shape, or skeleton. Their drawings should show how they plan to use the three wires.

- If possible, encourage students to wear safety glasses.

- Model how to twist short pieces of wire around a longer piece to construct a sculpture.

- Invite students to bend parts of their sculptures to show movement. Encourage students to look at their sculptures from all sides to make sure the movement looks realistic from different points of view. They should adjust the wires until they have achieved the movement they want.

OPTIONAL: Quick Activity Students can use a black or brown marker to draw a wire figure in action. Remind students that diagonal lines help show movement.

WRAP-UP

INFORMAL ASSESSMENT

- **How did you make your animal appear to be moving?** (Possible responses: by experimenting with moving parts of the sculpture until it appeared to be moving; by using diagonal lines) PRODUCTION: PROBLEM SOLVING

- **How did looking at sculpture A help you make your sculpture?** (Possible responses: It showed me how to twist one piece of wire around another; it showed me how to make simple shapes.) PRODUCTION: APPLICATION

LESSON 6: *Showing Movement*

UNIT 1
REFLECTING AND REVIEWING

Pages 32–33	**Reflect on the unit theme.** Have students read the first paragraph on page 32. Point out that the artworks in this unit show some of the ways artists represent natural and human-made environments. **Ask students to discuss the sculpture.** Encourage students to speculate about the ideas the artist wanted to communicate with this sculpture. Ask them to describe techniques the artist used to make the cattle and cowboys appear more realistic.
About the Artist	Robert Summers (1940–) is a native of Glen Rose, Texas, where he grew up surrounded by the lore and legends of the Western range. As a boy, he loved John Wayne movies and listened with fascination to his grandmother's stories about cowboys and trail drives. His uncle was said to have ridden with Will Rogers in the Texas Panhandle and Oklahoma. Summers's interest in art began at an early age, although he never received much formal training. He advises young aspiring artists to "learn to *see* things, not just look at them. Observation," he says, "is one of the best teachers."
About the Art	This re-creation of a trail drive extends over 2.8 acres of downtown Dallas, just a few blocks from where the Shawnee Trail once ran. The bronze figures, which include dozens of cattle and three drovers (a trail boss, a vaquero, and a cutter) are 30 percent larger than life, though they appear startlingly lifelike and often make passersby stop in amazement.

UNIT 1 REFLECTING AND REVIEWING

Artists use illusions to create images of their environments.

In this unit, you have learned about some of the ways artists show movement, texture, and distance. These techniques can make a work of art come to life. Look at this sculpture in Dallas, Texas. The artist is showing an important part of Texas heritage in an unusual way. This life-size cattle drive is placed in the middle of a large, bustling city!

Pioneer Plaza, Robert Summers
Under construction. Dallas, TX.

ART ACROSS THE CURRICULUM

MUSIC: RUMBLING ON THE RANGE Ask small groups of students to imagine the sound of the cattle running. Encourage students to think of musical instruments and other sound makers that might simulate the sound of the cattle running across the range followed by cowboys on horseback. The list may include drums, an organ, and stamping feet. Invite groups to explain the items on their lists.
COOPERATIVE LEARNING

What Did I Learn?

- **HOW** did this artist make the cattle seem to move? How would this sculpture be different if the cattle seemed to be standing still?
- **FIND** an artwork in this unit that is like this sculpture in some way. How are the two pieces alike? How are they different?
- **THINK** about the art you created in this unit. How did you show movement? How did you show texture and distance? What other techniques did you use?
- **FIND** an example of an artwork in this unit that shows distance. Explain what techniques the artist used.

Just for Fun — TREASURE HUNT

TO ENCOURAGE STUDENTS to take another close look at the artworks in this unit, ask them to respond to the following questions and statements:

- Name some of the objects from nature that you see in this unit.
- Which one of the scenes in this unit would you like to be in?
- Find three images that show movement. Tell what might happen next in each image.
- As you look through the artworks, find objects that seem far away. Did the artists use the same techniques to show distance?

What Did I Learn?

Encourage students to work in small groups to discuss their answers to these questions that appear on page 33.

- **How did this artist make the cattle seem to move? How would this sculpture be different if the cattle seemed to be standing still?** (Possible response: The artist sculpted the cattle in running or walking positions rather than standing. If the cattle seemed to be still, the sculpture would not seem as lifelike or exciting.) ART CRITICISM: EVALUATION

- **Find an artwork in this unit that is like this sculpture in some way. How are the two pieces alike? How are they different?** (Responses will vary. Encourage students to give specific examples.) ART CRITICISM: COMPARE/CONTRAST

- **Think about the art you created in this unit. How did you show movement? How did you show texture and distance? What other techniques did you use?** (Responses will vary.) PRODUCTION: DESCRIPTION

- **Find an example of an artwork in this unit that shows distance. Explain what techniques the artist used.** (Responses may include overlapping, linear perspective, and atmospheric perspective.) ART CRITICISM: ANALYSIS

Students may select images from this unit to add to their portfolios.

Reflecting and Reviewing 33

UNIT 2

Viewpoints

Art can be a powerful tool to help people express their ideas and feelings. An artist's work shows his or her viewpoint or attitude about a particular person, place, or thing. A sculptor, for example, might create a statue in honor of a hero, or a painter might record the story of a people or an event. An artist can choose his or her medium or subject to make a statement on an issue.

In this unit, students will discover some of the ways viewpoints can be expressed in art.

ART PRINT 3 *Martin Luther King, Jr.* statue by Selma Hortense Burke

ART PRINT 4 *Good Neighbors* by Jane Wooster Scott

Using the Art Prints

Display and introduce *Art Prints 3* and *4.* (Discussion suggestions appear on the back of each *Art Print.*) Invite students to discuss the viewpoints expressed in each work.

RESPONSE CARD OPTION Have students select an artwork from the unit and use Response Card 1, *Portraits,* on page R56 of this *Teacher's Edition* to compare the artwork with *Art Print 3.*

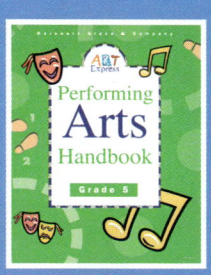

Performing Arts Handbook

Dance, theater, and music activities to extend and enrich students' experiences with these *Art Prints* can be found in the *Performing Arts Handbook.*

UNIT 2: *Viewpoints* 34B

UNIT 2 VIEWPOINTS

Introducing the Unit pp. 34A–35

LESSON	VIEWING	CREATING	CURRICULUM CONNECTIONS
7 PORTRAITS PP. 36–37 • portrait of George Washington by Gilbert Stuart • portrait of Mary McLeod Bethune by Betsy Graves Reyneau	*Understand that portrait artists can depict people in ways that emphasize their importance and dignity.* **VOCABULARY:** portrait, pose, symbols, emphasis, proportions	*Choose a personal hero and draw that person's portrait. Include a symbol in the portrait.* **MATERIALS:** pencils, scissors, glue, pastels or crayons, rulers, paper	**Language Arts** Writing about Heroes, p. 37 **Social Studies** American Heroes, p. 37
8 COLORS AND FEELINGS PP. 38–39 • *A Really Swell Parade Down Main Street* by Jane Wooster Scott • *The Country School* by Winslow Homer	*Examine how artists use color to convey feelings about special times and places.* **VOCABULARY:** mood, warm colors, cool colors	*Make a painting of life today from the perspective of someone living in the future.* **MATERIALS:** paper, watercolors, paintbrushes	**Performing Arts** Music: Discuss songs and memories, p. 39 **Social Studies** A Picture Is Worth a Thousand Words, p. 39

CONNECTIONS: ART AND CULTURE Magazine Art pp. 40–41

LESSON	VIEWING	CREATING	CURRICULUM CONNECTIONS
9 MOSAICS PP. 42–43 • Detail from Shalom Mayer Tower, by Nachum Gutman • Detail from the Greca Mausoleum of Galla Placidia	*Understand that mosaics can decorate and honor special places.* **VOCABULARY:** mosaics, tesserae, abstract, nonrepresentational	*Work with a group to make a mosaic.* **MATERIALS:** colored stones, beads, cut paper, strong glue, large sheet of cardboard as backing	**Mathematics** Geometry in Mosaics, p. 43 **Language Arts** Write a Poem, p. 43
10 IMAGES THAT INSPIRE PP. 44–45 • *Liberty Enlightening the World* by Frédéric-Auguste Bartholdi • Panel from *The Migration Series* by Jacob Lawrence • *The Marine Corps Memorial* by Felix W. de Weldon	*Examine how works of art celebrate cultural values and heroes.* **VOCABULARY:** scale, statues	*Create a photomontage that expresses an American value.* **MATERIALS:** old magazines, scissors, poster board, glue	**Social Studies** Painting History, p. 45 **Language Arts** Inspiring Poems, p. 45

CONNECTIONS: COMMUNITY ART Heroic Statues pp. 46–47

LESSON	VIEWING	CREATING	CURRICULUM CONNECTIONS
11 THE POWER OF THE POSTER PP. 48–49 • *Uncle Sam Wants You* by James Montgomery Flagg • *1964 Tokyo Olympic Games* by Yusaku Kamekura • *1968 Mexico City Olympic Games* by Lance Wyman	*Examine how words and images are used in poster art to persuade people.* **VOCABULARY:** foreshortened, type	*Design a persuasive poster using simple, powerful images and words.* **MATERIALS:** brightly colored paper, poster paints, paintbrushes, markers, poster board, glue, scissors	**Health** Get Involved, p. 49 **Language Arts** Who's Who, p. 49
12 POP ART PP. 50–51 • *Peach Halves* by Andy Warhol • *Untitled* by Wayne Thiebaud	*Explore how artists comment on our culture.* **VOCABULARY:** Pop Art, impasto painting, unity, variety	*Make an impasto painting of a common object.* **MATERIALS:** tempera paints, paintbrushes, dry wheat paste, cardboard, craft sticks, newsprint	**Social Studies** Mass Production, p. 51 **Language Arts** Write Pop Poems, p. 51

Unit 2 Reflecting and Reviewing pp. 52–53

Integrating Your Day

SUGGESTED READING	OPTIONAL VIDEOS/TECHNOLOGY
A Victorian Cat's Journal by Stanley Baron, illus. by Susan Herbert. Bulfinch Press, 1991. **EASY** *Navajo: Visions and Voices Across the Mesa* by Shonto Begay. Scholastic, 1995. **AVERAGE** 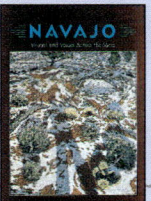	Students can use the *Monstrous Media Kit* to compose an illustrated story about their personal hero.
A Weekend with Winslow Homer by Ann Beneduce. Rizzoli, 1993. **AVERAGE** *The Science Book of Color* by Neil Ardley. Gulliver, 1991. **EASY**	Students can view excerpts from the video *Winslow Homer: The Nature of the Artist* to learn more about the art of this well-known artist.
Art from Rocks and Shells: with projects using pebbles, feathers, flotsam, and jetsam by Gillian Chapman and Pam Robson. Thomas Learning, 1995. **EASY** *A Collage of Crafts* by Charlie Guerrier. Ticknor and Fields, 1994. **AVERAGE**	Have students use *kidDraw* with *The New Kid Pix* to create an animated multi-media mosaic.
Eyewitness Books: Flag by William Crampton. Knopf, 1989. **CHALLENGE** *Texas: A Picture Memory* by Bill Harris. Crescent, 1990. **CHALLENGE** 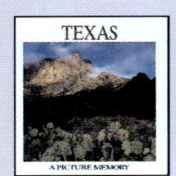	Students can learn about some of Lawrence's artistic techniques by watching excerpts from the video *Jacob Lawrence: The Glory of Expression*.
Great Winter Olympic Moments by Nate Aaseng. Lerner, 1990. **AVERAGE** *Great Summer Olympic Moments* by Nate Aaseng. Lerner, 1990. **AVERAGE**	Small groups of students can use *HyperStudio* to create a web page or an interactive presentation that encourages the study of art.
Roy Lichenstein: The Artist at Work by Lou Ann Walker. Lodestar, 1994. **AVERAGE** *Wild Wheels* by Harrod Blank. Pomegranate, 1994. **CHALLENGE**	Have students use *Crayola Art Studio 2* to draw an everyday object from their classroom.

Art Minutes

Present one of these puzzles or activities for students to solve by the end of the week.

■ **Draw** a picture that tells the story of your last birthday or another important day in your life. APPLICATION

■ Look at the two *Art Prints* in this unit. **Explain** why you feel that the artists are successful or unsuccessful in conveying their viewpoints in these works. ANALYSIS

■ **Name** and describe another work of art you have seen recently that expresses the artist's viewpoint. ANALYSIS

■ Choose a person you admire or someone you consider a hero. **Describe** a statue you would make in that person's honor. SYNTHESIS

■ **Find** a patriotic poster or advertisement. Identify three things that make it patriotic. ANALYSIS

■ **Critically view** at least three TV commercials. Identify one way each commercial tries to persuade the viewer. APPLICATION

SCHOOL-HOME CONNECTION

After completing Lesson 7, distribute School-Home Connection 2, found on page R51. Students can work with a family member to draft a list of admirable people to sketch a portrait of.

Activities and Resources CD-ROM provides additional teaching materials and interactive student activities for use with Unit 2.

UNIT 2: *Viewpoints* 34D

UNIT 2

INTRODUCING THE UNIT

Pages 34–35

Discuss the image of Franklin Delano Roosevelt. Have students read pages 34 and 35. Point out to students that the image is a tribute to a former President of the United States. Ask volunteers to explain why it might be appropriate to honor a leader in this manner. Ask students what they think of the plaque.

Examine the process. Tell students that Burke visited the White House and sketched the President while planning the plaque. Burke actually completed the plaque after Roosevelt's death, using her sketches and her memory. Ask students what viewpoints they think Selma Burke expresses in this plaque.

About the Art

This plaque is one of many sculptures by Selma Burke. Burke entered and won a national competition, after which she was commissioned to create a profile of the President. Have students examine the profile, and point out that this image is the basis for the image on the dime.

Another example of Selma Burke's sculpture can be found on *Art Print 3*.

Roosevelt dime based on Burke

Franklin Delano Roosevelt, Sel
Bronze, 3 ft. 6 in. X 2 ft. 6 in.

TIME LINE

You may wish to have pairs of students select two artworks from the unit from different time periods. Suggest that they use the *Time Line* to compare the two periods.

34 UNIT 2: *Viewpoints*

UNIT 2

Viewpoints

How can art express how people feel about a country and its history?

Throughout the history of the United States, artists have shown their patriotism through art. They have made pictures and sculptures that tell about important American heroes, ideas, and events.

This plaque was made by artist Selma Burke to honor President Franklin Delano Roosevelt. Burke said she wanted this to be the best piece of sculpture she had ever done? Why do you think she felt this way?

ABOUT SELMA BURKE

Dr. Selma Burke studied art at Sarah Lawrence College and Columbia University. She was in the Navy during World War II when she created her sculpture of the president.

Meet the Artist

Selma Hortense Burke (1900–1995) grew up in a family of ten children in Mooresville, North Carolina. Her father and two brothers did extensive traveling and collected fine art objects. Because of this, Selma discovered the wonders of art at a young age. Selma studied to be a nurse but decided to pursue her artistic talent instead. She graduated with a Master of Fine Art degree from Columbia University. While in the hospital for a back injury, Selma learned of a national competition to create a profile of President Roosevelt. She entered and won. The plaque she created was unveiled at a ceremony in 1945, and its image was chosen for use on the dime.

Burke is best known for this plaque, but she has also created sculptures of such people as Dr. Martin Luther King, Jr., Dr. Mary McLeod Bethune, and Booker T. Washington.

LITERATURE CONNECTION

Grandma Moses: Painter of Rural America by Zibby Oneal. Viking, 1986. AVERAGE

This book tells the story of artist Grandma Moses, who painted scenes of early rural America.

CLASSROOM MANAGEMENT

VIEWING: Response Cards To provide students with additional opportunities to view and discuss art, have students use appropriate Response Cards as they think about art from the unit and from other sources. For example, have students use Response Card 3, Stories in Art, with Lesson 9, Mosaics. Then have them use the Response Card as they view other examples of storytelling in artwork. The Response Cards begin on page R56 of this Teacher's Edition.

CREATING: Studio Activity Options Each lesson in the unit contains two options for the In the Studio activity. If your time is limited, choose the Quick Activity for one or more lessons. Each Quick Activity provides students with an experience that will deepen their understanding of the lesson concepts and skills.

LESSON 7 Portraits

OBJECTIVES: Understand that portrait artists can depict people in ways that emphasize their importance and dignity. Choose a personal hero and draw that person's portrait. Include a symbol in the portrait.

MOTIVATE

Share personal heroes. Tell students about someone you admire. Then invite students to tell who their personal heroes are and why they admire them.

VIEWING ART

TEACH

Discuss the importance of portraits. Explain that artists can honor people by painting portraits of them. Point out that before photography was invented, artists were often asked to paint portraits of important people.

Discuss the art. Have students read pages 36 and 37. Ask how the artist showed George Washington's dignity. (Possible response: Washington is standing up straight and holding his hand out.) Ask what the sword and the pen might stand for. (Possible response: his skills as a soldier and a writer) Ask where in B the painter placed emphasis. (on Bethune's face and on the globe) Ask what kind of person students think Bethune was. (Possible responses: respectable; intelligent; a teacher)

Critical Thinking Questions

- **How are A and B similar? How are they different?** (Possible responses: Both persons are standing in dignified poses. Bethune's portrait seems more recent.) ART CRITICISM: COMPARE/CONTRAST

- **Based on their portraits, which of these persons would you like to know? Why?** (Responses will vary.) AESTHETICS: PERSONAL RESPONSE

CHALLENGE Ask students to list two objects in B and explain what each might stand for.

LESSON 7 DRAWING A PORTRAIT

Portraits

What can you tell about these two people from their pictures?

A **portrait** is a picture of a person. Portraits are often created to tell about an important person's life and work. Why do you think the artist decided to show President George Washington in this **pose**, or position? The sword and the pen in portrait A are **symbols** of Washington's special skills and talents. What special skill do you think each symbol stands for?

Mary McLeod Bethune started a women's college in Florida. On which parts of her portrait B did the painter put the most **emphasis**, or importance? What kind of person do you think Bethune was, judging from her portrait?

A *George Washington*, Gilbert Stuart

B *Mary McLeod Bethune*, Betsy Graves Reyneau
1943–44. Oil on canvas. National Portrait Gallery, Washington, D.C.

36

SHARE ART HISTORY

A Gilbert Stuart (1755–1828) was born in Rhode Island before the United States became a nation. He painted several of our earliest presidents: George Washington, John Adams, Thomas Jefferson, and James Madison. Stuart's portraits were not only good likenesses; they also captured the character of his subjects. Stuart also created a very famous engraving—the relief portrait of George Washington on our one-dollar bill.

B Betsy Graves Reyneau [ray•NOH] (1888–1964) was born in Battle Creek, Michigan, and studied in Boston, Paris, and Rome. She painted many portraits of well known African Americans. This portrait, along with a portrait of boxer Joe Louis, hangs in the National Portrait Gallery.

You may wish to share another image of a heroic African American, *Art Print 3*, a statue of Martin Luther King, Jr., by Selma Burke.

36 UNIT 2: *Viewpoints*

IN THE STUDIO BIG BOOK p.7

When you draw a portrait, look carefully at the person's face. Do not try to draw from memory. Notice the **proportions** of the face. Proportion is the size and placement of the features when you compare them with each other. Where are the eyes compared with the ears? How big is the forehead compared with the whole head? A grid like the one shown here can help you draw portraits.

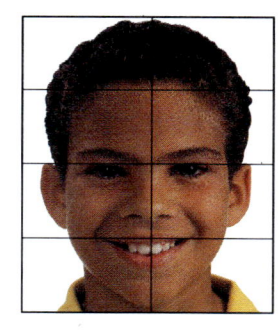

IN THE STUDIO

MATERIALS
- model
- white paper for background, neck, and shoulders
- smaller white paper for face
- soft pencil
- ruler
- watercolors
- paintbrushes
- pastels (oil or chalk) or crayons
- scissors
- glue

Draw a portrait of a person. Show the person's head and shoulders. Use natural-looking proportions.

1. First, choose a model (a person to pose for you). Then use watercolors to paint a background on the large sheet. Choose colors that express a feeling or an attitude about the person.

2. Use a ruler and a pencil to draw a light grid. Draw the person's face in the grid. Then use pastels or crayons to redraw your lines, adding color and details.

3. Cut out the face, and glue it to the background, leaving room for the neck and shoulders. Remember to look at your model carefully. Use pastels or crayons to draw in the neck and shoulders.

ART ACROSS THE CURRICULUM

LANGUAGE ARTS: WRITING ABOUT HEROES Ask students to research and write essays about the lives of the people they admire. Students can interview subjects whom they know personally. If the subject is well known, students can read about him or her at the local or school library, or on the World Wide Web. Display students' essays on a bulletin board.

SOCIAL STUDIES: AMERICAN HEROES Ask students to read about the life of George Washington, Mary McLeod Bethune, or another hero of their choice. Have them find biographies of these people and locate entries in encyclopedias. Ask students to prepare oral presentations about the people they have researched.

IN THE STUDIO

MATERIALS: pencils, scissors, glue, pastels (chalk or oil) or crayons, rulers, large sheets of white paper, smaller sheets of white paper, models for portraits

Drawing a Portrait

CREATING ART

- Have students read page 37. Then have them use watercolors to paint a background on the large sheet. They can use more than one color.

- Direct students to draw their grids lightly. Then have students lightly sketch their portraits with pencils, using the proportion grid as a guide. Remind them to look carefully at their model.

- Direct students to add color to their sketches. If students are using oil pastels, show them how to blend thick layers of color by rubbing them with their fingers or a paper towel.

- Have students cut out their portrait and glue it to the background, leaving space at the bottom. Then have them add the neck and shoulders.

OPTIONAL: Quick Activity Invite students to make quick sketches of people without a proportion grid. Encourage them to solve proportion problems by looking at each other's faces.

WRAP-UP

INFORMAL ASSESSMENT

- **How did the grid help you draw your portrait?** (Responses will vary. Students may suggest that it helped them draw more natural-looking proportions.) PRODUCTION: APPLICATION

- **Find a symbol in another student's portrait. What do you think the symbol stands for?** (Responses will vary.) ART CRITICISM: INTERPRETATION

LESSON 7: *Portraits*

LESSON 8

Colors and Feelings

OBJECTIVES: Examine how artists use color to convey feelings about special times and places. Make a painting of life today from the perspective of someone living in the future. Use warm colors to convey a happy mood.

MOTIVATE

Share visual memories. Ask students to think of a happy scene. Then ask each student to tell about the colors he or she would use to paint that scene.

VIEWING ART

TEACH

Discuss how colors create a mood. Read aloud pages 38–39. Ask how students would feel if they were watching the parade shown in A. (Possible response: excited) Point out that the artist used bright colors—yellow, green, and red—and patriotic colors—red, white, and blue. You may wish to display *Art Print 4,* another example of Jane Wooster Scott's work.

Discuss warm colors and the feelings they evoke. Ask students how it would feel to be a student in *The Country School* and why. (Possible response: comfortable and safe) Ask what colors the artist used to help create this feeling. (oranges, yellows, reds, and browns)

Critical Thinking Questions

- **When might you want to use blues, purples, and grays in a painting?** (Possible response: to make a sad or cold painting) PRODUCTION: APPLICATION

- **Why doesn't the blue background in picture A create a cool mood?** (Possible response: because it makes the bright, warm colors stand out) ART CRITICISM: ANALYSIS

MEETING INDIVIDUAL NEEDS

STUDENTS ACQUIRING ENGLISH Work with students to name the colors on a color wheel and to identify warm and cool colors. Then have them identify the warm and cool colors in each painting.

LESSON 8 PAINTING THE PAST

Colors and Feelings

How do you think the artists felt about these scenes of the past?

American flags! Balloons! A band marching down Main Street! How would you feel if you were standing on the curb watching the parade in picture **A**? Artists can use bright colors to create a **mood**, or feeling, of excitement. They can use the colors of the American flag to make Americans feel proud.

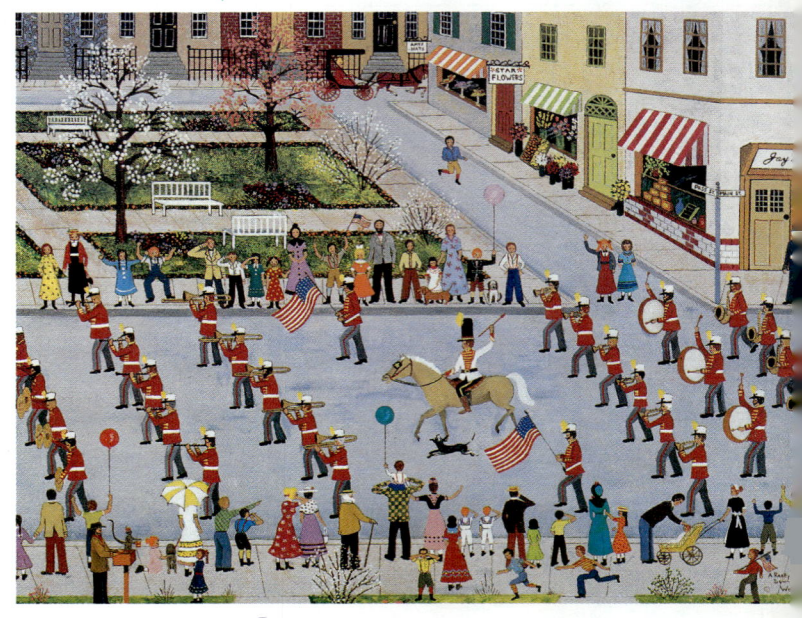

A *A Really Swell Parade Down Main Street,* Jane Wooster Scott

38

SHARE ART HISTORY

A **Jane Wooster Scott** has had two careers in the arts. She started out as a film and television actress. When she had children, she stopped acting and began to paint as a hobby. Before long she became a well-known artist. In her work, Scott tries to capture the simple life she knew as a child. She says, "I travel to New England and southward along the Atlantic Coast, scouring the back roads and country lanes searching for the past."

B **Winslow Homer** (1836–1910) had no formal art training. He worked as a magazine illustrator and painted realistic scenes while working as a pictorial reporter during the Civil War. During his life, artists such as the Impressionists were experimenting with new styles. But Homer was interested in depicting typically American scenes realistically. Homer's style is rooted in the movement known as American Realism.

38   UNIT 2: *Viewpoints*

IN THE STUDIO BIG BOOK p.8

What do you think it would feel like to be a student in picture **B**, *The Country School*? Why? What colors did the artist use to create this mood? **Warm colors** (reds, oranges, yellows) can make us feel warm and happy. **Cool colors**, such as blues and violets, can make us feel cool. How else did the artist show his feelings about this old-fashioned school?

B

The Country School, Winslow Homer
1871. Oil on canvas, 21 3/8 X 38 3/8 in.
The Saint Louis Art Museum, St. Louis, MO.

IN THE STUDIO

MATERIALS
- watercolor paper
- watercolors
- paintbrushes

Paint with the colors of the past.

Imagine you are living far in the future. Paint a picture that makes some part of life today seem like "the good old days." Use warm colors to make viewers feel good about what is happening in your scene.

ART ACROSS THE CURRICULUM

PERFORMING ARTS: MUSIC Encourage students to ask older family members to play favorite songs for them from twenty years ago or more. Family members may wish to share memories that are associated with these songs. If possible, arrange for students to sing or play recordings of these songs for classmates and to retell their family members' nostalgic stories.

SOCIAL STUDIES: A PICTURE IS WORTH A THOUSAND WORDS Local historical museums are full of memories of the past. Arrange a field trip to a local museum, and invite students to look at photographs of your community as it was many years ago. Encourage students to choose one photograph and write a short essay describing what they see happening in the picture and telling how the images make them feel.

IN THE STUDIO

MATERIALS: watercolor paper, watercolors, paintbrushes

Painting the Past

CREATING ART

- Ask students to imagine that they are older and are remembering life as it is today. Encourage them to visualize a scene that makes them feel happy. Ask what images and colors they might include in a painting of the scene.

- Students can begin by choosing several colors that convey the mood of the scene they visualized.

- Have students mix one color with water and create a sketch with this pale color. Explain to students that at this point, changes in images or their placement are easy to make; suggest that they add brighter and darker colors gradually.

OPTIONAL: Quick Activity Invite students to draw one simple cityscape in cool colors and one in warm colors, using crayons. Then ask them to discuss the differences in mood created by the colors.

WRAP-UP

INFORMAL ASSESSMENT

- **Look at a classmate's painting. How does it make you feel? What colors and images did the artist use to create this mood?** (Responses will vary.) ART CRITICISM: ANALYSIS

- **Why do you think artists paint pictures such as A and B?** (Possible response: They want to make a record of the world during their lifetime; they want to share good feelings.) ART HISTORY: GENERALIZE

LESSON 8: *Colors and Feelings*

CONNECTIONS

ART AND CULTURE

Identify popular children's magazines. Have students name children's magazines that they have read. Ask them what they liked in particular about the magazines. (Possible responses: *Sports Illustrated for Kids*—I liked the photographs; *Cricket Magazine*—the drawings can be funny, or dreamlike.) Then have students read pages 40–41.

Discuss the magazine cover. Ask students to look at the *St. Nicholas Magazine* cover art and discuss how color affects their appreciation of it. (Possible response: The color is part of what makes it look old and from another time.)

CONNECTIONS — ART AND CULTURE

Magazine Art

Children's magazines have been popular in the United States since 1829.

Nineteenth-century children did not have TVs or videos, but they did have wonderful books and magazines. In fact, many of the books they read, such as *Alice in Wonderland* and *The Adventures of Tom Sawyer,* are still popular with young readers today.

The most popular children's publication back then was called *St. Nicholas Magazine.* Look at this cover and these illustrations. If you didn't look at the date, how could you tell that this art was done long ago?

▶ Cover of *St. Nicholas Magazine,* July 1926

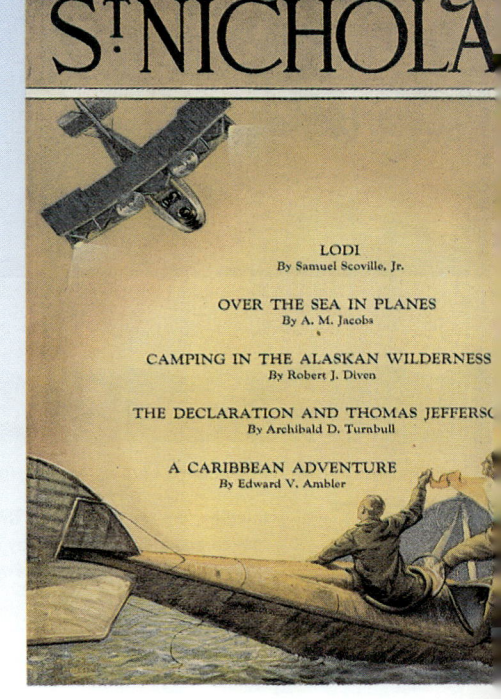

40

SHARE ART HISTORY

Past Authors and Illustrators

Contributors to *St. Nicholas Magazine* included many famous writers and illustrators. Louisa May Alcott, Mark Twain, and Robert Louis Stevenson were writers known all over the English-speaking world. Howard Pyle and Thomas Nast were equally famous illustrators. These writers and artists helped influence the development of children's literature in the twentieth century. You may want to read aloud some poems by Robert Louis Stevenson or share a cartoon by Thomas Nast.

HEALTH

Temperature Test

Have students draw a piece of art for their own *Classroom Health Magazine.* Ask students to illustrate a group of healthful fruits and vegetables. Challenge students to use warm or cool colors to influence the feelings of the viewer. Have volunteers share their illustrations.

40 UNIT 2: *Viewpoints*

▲ "Great Grandmother's Girlhood"    ▲ "The Mistletoe Hung in the Castle Hall…"

WHAT DO YOU THINK?
- How would you describe the colors in these illustrations?
- Do you think a publisher would use this type of art today? Explain.

WHAT DO YOU THINK?
- How would you describe the colors in these illustrations? (Possible responses: soft, warm, quiet) AESTHETICS: ANALYSIS
- Do you think a publisher would use this type of art today? Explain. (Possible response: No, today publishers use brighter, livelier colors and pictures.) ART CRITICISM: MAKE JUDGMENTS

41

THEATER

Mood Colors

Discuss with students how different moods are associated with different colors. For example, the color yellow might indicate joy. Have students take turns selecting colors and then pantomiming moods appropriate for them. Color combinations, such as red, white, and blue, might be interesting, too. Students of various cultural backgrounds might share ways in which color associations differ in the countries of their heritage.

IN THE STUDIO

Playground Puzzle

COOPERATIVE LEARNING Have students work in pairs to design a playground with the following requirements:

- The playground must have three pieces of playground equipment.
- The designers must use color to influence people's feelings.
- The design must create an image of activity and fun.

Have volunteers share their playground designs.

CONNECTIONS: *Art and Culture*   41

LESSON 9

Mosaics

OBJECTIVES: Understand that mosaics can decorate and honor special places. Work with a group to make a mosaic.

MOTIVATE

Discuss some murals in the local community. Invite students to describe murals they have seen on the walls of buildings or in other public places.

VIEWING ART

TEACH

Define the term *mosaic*. Encourage students to view the mosaics and read about them. Explain that mosaic tesserae can be small pieces of stone, glass, or pottery. Make sure that students can tell the difference between abstract works such as A and works that are entirely nonrepresentational, such as B.

Discuss the art. Ask students what they think the artist wanted viewers to feel when looking at A. *(Possible response: hopeful)* Invite students to explain their answers. *(Possible response: The shadows show that there is a strong light, which might stand for hope.)* Ask students why the mosaic-covered wall shown in B might honor the dead more than a plain wall. *(Possible response: The mosaic looks as if it took much time, effort, and care to make.)*

Critical Thinking Questions

- **Why might an artist decorate an outdoor wall with a mosaic rather than with a painting?** *(Possible response: Mosaic would last longer.)* PRODUCTION: COMPARE/CONTRAST

- **Name two ways in which mosaic artists can "draw" lines.** *(Possible response: by using long, thin tesserae or by lining up many small tesserae)* PRODUCTION: DESCRIPTION

CHALLENGE Invite students to find more reproductions of mosaics in library books. Ask them to retell for the class any stories these mosaics illustrate.

LESSON 9 MAKING A MOSAIC

Mosaics

How do artists turn walls into special places of honor?

Mosaics are pictures made with many small pieces called **tesserae** [TEH•suh•ree]. Mosaic **A** tells the story of the beginning of a city. It was created in an **abstract** style. The people in A do not look like people do in the natural world. What feeling might the artist want viewers to have about this new city? How do you know?

Mosaic **B** was made to decorate a Roman tomb. It was created in a **nonrepresentational** style. The shapes and colors in B do not look like objects you recognize. Why might this wall honor the dead more than a plain wall?

A Detail from a mural in Shalom Mayer Tower, Nachum Gutman 1965–66. Tile, about 15 ft. 8 in. X 55 ft. 8 in. (entire), Tel Aviv, Israel.

SHARE ART HISTORY

A Nachum Gutman (1898–1981) was born in Russia and immigrated to Israel. His paintings have been exhibited in many major cities. Gutman made this huge mosaic with the help of master craftspeople from Ravenna, Italy; they showed Gutman how to raise parts of the mosaic and how to color some of the grout between the tiles. This section of the mosaic commemorates the first streetlight in Tel Aviv.

B This mosaic was hand set in Ravenna, Italy, over 1,500 years ago. The picture shown is a small detail from an arch in a tomb. It was built for the daughter of Emperor Theodosius the Great, Galla Placidia, who grew up to rule the Western Roman Empire. This mosaic design, called the meander ornament, can be looked at as flat or three-dimensional. This makes it similar to Op Art.

IN THE STUDIO BIG BOOK p. 9

Detail from the *Greca* Mausoleum of Galla Placidia
A.D. 424–450. Tile, width about 2 ft.
Ravenna, Italy.

IN THE STUDIO

MATERIALS
- colored stones
- beads
- cut paper
- glue
- large sheet of heavy cardboard

Work with a group to make a mosaic.

First, plan your mosaic together. Decide if you want to tell a story or make an abstract design. Then sketch your plan in pencil on a sheet of heavy cardboard. Glue colored stones, beads, and cut paper to the cardboard to make your mosaic.

43

ART ACROSS THE CURRICULUM

MATHEMATICS: GEOMETRY IN MOSAICS

Invite students to look closely at B and find examples of the following geometric shapes: squares, rectangles, triangles, parallelograms, rhombuses, and trapezoids. Students may need to look up the properties of some of these shapes in a dictionary or a textbook. Challenge interested students to create their own design that includes several of these shapes.

LANGUAGE ARTS: WRITE A POEM Invite students to write a poem inspired by A. Before they write their poems, they may wish to do some research on Tel Aviv, Israel, the city whose founding this mosaic celebrates.

IN THE STUDIO

MATERIALS: colored stones, beads, cut paper, strong glue, large sheet of cardboard as backing

Making a Mosaic

CREATING ART

- Have students read the instructions. Then have students form small groups.

- Ask group members to plan their mosaic design. Tell them to decide whether it will show recognizable objects. Have students sketch their design in pencil on the backing. Have students label different areas with the colors they plan to use.

- Suggest that students lay out several tesserae on the backing to judge how the pieces fit into part of the design. Remind them to consider texture as well as color.

- After students are satisfied with a section, they should carefully pick up one tessera at a time, put glue on the back of it, and press it into place.

OPTIONAL: Quick Activity Invite students to draw plans for a mosaic for your school. Encourage students to think of an important person or event they want to honor and to consider where the mosaic might be located.

WRAP-UP

INFORMAL ASSESSMENT

- **How did you work as a group to solve problems that came up as you made your mosaic?** (Responses will vary.) PRODUCTION: PROBLEM SOLVING

- **How are mosaics and paintings similar? How are they different?** (Possible responses: Mosaics and paintings can be abstract or nonrepresentational and can have areas of color; in mosaics, the colored areas are broken up into little pieces.) ART CRITICISM: COMPARE/CONTRAST

LESSON 9: *Mosaics* 43

LESSON 10

Images That Inspire

OBJECTIVES: Examine how works of art celebrate cultural values and heroes. Create a photomontage that expresses an American value.

MOTIVATE

Discuss the values represented by heroes. Help students make a list of American heroes on the board. Ask what deeds or values makes each person they chose a hero.

VIEWING ART

TEACH

Discuss symbols in the art. Have students read the paragraphs and look at the images. Explain that symbols are images or objects that represent other things or ideas. Ask students what they think the torch in A stands for. (Possible response: the light of freedom) Ask what symbol students can find in C and what values they think it represents. (the flag; the United States, freedom, independence)

Point out diagonal lines in the art. Explain that the repeated diagonal lines in B and C help viewers feel the subjects' movement and struggle. Ask students what feelings these works of art inspire about the United States. (Possible response: pride, awareness of the struggles Americans have faced) You may wish to display **Art Print 3**. Ask students to identify diagonal lines. (the arms, legs, and torso)

Critical Thinking Questions

- Why do you think the creators of A and C made large-scale artworks? (Possible response: to show that courage and freedom are important) ART HISTORY: INTERPRETATION

- Do the diagonal lines in B and C reflect real life? Explain. (Possible response: Yes, people lean forward when they are walking or struggling.) ART CRITICISM: ANALYSIS

STUDENTS ACQUIRING ENGLISH Explain that the Statue of Liberty stands on an island in New York and welcomes immigrants to the United States.

LESSON 10   MAKING A PHOTOMONTAGE

Images That Inspire

How do these works of art make you feel about the United States?

These three works of art honor American values. They show ideas that are traditionally important to Americans. Find the torch in picture **A**. What do you think this symbol stands for? In picture **B**, the suitcases might be symbols of moving. The people in this picture are trying to move to a better place. What symbol can you find in picture **C**? What values do you think this scene represents?

Find some diagonal lines in pictures B and C. How do these repeated diagonal lines help you understand the people's struggle?

A *Liberty Enlightening the World*, Frédéric-Auguste Bartholdi
1886. Copper, 151 ft. 1 in. tall (toe to torch).
New York Harbor, New York.

B Panel 40 from *The Migration Series*, Jacob Lawrence
1940–41. Tempera and gesso on composition board, 18 in. X 12 in.
Museum of Modern Art, New York.

SHARE ART HISTORY

A **Frédéric-Auguste Bartholdi** [bar•TOHL•dee] (1834–1904), a French sculptor, may have modeled Liberty's face after his mother's. Bartholdi specialized in creating huge patriotic sculptures. He was influenced by the monuments of ancient Egypt.

B **Jacob Lawrence** (1917–) was born during the Great Migration. Like many African Americans, his family moved to the North in search of a better life. In New York City, young Jacob took after-school art classes. Lawrence's *Migration Series* is made up of 60 paintings.

C **Felix de Weldon** (1907–) used a photograph by Joe Rosenthal to design the Marine Corps Memorial. The photo shows six Marines raising the flag on Iwo Jima during World War II. Each morning, a Marine Corps color guard raises the flag on this famous sculpture.

UNIT 2: *Viewpoints*

IN THE STUDIO BIG BOOK p.10

Scale is the size of an object in an artwork compared to its real size. Many public **statues** have a powerful effect on people because they have such a grand scale—they are much larger than life. How large is the Statue of Liberty? About fifteen fifth graders can stand inside its crown!

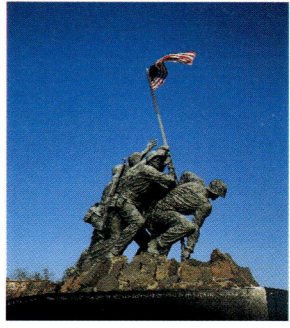

C *The Marine Corps Memorial*, Felix W. de Weldon
Bronze. Arlington, VA.

IN THE STUDIO

MATERIALS
- old magazines
- scissors
- poster board
- glue

Create a photomontage, a group of photos that form one picture. Express an American value.

1. Think about values such as freedom, courage, and equality. Choose one that you would like to express. Find and cut out magazine photos that show this value.
2. Arrange your photos on the poster board. Use overlapping. Try to give emphasis to photos that make a strong statement. Glue the pictures down. Give your photomontage a title.

45

ART ACROSS THE CURRICULUM

SOCIAL STUDIES: PAINTING HISTORY

Ask the class to create a series of collages, photomontages, or paintings about a historical event they are studying in class. Help students choose a topic and decide on four or five related scenes to illustrate. Ask them to brainstorm a list of values and heroes to include. Small groups can work together. Then students can write captions and display their work.

LANGUAGE ARTS: INSPIRING POEMS

Invite students to write a poem based on one of the artworks in this lesson. Read aloud excerpts from poems such as Longfellow's "The Midnight Ride of Paul Revere." Then encourage students to do research on Ellis Island immigrants, the Battle of Iwo Jima, or the Great Migration. Their poetry should express their feelings about the stories connected with the artwork they chose.

IN THE STUDIO

MATERIALS: old magazines, scissors, poster board, glue

Making a Photomontage

CREATING ART

- Ask students to read the instructions. Tell them that a photomontage is a collage of photographs. Because there are so many images in a photomontage, it can express many different ideas and feelings.

- Brainstorm with students some values they might focus on, such as honesty, justice, education, or health.

- Direct students to cut out photographs that make them think about the value they have chosen. Remind students to look for photos showing people, objects, and colors that can be meaningful symbols.

- Ask students to spend some time moving their images around on poster board. This will help them find strong lines and colors for their composition before they glue their photos in place.

OPTIONAL: Quick Activity Invite students to draw a symbol of a value they believe in. Students can choose a well-known symbol or create a new symbol that they feel people will understand.

WRAP-UP

INFORMAL ASSESSMENT

- **Look at your photomontage for a few minutes. What does it seem to say?** (Responses will vary.) PRODUCTION: REFLECTION

- **Find a classmate's work that emphasizes one of the values shown in this lesson. Compare the two artworks.** (Responses will vary.) ART CRITICISM: COMPARE/CONTRAST

LESSON 10: *Images That Inspire* 45

CONNECTIONS
COMMUNITY ART

Identify familiar statues. Ask students to think about statues that they have seen in parks, in buildings, or at monuments. Call on volunteers to identify their favorite ones, and ask them to describe what they like about those statues. Then have students read pages 46–47.

Discuss the statues. Ask students to summarize what they have learned about statues. (Possible response: Communities put up statues to honor people who are brave and hardworking.) Have them look at the statues and speculate about decisions each sculptor made. (Possible responses: Decisions had to be made about the settings, materials, poses, symbols, and so on.)

CONNECTIONS   COMMUNITY ART

HEROIC STATUES

Communities across America honor their heroes with statues.

One of the greatest honors a community can give someone is to put up a statue. Look at the statues on these pages. The people of Phoenix, Arizona, honored the Navajo Code Talkers—talented men from that area who served bravely in World War II. The people of Richmond, Virginia, honored Arthur Ashe—a local boy who grew up to be an international tennis star. Among the statues of heroes in our nation's capital is one that honors all the women who served the United States in the Vietnam War. What decisions did each sculptor have to make in order to create these statues?

▲ Navajo Code Talker

46

SHARE ART HISTORY
Pioneer Sculptor

Like Abraham Lincoln, Vinnie Ream was born in a log cabin to poor parents. She believed that this was why President Lincoln agreed to sit for her while she sculpted his likeness. After President Lincoln was assassinated, Ream was the first woman to receive an art commission from the U.S. government. Her statue of Abraham Lincoln stands in the Capitol Building in Washington, D.C.

SCIENCE
Animals in Clay

Many sculptors begin to practice their craft by sculpting small figures of animals. Have students choose one animal to sculpt. Have them mold clay into the animal's form and make the animal as realistic as possible. Challenge them to create a piece of work that will appeal emotionally to viewers.

46   UNIT 2: *Viewpoints*

▲ Vietnam Women's Memorial

▲ Arthur Ashe

WHAT DO YOU THINK?

▶ What qualities do the three statues have in common?

▶ Look at the setting, or background, of each statue. How does it contribute to the effect?

47

WHAT DO YOU THINK?

▶ **What qualities do the three statues have in common?** (Possible responses: They are made of bronze; they use symbols; the faces look dignified.) ART CRITICISM: ANALYSIS

▶ **Look at the setting, or background, of each statue. How does it contribute to the effect?** (Responses will vary.) AESTHETICS: EVALUATION

THEATER

Express Yourself

COOPERATIVE LEARNING Have students work in pairs to explore different emotions through physical poses. Students should take turns posing and sketching. They should strike different poses as different emotions, such as fear and joy, are named. Partners should then quickly sketch them. Have volunteers share their results.

IN THE STUDIO

Statue Proposal

COOPERATIVE LEARNING Have students work in small groups to complete a proposal for a statue. Provide these requirements:

- Select a local person as the subject, and give reasons for the choice.
- Choose a site for the statue.
- Choose the symbols to include on the statue, and explain their meanings.
- Include a rough sketch.

Encourage volunteers to share their group's statue proposals with classmates.

CONNECTIONS: *Community Art* **47**

LESSON 11

The Power of the Poster

OBJECTIVES: Examine how words and images are used in poster art to persuade people. Design a persuasive poster using simple, powerful images and words.

MOTIVATE

Discuss posters as a means of communication. Invite students to describe familiar posters and describe what they communicate.

VIEWING ART

TEACH

Discuss design elements in the posters. Invite students to look at the posters and read the paragraphs. Ask students to point out examples of simple, powerful pictures, bright colors, and bold words. To demonstrate foreshortening, hold your finger up sideways. Then point it straight at the class so they can see how foreshortening looks in real life.

Discuss feelings evoked by posters. Ask why B is so eye-catching. (Its repeated lines seem to vibrate.) Next, ask how the designer of C created suspense. (He showed a dramatic, close-up photograph of Olympic runners who seem about to take off.) Finally, ask how B and C make students feel about the Olympic games. (Possible response: excited)

Critical Thinking Questions

- **How does poster A get its message across?** (Uncle Sam is looking and pointing straight at the viewer. The word *YOU* stands out. The colors red, white, and blue encourage patriotism.) ART CRITICISM: ANALYSIS

- **Describe how the black lines in B are arranged.** (The lines work both to spell *MEXICO* and form the Olympic rings.) ART CRITICISM: DESCRIPTION

MEETING INDIVIDUAL NEEDS

EXTRA SUPPORT Explain that Uncle Sam, the man in poster A, is a symbol of the United States. This poster was used to recruit soldiers during World War I.

LESSON 11 DESIGNING A PERSUASIVE POSTER

The Power of the Poster

What were these posters designed to do?

Most posters are meant to attract people's attention. They use bright colors, bold words, and simple, powerful pictures. What did the artist do with poster **A** to attract your attention?

Look at Uncle Sam's finger. It's been **foreshortened**, or made shorter, to appear to be pointing *right at you*. Now look at the **type**, or printing. How does it get your attention? This poster is persuasive. The artist wanted people to join the army. He wanted them to feel a personal duty to their country.

How does poster **B** make you keep looking at it? Now look at poster **C**. How did the artist create suspense? How does this poster make you feel about the Olympic Games?

A *Uncle Sam Wants You*, James Montgomery Flagg

SHARE ART HISTORY

A **James Montgomery Flagg** (1877–1960) was an American poster designer and illustrator. During World War I, as the official New York State military artist, Flagg designed posters to recruit men and women for the army. This famous poster was displayed in post offices across America.

B **Lance Wyman** (1937–) teaches in the Communication Design Department of the Parsons School of Design in New York. His graphic design clients include the Washington and Minnesota Zoos, the Baltimore subway system, and UNICEF.

C **Yusaku Kamesura** [yoo•SAH•koo kah•meh•SOO•ruh] (1915–) is a famous Japanese graphic designer. Among his colleagues, he is known as "the boss." Posters made for the 1964 Tokyo Olympics were the first Olympic posters to include photography.

48 UNIT 2: *Viewpoints*

IN THE STUDIO BIG BOOK p.11

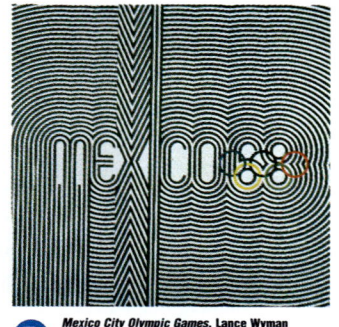

B Mexico City Olympic Games, Lance Wyman 1968.

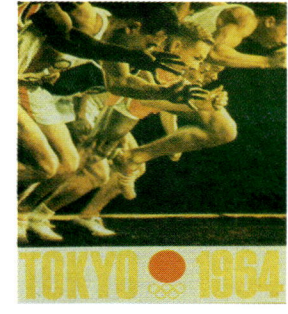

C Tokyo Olympic Games, Yusaku Kamekura 1964.

IN THE STUDIO

MATERIALS
- brightly colored paper
- poster paints
- paintbrushes
- markers
- poster board
- glue
- scissors

Design a poster that persuades viewers to feel or to do something.

1. Decide on the purpose of your poster.
2. Sketch a poster design. View your sketch from a distance. Are your pictures simple and powerful? Are your words exciting and easy to read?
3. Complete your poster, using colored paper, paints, and markers.

49

ART ACROSS THE CURRICULUM

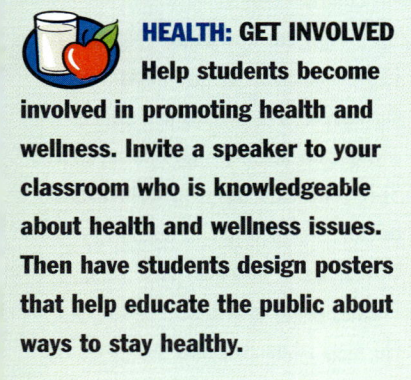

HEALTH: GET INVOLVED Help students become involved in promoting health and wellness. Invite a speaker to your classroom who is knowledgeable about health and wellness issues. Then have students design posters that help educate the public about ways to stay healthy.

LANGUAGE ARTS: WHO'S WHO Have students find information and write about an Olympic athlete. The athlete may be one who broke many records (Mark Spitz, Jesse Owens, Florence Griffith-Joyner, Mary Lou Retton), or someone who competed but did not win. They should include current information about the athlete. Encourage students to include a photograph.

IN THE STUDIO

MATERIALS: brightly colored paper, poster paints, paintbrushes, markers, large sheets of poster board, glue, scissors

Designing a Persuasive Poster   CREATING ART

- Ask students to begin by deciding on an event or a cause to advertise. Then have them brainstorm a list of simple, powerful symbols that will communicate information and feelings.

- You may want to provide a book on typefaces to help students design lettering that is interesting and easy to read. Tell them that most eye-catching posters have few words.

- Invite students to sketch their posters on poster board and imagine viewing them from a distance. Ask them to think about whether they would stop to look at this poster if they saw it on the street.

- If students are planning to combine collage and paint on their posters, encourage them to glue paper down first and to paint when the glue is dry.

OPTIONAL: Quick Activity   Small groups can sketch several poster designs and discuss the elements that make each design powerful and interesting.

WRAP-UP   INFORMAL ASSESSMENT

- How is your poster different from other artwork you have created? What choices did you make because it was a poster? (Possible response: I made objects simpler, more colorful, and bigger.) PRODUCTION: PROBLEM SOLVING

- Look at the class posters and the posters in the lesson. Which posters do you think are the most powerful? Why? (Responses will vary.) ART CRITICISM: EVALUATION

LESSON 11: *The Power of the Poster*

LESSON 12 Pop Art

OBJECTIVES: Explore how artists comment on our culture by basing their work on everyday objects. Make an impasto painting of a common object. Show the object's color and texture.

MOTIVATE

Discuss ordinary objects as art. Ask students to imagine a painting of an object such as a soda can. Encourage students to tell whether they think such a painting would be art.

VIEWING ART

TEACH

Discuss Pop Art. Have students read the paragraphs. Ask if students agree that anything can become art if an artist sees it that way.

Discuss the art. Ask students how the paint in A looks different from the paint in B. (Possible response: In B the paint is thicker.) Then ask what colors and shapes are repeated in B. (Possible responses: circles; the colors blue, green, and red) Discuss how the artist added variety to B. (Each ball has a different design and colors.) Tell students that many Pop Artists paint things that are mass-produced. Ask them what these artists might be saying about modern culture. (Possible response: People like things that are common.)

Critical Thinking Questions

- If a museum exhibited a *real* can of peaches, would you consider it a work of art? Explain. (Responses will vary. Encourage students to support their opinions.) AESTHETICS: MAKE JUDGMENTS

- What do you think people said about Pop Art at first? Why? (Possible response: They did not think it was art because it was so different.) ART HISTORY: REFLECTION

MEETING INDIVIDUAL NEEDS

STUDENTS ACQUIRING ENGLISH Explain that *popular* can mean "having to do with a lot of people." List examples of popular culture such as television sitcoms, blue jeans, and fast-food restaurants.

50 UNIT 2: *Viewpoints*

LESSON 12 CREATING AN IMPASTO PAINTING

Pop Art

What does this can of peaches mean to you?

Can a painting of a can of peaches be a work of art? What about six rubber balls? In the world of **Pop Art**, the answer is yes. *Pop* is short for *popular*. Pop Art often shows things that are popular, such as the canned food in picure **A**. Pop artists have a message: Anything in our culture can become art, if an artist sees it that way. Do you agree? Why or why not?

Notice the thick, textured paint in picture **B**. This technique is called **impasto** painting. How does the paint in picture B look different from the paint in picture A? Which colors and shapes are repeated in B? Repeated objects and elements give a painting **unity**. They make it come together as a whole. What differences can you find among the balls? Differences, or **variety**, can make a painting more interesting.

A

Peach Halves, Andy Warhol
1960. Synthetic polymer paint on canvas, 70 in. X 54 in.

50

SHARE ART HISTORY

A **Andy Warhol** (1928–1987) was a leader of the Pop Art movement. He is famous for instantly recognizable images, such as a Campbell's Soup can and the face of Marilyn Monroe. He said that common objects were the true American art. Many of his works reflect the mass-produced quality he saw in American culture.

B **Wayne Thiebaud** [TEE•boh] (1920–) lives in northern California. He began his career as a cartoonist and advertising artist. Thiebaud has painted colorful, detailed paintings of everyday things such as rows of shoes, cakes, pies, and banana splits. He also likes to paint pictures of the steep streets of San Francisco.

IN THE STUDIO BIG BOOK p.12

Untitled, Wayne Thiebaud
1967. Oil on canvas, 12 1/4 in. X 14 1/4 in.
Private collection.

IN THE STUDIO

MATERIALS
- tempera paints
- paintbrushes
- dry wheat paste
- cardboard
- craft sticks
- newsprint

Make an impasto painting of a common object. Show the object's color and texture.

1. Paint the back of your cardboard. Attach a piece of newsprint to the wet paint. This will help keep the cardboard from bending when you paint the front of it.
2. Choose an object you look at every day. (This should be a human-made object.)
3. Mix wheat paste with your paint. Paint a picture of your object, using the side of a craft stick.

51

ART ACROSS THE CURRICULUM

SOCIAL STUDIES: MASS PRODUCTION

Have students select a mass-produced commodity, such as canned foods, basketballs, or pencils, and research the process used to produce it. Students can present their findings in an illustrated flow chart or diagram.

LANGUAGE ARTS: WRITE POP POEMS

Ask students to write poems using popular sayings. Students can cut words and phrases from magazines or write them on slips of paper. They may find advertising slogans, comic strip quotations, and quotations from famous people. Invite students to choose ten phrases and arrange them into a poem.

IN THE STUDIO

MATERIALS: tempera paints, paintbrushes, dry wheat paste, cardboard, craft sticks, newsprint

Creating an Impasto Painting — CREATING ART

- Have students cut newsprint and cardboard sheets into pieces of the same size.
- Direct students to read the steps on page 51. Then demonstrate how to prepare a painting board to prevent bending.
- Tell students that the object they choose to paint does not have to be beautiful. Help them choose an object that has strong visual texture. You may want to provide magazines for students to look through.
- Direct students to mix a small amount of wheat paste into each color of paint. The paint should be about the consistency of cake frosting. Students will have best results if they make a light pencil sketch before filling in shapes with thickened paint.
- Encourage students to experiment with their craft sticks. They can spread paint with the side of the stick, lay on thin lines with the narrow end, and scratch lines into the paint with the tip.

OPTIONAL: Quick Activity Give students 8-inch squares of paper and ask each of them to make crayon drawings of a human-made object. Tape the drawings together in a quilt-like collage to display the unity and variety in the images.

WRAP-UP — INFORMAL ASSESSMENT

- **How did you use impasto painting to show the texture and weight of your object?** (Responses will vary.) PRODUCTION: PROBLEM SOLVING
- **Has making and looking at Pop Art made you see common objects differently? Why or why not?** (Responses will vary. Students may indicate that they will notice common objects more.) AESTHETICS: SYNTHESIZE

Lesson 12: *Pop Art* 51

UNIT 2

REFLECTING AND REVIEWING

Pages 52–53	**Reflect on the unit theme.** Have students read the first paragraph on page 52. Point out that all the artworks in this unit show how artists use their work to convey viewpoints about people, places, or events.
	Ask students to discuss the photograph. Students might speculate as to how such a photograph could be accomplished. Ask students why they think Arthur Mole chose this manner to express pride in his country. Students should discuss the fact that Mole's unique tribute to an American symbol leaves a lasting impression on viewers.
About the Artist	Arthur Mole (1889–1947) began his career when he became the apprentice to a Chicago photographer at the age of seventeen. Just six months later, Mole established his own photography business. Mole's friend, an assistant fire chief, gave him access to a local fire tower. It was from this great height that the idea for "living photography" occurred to him.
About the Art	To create the *Living American Flag,* Mole arranged 10,000 sailors into a flag and flagpole formation. The photo was taken in 1917 at the U. S. Naval Training Station in Great Lakes, Illinois, using an 11- × 14-inch camera. Before arranging the men, Mole and an assistant spent over a week laying lace edging on the ground to mark the borders of the image.

52   UNIT 2: *Viewpoints*

UNIT 2   REFLECTING AND REVIEWING

Art can convey attitudes about people, places, and events.

Think about some of the artwork you saw in this unit. How did the artists show they were proud of their country? The artwork on this page shows a great deal of pride, too. This "living flag" is made of 10,000 sailors. The artist, Arthur Mole, created patriotic photographs like this in many parts of the country.

The Living American Flag, Arthur Mole
Circa World War I. 10,000 men. U.S. Naval Training Station, Great Lakes, IL.

52

ART ACROSS THE CURRICULUM

DANCE: SHAPE SHUFFLE Ask students to work in groups to design and perform a dance in which they form shapes. Encourage students to pick shapes that can be easily identified by the other students. Students may perform their dance to music or they may have the audience clap a certain beat. **COOPERATIVE LEARNING**

What Did I Learn?

- **THINK** about the artwork you created in this unit. What feelings did you express about people and places?

- **LOOK** back through the unit. Find examples of symbols in the art. What do these symbols stand for? Why do you think the artists chose these symbols?

- **FIND** two artworks in this unit that you especially like. Tell what you think the artists' viewpoints are. How did they show those viewpoints?

- **NAME** an artwork that tells about a time in American history. How does the artist help you understand more about that time?

Just for Fun

WHERE AM I?

TO ENCOURAGE STUDENTS to take another close look at the artworks in this unit, demonstrate how to play "Where Am I?" Choose an image from the unit and pretend you are "inside" the image. Name details from the image, and have students guess which image you are "in." Allow them to look through their books to help them. Then have pairs of students play the game together.

What Did I Learn?

Encourage students to work in small groups to discuss their answers to these questions that appear on page 53.

- **Think about the artwork you created in this unit. What feelings did you express about people and places?** (Responses will vary.) PRODUCTION: DESCRIPTION

- **Look back through the unit. Find examples of symbols in the art. What do these symbols stand for? Why do you think the artists chose these symbols?** (Possible responses: lesson 7—a globe is a symbol that Mary McLeod Bethune wanted to help all people of the world; lesson 10—the Statue of Liberty's lamp is a symbol of freedom.) ART CRITICISM: ANALYSIS

- **Find two artworks in this unit that you especially like. Tell what you think the artists' viewpoints are. How did they show those viewpoints?** (Responses will vary.) ART CRITICISM: DRAW CONCLUSIONS

- **Name an artwork that tells about a time in American history. How does the artist help you understand more about that time?** (Responses will vary. Encourage students to discuss specific examples and details.) ART HISTORY: ANALYSIS

Students may select images from this unit to add to their portfolios.

Reflecting and Reviewing

UNIT 3

Unexpected Art

Artists do not always do as people expect. Sometimes they make art to surprise and amuse the viewer. Artists may create unusual images, or they may give an unusual treatment to a common image.

In this unit, students should expect the unexpected.

ART PRINT 5 *The Elephants* by Salvador Dalí

ART PRINT 6 *Watts Towers* by Simon Rodia

Using the Art Prints

Display and introduce *Art Prints 5* and *6*. (Discussion suggestions appear on the back of each *Art Print*.) Have students discuss what is surprising or unusual about each image.

RESPONSE CARD OPTION You may also have students use Response Card 7, *Everyday Art*, on page R62 of this *Teacher's Edition* as they view Art Print 6.

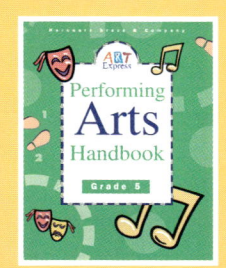

Performing Arts Handbook

Dance, theater, and music activities to extend and enrich students' experiences with these *Art Prints* can be found in the *Performing Arts Handbook*.

UNIT 3: *Unexpected Art* **54B**

UNIT 3 UNEXPECTED ART

Introducing the Unit pp. 54A–55

LESSON	VIEWING	CREATING	CURRICULUM CONNECTIONS
13 EXPERIMENTING WITH SPACE PP. 56–57 • Vase or faces? • *The Swimmer in the Pool* by Henri Matisse	Observe how artists use simple shapes to create positive and negative space. **VOCABULARY:** positive space, negative space, collage	Make a paper cutout that shows positive and negative space. **MATERIALS:** white paper, dark-colored paper, scissors, glue	**Social Studies** Research Mexican Cutouts, p. 57 **Performing Arts** Dance: Dance in positive and negative spaces, p. 57
14 THE ART OF ILLUSION PP. 58–59 • optical illusion • *Suspension* by Bridget Riley • *Plus Reversed* by Richard Anuskiewicz	Examine techniques in art that fool the eye and the brain. **VOCABULARY:** optical illusion, Op Art, complementary colors	Make a collage that vibrates, using complementary colors. **MATERIALS:** poster board, brightly colored construction paper, scissors, glue	**Science** The Colors of Light, p. 59 **Mathematics** Signs and Symbols, p. 59
CONNECTIONS: EVERYDAY ART	**Can You Believe Your Eyes? pp. 60–61**		
15 IMAGINARY WORLDS PP. 62–63 • from *Dinotopia* by James Gurney	Understand how artists' imaginative illustrations help to tell fantasy stories.	Work in a group to create a diorama of an imaginary world. **MATERIALS:** cardboard box (shoe box or larger), colored paper, colored markers, scissors, modeling clay, string, tape	**Reading** Explore *Dinotopia*, p. 63 **Science** Dinosaur Research, p. 63
16 ASSEMBLED ART PP. 64–65 • *California Crosswalk* by John Outterbridge • *Royal Tide IV* by Louise Nevelson	Recognize that artists can make everyday objects into surprising or interesting artworks. **VOCABULARY:** assemblage	Create an assemblage. **MATERIALS:** unwanted objects, strong glue, large sheets of cardboard or foamcore	**Social Studies** Recycling, p. 65 **Language Arts** How-to Paragraph, p. 65
CONNECTIONS: COMMUNITY ART	**The Power of Art pp. 66–67**		
17 DOUBLE TAKES PP. 68–69 • *The Castle in the Pyrenees* by René Magritte • *Niña con su pescado rojo (Girl and Her Red Fish)* by Liliana Wilson Grez	Understand that artists can create surprises by depicting possible objects in impossible ways. **VOCABULARY:** Surrealism	Make a Surrealist painting. **MATERIALS:** large sheets of poster board or white paper, tempera paints, paintbrushes	**Social Studies** Surrealism Today, p. 69 **Language Arts** Description of a Surreal Scene, p. 69
18 OUTDOOR SPECTACLES PP. 70–71 • *Spoonbridge and Cherry* by Claes Oldenburg and Coosje van Bruggen • *Cadillac Ranch* by Stanley Marsh 3 and the Ant Farm	Understand how artists use unexpected sites, scale, media, and subjects to surprise us.	Make a papier-mâché model of a large-scale outdoor sculpture for the community. **MATERIALS:** soft pencils, drawing paper, old newspapers, thin glue, tempera paints, paintbrushes, objects such as boxes or balloons to use as cores	**Social Studies** Car Talk, p. 71 **Reading** Tiny People in a Huge World, p. 71

Unit 3 Reflecting and Reviewing pp. 72–73

Integrating Your Day

SUGGESTED READING	OPTIONAL VIDEOS/TECHNOLOGY
Color by Ruth Heller. Putnam, 1995. EASY *3-D Planet* by Hiroshi Kunoh and Eiji Takaoki. Cadence, 1994. EASY	Students can experiment with *BLOX-Flying Shapes* from *Thinkin' Things Collection 1* to experiment with spacial relationships.
Arithmetic by Carl Sandburg. Harcourt Brace, 1993. EASY *Visual Magic* by Dr. David Thomson. Dial, 1991. AVERAGE	Small groups of students can work with *kidDraw* from *Art Explorer* to create illusion images.
Dinotopia: The World Beneath by James Gurney. Dorling Kindersley, 1995. AVERAGE *Imaginary Gardens* by Charles Sullivan. Abrams, 1989. AVERAGE	Have students view *Get to Know Keith Baker* to learn about another author who draws his own illustrations.
Garden Crafts for Kids by Diane Rhoades. Sterling, 1995. AVERAGE *Art from Wood: With Projects Using Branches, Leaves, and Seeds* by Gillian Chapman. Thomson Learning, 1995. EASY	Students can watch excerpts from the video *Louise Nevelson in Process* to learn more about this sculptor.
Dinner at Magritte's by Michael Garland. Dutton Children's Books, 1995. EASY *Miss Piggy's Treasury of Art Masterpieces from the Kermitage Collection* by Henry Beard. Holt Rinehart Winston, 1984. EASY	Students can use *kidDraw* with *The New Kid Pix* to create some surprising artworks of their own.
The Borrowers by Mary Norton. Harcourt Brace, 1991. AVERAGE *Art from Paper: With Projects Using Waste Paper and Printed Materials* by Gillian Chapman and Pam Robson. Thomson Learning, 1995. EASY	Have students use *The Monstrous Media Kit* to write a story and illustrate it with unexpected clip art and sounds.

Art Minutes

Present one of these puzzles or activities for students to solve by the end of the week.

- ■ **Find** an everyday object in the room. **List** three unusual ways you could draw this object. ANALYSIS

- ■ **Draw** the same image in two different ways. List the differences between the two. APPLICATION

- ■ **Look** through the newspaper or a magazine to find an unusual image of a common object. Name ways you could make the image appear more usual. SYNTHESIS

- ■ **Draw** a picture in which an image is hidden within another image. APPLICATION

- ■ **List** ways you could change the appearance of your school to make it look as if it were in an imaginary world. APPLICATION

- ■ **Read aloud** a surprising scene from a favorite poem or story. Explain why it is surprising to you. ANALYSIS

SCHOOL-HOME CONNECTION

After completing Lesson 17, distribute School-Home Connection 3, found on page R52. Students can ask a family member to help them find photographs that they can include in a scene with their own drawings.

Activities and Resources CD-ROM provides additional teaching materials and interactive student activities for use with Unit 3.

UNIT 3: *Unexpected Art* 54D

UNIT 3

INTRODUCING
THE UNIT

Pages 54–55

Discuss *Clothed Automobile*. Have students read pages 54 and 55. Ask volunteers to list some of the unusual aspects of the image and to tell why they think the artist presented the car in this manner.

Examine the unexpected. Point out to students that this painting combines the ordinary (such as bricks, clothing, and cars) in an extraordinary way. Dalí [dah•LEE] is well known for his strange, sometimes dreamlike images. Have students think of other ways Dalí might have painted this image to make it surprise or amuse the viewer.

About the Art

Clothed Automobile catches the eye because it is such an unusual image. This work, like many others by Dalí during this period, was a statement on the political situation in Europe.

Another example of a Salvador Dalí painting can be found on **Art Print 5**.

Clothed Automobile, Salvador Dalí
1941. Oil on cardboard, 15 1/2 in. X 10 1/2 in.
Fundación Gala–Salvador Dalí, Figueras, Spain.

TIME LINE

Suggest that students select two or three artworks from the unit and locate the periods of their creation on the *Time Line*.

54   **UNIT 3:** *Unexpected Art*

UNIT 3

Unexpected Art

How can art be funny or surprising?

Every artist must have an active imagination. Some artists also have a good sense of humor. What is amusing about this painting? How is it different from what you might expect?

Salvador Dalí (SAHL•vuh•dawr dah•LEE) is one of many painters whose works often surprise us. He liked to show ordinary objects in unexpected ways. Sometimes he combined two or more ordinary things to create something extraordinary.

As you look at and create art in this unit, keep your eyes open for surprises. You might even surprise yourself!

ABOUT SALVADOR DALÍ

Salvador Dalí was born in Spain but moved to the United States during World War II. He is known for his strange, dream-like images.

Meet the Artist

Salvador Dalí (dah•LEE) (1904–1989) was born in the foothills of the Pyrenees in Figueras, Spain. His parents built him his first studio when he was just a boy attending the San Fernando Academy of Fine Arts in Madrid. Dalí became a well-known artist at a young age, having his first solo show at age twenty-one. Dalí and his wife, Gala, emigrated to the United States during World War II. Dalí's work was strongly influenced by the Surrealist movement, but he was also influenced by the Italian Renaissance masters and Italian metaphysical painters.

Although Dalí is best known for his strange, dreamlike paintings, he also completed several publications, book illustrations, jewelry designs, and films.

LITERATURE CONNECTION

Visual Magic by Dr. David Thomson. Dial, 1991.
AVERAGE

This book offers several challenging optical illusions, or tricks of the eye, for the reader to solve.

CLASSROOM MANAGEMENT

VIEWING: Response Cards You may wish to select one or more Response Cards for students to use with the artworks in the unit. For example, have each student in a small group choose an artwork from the unit. Provide Response Card 8, Art Critics' Circle, to guide their discussion of the artworks. The Response Cards begin on page R56 of this Teacher's Edition.

CREATING: Studio Activity Options If any students have limited time for art activities because of illness, pull-out classes, or other school demands, have them complete the Quick Activity in a lesson to reinforce lesson skills and concepts.

LESSON 13

Experimenting with Space

OBJECTIVES: Observe how artists use simple shapes to create positive and negative space. Make a paper cutout that shows positive and negative space.

MOTIVATE

Discuss subjects and backgrounds. Display a still life or another image with a clear subject and a plain background. Point out that in most paintings, the background is plain and the subject is more colorful and detailed. However, some artists experiment with subjects and backgrounds.

VIEWING ART

TEACH

Define positive and negative space. Ask students to read pages 56–57. Invite them to make up two different titles for A, one based on what they see in the black shape and one based on the white shapes. (Responses should show recognition of the faces and the vase.)

Discuss positive and negative space in B. Ask students where they think the positive space is. (Possible response: The swimmer seems to form the positive space, even though it is plainer than the background.)

Critical Thinking Questions

- **How are A and B alike?** (Both use positive and negative space in interesting ways.) ART CRITICISM: COMPARE/CONTRAST

- **The swimmer in B seems to move. How do you think the artist made this happen?** (Possible response: The shape is curved and points upward.) ART CRITICISM: PROBLEM SOLVING

MEETING INDIVIDUAL NEEDS

EXTRA SUPPORT Point out that here, the terms *positive* and *negative* do not mean "good" and "bad." Use picture A to help students understand the meanings of these terms as they are used in this lesson.

56 UNIT 3: *Unexpected Art*

LESSON 13 USING POSITIVE AND NEGATIVE SPACE

Experimenting with Space

How can simple shapes create big surprises?

Look at the black shape in picture **A**. Now look at the white shapes. Do you see two different pictures? If you could make up two different titles for A, what would they be? **Positive space** describes the shapes, lines, and forms in a work of art. **Negative space** describes the empty space around them. Picture A is playing with positive and negative space. You see something different depending on which space you look at.

A Vase or f[...]

B
The Swimmer in the Aquarium,
Henri Matisse
Circa 1944. Gouache on paper cutouts,
16 5/8 in. X 25 5/8 in.
Museum of Modern Art, New York.

56

SHARE ART HISTORY

Henri Matisse [ahn•REE mah•TEES] (1869–1954) was a French artist who is famous for his simplified shapes and flat colors. Matisse did not become interested in art until he was twenty-one. While he was recovering from an illness in the hospital, his mother brought him a paint set. He later said, "Somehow I knew I had finally found my true path."

Matisse was inspired by the shapes and contrasts in African masks and sculptures. Late in his career he began making paper cutouts. He painted paper many colors and then cut out simple shapes of figures, plants, and designs. When he became too ill to leave his bed, he attached charcoal to a long stick and made large drawings on the ceiling. His assistants helped him arrange his cutouts into collages.

IN THE STUDIO BIG BOOK p.13

Picture **B** is a ==collage==. It was made by pasting pieces of cut paper together. The background of this picture is made of bright colors. The shape of the swimmer is simply white. Usually, the shapes and objects in a picture are filled with color, and the background is empty. What part of this collage is empty? What part is the negative space? It's hard to say!

IN THE STUDIO

MATERIALS
- white paper
- dark paper
- scissors
- glue

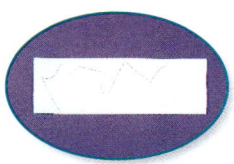

Make a white cutout against a dark background. Make both the positive and the negative space interesting.

1. Fold a sheet of white paper the long way. Draw one half of a design on your folded paper. Get fancy! Think about what shapes and spaces you want the viewer to see.

2. Cut out your design, and unfold the paper.

3. Glue your white paper against a piece of dark paper. How is the design different when you look at the space in different ways?

57

ART ACROSS THE CURRICULUM

SOCIAL STUDIES: RESEARCH MEXICAN CUTOUTS Invite students to do research on *papel picado* (pah•PEL pee•CAH•doh). The Spanish term refers to the cut-paper designs made by many Mexican and Mexican American families for special occasions. Examples of these tissue-paper decorations can be seen in the paintings of Carmen Lomas Garza. Encourage students to give an oral presentation about these cutouts.

PERFORMING ARTS: DANCE Hang up two large cloths or sheets, one white and one a dark solid color. Invite a few students to dress all in white and a few to dress all in black. Challenge them to choreograph a dance in front of the dark and light backdrops. Their dance might consist of a series of poses that let viewers see positive and negative spaces. Encourage students to work together to form designs.

IN THE STUDIO

MATERIALS: white paper, dark-colored paper, scissors, glue

Using Positive and Negative Space   CREATING ART

- Invite students to read the steps on page 57. Make sure they fold their white paper in half lengthwise. As they plan their design, encourage them to be elaborate and detailed. You might direct students to color in the negative spaces in their design. This will help them remember what to cut out.

- Direct students to cut out the design and unfold their white paper. If they are not satisfied with their design, they might alter it or start over with another sheet of paper.

- Ask students to coat the back of their cutout evenly with a thin layer of glue. Then direct them to lay the cut-paper shape carefully onto the dark paper.

- Encourage students to find positive and negative space in their own and in classmates' cutouts.

OPTIONAL: Quick Activity Have students cut out two simple shapes and place them against paper of a contrasting color. Invite students to identify the positive and negative spaces in each other's work.

WRAP-UP   INFORMAL ASSESSMENT

- **Which color in your cutout shifts to positive space most often? Why do you think this happens?** (Responses will vary. Larger or more recognizable shapes will probably appear more often as positive space.) PRODUCTION: ANALYSIS

- **How do you feel when you look at Matisse's collage? How do you feel about your own work?** (Responses will vary.) AESTHETICS: PERSONAL RESPONSE

LESSON 13: *Experimenting with Space*

LESSON 14

The Art of Illusion

OBJECTIVES: Examine techniques in art that fool the eye and the brain. Make a collage that vibrates, using complementary colors.

MOTIVATE

Demonstrate an illusion. Lightly hold a pencil by the end, and move your hand slowly up and down so the pencil bobs. The pencil will appear to turn to rubber. Ask students to describe other illusions they have seen.

VIEWING ART

TEACH

Discuss the illusions and the Op Art. Have students read the first paragraph and describe what they see when they stare at pictures A, B, and C. (In the white space of A, students should see a green star; in B they may see lines appearing to vibrate and resemble steps; in C they should see the plus shapes vibrating, moving, and changing.) Help students see that there are only straight lines in B. Have them note where the plus shapes change from red to green in C.

Define complementary colors. As students look at the color wheel, help them identify pairs of complementary colors. Explain that artists can place complementary colors next to each other to make their paintings seem to move.

Critical Thinking Questions

- **Did pictures B and C stop vibrating when you knew how the artist created the effect? Why or why not?** (Possible response: No; the colors and lines still fooled my eye.) AESTHETICS: REFLECTION

- **Why do you think artists make Op Art?** (Possible responses: to play with colors and shapes.) AESTHETICS: HYPOTHESIZE

MEETING INDIVIDUAL NEEDS

CHALLENGE Ask students to research optical illusions and how they work. Invite them to present their findings to their classmates.

LESSON 14 EXPERIMENTING WITH COLORS

The Art of Illusion

How can colors and shapes trick your eyes?

Stare at the center of the red star picture in **A** while you count to thirty. Then look at the black dot in the white space. What do you see? Are you sure? If it's not really there, it is an **optical illusion**. What do you see when you stare at picture **B**? At picture **C**? Art that plays tricks on your eyes is called **Op Art**. Op (short for *optical*) Art is meant to dazzle your eyes and fool your brain.

A Optical illusion

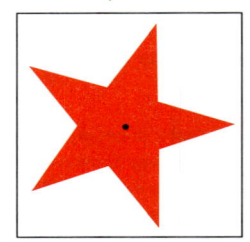

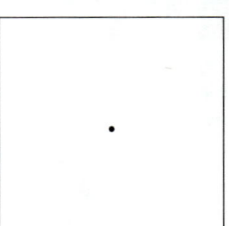

B *Suspension*, Bridget Riley
1964. Emulsion on wood, 45 3/4 in. X 45 7/8 in. Walker Art Center, Minneapolis, MN.

58

SHARE ART HISTORY

A **Bridget Riley** (1931–) is a British artist. While traveling in Italy, Riley noticed black and white interlocking marble stones on the ground. They seemed to be vibrating. This inspired her to make similar patterns in her artwork. Riley does not think of her paintings as pictures; she calls them "visual prickles." To make a painting, she experiments with lines until shapes begin to move and change before her eyes.

B **Richard Anuszkiewicz** [ah•noo•SKAY•vich] (1930–) has been called a "scientific" painter because he is interested in how our eyes work and how our brains organize what we see. Like Riley, he was a leader of the Op Art movement of the 1960s. A reviewer once called Anuszkiewicz "a master magician of cool pyrotechnics."

58 UNIT 3: *Unexpected Art*

IN THE STUDIO BIG BOOK p.14

Colors that are across from each other on the color wheel are called **complementary colors**. These colors seem to move and change when they are next to each other, as you can see in picture C. How else does this painting fool your eyes?

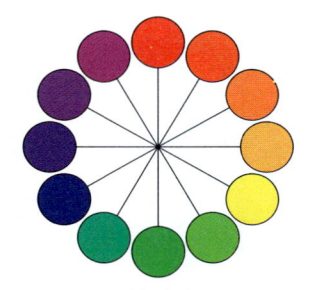

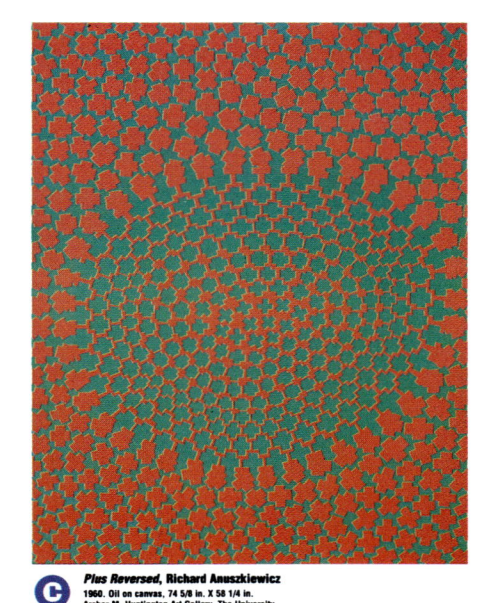

Color wheel

Plus Reversed, Richard Anuszkiewicz
1960. Oil on canvas, 74 5/8 in. X 58 1/4 in.
Archer M. Huntington Art Gallery, The University of Texas at Austin.

IN THE STUDIO

MATERIALS
- poster board
- brightly colored construction paper
- scissors
- glue

Make a cut-paper collage.

Cut shapes out of paper, and glue them onto a background. Use complementary colors. Can you make the shapes seem to move?

ART ACROSS THE CURRICULUM

SCIENCE: THE COLORS OF LIGHT Have students study how light is broken into colors when it passes through a prism. Hang a prism in the sunlight, and ask students to record the order in which the colors appear. Ask them to compare the relationship of colors in a rainbow to those in the color wheel. Students might read more about light and color and share what they learn with classmates.

MATH: SIGNS AND SYMBOLS The plus sign and the minus sign are but two of the many symbols that make up the language of mathematics. Call on volunteers to draw other math symbols on the board such as the symbols for *multiplied by, divided by, is greater than, is less than,* and *equals*. Then have each student choose a symbol and render it in an artistic way.

IN THE STUDIO

MATERIALS: poster board, brightly colored construction paper, scissors, glue

Experimenting with Colors

CREATING ART

- Invite students to read the In the Studio activity.

- Encourage students to think about composition when they are creating their collages. Explain that a composition works best when the colors and shapes are balanced and interesting. Suggest that students cut shapes that interact in an unusual way.

- If students are not sure how to choose complementary colors, remind them to look for colors that are opposite each other on the color wheel. Suggest that they experiment with colors and shapes until they are satisfied with their compositions.

- Students might want to show their compositions to partners before they glue down their shapes.

OPTIONAL: Quick Activity Invite students to stare at simple shapes cut from brightly colored paper and then look at white paper. Ask them to note the colors of the afterimages and decide whether they are complements of the paper colors.

WRAP-UP

INFORMAL ASSESSMENT

- **How did looking at pictures B and C help you to create your own work?** (Responses will vary.) PRODUCTION: APPLICATION

- **Look at your classmates' collages. Which colors vibrate most? Why?** (Responses will vary. Combinations of very bright complementary colors, especially those set off in complex designs, will probably vibrate most.) ART CRITICISM: DRAW CONCLUSIONS

LESSON 14: *The Art of Illusion*

CONNECTIONS

EVERYDAY ART

Tap prior knowledge about optical illusions. Challenge students to brainstorm optical illusions that they have witnessed in nature. *(Possible responses: Heat radiates from the pavement and makes the pavement appear to move; water appears on the horizon as a mirage.)* You may also want to remind students of the illusions in Lesson 14. Then have them read pages 60–61.

Discuss the painting. Ask students what illusions the artists created. *(Possible responses: Boys climbing a staircase; cattle charging into a street.)* Ask why the Ft. Worth scene might make people stop. *(Possible response: It looks as if there is a tunnel through the wall.)*

CONNECTIONS — EVERYDAY ART

Can You Believe Your Eyes?

Some works of art make you stop and stare.

Over two hundred years ago, an American artist named Charles Willson Peale decided to fool visitors to his home. Peale painted a life-size staircase on one wall. Then he framed the painting with a real step and a real doorway. Peale fooled many, many visitors, including George Washington.

Artists today still enjoy fooling their viewers. Look at the outdoor scene painted on a building in Fort Worth, Texas. How does it fool the eye?

◀ *The Staircase Grou[p]*
Charles Willson Pe[ale]
1795. Philadelphia
Museum of Art: Th[e]
George W. Elkins
Collection

60

SHARE ART HISTORY

Art Tricks

Trompe l'oeil [trom•LOY] is a French phrase that means "fool the eye." This technique was used by ancient Greek and Roman artists. It was revived during the Renaissance when entire rooms were painted with murals which conveyed three-dimensional illusions.

SOCIAL STUDIES

Ranching in Texas

Share with students that the first cattle were brought to Texas when it was still controlled by Spain. Spanish missionaries and explorers brought cattle with them for food. Later, Mexican and American settlers began many ranches. After the Civil War, the ranchers began driving cattle to the North to sell. Invite students to research the cattle drives and to outline some of the routes on a map.

UNIT 3: *Unexpected Art*

Chisholm Trail facade, Jet Building
Fort Worth, Texas

WHAT DO YOU THINK?

▶ How does the setting of each painting help the artist fool the viewer?

▶ Do you think people enjoy being fooled this way? Why or why not?

61

WHAT DO YOU THINK?

▶ How does the setting of each painting help the artist fool the viewer? (Responses will vary. Possible response: Houses do have staircases; Ft. Worth, Texas, did have cattle drives.) PRODUCTION: ANALYSIS

▶ Do you think people enjoy being fooled this way? Why or why not? (Responses will vary.) AESTHETICS: SPECULATE

THEATER

Mime Time

Mimes are performers who use exaggerated facial expressions and gestures rather than words to communicate. They can create the illusion that they are touching real objects, even though they use no props. Have volunteers take turns pantomiming familiar situations, such as walking a dog, opening a window, or swatting a mosquito. Remind students that exaggerated expressions and gestures will help create their illusions.

IN THE STUDIO

An Illusion in the Classroom

COOPERATIVE LEARNING   Have students work in small groups to create trompe l'oeil art for the classroom walls. Provide large sheets of butcher paper or newsprint, and brainstorm ideas with students. They might try concepts such as these:

- a false window with an outdoor view or a view of a fantasy land
- a false door open to a hallway or to another room
- a false mirror

CONNECTIONS: *Everyday Art*   **61**

LESSON 15

Imaginary Worlds

OBJECTIVES: Understand how artists' imaginative illustrations help to tell fantasy stories. Work in a group to create a diorama of an imaginary world.
MATERIALS: two copies of a comic strip; on one copy, block out the dialogue with a black marker

MOTIVATE

Use pictures to predict a story. Display the comic strip with no dialogue. Ask students to try to predict what the words might say. Then display the copy with dialogue, and have students evaluate their predictions.

VIEWING ART

TEACH

Discuss realistic and unrealistic details in the art. Direct students to look at the illustration and read the paragraphs. Ask which parts of the painting might or might not exist in the real world. (Possible responses: Buildings and waterfalls exist; people riding flying dinosaurs don't.) You may wish to display **Art Print 5**. Ask how it is similar to Gurney's illustration. (Each shows an imaginary world.)

Discuss highlighting and warm colors. Have students point to places in the art where the sun lights up parts of the water. Ask them to find some warm colors. (yellows and golds) Ask what mood these warm colors create. (Possible response: a peaceful mood) Encourage students to speculate about the plot of the book.

Critical Thinking Questions

- **Does this picture make you want to read the book? Why or why not?** (Responses will vary.) AESTHETICS: PERSONAL RESPONSE

- **In what way is this painting like some Impressionist paintings?** (Possible response: It emphasizes the way light hits objects.) ART CRITICISM: COMPARE/CONTRAST

EXTRA SUPPORT Explain that *Dino* comes from *dinosaur* and *topia* comes from the word *utopia*. Explain that a utopia is a perfect place.

LESSON 15 MAKING A DIORAMA

Imaginary Worlds

How can an artist tell a fantasy story?

Rumble and Mist, James Gurney 1995.

This painting shows a scene from James Gurney's book *Dinotopia: The World Beneath*. Illustrators can create make-believe worlds, filled with fantastic scenes. Which things in this painting might exist in the real world? Which parts tell us that the scene is imaginary?

Look at the water in this scene. Find some places where the artist used highlighting to show where sunlight hits the water. Find some warm colors in the painting. What kind of mood do these colors help create?

Where do you think the flying creatures with riders might be going? What do you think might happen when they get there? What else can you learn about this story from the art?

62

SHARE ART HISTORY

Even as a boy, author/illustrator **James Gurney** (1958–) dreamed of "creating a world." In Gurney's imaginary world—Dinotopia— dinosaurs and humans participate in exciting adventures together. Gurney says, "I want [Dinotopia] to be a terrific place for viewers to conjure their own dreams, to participate in high adventure, and to see our own world through new eyes." Gurney has written and illustrated two Dinotopia books.

IN THE STUDIO BIG BOOK p.15

IN THE STUDIO

MATERIALS: cardboard box (shoe box or larger), colored paper, colored markers, scissors, modeling clay, string, tape

Making a Diorama

CREATING ART

- Direct students to read the steps in the activity and then work alone or in small groups.
- Encourage students to discuss their make-believe world. You may wish to provide them with illustrated fantasy stories to help them generate ideas. Direct students to use markers or colored paper to create a background on the back wall of their box.
- Students can use modeling clay to create characters, buildings, or other scenery items for their diorama. If students are working in a group, each member should contribute at least one figure or object.
- Suggest that students may want to use string and tape to hang flying creatures or objects from the ceiling of their diorama.

OPTIONAL: Quick Activity Students can use markers or colored pencils to draw an imaginary world on white paper.

WRAP-UP

INFORMAL ASSESSMENT

- **How did you or your group decide on a scene to create?** (Responses will vary. Students may mention that they looked at fantasy stories for ideas.) PRODUCTION: PROBLEM SOLVING

- **How does the mood of your diorama compare with the mood of the illustration of Dinotopia? Identify the colors, shapes, or other parts of your diorama that help create its mood.** (Responses will vary.) ART CRITICISM: ANALYSIS

ART ACROSS THE CURRICULUM

READING: EXPLORE DINOTOPIA Encourage students to borrow a copy of *Dinotopia: The World Beneath* from a library. After reading, students can perform "book-in-a-can" book reports. To do this, they should decorate a coffee can with images from the book and fill the can with objects that stand for characters, places, or events. Students present their reports by pulling objects from the can and explaining how they relate to the book.

SCIENCE: DINOSAUR RESEARCH Assign pairs of students a research topic related to dinosaurs, such as what dinosaur habitats were like, how dinosaurs cared for their young, and how dinosaurs became extinct. If possible, have students use the Internet to find current information. Partners can make posters to display the information they find.

LESSON 15: *Imaginary Worlds*

LESSON 16

Assembled Art

OBJECTIVES: Recognize that artists can make everyday objects into surprising or interesting artworks. Create an assemblage.

MOTIVATE

Ask students to list everyday objects that could be used in works of art. They might begin with objects in the classroom.

VIEWING ART

TEACH

Explain that some artists use unusual objects to create artwork. Invite students to view the artwork as they read the page. Discuss the process of turning everyday objects into art. Ask: What is the difference between an *assemblage* and just a collection of things? (An assemblage is arranged artistically.)

Discuss the art. Tell students to list any familiar objects they see in the two assemblages. Have students speculate about where the artists might have found their materials. Discuss what each artist did to make a variety of objects work together as a work of art.

Critical Thinking Questions

- **What would be another good title for *California Crosswalk*?** (Responses will vary. Ask students to explain their titles.)
  ART CRITICISM: DESCRIPTION

- **Do you think these artworks are art in the same way that paintings are art? Why or why not?** (Responses will vary. Encourage students to recognize that both forms of art are creative expressions of ideas and feelings.) AESTHETICS: EVALUATION

EXTRA SUPPORT Help students understand the difference between unwanted objects and fine-art materials. Work together to make a list of unwanted objects such as metal or wood scraps, bottles, and cans. Then make a list of fine-art materials such as tubes of paint, colored pencils, and canvas.

LESSON 16 CREATING AN ASSEMBLAGE

Assembled Art

How can an artist use unusual objects to create art?

An **assemblage** is a group of objects that are put together, or assembled. Where would you look for objects to create an assemblage like **A** or **B**? Where do you think these artists found these objects?

We often use the word *junk* to describe things that are unwanted. But artists can use unwanted objects to create some exciting surprises. John Outterbridge combined unwanted metals and fabric into an assembled sculpture. This assemblage expresses ideas about cars and about California.

Louise Nevelson made her wall-sized sculpture from furniture pieces and other wooden items. After she assembled the pieces, she painted them all gold to give the assemblage unity. How else does the assemblage show unity?

A *California Crosswalk,* **John Outterbridge**
1979. Metals, wire, cloth, other mixed media, 3 ft. 6 in. X 3 ft. California Afro-American Museum Foundation, Los Angeles.

SHARE ART HISTORY

A **John Outterbridge** (1933–) is an African American artist who grew up in Greenville, North Carolina. Outterbridge was influenced by his father, who collected junk, made it into new items, and sold them, and his mother, who made quilts from scraps of cloth. For many years Outterbridge was a teacher and a bus driver as well as an artist, but he now creates art full-time.

B **Louise Nevelson** (1899–1988) moved from Russia to Rockland, Maine, as a young girl. She studied music and dance but was most drawn to visual art. In 1932 Nevelson worked as an assistant to muralist Diego Rivera. Nevelson is well known for her large sculptures, some of which take up whole walls and even entire rooms. Much of her art was influenced by Cubism.

UNIT 3: *Unexpected Art*

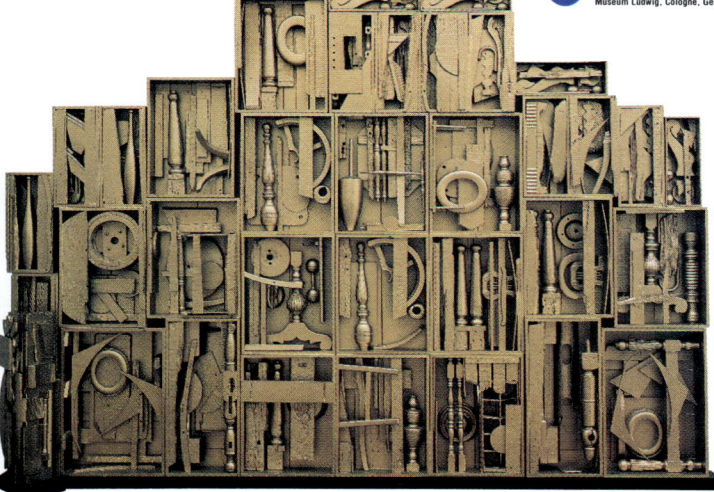

IN THE STUDIO BIG BOOK p.16

B *Royal Tide IV*, Louise Nevelson
1960. Wood painted gold, 11 ft. X 14 ft.
Museum Ludwig, Cologne, Germany.

IN THE STUDIO

MATERIALS
- unwanted objects
- strong glue
- large sheets of cardboard or foamcore

Create an assemblage.

Collect objects of different shapes and sizes. (First check to be sure nobody wants these items.) Experiment with your objects. Find interesting ways to fit them together to express unity and variety. Glue your objects to the cardboard or foamcore in the arrangement you like best.

65

ART ACROSS THE CURRICULUM

SOCIAL STUDIES: RECYCLING Encourage students to research recycling. Encourage students to learn about how familiar materials as well as not-so-familiar materials are recycled and made into clothes or other things. Ask questions such as these: Why do we recycle used items? What happens to recyclables once they leave our homes? If possible, arrange for a class trip to a local recycling plant.

LANGUAGE ARTS: HOW-TO PARAGRAPH Have students work with partners. Have them interview each other. Then have each partner write a how-to paragraph in which they give instructions and advice for making the other partner's assemblage.

IN THE STUDIO

MATERIALS: unwanted objects, strong glue, large sheets of cardboard or foamcore

Creating an Assemblage   CREATING ART

- Have students collect small objects such as shells, wood scraps, and ballpoint pen caps. Emphasize that they need to make sure nobody wants these objects anymore.

- Ask students to read the instructions. Encourage them to experiment with their objects to find interesting ways to fit them together. Students may want to create an abstract design or a design that represents a real object or person.

- Instruct students to use strong glue (very carefully) to attach their objects to cardboard or foamcore in the arrangement they like best. Tell students that if one of their objects is heavy, they may need to apply glue to both the object and the surface they are gluing it to, wait a few minutes for the glue to become tacky, and then firmly press the object against the surface.

OPTIONAL: Quick Activity Have students gather several small objects. They can add glue to the cardboard and drop the objects onto the glue to create an unexpected assemblage.

WRAP-UP   INFORMAL ASSESSMENT

- **Does your assemblage represent something real, or is it an abstract design? Why did you choose this kind of design?** (Responses will vary.) PRODUCTION: REFLECTION

- **Think about items that people often recycle, such as cans, bottles, and plastic jugs. Describe a sculpture that an artist could make with these items.** (Responses will vary. Ask students to suggest how the sculpture might show unity and variety.)
ART CRITICISM: SYNTHESIZE

LESSON 16: *Assembled Art*

CONNECTIONS

COMMUNITY ART

Identify art in the students' community. Ask students to tell where they have seen art in their neighborhoods, and discuss what they liked or disliked about it. (Responses will vary: billboards, statues, architecture; colors, images, style) Then have students read pages 66–67.

Discuss the artwork. Share with students that Lily Yeh founded the Village of Arts and Humanities in North Philadelphia. She first designed a park for a vacant lot. A construction crew of local adults made the design a reality. Many children also helped. The park triggered an artistic renaissance in the community. Ask students to look at the completed projects and to discuss what message they send. (Possible responses: People are proud to live in this neighborhood; people can work together.)

SHARE CULTURAL BACKGROUND

Lily Yeh was born in China and raised in Taiwan. She attended Taiwan University and later earned a master's degree in fine arts from the University of Pennsylvania. Yeh is partial to African art. Her philosophy of using art to rebuild a community is based on the African proverb "It takes a village to raise a child." Discuss the meaning of this proverb with students. (Everyone in the village has something of value to teach a child; every child is important to the village.)

CONNECTIONS COMMUNITY ART

The Power of Art

Art can bring beauty to a neighborhood. It can also bring people together.

Lily Yeh is an artist who cares about communities. Many young artists show they also care by working with her.

This neighborhood is in Philadelphia. It was once very run-down, and many people who lived there wished they could move. Lily Yeh helped them change all that. Many people in the neighborhood, including young people, worked together. First they built an "art park." Later, they went on to the other projects shown here. What messages do these projects send about this community?

◀ Lily Yeh working on the *Tree of Life* mural

SOCIAL STUDIES

Community Spaces

Discuss with students why public areas sometimes become run-down and littered. Point out that people often take better care of their own property than of public property, because they do not feel truly responsible for the public property. This tendency is called "the law of the commons" by economists. Have students suggest ways to encourage better treatment of public property, such as posting signs, starting neighborhood improvement programs, and setting a good example.

▲ **Meditation Park**

WHAT DO YOU THINK?

▶ Why do you think Lily Yeh chose the title *Tree of Life* for this mural?

▶ Do you think this community art will still be valuable to future generations? Explain.

WHAT DO YOU THINK?

▶ Why do you think Lily Yeh chose the title *Tree of Life* for this mural? (Possible response: The title suggests that art can bring the community back to life.) ART CRITICISM: ANALYSIS

▶ Do you think this community art will still be valuable to future generations? Explain. (Possible response: Yes, the art has a timeless look; people will be proud of the community spirit behind it.) ART CRITICISM: MAKE PREDICTIONS

MUSIC

Music in the Air

Ask students to think about music to accompany works of art. What music is suggested by the *Meditation Park*? What music is suggested by other works of art? Have students answer these questions and then share their answers with the class.

IN THE STUDIO

Before-and-After Parks

COOPERATIVE LEARNING Have students work in pairs to sketch two scenes of a community park.

- One scene should show the park before art is added; one scene should show the park after art is added.
- Students should add at least three artworks.
- Students should think of a new name for the park.

Have volunteers share their sketches.

CONNECTIONS: *Community Art*

LESSON 17

Double Takes

OBJECTIVES: Understand that artists can create surprises by depicting possible objects in impossible ways. Make a Surrealist painting.

MOTIVATE

Discuss dreams. Share a dream you had in which ordinary objects or events were combined in a strange way. Point out that in dreams, people encounter many images and events that don't make sense.

VIEWING ART

TEACH

Identify realistic and unrealistic elements. Have students read the paragraphs and look at the paintings. Ask students what is strange about A. (Possible response: A huge rock is floating in the air; there is a castle on top of the rock.) Ask what is strange about B. (Possible response: The girl is holding the fish as if it were a pet or a doll.)

Compare Surrealist paintings. You may want to display **Art Print 5** and have students identify realistic and unrealistic elements in it.

Critical Thinking Questions

- **Compare these artworks to the scene from *Dinotopia* on pages 62–63. Which things are ordinary in each? Which are fantastic?** (Possible response: *Dinotopia* shows places and animals that don't exist; the artworks in this lesson distort objects that do exist.) ART CRITICISM: COMPARE/CONTRAST

- **Why do you think artists create surreal paintings like these?** (Possible response: It's fun to create and play with unexpected images and combinations that will surprise viewers.) ART HISTORY: HYPOTHESIZE

MEETING INDIVIDUAL NEEDS

CHALLENGE Ask students to write a short description of each painting and tell what each image makes them think about.

LESSON 17 MAKING IMPOSSIBLE PAINTINGS

Double Takes

What is strange about each of these paintings?

A double take is a quick second look. You might look at something once and not see anything odd. Then you look again and think, "That's impossible!"

You have seen castles before, and you have seen oceans before. But have you ever seen them combined as in painting **A**? In **B**, the fish is a lot bigger than you would expect. Why has the artist changed the proportions this way? What else is strange about picture B?

A *The Castle in the Pyrenees*, René Magritte
1959. Oil on canvas, 78 3/8 in. X 55 in.

SHARE ART HISTORY

A **René Magritte** [ruh•NAY muh•GREET] (1898–1967) was a Belgian Surrealist. Magritte's paintings showed what things are not. He painted a bird made of stone, an apple filling an entire room, and mysterious men in bowler hats floating in the sky. The term *Surrealism* is an invented word made by combining the prefix *sur-*, meaning "above," and *realism*. Surrealists wanted to shock viewers and readers into looking at the world in a different way.

B **Liliana Wilson Grez** studied art at the Instituto de Bellas Arte in Chile and at Southwest Texas University in the United States. In 1993, she won first prize at the Juried Women's Art Exhibit in San Antonio, Texas.

UNIT 3: *Unexpected Art*

IN THE STUDIO BIG BOOK p.17

This style of painting is called **Surrealism**. Surrealism mixes and matches possible objects in impossible ways. Separately, the castle and the ocean in picture A are possible. Together, they are just—impossible! Many Surrealist paintings look like dream scenes. Like many dreams, they don't seem to make much sense.

B
Niña con su pescado rojo (Girl and Her Red Fish), Liliana Wilson Grez
1993. Acrylic, 48 in. X 36 in.

IN THE STUDIO

MATERIALS
- large sheets of poster board or white paper
- tempera paints
- paintbrushes

Make a Surrealist painting.

Think of one or two real things you see every day. Make a painting that puts these things together in an impossible way. You might "play with reality" by putting the objects in strange places or giving them odd proportions.

69

ART ACROSS THE CURRICULUM

SOCIAL STUDIES: SURREALISM TODAY
Ask students to investigate ways in which Surrealism has become a part of our everyday lives. Point out dreamlike images in advertising. As a homework assignment, ask students to be on the lookout for surreal images in television advertisements, on billboards, and in films. Encourage them to create lists and share their examples with classmates.

LANGUAGE ARTS: DESCRIPTION OF A SURREAL SCENE Have students imagine a surreal scene and then write a description of it. They may wish to include a drawing. Encourage students to display their surreal writings on a bulletin board and to read each other's work.

IN THE STUDIO

MATERIALS: large sheets of poster board or white paper, tempera paints, paintbrushes

Making Impossible Paintings

CREATING ART

- Help students brainstorm a list of familiar objects such as a tube of toothpaste, a piece of luggage, an apartment building, and a bus.

- Model for students ways to combine two of the objects in a surreal way. For instance, they might show a giant tube of spreading toothpaste on the top of an apartment building, or a bus driving into an open piece of luggage.

- Invite students to make rough sketches before they begin to paint. Encourage them to experiment with proportion and placement.

- Students might display their work in a Surrealist art exhibit.

OPTIONAL: Quick Activity Invite students to choose one everyday object and draw it much larger or much smaller than it is in real life. They should include another, normal-size object in their drawings to show the scale.

WRAP-UP

INFORMAL ASSESSMENT

- **What objects did you combine in your painting? Do you think differently about the objects now? Explain.** (Responses will vary. Help students realize that unusual relationships between objects can make us think differently about them.) PRODUCTION: REFLECTION

- **Judging from the works you have seen so far, do you like Surrealism? Why or why not?** (Responses will vary.) AESTHETICS: PERSONAL RESPONSE

LESSON 17: *Double Takes*

LESSON 18

Outdoor Spectacles

OBJECTIVES: Understand how artists use unexpected sites, scale, media, and subjects to surprise us. Make a papier-mâché model of a large-scale outdoor sculpture for the community.

MOTIVATE

Engage students' attention by doing something out of the ordinary. You might, for example, put on a huge pair of eyeglasses or turn a large poster or object upside down. Then discuss how surprises catch our attention.

VIEWING ART

TEACH

Discuss the element of surprise. Ask students to view the art and read the paragraphs. Have them tell what surprised them when they first looked at the pictures. Encourage them to point out the unusual scale of sculpture A.

Discuss the message of *Cadillac Ranch*. Ask students what position the cars are in and why they think the artists chose this position. (Possible responses: The cars are nose down. Maybe the artists wanted us to really look at and think about cars.) Point out that some of these Cadillacs have the big tailfins that were popular in the 1950s. Stanley Marsh 3 considers cars part of the American Dream.

Critical Thinking Questions

- **How do you think you would feel standing next to the fifty-foot spoon? Why?** (Possible responses: very small; amused)
  AESTHETICS: PERSONAL RESPONSE

- **What do you think an artist living 200 years ago would say about these sculptures? Explain.** (Possible responses: He or she would probably not understand B because it is about cars. He or she might not consider either sculpture to be a work of art.) ART HISTORY: COMPARE/CONTRAST

MEETING INDIVIDUAL NEEDS

EXTRA SUPPORT You may wish to cut out a small figure of a teaspoon and place it next to the picture of sculpture A to show how big the sculpture is.

LESSON 18   MAKING A PAPIER-MÂCHÉ MODEL

Outdoor Spectacles

What is surprising about these sculptures?

Wait a minute! What's a giant spoon holding a cherry doing in a city park? Why are those rusty cars planted in a Texas wheat field?

Each of these sculptures shows a familiar object that has been changed in some way. The spoon in sculpture **A** is almost 50 feet long. The scale of this sculpture makes us stop and take a second look.

A group of artists created sculpture **B** from unusual materials—cars! Why do you think they placed the old cars in the middle of a country landscape? Do you think they were trying to make a point? Why do you think so?

A

Spoonbridge and Cherry,
Claes Oldenburg and
Coosje van Bruggen
1985–88. Stainless steel, painted aluminum,
29 1/2 ft. X 51 1/2 ft. X 13 1/2 ft.
Minneapolis Sculpture Garden, Minneapolis, MN.

SHARE ART HISTORY

A **Claes Oldenburg** [KLAHS OHL·dun·burg] (1929–) is from Sweden, and his wife, Coosje van Bruggen [KOOS·yeh van BROO·gen] (1942–), is from the Netherlands. They live in the United States, where they build large public sculptures. Oldenburg designed the *Spoonbridge,* and van Bruggen added the cherry. Oldenburg draws constantly to develop new ideas. He and van Bruggen once built a 36-foot pickax and a giant boat in the shape of a Swiss Army knife.

B **Stanley Marsh 3**, a Texas sculptor, and a San Francisco-based design group called the **Ant Farm** worked together to help create *Cadillac Ranch.* Ant Farmer Doug Michels says, "To me, it was a dolphin idea . . . the dolphin tail became a Cadillac tailfin." Marsh liked the idea of placing the ten Cadillacs near old Route 66. Marsh says, "What makes America the best country in the world is the car."

UNIT 3: *Unexpected Art*

IN THE STUDIO BIG BOOK p.18

Cadillac Ranch, Stanley Marsh 3 and the Ant Farm
1974. Car bodies. Near Amarillo, TX, off old Route 66.

IN THE STUDIO

MATERIALS
- soft pencils
- drawing paper
- old newspapers
- thin glue
- boxes, balloons, other unneeded objects
- tempera paints
- paintbrushes

Work by yourself or with a group. Plan a large piece of public art for your community.

1. Think of a special place in your community. Imagine a large sculpture that would fit well there. Draw a sketch of your sculpture and its setting.

2. Make a model of your plan, using papier-mâché. Use a box, a balloon, or some other object for the base of your model. Cover the base with strips of newspaper dipped in thin glue. Let dry, and repeat at least once. Paint your model after it dries again.

71

ART ACROSS THE CURRICULUM

SOCIAL STUDIES: CAR TALK Ask students to interview adult relatives or friends about their cars. Students can compile a list of questions, such as "How do you think most Americans feel about their cars? Why do you like or dislike your car? Where have you traveled in your car?" Encourage students to record the results of their interviews and to illustrate them with surprising pictures of cars.

READING: TINY PEOPLE IN A HUGE WORLD Suggest that students read one or more of *The Borrowers* series by Mary Norton. When students are finished, they can make posters that show some of the furniture pieces and other items that the tiny Borrowers make out of things from the human world

---

IN THE STUDIO

MATERIALS: soft pencils, drawing paper, old newspapers, thin glue, tempera paints, paintbrushes, objects such as boxes, balloons, or other unneeded objects to use as cores

Making a Papier-Mâché Model   CREATING ART

- Have students tear newspapers into strips. In a large container, mix glue with two parts water. Demonstrate how to dip strips of newspaper into the glue and lay the wet strips down over a core.

- Ask students to work alone or in groups of three or four. Read aloud the directions on page 71, and remind students to plan sculptures that will surprise viewers. They should decide where in their community they would place the sculptures.

- If students' models require unusual shapes, they can create malleable papier-mâché by letting newspaper strips soak for five minutes in glue and then squishing the strips together and shaping them.

- Students can add small cardboard trees or people to show setting and scale.

- Allow the papier-mâché to dry before having students paint their models.

OPTIONAL: Quick Activity Students can sketch ideas for large sculptures. Ask them to show the sculptures' scale by drawing them next to people.

WRAP-UP   INFORMAL ASSESSMENT

- **How do you think your sculpture would make people feel?** (Responses will vary. Students might say that their sculptures would amaze viewers.) AESTHETICS: MAKE PREDICTIONS

- **How did looking at the two sculptures help you plan your own large-scale sculpture?** (Responses will vary.) PRODUCTION: APPLICATION

LESSON 18: *Outdoor Spectacles*

UNIT 3
REFLECTING AND REVIEWING

Pages 72–73	**Reflect on the unit theme.** Have students read the first paragraph on page 72. Point out to students that the artworks in this unit surprise or amuse the viewer, often by presenting common objects in unusual ways.
	Ask students to discuss the artwork. Students might describe what the artwork reminds them of. Ask students why they think Christo and Jeanne-Claude chose these particular islands to surround with pink material. Students might reason that they probably picked these islands because they are small and they are all in a row.
About the Artist	Christo and Jeanne-Claude (1935–) Christo worked for the Bulgarian government improving the scenery along the route of the Orient Express while he studied at the Fine Arts Academy in Sofia, Bulgaria. He and Jeanne-Claude began wrapping found objects such as bottles, cans, and magazines in cloth in 1960. They then moved to New York and began larger projects, including wrapping and transforming monuments, buildings, and bridges.
About the Art	*Surrounded Islands* is a work in which Christo and Jeanne-Claude encircled eleven islands with 6.5 million square feet of pink material. These islands are located near Miami in Biscayne Bay, Florida. The material he used is called polypropylene, which is a very light plastic material normally used in packaging.

UNIT 3   REFLECTING AND REVIEWING

Artists use the unexpected to surprise and amuse us.

Did you find any of the artwork in this unit surprising? The work on this page is so surprising that some people do not even call it art. What do *you* think? Are these islands—surrounded by pink fabric—art? Why or why not?

Surrounded Islands, Christo and Jeanne-Claude
1980–1983. Polypropylene fabric,
11 islands. Biscayne Bay, FL.

72

ART ACROSS THE CURRICULUM

THEATER: WRAP REVIEWS Ask small groups of students to pretend they are residents in the Biscayne Bay area seeing the surrounded islands for the first time. Have them perform a play in which the residents react to the artwork. Encourage students to have an even mix of positive and negative reactions by the characters.
COOPERATIVE LEARNING

72   UNIT 3: *Unexpected Art*

What Did I Learn?

- **ARTISTS** can surprise us by using unexpected subjects, scale, or media. Find an artwork in this unit that is surprising in one of these ways. Explain why you chose the artwork you did.
- **CHOOSE** an artwork in this unit that fools your eyes and your brain. Why do you think many people enjoy looking at artwork like this?
- **WHICH** artwork in this unit was the most amusing? Explain your opinion.
- **YOU** made some surprising artwork of your own in this unit. How did you use materials, techniques, subjects, or ideas in unexpected ways?

Just for Fun — TREASURE HUNT

TO ENCOURAGE STUDENTS to take another close look at the artworks in this unit, ask them to respond to the following questions and statements:

- How can you tell that the scene in *Dinotopia* is an imaginary world? (Possible responses: The creatures flying do not exist; there is water pouring from the building.)
- Find one image that shows two separate scenes. (page 56)
- Name some of the everyday objects used in the artworks in this unit. (Possible responses: cars, a spoon, a fish)
- Find three images that show unexpected objects. (Possible responses: the *Dinotopia* image, *The Castle in the Pyrenees*, *Spoonbridge and Cherry*, *Cadillac Ranch*)

What Did I Learn?

Encourage students to work in small groups to discuss their answers to these questions that appear on page 73.

- **Artists can surprise us by using unexpected subjects, scale, or media. Find an artwork in this unit that is surprising in one of these ways. Explain why you chose the artwork you did.** (Responses will vary.) AESTHETICS: ANALYSIS
- **Choose an artwork in this unit that fools your eyes and your brain. Why do you think many people enjoy looking at artwork like this?** (Possible responses: Because it is a challenge to the viewer; because being fooled can be amusing.) AESTHETICS: MAKE JUDGMENTS
- **Which artwork in this unit was the most amusing? Explain your opinion.** (Responses will vary.) AESTHETICS: MAKE JUDGMENTS
- **You made some surprising artwork of your own in this unit. How did you use materials, techniques, subjects, or ideas in unexpected ways?** (Responses will vary.) PRODUCTION: DESCRIPTION

Students may select images from this unit to add to their portfolios.

Reflecting and Reviewing

UNIT 4

Harmony and Conflict

Art can convey a wide range of human feelings. Some works of art try to make a viewer feel calm, while others deliberately create tension. Artists use a wide range of colors—from a peaceful blue lake to a fiery red inferno—to achieve this end.

In this unit, students will see how artists project feelings of harmony and conflict into their work.

ART PRINT 7 *The Wreck of the "Covenant"* by N. C. Wyeth

ART PRINT 8 *Instruments of Dixieland* by Romare Bearden

Using the Art Prints

Display and introduce *Art Prints 7* and *8*. (Discussion suggestions appear on the back of each *Art Print*.) Have students discuss what feelings each image expresses.

RESPONSE CARD OPTION Have pairs of students use Response Card 6, *Nonrepresentational Art,* on page R61 of this *Teacher's Edition* to guide a discussion of *Art Print 8*.

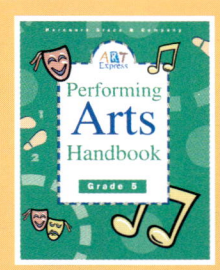

Performing Arts Handbook

Dance, theater, and music activities to extend and enrich students' experiences with these *Art Prints* can be found in the *Performing Arts Handbook*.

UNIT 4: *Harmony and Conflict*   **74B**

UNIT 4 — HARMONY AND CONFLICT

Introducing the Unit pp. 74A–75

LESSON	VIEWING	CREATING	CURRICULUM CONNECTIONS
19 FEELINGS OF HARMONY PP. 76–77 • *Trail Riders* by Thomas Hart Benton • *Squaw Creek Valley* by Florence McClung	Understand how artists use related colors and shapes to create a harmonious scene. **VOCABULARY:** harmony, analogous colors, tints, shades	Paint a harmonious scene that includes analogous colors and repeated lines and shapes. **MATERIALS:** watercolors, paintbrushes, water container and water	**Performing Arts** Music: Listen to Beethoven while painting, p. 77 **Social Studies** Discover Regional Art, p. 77
20 A SENSE OF EXCITEMENT PP. 78–79 • *Nichols Canyon* by David Hockney • *The Toboggan* by Henri Matisse	Observe how artists use contrasting colors to show excitement and curved lines to show movement. **VOCABULARY:** contrast	Create a scene that shows movement. Use complementary colors to add contrast and excitement. **MATERIALS:** soft pencils, colored markers, white paper	**Performing Arts** Music: Study traveling music, p. 79 **Physical Education** Winter Sports, p. 79
CONNECTIONS: ART AND LITERATURE The Lively Art of David Diaz pp. 80–81			
21 IN BALANCE PP. 82–83 • *Victorian Interior* by Horace Pippin • *Untitled* by Alexander Calder	Understand how artists create balance in their artwork. **VOCABULARY:** symmetrical, balance, mobile, asymmetrical	Use objects from nature to create a mobile that is in balance. **MATERIALS:** branches and twigs, strong thread or fishing line, natural objects	**Reading** Balance and Imbalance in Poetry, p. 83 **Mathematics** Weighing In, p. 83
22 COLORS IN CONFLICT PP. 84–85 • *Confusion of Shapes* by Diana Ong • student artwork	Recognize how artists show tension or conflict in their artwork. **VOCABULARY:** arbitrary colors	Create a collage that shows tension. **MATERIALS:** oaktag or white paper, tempera paints, paintbrushes, colored paper, scissors, glue	**Language Arts** Stream-of-Consciousness Writing, p. 85 **Science** Computer Graphics, p. 85
CONNECTIONS: CELEBRATION ART Art on Parade pp. 86–87			
23 VISUAL RHYTHMS PP. 88–89 • *Broadway Boogie Woogie* by Piet Mondrian • *Rhythme Colore* by Sonia Terk Delaunay • *Atmospheric Effects II* by Alma Woodsey Thomas	Learn how artists use repetition to create a feeling of rhythm. **VOCABULARY:** rhythm, pattern	Use repeated colors and shapes to create a print with visual rhythm. **MATERIALS:** tempera paints, dry sponges, scissors, white paper, flat paint containers	**Performing Arts** Music: Listen to the beat, p. 89 **Science** Rhythm of the Heart, p. 89
24 LINES OF EXPRESSION PP. 90–91 • *The Starry Night* by Vincent van Gogh	Understand that artists can paint objects in ways that show how they feel about them. **VOCABULARY:** expressive, Expressionists	Paint a favorite landscape or cityscape in a way that expresses feelings. **MATERIALS:** tempera paints, paintbrushes, large sheet of white paper	**Language Arts** Writing a Description, p. 91 **Science** Constellations, p. 91

Unit 4 Reflecting and Reviewing pp. 92–93

Integrating Your Day

SUGGESTED READING	OPTIONAL VIDEOS/TECHNOLOGY
Rough Sketch Beginning by James Berry. Harcourt Brace, 1996. EASY *Mattie Lou O' Kelley: Folk Artist* by Mattie Lou O' Kelley. Little, Brown and Company, 1989. AVERAGE	Students can use *Crayola Art Studio 2* to draw an image from nature that conveys a sense of harmony.
Fireworks: The Science, the Art, and the Magic by Susan Kuklin. Hyperion, 1996. AVERAGE *Going Home* by Eve Bunting, illus. by David Diaz. HarperCollins, 1996. EASY	Students can watch *Get to Know Gerald McDermott* to learn how the artist uses color to show movement and excitement in his books.
Drawing by Jude Welton. Dorling Kindersley, 1994. AVERAGE *The Piñata Maker/El Piñatero* by George Ancona. Harcourt Brace, 1994. AVERAGE	Small groups of students can use BLOX-Flying Shapes from the *Thinkin' Things Collection 1* to explore shapes and balance.
Making Prints by Deri Robins. Kingfisher, 1993. AVERAGE *I Live in Music* by Ntozake Shange, paintings by Romare Bearden. Welcome Enterprises, 1994. EASY	**INTERNET** Have students use the *Strange Combinations* activity in the Art section of *Just For Kids* to explore how artists show conflict using shapes and color. http://www.hbschool.com
Five Minute Art Ideas: Print by Nicola Wright. Ideals Children's Books, 1995. EASY *Rainbow Warrior Artists: Native Artists of North America* by Reavis Moore. Muir, 1993. AVERAGE	Encourage students to experiment with BLOX-Flying Spheres in *Thinkin' Things Collection 2* to create rhythmic images.
Talking with Artists ed. by Pat Cummings. Bradbury Press, 1992. AVERAGE *A Young Painter, Wang Yani* by Zhen Zhensun and Alice Low. Scholastic, 1991. AVERAGE	Have students explore Moods in *Look What I See!* to learn more about how artists express themselves.

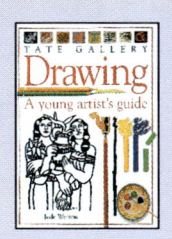

Art Minutes

Present one of these puzzles or activities for students to solve by the end of the week.

■ **Think** of a time when you were happy or sad. Draw a picture of your face at that time. SYNTHESIS

■ **Look** at an image that expresses a particular feeling. Name ways you could change the image so that it expresses a different feeling. SYNTHESIS

■ **Find** a picture of a happy scene. Describe what makes the scene happy. ANALYSIS

■ **Name** some of the colors you associate with happiness. With sadness. With excitement. APPLICATION

■ **Create** a construction-paper mask that uses arbitrary, or nonnatural, colors. APPLICATION

■ **Think** of as many color emotion sentences as you can. For example, "He's *red* with anger." APPLICATION

SCHOOL-HOME CONNECTION

After completing Lesson 23, distribute School-Home Connection 4, found on page R53. Students and family members can collect objects to make an interesting print.

Activities and Resources CD-ROM provides additional teaching materials and interactive student activities for use with Unit 4.

UNIT 4: *Harmony and Conflict*

UNIT 4

INTRODUCING
THE UNIT

Pages 74–75

Discuss *Faraway*. Have students read pages 74 and 75. Invite volunteers to respond to the painting by suggesting the feelings expressed in it.

Examine the artist's technique. Ask students what techniques contribute to feelings of peaceful rest, dreaming, and harmony in the painting. Discuss the harmony created by the repeated lines in the twigs, grass, and cap, and the harmony created by the brown, gold, and yellow colors.

About the Art

Andrew Wyeth, looking to stretch his skills beyond the watercolor medium, used a brush squeezed almost dry of paint to create *Faraway*. Wyeth's use of the "dry brush" method produced the extraordinary texture of the field and of the raccoon hat. The model with the dreaming eyes is Andrew's six-year-old son, Jamie, who is now a successful painter in his own right.

Another example of a Wyeth family painting, this by N. C. Wyeth, can be found in **Art Print 7**.

Faraway
drybrush, 1952
copyright 1998 Andrew Wyeth

TIME LINE

Have students choose one artwork from the unit, locate the period of its creation on the *Time Line*, and use other sources to find out more about the period.

UNIT 4: *Harmony and Conflict*

UNIT 4

Harmony and Conflict

How do artists bring out different feelings in viewers?

Some works of art can make you feel quiet and calm. Some can make you feel tense and excited. How do you feel when you look at *Faraway*?

In this painting, Andrew Wyeth has set his son Jamie in an empty world of grass and twigs. Yet the boy's thoughts seem to be far from empty.

When you look at this painting, can you sense what it would be like to be in the scene? What has the artist done to make you feel this way?

ABOUT ANDREW WYETH

Andrew Wyeth was born in 1917 into a remarkable family. His father, N.C. Wyeth, was one of the greatest illustrators of the day. His son, James, is a celebrated artist, too.

Meet the Artist

Andrew Wyeth (1917–) was born in Chadds Ford, Pennsylvania, the youngest of the five children of the famous illustrator N. C. Wyeth. Andrew was also the pupil of N. C. Wyeth, who encouraged him to exhibit his first collection of watercolors (very successfully) at the age of twenty-one. Since then, Andrew Wyeth has produced thousands of images, nearly all based upon life in and around the Wyeth homesteads in Pennsylvania and Maine.

LITERATURE CONNECTION

Seasons by Warabé Aska. Doubleday, 1990. EASY

This book combines beautiful oil paintings with poems about the seasons from around the world.

CLASSROOM MANAGEMENT

VIEWING: Response Cards Have students use appropriate Response Cards as they think about art from the unit and from other sources. For example, have students use Response Card 4, Still Lifes and Objects in Nature, with Lesson 19, Feelings of Harmony. Then have them use the Response Card as they view other examples of special clothing in magazines or library books. The Response Cards begin on page R56 of this Teacher's Edition.

CREATING: Studio Activity Options If your classroom resources are limited, you may wish to have students complete the Quick Activity for one or more lessons. The Quick Activity in each lesson reinforces lesson concepts and skills but usually requires fewer materials.

LESSON 19

Feelings of Harmony

OBJECTIVES: Understand how artists use related colors and shapes to create a harmonious scene. Paint a harmonious scene that includes analogous colors and repeated lines and shapes.
MATERIALS: tape player, harmonious music

MOTIVATE

Discuss how musical harmony affects a person's feelings. Play for students an audiotape of harmonic vocal music. Have students share their reactions. Explain that voices that blend create harmony.

VIEWING ART

TEACH

Discuss repetition in the paintings. Read about the artworks. Explain that harmony can be created by colors and shapes. Point out the repeated shapes in A such as the pointed rocks and the trees, and the rounded, low rocks and the riders. Ask them which shapes are repeated in B. (shapes of the haystacks, hills, and houses)

Discuss analogous colors. On a color wheel, point out analogous color pairs. Explain that yellow and green are related, so they are easy to look at together. In A, point out tints and shades that create smooth transitions between light and dark areas. You may want to display *Art Print 7* and ask students to point out areas of transition between colors.

Critical Thinking Questions

- **How do you think these artists felt about these scenes?** (Possible response: peaceful)
  ART CRITICISM: DRAW CONCLUSIONS

- **Which painting gives you the greatest feeling of harmony? Why?** (Responses will vary.) AESTHETICS: PERSONAL RESPONSE

EXTRA SUPPORT Mix blue paint with red to create two analogous colors: blue-purple and red-purple. Explain that these colors are analogous, or closely related.

LESSON 19 PAINTING WITH WATERCOLORS

Feelings of Harmony

How can colors and shapes express peaceful feelings?

The beauty of the American West has inspired strong feelings in many artists. What gives these paintings of the West such a feeling of harmony, or peace?

In picture **A**, sharp, pointed shapes and lines are repeated in the forest and the mountains. The painter also made the dull shapes of the rocks and the horses alike. Which shapes are alike in picture **B**? Which lines are repeated?

Both artists used yellow and green as important colors. This helps to create harmony, because yellow and green are analogous colors. This means that they are next to each other on the color wheel.

A
Trail Riders,
Thomas Hart Benton
Polymer tempera on canvas,
56 1/8 in. X 74 in.
National Gallery of Art,
Washington, D.C.

SHARE ART HISTORY

A Thomas Hart Benton (1889–1975) was part of an art movement called Regionalism. Regionalist painters depicted rural American scenes. Benton was inspired by the work of Mexican muralists such as Diego Rivera. He decided to create similar paintings of scenes in the United States. Benton's works show Americans working hard to develop farms and build new cities.

B Florence McClung (1896–1992) matured as an artist as Regionalism was being embraced in American art. McClung liked to paint scenes that could be found only in Texas. Her landscapes, with manicured fields and sparkling white farmhouses, brought her national attention. She stated, "I wanted children a hundred years from now to know how Texas looked in this day and time."

UNIT 4: *Harmony and Conflict*

IN THE STUDIO BIG BOOK p.19

Notice how the artists blended the colors. They created **tints** by starting with white and adding color. They created **shades** by starting with color and adding black. Find some tints and shades in each painting. How does this blending add to the feeling of harmony?

Squaw Creek Valley, Florence McClung
1937. Oil on Canvas, 24 1/8 in. X 30 1/8 in.
Dallas Museum of Art, gift of Florence E. McClung

IN THE STUDIO

MATERIALS
- white paper
- watercolors
- paintbrushes

Paint a peaceful scene. Create a feeling of harmony with colors and shapes.

1. Before painting, choose two or more analogous colors. Then mix tints and shades. To mix tints with watercolors, add extra water to let the white paper show through. To mix shades, start with a color and add black.

2. Paint a natural scene. First, paint the large areas, such as sky, water, or forest. Use light colors. Then add details and darker colors. Try to repeat shapes, lines, and textures to add to the harmony.

ART ACROSS THE CURRICULUM

PERFORMING ARTS: MUSIC While students paint their watercolors, play a recording of the first movement of Beethoven's Sixth Symphony. Beethoven said the piece was "an expression of feeling [that] . . . is easy to recognize. . . . How happy I am to be able to wander among the bushes and herbs, under trees and over rocks." Ask students if they can recognize those feelings.

SOCIAL STUDIES: DISCOVER REGIONAL ART Help students discover painters in your community. Invite students to ask family members or a librarian for the names of local painters. If possible, invite one of these painters to talk with the class about art and show them his or her paintings. You might also plan a field trip to a local gallery.

IN THE STUDIO

MATERIALS: watercolors, paintbrushes, water container and water

Painting with Watercolors

CREATING ART

- Before students begin painting, ask them to create a palette of analogous colors by mixing different ratios of two primary colors. Also ask them to mix white with some colors to create tints, and black with some colors to create shades.

- Demonstrate an alternate method of making tints with watercolors: Mix large amounts of water with a color to create a *wash*, or a thin paint that allows the white paper to show through.

- Direct students to begin their paintings by painting large background areas of sky, forest, or water with tints or washes.

- Next, have students use colors from their palettes to add details to their artwork. Remind students to repeat shapes, lines, and textures in different areas of their paintings.

OPTIONAL: Quick Activity Invite students to create charts of analogous colors. Assign groups two primary colors; ask them to chart at least ten combinations of colors, tints, and shades that include one or both of their primary colors.

WRAP-UP

INFORMAL ASSESSMENT

- **Find a classmate's painting that makes you feel peaceful. How did the artist use colors and lines to express harmony?** (Responses will vary. Students should recognize analogous colors and repetition.) AESTHETICS: ANALYSIS

- **How are paintings A and B different from photographs?** (Possible responses: The paintings do not make the scenes look as realistic. The painters' colors and shapes tell us what they feel and think about the scenes.) AESTHETICS: COMPARE/CONTRAST

LESSON 19: *Feelings of Harmony*

LESSON 20

A Sense of Excitement

OBJECTIVES: Observe how artists use contrasting colors to show excitement and curved lines to show movement. Create a scene that shows movement. Use complementary colors to add contrast and excitement.

MOTIVATE

Visualize winding tracks or roads. Ask students to visualize traveling down a winding road. Have several volunteers come to the board and sketch the road or track they visualized.

VIEWING ART

TEACH

Discuss the effects of contrasting colors and curved lines. Invite students to read about the art. Ask them to point out complementary colors in A. (blue and orange, red and green) Explain that cool colors tend to recede and warm colors to advance, making the orange area at the top seem almost as close as the blue area at the bottom. Point out that curved or wiggly lines can make shapes in a picture seem to move. Ask students to point out the curving lines in A and B. (Possible response: in A—in the road and plants; in B—in the blue figure and the border)

Critical Thinking Questions

- Look at previous lessons in your book. Find other works of art with complementary colors. (Possible response: *Plus Reversed* in Lesson 14) ART CRITICISM: APPLICATION

- How could you use the title of picture B to explain what is happening in this collage? (Possible response: A person has fallen out of a toboggan and is rolling over on a snowy track with bushes on each side.) ART CRITICISM: DESCRIPTION

STUDENTS ACQUIRING ENGLISH Move toward students and then away from them to help them understand the meanings of *advance* and *recede*.

LESSON 20 SHOWING CONTRAST AND MOVEMENT

A Sense of Excitement

How can a painting show action and excitement?

Picture yourself on a bicycle, zooming down the road in picture **A**. Now imagine tumbling head over heels like the figure in picture **B**. These pictures give viewers a feeling of excitement and movement. How have the artists done this?

In picture A, the orange in the background advances, or seems to jump outward. The blue in the foreground recedes, or seems to move back. This helps to make the hill look very steep. The fact that painting A is long, rather than wide, also makes the hill seem steep.

A *Nichols Canyon*, David Hockney
1980. Acrylic on canvas, 84 in. X 60 in.

SHARE ART HISTORY

A **David Hockney** (1937–) is one of the most famous contemporary artists in the world. He has created photographs, drawings, and prints in addition to paintings. He started painting *Nichols Canyon* after he moved to a house in the Hollywood Hills. As he described it, he took a canvas and "drew a wiggly line down the middle, which is what the roads seemed to be." Many of his paintings reflect images of Southern California, where he makes his home.

B **Henri Matisse** [ahn•REE mah•TEES] (1869–1954), a French painter and sculptor, is also famous for colorful cut-paper collages. He originally made paper cutouts as a method of repairing parts of his paintings. However, near the end of his life, Matisse became ill and could no longer get out of bed to paint. After a lifetime of painting, he said: "The cutout is what I have now found to be the simplest and most direct way of expressing myself."

78   UNIT 4: *Harmony and Conflict*

IN THE STUDIO BIG BOOK p.20

When complementary colors are put together, they create **contrast**. They can surprise the eyes and make a scene look exciting. Find some complementary colors in each picture.

Curving lines can also create excitement. What curving lines can you find in each picture?

B *Tobaggan*, Henri Matisse
1947. Cut and pasted paper, 16 5/8 in. X 25 5/8 in. Museum of Modern Art, New York.

IN THE STUDIO

MATERIALS
- soft pencils
- colored markers
- white paper

Create a scene that shows movement. Use complementary colors to add contrast and excitement.

1. Think of a scene in which someone or something is moving. Sketch the scene in pencil. Use curves to create a sense of movement.

2. Add color to the sketch. Choose colors that create contrast. You might choose complementary colors from the color wheel, such as orange and blue or violet and yellow.

79

ART ACROSS THE CURRICULUM

PERFORMING ARTS: MUSIC Invite students to play audiotapes or sing songs about traveling. Discuss the kinds of melodies and rhythms that songs about movement typically have. Ask students to draw a scene, showing movement, from a traveling song.

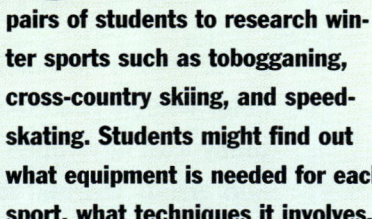

PHYSICAL EDUCATION: WINTER SPORTS Invite pairs of students to research winter sports such as tobogganing, cross-country skiing, and speed-skating. Students might find out what equipment is needed for each sport, what techniques it involves, and what records have been set in it, if it is a competitive sport. Have students make posters that show their findings.

IN THE STUDIO

MATERIALS: soft pencils, colored markers, white paper

Showing Contrast and Movement

CREATING ART

- Invite students to read the directions on page 79. Encourage them to imagine an active, colorful scene that includes moving people, animals, or objects.

- Have students sketch their scenes lightly in pencil. Remind them to use curved lines to show movement.

- When students have completed a rough sketch, tell them to color their sketch with markers and to include at least one pair of complementary colors in their picture.

- Remind students that using receding colors in the foreground and advancing colors in the background can help make their pictures more lively.

OPTIONAL: Quick Activity Ask students to draw simple abstract designs that include curved lines and complementary colors. Have them share their work and discuss the movement in classmates' designs.

WRAP-UP

INFORMAL ASSESSMENT

- **Imagine that you are teaching someone how to draw. What instructions would you give for drawing an exciting scene that shows movement?** (Possible response: Use contrasting or complementary colors and curving lines.) PRODUCTION: APPLICATION

- **Why do you think curved lines in a picture create a feeling of movement?** (Responses will vary. Students might suggest that viewers' eyes follow the curves and that this makes objects in the artwork seem to move.) ART CRITICISM: ANALYSIS

LESSON 20: *A Sense of Excitement*

CONNECTIONS

ART AND LITERATURE

Identify "energetic" artwork. Have students think about exciting book covers, magazine covers, posters, and advertisements that they have seen recently. Ask students what colors and styles attracted them to these artworks. Then have students read pages 80–81 to learn about illustrating a short story.

Discuss the illustration. Share with students that David Diaz won the Caldecott award in 1995 for *Smoky Night*. This yearly award honors the children's book published with the best illustrations. Ask students to look at the illustration for "La Bamba" and speculate as to what techniques David Diaz used. (Possible responses: He used paper cutouts that are sharp and jagged, to provide contrast; he used the contrast of the complementary colors to give the art a sense of energy.) Ask what the story might be about. (Responses will vary.)

CONNECTIONS — ART AND LITERATURE

The Lively Art of David Diaz

Artists can create a sense of movement and excitement on the page.

David Diaz often works with bold, striking colors and sharply cut edges. Look at the colors he used to illustrate Gary Soto's short story "La Bamba." What has David Diaz done to make this title page as exciting as possible?

▲ David Diaz

Artists who illustrate stories face a special challenge. The style and mood of their art must match the style and mood of the story. You can probably guess that "La Bamba" is a lively story. What else can you tell about the story from the art?

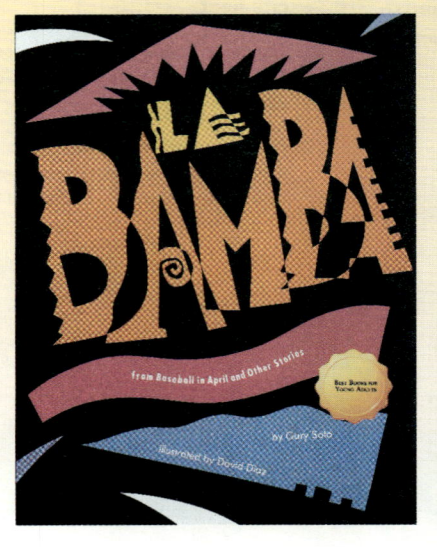

SHARE ART HISTORY

Papier Collé

The art of using cut pieces of paper to create an image is called papier collé [pahp•YAY koh•LAY]. Matisse was well-known for using papier collé. Picasso and other Cubists also used this technique to add dimension, movement, and excitement to their works.

SCIENCE

The Color Wheel

David Diaz used colors that are far apart on the color wheel. The color wheel most people refer to today was developed over centuries, as scientists and artists learned more about colors and their relationships. Have students do research to find an old version of the color wheel. Ask them to share it with their classmates and to explain how it is different from most color wheels today.

80 UNIT 4: *Harmony and Conflict*

WHAT DO YOU THINK?

▶ **What do you think of when you look at the art for "La Bamba"?** (Responses will vary: a wild dance, lively music, fun) AESTHETICS: INTERPRETATION

▶ **How do you think David Diaz's art would look if he had used analogous colors? Explain.** (Possible responses: Less exciting; less interesting; the bright complementary colors give a sense of movement and excitement.) PRODUCTION: COMPARE/CONTRAST

DANCE

Title Art

"La Bamba" was the name of a rock-and-roll song written by Ritchie Valens in the 1950s. The title seems to move like the names of such Latin American dances as the samba, the cha-cha, the tango, or the macarena. Have students use names of Latin American dances to design title art. Remind students to use sharp lines and complementary colors. If resources are available, have students play samples of appropriate music while they share their artwork.

IN THE STUDIO

Cut-Paper Illustrations

Challenge students to create an illustration for a children's book. Give them these requirements:

- They must choose a familiar and lively children's book.
- Their illustration must be made of cut paper.
- They must use complementary colors.
- They must show a main character.

Have students display their illustrations while their classmates try to guess the titles.

CONNECTIONS: *Art and Literature*

LESSON 21

In Balance

OBJECTIVES: Understand how artists create balance in their artwork. Use objects from nature to create a mobile that is in balance.

MOTIVATE

Have students study a face in a magazine or book. Ask them to imagine a line down the middle of the forehead, nose, mouth, and chin. Ask students whether the face is exactly the same on each side of this imaginary line.

VIEWING ART

TEACH

Discuss symmetry. Ask students to read about the artworks. Have volunteers point out "twins" in A. (the framed pictures, the armchairs, the two halves of the flower arrangement) Explain that this painting is almost symmetrical because its two sides are almost the same.

Discuss balance. Point out that the bookcase and the table with the lamp in A are not "twins" but that they balance each other. Invite students to cover the bookcase with one hand. Ask: Which way does the painting "tip"? (to the left) Then have students study the mobile. Ask them to cover different elements of the mobile and to note the effect this has on its balance. Ask them how watching this mobile in motion might make them feel.

Critical Thinking Questions

- **How do you think the painter of A wanted viewers to feel about this room?** (Possible response: that it is an orderly place) ART CRITICISM: INTERPRETATION

- **Mobile B hangs in The National Gallery of Art in Washington, D.C. Do you think this is a good place for it? Why or why not?** (Responses will vary.) AESTHETICS: PERSONAL RESPONSE

STUDENTS ACQUIRING ENGLISH Clarify that the word *balance* has several meanings. Explain that in this lesson, it involves the placement of shapes in artwork.

LESSON 21 CREATING A MOBILE

In Balance

How do artists create balance in their works?

Use your finger to draw an imaginary line down the center of picture **A**. Which objects in the left half of the painting have a twin or near-twin in the right half? When an artwork is exactly the same on both sides, it is **symmetrical**. Picture A is almost symmetrical, but not quite. The objects without twins **balance** each other. With your hand, take turns covering up the bookcase and the table with the lamp. Each way, the painting looks lopsided, too heavy on one side or the other.

A **mobile** is a hanging sculpture that moves. Even though mobile **B** is **asymmetrical** (not symmetrical), it is still in balance. This balance can make us feel calm when we watch the mobile's slowly circling shapes.

A *Victorian Interior*, Horace Pippin 1945. Oil on canvas, 25 1/4 in. X 30 in. Metropolitan Museum of Art, New York.

SHARE ART HISTORY

A **Horace Pippin (1888–1946)** was an African American painter. Pippin used simple, flat-looking shapes and unusual color combinations in his paintings. He painted a well-known series of works about John Brown, an abolitionist. One painting in this series, *John Brown Going to His Hanging*, was partly based on a first-hand account by Pippin's mother, who witnessed Brown's trial in 1859.

B **Alexander Calder (1898–1976)** is one of the most famous sculptors of the twentieth century. Calder began to experiment with mobiles in the 1930s. These sculptures rotate slowly, pushed by moving air. Calder also made stationary sculptures called **stabiles**. Many of Calder's pieces are displayed in public places around the world. He was influenced by the abstract painters Piet Mondrian [PEET MAWN•dree•ahn] and Joan Miró [hoh•AHN mee•ROH].

UNIT 4: *Harmony and Conflict*

IN THE STUDIO BIG BOOK p.21

B Untitled, Alexander Calder
National Gallery of Art, Washington, D.C.

IN THE STUDIO

MATERIALS
- branches and twigs
- strong thread or fishing line
- natural objects such as feathers, shells, small rocks, and pieces of wood
- scissors

Create a mobile that is in balance.

1. Use a thick branch for your main crosspiece. Tie thread in the middle of the branch.

2. Hang your branch in a place where you can work on it easily. Tie threads to the ends, and hang objects from them. Your threads can be different lengths. Add and take away threads and objects until your mobile is in balance and moves freely.

83

ART ACROSS THE CURRICULUM

READING: BALANCE AND IMBALANCE IN POETRY Have students read several short poems from their reading textbook or a children's poetry anthology. Ask them to look for poems that seem to be in balance and others that seem out of balance in their structures. Encourage students to copy one of the poems on the board, read it aloud, and explain to the class why they think it is or is not balanced.

MATHEMATICS: WEIGHING IN Provide small groups of students with scales and substances to weigh, such as toothpicks, small rocks, and shells. Challenge them to calculate as precisely as possible how many of the various items it takes to balance with another substance. They should share their findings in the form of a chart.

IN THE STUDIO

MATERIALS: branches and twigs; strong thread or fishing line; natural objects such as feathers, shells, small rocks, pieces of wood, and scissors

Creating a Mobile

CREATING ART

- Direct students to read the steps on page 83.
- Have students use strong thread or fishing line to hang the main crosspiece from the ceiling or from the back of a chair while they work.
- Demonstrate how to suspend objects from the crosspiece. Students can then suspend a second or third crosspiece from the first one to create a multitiered mobile.
- Invite students to experiment with objects of different weights in order to create a balanced mobile that moves freely.

OPTIONAL: Quick Activity Students can create a balanced mobile by hanging natural objects from just one wooden crosspiece.

WRAP-UP

INFORMAL ASSESSMENT

- **How is your mobile similar to Calder's mobile? How is it different?** (Possible response: They are both balanced and move freely. They are made of different materials.) ART CRITICISM: COMPARE/CONTRAST

- **How did you solve the problem of balancing objects of different weights?** (Responses will vary. Students may note that they balanced two or more lighter objects against one heavier one or moved the thread toward one end of the crosspiece.) PRODUCTION: PROBLEM SOLVING

LESSON 21: *In Balance*   83

LESSON 22

Colors in Conflict

OBJECTIVES: Recognize how artists show tension or conflict in their artwork. Create a collage that shows tension.

MATERIALS: fabric or paper of many different colors: pastels, primary colors, dark and light shades

MOTIVATE

Identify colors that contrast strongly. Display fabric or paper of various colors. Ask students which colors seem closely related and which are very different.

VIEWING ART

TEACH

Discuss how contrasting colors in artwork show feelings of tension and conflict. Invite students to read pages 84 and 85. Direct them to compare A and B to the artwork on pages 76 and 77. Ask students to contrast how they feel when they look at each pair of pictures. (Possible responses: A and B are jumbled; the paintings on pages 76 and 77 are peaceful.)

Discuss how jumbled shapes and arbitrary colors can create feelings of uneasiness. Ask students to figure out how the artist made A look jumbled. (Possible response: She made a picture of a face, cut it into strips, and then slid the strips apart.) Ask whether the colors in B are like colors seen in real life. (no) Explain that such colors are called *arbitrary* colors. Long ago, very few artists dared to use such arbitrary, or nonnatural, colors.

Critical Thinking Questions

- **Think of a good title for picture B, and explain your choice.** (Responses will vary. Students' titles will probably express conflict or confusion.) ART CRITICISM: DESCRIPTION

- **Do you think A or B shows more tension and conflict? Why?** (Responses will vary.) ART CRITICISM: COMPARE/CONTRAST

MEETING INDIVIDUAL NEEDS

EXTRA SUPPORT Point to places in A and B where lines end abruptly instead of continuing as viewers might expect. Have students trace these lines with their fingers.

LESSON 22 MAKING A COLLAGE

Colors in Conflict

How do artists show tension or conflict in their works?

Look at pictures **A** and **B**. How do these pictures make you feel? Then look back at the pictures on pages 76 and 77. Compare the feelings you get when you look at the two pairs of pictures.

Some artists use shapes that do not seem to go together. Picture A is titled *Confusion of Shapes*. Look closely. How

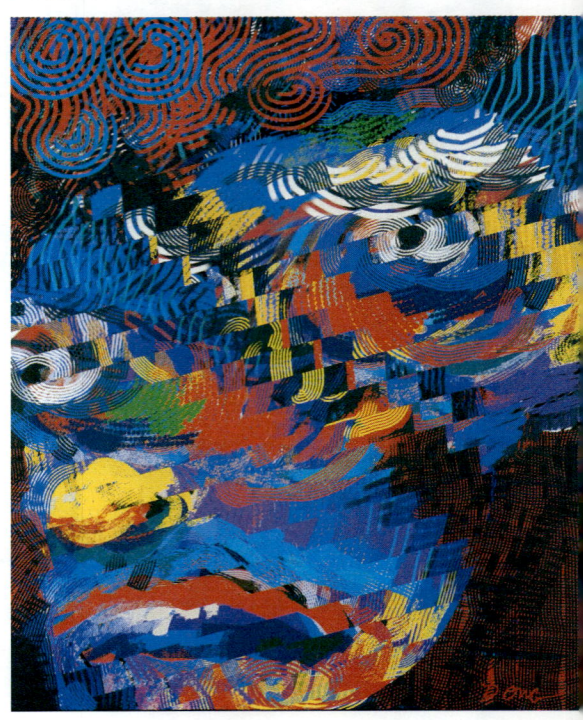

A
Confusion of Shapes,
Diana Ong

84

SHARE ART HISTORY

Diana Ong (1940–), born in New York City, is a multi-media artist. She has produced works in watercolor, acrylic, etching, woodcuts, silkscreens, computer art, and ceramic art. Her artworks have been exhibited in more than thirty countries. In many of her works, she has combined different media. Her art has also been displayed on hundreds of book jackets by publishers around the world.

---

84 UNIT 4: *Harmony and Conflict*

IN THE STUDIO BIG BOOK p.22

did the artist make the shapes look jumbled and confused? What words would you use to describe the way picture A makes you feel?

Some artists use colors that are not seen in nature. These colors, called **arbitrary colors**, can seem as if they don't belong. Surely you have never seen an animal the colors of picture B!

B Student Artwork

IN THE STUDIO

MATERIALS
- oaktag or white paper
- tempera paints
- paintbrushes
- colored paper
- scissors
- glue

Create a collage that shows tension or conflict.

1. Cut colored paper into different shapes. Create shapes that do not seem to belong together.
2. Place your shapes in a mixed-up arrangement on a sheet of oaktag. Then glue them down.
3. Add paint to your collage. Use bold strokes of color.

85

ART ACROSS THE CURRICULUM

LANGUAGE ARTS: STREAM-OF-CONSCIOUSNESS WRITING Explain that writing in stream of consciousness means jotting down whatever random thoughts come into one's mind. Direct students to turn to pages 84–85, focus on A or B, and write down the thoughts that come into their minds. Ask students to write without stopping for two minutes.

SCIENCE: COMPUTER GRAPHICS Tell students that picture A was created on a computer. Ask students to research different uses of computer graphics. Encourage them to find out how people with different jobs (scientists, architectural designers, animators) use computers to generate images. If possible, help students use a computer graphics program to create their artwork.

IN THE STUDIO

MATERIALS: oaktag or white paper, tempera paints, paintbrushes, colored paper, scissors, glue

Making a Collage

CREATING ART

- Direct students to read page 85. Ask students to choose colors as you distribute colored paper.

- Ask students to cut a variety of shapes out of the colored paper. Point out that jagged or geometric shapes might suggest more tension than rounded, organic ones. Invite students to arrange their shapes on sheets of oaktag in ways that show conflict.

- Encourage students to experiment with their shapes. Have them glue the shapes down after they find an arrangement they like.

- Suggest that students use paint to make their collages show even more conflict. Demonstrate different types of brushstrokes they might use. (For example, diagonal brushstrokes that are not blended can create tension.)

OPTIONAL: Quick Activity Students might cut a face or other image from a magazine illustration, cut it into strips, and slide every other strip slightly as Diana Ong seems to have done to create picture A. Students can then glue the strips to a sheet of cardboard.

WRAP-UP

INFORMAL ASSESSMENT

- **How did viewing pictures A and B help you create a collage that shows tension and conflict?** (Possible responses: Pictures A and B show which types of colors can create tension; A shows that jumbled shapes look confusing together.) PRODUCTION: APPLICATION

- **Look at a classmate's collage. How did he or she create feelings of tension or uneasiness?** (Responses will vary.) ART CRITICISM: ANALYSIS

LESSON 22: *Colors in Conflict* **85**

CONNECTIONS

CELEBRATION ART

Discuss parades. Have students think about parades they have seen. Ask them to discuss what parts of the parades they liked and why. (Possible responses: bands—music; balloons—funny shapes; floats—interesting themes and details) Have students read pages 86–87 to find out about a unique parade.

Discuss color combinations. Ask students to look at the float and speculate as to why the designer chose those colors. (Possible response: The designer chose light and dark colors to create an exciting visual impact.)

CONNECTIONS: CELEBRATION ART

Art on Parade

Communities organize unique events to celebrate their home, their work, and themselves!

The New Year's Day Tournament of Roses Parade is a great American tradition. Thousands upon thousands of colorful flowers and leaves cover the festive and imaginative floats. In the last few days before the parade, crews work around the clock to add the flowers. Look at this float from the parade. Why might the designer have chosen these colors?

▶ At work on the *Treasure Island* float

86

SHARE CULTURAL INFORMATION

The Rose Parade first began in 1890 in Pasadena, California. The Valley Hunt Club organized the festival to celebrate and advertise the area's mild winter weather. Professor Charles Holder suggested that they name it the "Rose Parade" because of the abundance of blooming flowers and laden orange trees. Flower-covered carriages were featured in the first parade. The carriages were soon replaced by motorized vehicles.

SCIENCE

Garden Art

COOPERATIVE LEARNING Have students work in pairs to design flower gardens. Encourage students to use paper cutouts and paint to create colorful patterns in their gardens. Have volunteers share their plans.

86 UNIT 4: *Harmony and Conflict*

▲ The *Treasure Island* float on parade

WHAT DO YOU THINK?
- What is unusual about an artwork made of flowers?
- What other celebrations have you seen that included works of art?

87

WHAT DO YOU THINK?
- What is unusual about an artwork made of flowers? (Possible responses: It is temporary, made only for this event; it has a scent.) ART CRITICISM: COMPARE/CONTRAST
- What other celebrations have you seen that included works of art? (Responses will vary.) AESTHETICS: DESCRIPTION

READING

Character Parade

Have students brainstorm characters from literature who would be good subjects for parade floats. Encourage students to discuss how they would use symbols and color to depict different characters.

IN THE STUDIO

Parade Floats

COOPERATIVE LEARNING Have students work in groups to design a parade float. Provide these requirements:

- The float must express pride in your city, area, or state.
- The float must be made of natural materials from your area.
- The float must be colorful and create a feeling of excitement.

Have volunteers share their designs.

CONNECTIONS: *Celebration Art* **87**

LESSON 23

Visual Rhythms

OBJECTIVES: Learn how artists use repetition to create a feeling of rhythm. Use repeated colors and shapes to create a print with visual rhythm.
MATERIALS: tape player, tape of strongly rhythmic or percussive music

MOTIVATE

Visualize rhythm in music. Play some rhythmic music for students and encourage them to visualize colors and shapes. Explain that rhythm is a repetition of beats.

VIEWING ART

TEACH

Discuss rhythm in the art. Invite students to read about the artworks. Have them compare the rhythm in painting A to that in B. *(Possible response: B has a slower rhythm created by graceful curves and large areas of color; your gaze doesn't hop from place to place.)* Next, ask what kind of feeling students get from the pattern in C. *(Possible responses: The wide color bands create a slow, sad mood; the bright, narrow color bands create an excited, happy feeling.)* Point out that the wide bands seem to slow down the painting's rhythm. You may want to display **Art Print 8, Instruments of Dixieland**. Discuss how the repeated triangles and diagonal lines create rhythm.

Critical Thinking Questions

- **Why do you think some artists create nonrepresentational art?** *(Possible response: They want to show an idea or a feeling, not a particular object.)* AESTHETICS: HYPOTHESIZE

- **Imagine a painting with an even quicker rhythm than A has. What might such a painting have in it?** *(Possible response: smaller geometric shapes; brighter colors)* ART CRITICISM: SYNTHESIZE

EXTRA SUPPORT Have students move their fingers from left to right across painting C and name each color they touch, saying the name quickly when the color area is smaller and slowly when it is larger.

LESSON 23 — MAKING A PRINT WITH VISUAL RHYTHM

Visual Rhythms

How do artists create rhythm in artwork?

Bop biddly be bop! Your gaze bounces up and down and back and forth when you look at painting **A**. The artist has created a **rhythm** you can see. To do this, he used squares and rectangles of bright, contrasting colors. The **pattern**, or repeated shapes and colors, makes your gaze hop from place to place.

The rhythm is different in painting **B**. The large areas of color and the long curves make your eyes move at a slower pace. What kind of rhythm do you see in painting **C**? Paintings A, B, and C are examples of nonrepresentational art. They do not represent, or show, objects we can recognize. However, they

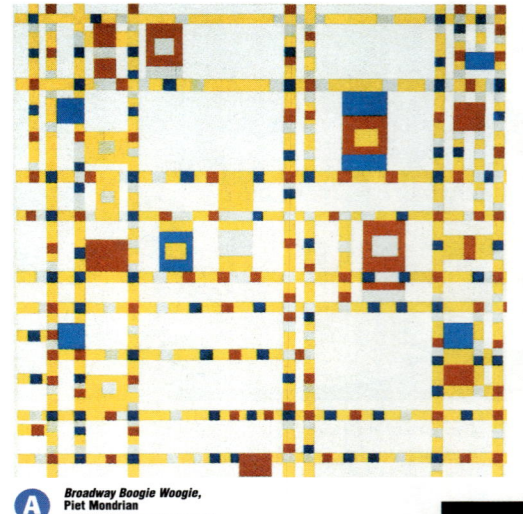

A *Broadway Boogie Woogie*, Piet Mondrian
1942–43. Oil on canvas, 50 in. X 50 in. Museum of Modern Art, New York.

B *Rhythme Colore*, Sonia Terk Delaunay

SHARE ART HISTORY

A With other Dutch artists, **Piet Mondrian** [PEET MOHN•dree•ahn] (1872–1944) created a school of nonrepresentational art that had a great influence on artists, architects, and designers. Mondrian wanted his paintings to show that people can exist in a state of harmony with the universe.

B **Sonia Delaunay** (1885–1979) moved from the Ukraine to Paris to work among French painters. In 1964 she became the first woman whose work was exhibited at the Louvre Museum while she was still alive. She strove to create abstract worlds where colors moved rhythmically.

C The art of African American **Alma Woodsey Thomas** (1891–1978) changed over the decades. She sculpted, painted, made marionettes, and taught art. In the 1960s she developed her own style, experimenting with pure colors.

UNIT 4: *Harmony and Conflict*

IN THE STUDIO BIG BOOK p.23

can still express feelings and ideas. Look again at painting C. If you were to put music to this painting, which would be the fast parts? Which would be the slow parts? Why?

C *Atmospheric Effects II,*
Alma Woodsey Thomas
1971. Watercolor, 22 in. X 30 in.
National Museum of American Art,
Smithsonian Institution, Washington, D.C.

IN THE STUDIO

Use repeated colors and shapes to make a print with rhythm.

MATERIALS
- tempera paints
- dry sponges
- scissors
- white paper

1. Cut sponges into simple shapes such as circles, squares, and triangles.
2. Dip the shapes into different colors of paint.
3. Dab the shapes onto your paper in a pattern that has its own rhythm. Is your rhythm fast or slow? 

89

ART ACROSS THE CURRICULUM

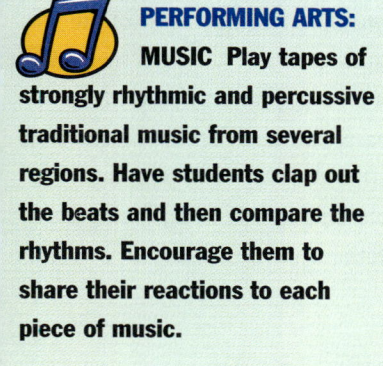

PERFORMING ARTS: MUSIC Play tapes of strongly rhythmic and percussive traditional music from several regions. Have students clap out the beats and then compare the rhythms. Encourage them to share their reactions to each piece of music.

SCIENCE: RHYTHM OF THE HEART Invite students to learn about the rhythm of the human heart. You might provide these questions to help them focus their research: How many times a minute does an average adult's heart beat? An average child's? What is the relationship between the size of a mammal and the rate of its heartbeat? What makes the heart beat faster and slower? Students can share their findings in an oral report.

IN THE STUDIO

MATERIALS: tempera paints, dry sponges, scissors, white paper, flat paint containers

Making a Print with Visual Rhythm — CREATING ART

- Have students read the directions on page 89. Demonstrate how to cut a shape from a sponge, and how to print with one. Emphasize that the sponge should be lightly dabbed in the paint and then pressed lightly against the paper to avoid smearing the print.

- Advise students that before beginning they should visualize a repetitive pattern and think about the colors and shapes they plan to use. Students may want to use their sketchbooks to plan their prints.

- Students can work in groups to share sponge shapes and paints.

OPTIONAL: Quick Activity Have students create repetitive patterns. They can trace coins and other geometrically shaped objects such as mathematics manipulatives, and then color the shapes.

WRAP-UP — INFORMAL ASSESSMENT

- **Think about the visual rhythm in your print. How is your print's rhythm like the rhythm in one of the three paintings? Explain why.** (Responses will vary. Ask students to support their responses with details.) PRODUCTION: COMPARE/CONTRAST

- **Look carefully at a classmate's print. How did your classmate use color and repetition to create rhythm?** (Responses will vary.) ART CRITICISM: DESCRIPTION

LESSON 23: *Visual Rhythms* 89

LESSON 24

Lines of Expression

OBJECTIVES: Understand that artists can paint subjects in ways that show how they feel about them. Paint a favorite landscape or cityscape in a way that expresses feelings.

MATERIALS: crayons, paper

MOTIVATE

Explore expressive lines. Ask students if they have ever been in a bad storm. Invite students to draw a scene that shows how they felt.

VIEWING ART

TEACH

Explain the differences between expressive and realistic styles of painting. Invite students to read about the artwork. Ask whether the painting is realistic. (Possible response: No; a realistic painting of this scene would look more like a real town and sky.) Discuss how the strong lines in this painting move viewers' eyes from the left to the right side of the image, in circles (the stars), and upward (the cypress tree). Ask what a realistic painting of the same scene might look like. (Possible responses: The stars and the moon would be smaller. You would not see big swirls in the sky.)

Critical Thinking Questions

- Why do you think van Gogh used oil paint rather than watercolors to paint *The Starry Night*? (Possible responses: Oil paints are thicker. Lines and brushstrokes show more feeling when painted in oils.) PRODUCTION: ANALYSIS

- Do you think van Gogh painted *The Starry Night* quickly or slowly? How can you tell? (Possible response: The brushstrokes look as if they were painted quickly.) ART CRITICISM: DRAW CONCLUSIONS

EXTRA SUPPORT Display magazine or newspaper photographs of landscapes. Invite students to compare the realistic details in a photograph with the expressive style of *The Starry Night*.

LESSON 24 PAINTING A LANDSCAPE

Lines of Expression

How can artists show things as *they* see them?

How do you think Vincent van Gogh [van GOH] might have been feeling when he painted this picture? Was he feeling quiet or full of energy? Why do you think so?

Instead of showing a night sky as it really looked, van Gogh showed his feelings about the scene. The huge yellow stars and swirling sky show a world full of movement and light.

The Starry Night, Vincent van Gogh
1889. Oil on canvas, 29 in. X 36 1/4 in. Museum of Modern Art, New York.

90

SHARE ART HISTORY

Dutch painter **Vincent van Gogh** [van GOH] (1853–1890) is one of the world's most famous modern artists. He is sometimes called a Post-Impressionist. The Post-Impressionists were more subjective than the Impressionists, more interested in feelings than in the objective natural world. Instead of depicting a scene realistically, they used vivid colors and thick brushstrokes to express strong feelings. Van Gogh was considered a forerunner of the Expressionists. Although he worked as an artist for only about ten years, van Gogh created more than 2,000 drawings and paintings. He sold only one painting during his lifetime.

---

90 UNIT 4: *Harmony and Conflict*

Works of art like *The Starry Night* are **expressive**. This means that they express, or show, the artists' feelings. Trace the strong lines around the stars and the moon. Does your gaze move from the right side of the painting to the left, or from left to right? Why? Explain how the lines make you move your eyes.

Van Gogh's expressive works influenced other artists. A later group of artists used colors and shapes as well as lines to express their feelings. These artists are called the **Expressionists**.

You can express your feelings in your artwork, too. Remember that you don't have to show things as they really look. Express yourself!

IN THE STUDIO

MATERIALS
- tempera paints
- paintbrushes
- large sheet of white paper

Paint a landscape or a cityscape.

Think of one of your favorite places in the country or in the city. Paint this scene, using strong lines to express your feelings about it. Try to lead the viewers' gaze from one section of your painting to another.

91

ART ACROSS THE CURRICULUM

LANGUAGE ARTS: WRITING A DESCRIPTION Ask students to study *The Starry Night* carefully and then write a vivid description of it. Tell them to describe the painting's colors, brushstrokes, and details, as well as the feelings it might give viewers. Encourage students to use a thesaurus to find words that convey exactly what they want to say about the painting.

SCIENCE: CONSTELLATIONS Invite students to research constellations. Students might find out how ancient peoples named constellations, the myths that the names of various constellations are based on, and how astronomers use constellations today. Ask students to draw diagrams of constellations. If possible, arrange for them to visit a planetarium or observatory to learn more about the locations of planets and stars.

IN THE STUDIO

MATERIALS: tempera paints, paintbrushes, large sheet of white paper

Painting a Landscape

CREATING ART

- Ask students to choose a favorite landscape or cityscape to paint.

- Distribute paper, paintbrushes, and paint. You may wish to have students paint with thick tempera paint to imitate van Gogh's thick oil paint.

- Remind students to use expressive brushstrokes to show their feelings. Suggest that they try to use strong lines to lead the viewer's eyes from one section of the painting to another.

- Display students' finished paintings. Ask students to tell what feelings they think are expressed in their classmates' work.

OPTIONAL: Quick Activity Invite students to draw landscapes, using colored markers. Encourage them to use expressive lines to convey feelings.

WRAP-UP

INFORMAL ASSESSMENT

- **Which colors and techniques did you use to help viewers understand your feelings about the scene you painted?** (Possible responses: I used bright colors to show happiness; I used dark colors to show how I feel on a rainy day.) PRODUCTION: PROBLEM SOLVING

- **What feeling do you think the artist expressed in *The Starry Night*? How might the painting have been different?** (Possible responses: I think he expressed tension. He probably would not have included the thick, swirling lines in the sky if he had been calm.) ART CRITICISM: HYPOTHESIZE

LESSON 24: *Lines of Expression*

UNIT 4
REFLECTING AND REVIEWING

Pages 92–93	**Reflect on the unit theme.** Have students read the paragraph on page 92. Point out that the artworks in this unit use rhythm, pattern, color, and balance to show feelings such as harmony or conflict. **Ask students to discuss the painting.** Students might describe how the painting seems to be a confusion of distorted images. Ask them whether they think the image conveys a sense of harmony or conflict and what about the painting makes them feel that way. Students should name specific aspects of the painting such as the colors, the shape of the figures, and the overlapping.
About the Artist	Spanish artist Pablo Picasso [pee•CAH•soh] (1881–1973) was born in Spain and educated in Paris. He founded a movement in painting called Cubism. Picasso's Cubist style was heavily influenced by the style of African sculpture. His works were enormously popular and changed the way many people thought about art.
About the Art	*Three Musicians* is an example of Picasso's Cubist art. The painting shows movement by juxtaposing planes in colors of orange, blue, yellow, and white. The figures in the painting are a Pierrot (a clown), a harlequin, and a monk. There are two versions of this painting; only one of them shows a shaggy dog in the lower left.

92 UNIT 4: *Harmony and Conflict*

UNIT 4 REFLECTING AND REVIEWING

Art can express feelings of harmony and conflict.

In this unit, you have learned about some of the ways artists show rhythm, pattern, and balance. These techniques, combined with the artist's choice of colors, can have a powerful effect on viewers. Look at this painting by the Spanish artist Pablo Picasso. The artist is showing three musicians. Perhaps they are making music in harmony. However, considering the way the artist has shown them, perhaps they are not.

Three Musicians, Pablo Picasso
1921. Oil on canvas, 6 ft. 7 in. X 7 ft. 3 3/4 in. Museum of Modern Art, New York.

92

ART ACROSS THE CURRICULUM

DANCE: PAINTED MELODY Ask small groups of students to imagine that they are dancing to the music played by the musicians in the painting. They should determine whether they think the music is harmonious or not and design a dance that conveys that feeling. Have the groups perform a dance that coincides with the type of music they imagine is being played. **COOPERATIVE LEARNING**

What Did I Learn?

- **WHAT** did Pablo Picasso do to create harmony in this painting? What did he do to create conflict?

- **FIND** an artwork in this unit that is like *Three Musicians* in some way. How are the two pieces alike? How are they different?

- **THINK** about the artwork you created in this unit. How did you use rhythm and patterns? How did you use shapes and colors? What other techniques did you use?

- **FIND** an artwork in this unit that shows balance. Explain how the artist created this balance.

Just for Fun — TREASURE HUNT

TO ENCOURAGE STUDENTS to take another close look at the artworks in this unit, ask them to respond to the following questions and statements:

- Which of the places pictured in this unit would you like to visit?
- What are some of the main colors in the painting *The Starry Night*? Find another painting in which these colors are important. (Possible responses: *The Toboggan, Atmospheric Effects II.*)
- Find three images that repeat the same type of shape or line.
- Name one image that makes you feel happy, and tell why it makes you feel that way.

What Did I Learn?

Encourage students to work in small groups to discuss their answers to these questions that appear on page 93.

- **What did Pablo Picasso do to create harmony in this painting? What did he do to create conflict?** (Possible response: To create harmony, he used repeated colors and shapes. To create conflict, he used brilliant colors; the figures have unusual shapes; the musicians appear to be on top of one another.) ART CRITICISM: EVALUATION

- **Find an artwork in this unit that is like *Three Musicians* in some way. How are the two pieces alike? How are they different?** (Responses will vary.) ART CRITICISM: COMPARE/CONTRAST

- **Think about the artwork you created in this unit. How did you use rhythm and patterns? How did you use shape and colors? What other techniques did you use?** (Responses will vary.) PRODUCTION: DESCRIPTION

- **Find an artwork in this unit that shows balance. Explain how the artist created this balance.** (Responses will vary. Encourage students to tell how the balanced parts are alike.) ART CRITICISM: APPLICATION

Reflecting and Reviewing

UNIT 5

New Ways to Create

Changes in technology affect all aspects of our lives, including art. Artists adapt to these changes by learning to create in different ways. For instance, an artist who used a pencil to draw may now be able to create the same drawing more quickly and precisely with a computer.

In this unit, students will discover how art has evolved and adapted to changes in technology.

ART PRINT 9 *Eagle Knight* by Flor Garduño

ART PRINT 10 *Sagrada Familia* by Antoni Gaudí

Using the Art Prints

Display and introduce *Art Prints 9* and *10*. (Discussion suggestions appear on the back of each *Art Print*.) Invite students to discuss how each artist made use of new technology.

RESPONSE CARD OPTION You may wish to have students use Response Card 8, *Art Critics' Circle,* on page R63 of this *Teacher's Edition* to compare the photography techniques of *Art Prints 9* and *10*.

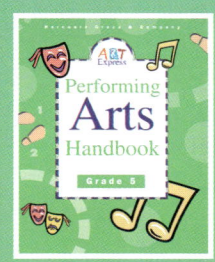

Performing Arts Handbook

Dance, theater, and music activities to extend and enrich students' experiences with these *Art Prints* can be found in the *Performing Arts Handbook*.

UNIT 5: *New Ways to Create*   **94B**

UNIT 5 NEW WAYS TO CREATE

Introducing the Unit pp. 94A–95

LESSON	VIEWING	CREATING	CURRICULUM CONNECTIONS
25 BOOK ART pp. 96–97 • illuminated page from *The Book of Lindisfarne* (AD 700) • illuminated page from the Haggadah (AD 1470) • *Old Man and Youth in Landscape*, Behzad (AD 1500)	Understand that artists decorate books to add beauty and meaning to words. **VOCABULARY:** illuminated pages	Make a cover for a book, diary, or portfolio. **MATERIALS:** heavy white paper, tempera paints, paintbrushes, colored pencils or fine-tipped marking pens	**Social Studies** Hieroglyphics, p. 97 **Language Arts** Writing an Essay, p. 97
26 IS PHOTOGRAPHY ART? pp. 98–99 • *A Child's Brilliant Smile* by Carol Guzy • *Point Lobos, at Carmel, California* by Leah Washington	Realize that photographs can be works of art. **VOCABULARY:** center of interest, frame, focus	Make a photogram that fits well within its frame and has a clear center of interest. **MATERIALS:** light-sensitive paper or photogram kits; pieces of cardboard; materials such as netting, lace, leaves and ferns; water	**Language Arts** Writing a Caption, p. 99 **Social Studies** Photojournalism, p. 99
CONNECTIONS: ART AND LITERATURE		The Photographic Art of George Ancona pp. 100–101	
27 SCULPTURES THROUGH TIME pp. 102–103 • *Draped, standing woman* terra-cotta • Queen Mother head Benin bronze • *Blue Girl on Park Bench* by George Segal	Understand that over the centuries sculptors have used similar ideas but different materials. **VOCABULARY:** synthetic	Use two different materials to sculpt the same subject. **MATERIALS:** milk cartons, mixed plaster of Paris, plastic knife, heavy-duty aluminum foil, scissors	**Language Arts** Writing a Description, p. 103 **Health and Safety** Artists' Safety Rules, p. 103
28 THE WORLD OF ANIMATION pp. 104–105 • Frame from *Pinocchio* • Frame from *Toy Story*	Understand how animators bring still pictures to life. **VOCABULARY:** animation, frame	Make a flip book that creates the illusion of movement. **MATERIALS:** unlined index cards, colored markers, stapler	**Language Arts** Writing a Film Scenario, p. 105 **Social Studies** Hollywood, p. 105
CONNECTIONS: CAREERS IN ART		Computer Animator pp. 106–107	
29 CELEBRATIONS IN STONE pp. 108–109 • Lincoln Cathedral, England • Taj Mahal, India	Understand that buildings express a culture's values. **VOCABULARY:** arch, spires, minarets	Make a scale drawing of a grand building. **MATERIALS:** large sheets of white paper, colored pencils, ruler, compass	**Language Arts** Writing a Travel Brochure, p. 109 **Social Studies** Building Across Cultures, p. 109
30 UNUSUAL ARCHITECTURE pp. 110–111 • The Grand Louvre by I.M. Pei & Associates • The Solomon R. Guggenheim Museum by Frank Lloyd Wright	Understand that bold modern architecture can be exciting and controversial.	Make a foil model of a modern-style building. **MATERIALS:** foam board or cardboard, aluminum foil, paper towel rolls, small boxes or blocks, balloons or small balls, tape or wire, tempera paints, paintbrushes	**Mathematics** Geometric Display, p. 111 **Performing Arts** Theater: Stage a debate about architecture, p. 111

Unit 5 Reflecting and Reviewing pp. 112–113

Integrating Your Day

SUGGESTED READING

Bibles and Bestiaries: A Guide to Illuminated Manuscripts by Elizabeth Wilson. Farrar, Straus, and Giroux, 1994. CHALLENGE

Bookworks: Making Books by Hand by Gwenyth Swain. Carolrhoda Books, 1995. EASY

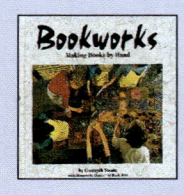

Black Artists in Photography by George Sullivan. Cobblehill, 1996. CHALLENGE

A Female Focus: Great Women Photographers by Margot F. Horitz. Franklin Watts, 1996. CHALLENGE

The Sculptor's Eye by Jan Greenberg and Sandra Jordan. Delacorte, 1993. CHALLENGE

Totem Pole by Diane Hoyt-Goldsmith. Holiday House, 1990. AVERAGE

Animation Magic: A Behind-the-Scenes Look at How an Animated Film Is Made by Don Hahn. Disney Press, 1996. CHALLENGE

Animation: How to Draw Flipbooks by Patrick Jenkins. Kids Can Press, 1991. AVERAGE

Structures That Changed the Way the World Looked by Donna Singer. Raintree, 1995. CHALLENGE

Castle by David Macaulay. Houghton Mifflin, 1977. CHALLENGE

Frank Lloyd Wright for Kids by Kathleen Thorne-Thomsen. Chicago Review Press, 1994. AVERAGE

The Seven Wonders of the Modern World by Reg Cox and Neil Morris. Silver Burdett, 1996. AVERAGE

OPTIONAL VIDEOS/TECHNOLOGY

Groups of students can use *HyperStudio* to create a multimedia book or story.

INTERNET Have students use the *Like a Picture Postcard* activity in the Art Section of *Just For Kids* to learn more about how photographers create a center of interest.
http://www.hbschool.com

Students can view *Stay Away from the Junkyard!* to see how one young girl makes artistic use of materials that are considered junk.

Encourage small groups of students to use *kidDraw* with *The New Kid Pix* to create an animated slide-show.

Students can explore and write about some grand stone structures in *Imagination Express, Destination: Castle*.

Small groups of students can use *Imagination Express, Destination: Pyramids* to learn more about pyramids.

Art Minutes

Present one of these puzzles or activities for students to solve by the end of the week.

■ **Find** an artwork that was drawn by hand. Name ways the artist could have created the artwork using new technology. SYNTHESIS

■ **Choose** five unusual things that could be used as paintbrushes. Describe the brushstrokes they would make and what you could paint with them. ANALYSIS

■ **Locate** a picture of something that was drawn with a computer. Identify how you can tell the picture was not drawn by hand. ANALYSIS

■ **Create** a miniature found-object assemblage using objects that are no more than one inch tall. APPLICATION

■ **Draw** a picture that shows some new technology you think might exist in the future. Write a description of what the technology will do. APPLICATION

■ **Make** a small paper frame. Pretend that it is a camera, and take a photograph of your favorite part of the classroom. APPLICATION

SCHOOL-HOME CONNECTION

After completing Lesson 25, distribute School-Home Connection 5, found on page R54. Students can ask a family member to help collect pictures from old magazines and newspapers to make a collage.

Activities and Resources CD-ROM provides additional teaching materials and interactive student activities for use with Unit 5.

UNIT 5: *New Ways to Create* 94D

UNIT 5

INTRODUCING THE UNIT

Pages 94–95

Discuss *Basket of Light*. Have students read and view pages 94 and 95. Ask students what about the photograph catches their eyes when they first look at it. Invite them to discuss how the photograph is more than just a snapshot. For example, they might discuss the unusual lighting that makes the flowers seem to glow.

Compare photographic techniques. Discuss with students why Garduño may have chosen to create the photograph in black and white. Ask students what effect the image would have if it were in color. Have students compare the two techniques. They might note that the use of black and white makes the flowers stand out.

About the Art

Inform students that Garduño took the picture *Basket of Light* while visiting Guatemala, a small country on the southern border of Mexico. Garduño was struck by the sight of a young girl walking with a basket of lilies balanced on her head. She took the picture with the girl standing half in shadow and half in light to create a good contrast.

Another example of a Flor Garduño photograph can be found on **Art Print 9**.

Basket of Light, Flor Garduño 1989.

TIME LINE

Suggest that students select two or three artworks from the unit and locate the periods of their creation on the *Time Line*.

94   UNIT 5: *New Ways to Create*

UNIT 5

New Ways to Create

How do artists see things in new and different ways?

Two people can pick up the same camera and point it in the same direction, but they may see very different things through its lens.

The women of Guatemala carried baskets of flowers for centuries before the camera was invented. When photographer Flor Garduño looked through a lens at this young woman, she saw more than a traditional, everyday scene. She saw a work of art. What makes *Basket of Light* more than a snapshot? What makes it a new way of seeing a familiar scene?

ABOUT FLOR GARDUÑO

Flor Garduño was born in Mexico in 1957. She studied photography at the National University in Mexico City. She worked with a master photographer and then set out on an independent career.

Meet the Artist

Flor Garduño (gahr•DUHN•yoh) (1957–) was born in Mexico City, Mexico. She was the youngest of three children. Ever since she was a young girl, Garduño knew she wanted to be an artist. She studied art at the San Carlos School of Fine Arts, and it was there that a teacher named Kati Horna introduced Garduño to photography. Garduño later became an assistant to Alvarez Bravo, a master of Mexican photography. She began working as a professional photographer when she was twenty-two. Then a friend of hers, Francisco Toledo, offered to publish a book of her photographs. Now she has published three books and taken photographs of people all over the world.

Garduño lives with her husband, Adriano, and her son, Azul, in the Mexican village of Tepoztlán.

LITERATURE CONNECTION

Prairie Visions: The Life and Times of Solomon Butcher by Pam Conrad. HarperCollins, 1991.
AVERAGE

This book tells the true story of Solomon Butcher, a photographer on the American frontier.

CLASSROOM MANAGEMENT

VIEWING: Response Cards You may wish to select one or more Response Cards for students to use with the artworks in the unit. For example, have each student in a small group choose an artwork from the unit. Provide Response Card 8, Art Critics' Circle, to guide their discussion of the artworks. The Response Cards begin on page R56 of this Teacher's Edition.

CREATING: Studio Activity Options Each lesson in the unit contains two options for the In the Studio activity. If your time is limited, choose the Quick Activity for one or more lessons. Each Quick Activity provides students with an experience that will deepen their understanding of the lesson concepts and skills.

LESSON 25

Book Art

OBJECTIVES: Understand that artists decorate books to add beauty and meaning to words. Make a cover for a book, diary, or portfolio. Use inviting designs, images, and words that suggest what will be inside.

MATERIALS: various books and magazines containing photographs and creative layouts

MOTIVATE

Explore the design of books and magazines. Invite students to look at the covers and contents of different books and magazines. Ask if the pages are eye-catching. Why or why not?

VIEWING ART

TEACH

Discuss the illuminated pages. Ask students to read the text and look at pictures A, B, and C. Have them name any letters they recognize in A. (Possible responses: *I, R, U*) Encourage students to describe some of the detailed pictures and patterns in B. Ask if B is symmetrical, and have students explain their answers. (Possible response: Yes, because the main shape is the same on both sides.) Invite students to describe details in and around the illustration in C. Have them speculate about what the writing is about. (Possible response: Perhaps it is a story about a young man who learns a lesson.)

Critical Thinking Questions

- **In A and B, are the words or the designs more important?** (Possible response: They are equally important. The designs make the words look more beautiful.) ART CRITICISM: ANALYSIS

- **Why do you think many books are not made by hand today?** (Possible response: It is easier, cheaper, and takes less time to print them with machines.) ART HISTORY: DRAW CONCLUSIONS

MEETING INDIVIDUAL NEEDS

EXTRA SUPPORT Point out that before the invention of the printing press, every book was created by hand, and the pages of holy books were often elaborately decorated.

LESSON 25 DESIGNING A BOOK COVER

Book Art

How did artists long ago decorate books to add beauty and meaning to words?

Pictures **A**, **B**, and **C** show pages from ancient books. All the letters, shapes, and patterns were created by hand.

The printing on picture A is in Latin. Which letters do you recognize? Real gold was used to decorate this page. Pages of this kind are called **illuminated pages** because they look as if they are lit up.

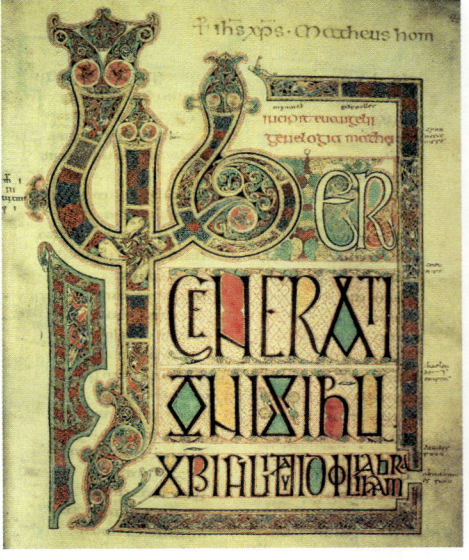

A Illuminated page from *The Book of Lindisfarne*
A.D. 700.

B Illuminated page from the Haggadah
Circa 1470. Parchment. The Israel Museum, Jerusalem.

SHARE ART HISTORY

A This illuminated page from the Book of Lindisfarne (700) was decorated with gold leaf. It shows the first words of the Gospel of St. Matthew, "Liber generationum." Eadfrith, Bishop of the English island of Lindisfarne, wrote and probably also decorated this page.

B This artwork is an illuminated page from a Haggadah [huh·GAH·duh] (circa 1470). A Haggadah is read on the Jewish holiday of Passover. It tells the story of how the Jewish people gained freedom from slavery in Egypt over 3,000 years ago.

C *Old Man and Youth in Landscape* (circa 1500) was illuminated by Behzad [bay·ZAHD], a well-known Persian artist. It is the first page of an anthology written in Persian.

96 UNIT 5: *New Ways to Create*

IN THE STUDIO BIG BOOK p.25

The printing on picture B is in Hebrew. Describe some of the patterns and detailed pictures on the page. Is picture B symmetrical? Why or why not?

The printing on picture C is in Persian. What details do you see in and around the illustration? What do you think the writing might be about?

Old Man and Youth in Landscape, Behzad
Circa 1500. Gold and silver on paper, 3 1/4 in. tall.
Smithsonian Institution, Washington, D.C.

IN THE STUDIO

MATERIALS
- heavy white paper
- colored pencils or fine-tipped marking pens
- tempera paints
- paintbrushes

Create a book cover.

Design a cover for a book, diary, or portfolio. Decorate the title with beautiful patterns and pictures. Try to show what will be inside your cover.

ART ACROSS THE CURRICULUM

SOCIAL STUDIES: HIEROGLYPHICS

Explain that ancient Egyptians developed a writing system in which pictures symbolized ideas or sounds. A *cartouche* was a set of symbols enclosed in an oval shape that represented a person's name. Invite students to visit a library and find out more about hieroglyphics. Students also might want to find examples of cartouches and create some for their own names.

LANGUAGE ARTS: WRITING AN ESSAY Ask students to write an essay about the importance of Johannes Gutenberg [yoh•HAHN•uhs GOOT•uhn•berg] (1395?–1468). Explain that Gutenberg developed a way of printing books from molds of individual letters, which made it possible to print multiple copies much more quickly than by hand. Ask students to do research to find out more about how Gutenberg printed his first book.

IN THE STUDIO

MATERIALS: heavy white paper, tempera paints, paintbrushes, colored pencils or fine-tipped marking pens (if possible, include gold, silver, copper, and bronze)

Designing a Book Cover

CREATING ART

- Students' covers can be for a book, a diary, or a portfolio. Encourage them to think of a design that will make viewers want to look inside and will suggest what the book is about.

- Distribute the paper and the other materials. Before students begin, they should determine the dimensions of the cover.

- Students should fold their paper according to their cover's dimensions and then unfold it to create their designs.

- Ask students to display their finished covers. Invite classmates to guess whether each cover is for a book, a diary, or a portfolio. If it is for a book, classmates should try to guess what the book is about.

OPTIONAL: Quick Activity Invite students to embellish their initials or the letters of their first name with ornate designs and geometric patterns.

WRAP-UP

INFORMAL ASSESSMENT

- **Why did the makers of illuminated manuscripts combine images and words?** (Possible responses: They wanted to add beauty and meaning to the words; they wanted to encourage readers to read further.) ART HISTORY: DRAW CONCLUSIONS

- **How did you solve the problem of making the cover of your book reflect what is inside?** (Responses will vary.) PRODUCTION: PROBLEM SOLVING

LESSON 25: *Book Art*

LESSON 26

Is Photography Art?

OBJECTIVES: Realize that photographs can be works of art. Make a photogram that fits well within its frame and has a clear center of interest.
MATERIALS: newspapers, textbooks, and magazines

MOTIVATE

Discuss photographs as art. Display various photographs. Ask whether students consider each a work of art, and why or why not.

VIEWING ART

TEACH

Discuss the choices photographers make. Explain that photographers carefully choose what to include in their photographs, and what angle to shoot them from; they also choose camera settings and lenses that produce the effects they want.

Discuss the photographs. Have students identify the center of interest in A (the child's face), and tell where it is in relation to the frame. (on the left side) Ask students to speculate why the photographer made the background fuzzy. (Possible response: to make the child's face stand out) Then ask what the center of interest is in B. (the figures of people against the shining water) You may want to display **Art Print 9.** Ask how the lighting draws attention to the center of interest. (It makes the face and headpiece stand out.)

Critical Thinking Questions

- **Find some diagonal lines in picture B. Why do you think the photographer wanted them in her composition?** (Possible response: The clouds, waves, and water make a zigzag path. This adds motion to the photograph.) ART CRITICISM: ANALYSIS

- **How do you think the photographer of A felt about the child?** (Possible response: She liked the child's smile and happy eyes.) AESTHETICS: DRAW CONCLUSIONS

EXTRA SUPPORT Cut out small frames of stiff white paper. Have students look through the frames in various positions as you clarify the meaning of *frame*.

LESSON 26 MAKING A PHOTOGRAM

Is Photography Art?

How does photography use technology to make art?

Like paintings, photographs can show feelings and tell stories. Photographers must make many choices in order to create interesting pictures.

Where does your eye go first in picture **A**? This is the **center of interest** in this photograph. Where is the child's face in relation to the picture's **frame**, or edge? Why do you think the photographer made the background look fuzzy or out of **focus**?

Notice the difference between the dark and light areas in picture **B**. This photographer used contrast to separate the sky, the water, and the land. What is the center of interest in picture B? Notice how the viewer's attention is drawn to the center of interest.

A *A Child's Brilliant Smile,* Carol Guzy

SHARE ART HISTORY

A Photojournalist **Carol Guzy** gave up a nursing career to pursue a degree in photography. She worked for eight years on a Miami newspaper. She now works as a staff photographer for the *Washington Post.* Guzy's job has taken her to places such as Haiti and Colombia to photograph major news events. This photograph (taken in Haiti) was awarded the 1995 Pulitzer Prize for Spot News Photography.

B Photographer **Leah Washington** was the first African American woman to graduate from the Brooks Institute of Photography. When Washington was a child, her mother owned and ran a photography studio. Washington's mother reminisces, "I guess Leah was destined to work in photography. The very night she was born, I worked in the darkroom processing film and making prints."

UNIT 5: *New Ways to Create*

IN THE STUDIO BIG BOOK p.26

B Point Lobos, at Carmel, California, Leah Washington

IN THE STUDIO

MATERIALS
- light-sensitive sun print paper or photogram kit
- materials such as netting, lace, leaves, and ferns
- pieces of cardboard

Make a photogram. Plan a design that fits well within its frame and that has a clear center of interest.

1. In a darkened room, arrange materials on a piece of light-sensitive paper to form an interesting design. Carefully cover the materials with a piece of cardboard.

2. Carry your design outside, or place it under a desk lamp. Lift the top piece of cardboard for two minutes.

3. Your teacher will help you develop your photogram.

ART ACROSS THE CURRICULUM

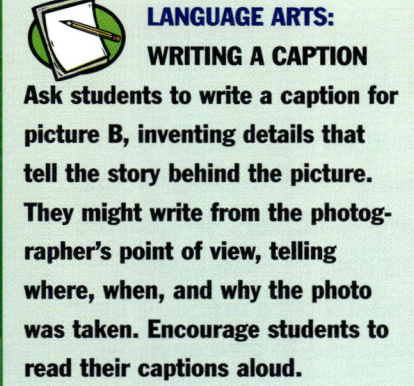

LANGUAGE ARTS: WRITING A CAPTION

Ask students to write a caption for picture B, inventing details that tell the story behind the picture. They might write from the photographer's point of view, telling where, when, and why the photo was taken. Encourage students to read their captions aloud.

SOCIAL STUDIES: PHOTOJOURNALISM

Photojournalists sometimes take pictures because they want to make the public aware of social problems or significant events. Direct students to do research in the library or on the Internet (with supervision) to find a photograph taken for one of these reasons. Students should display the photograph, tell why it was taken, and explain its probable effect on the public.

IN THE STUDIO

MATERIALS: light-sensitive paper or photogram kits; pieces of cardboard; materials such as netting, lace, leaves, and ferns; water

Making a Photogram

CREATING ART

- Read aloud and model the steps on page 99. Invite students to choose the materials they want to use.

- Students can experiment with arrangements on ordinary paper before placing the materials on the light-sensitive paper.

- Turn down the lights. Have students arrange objects on their paper to make creative designs. Cover the designs with cardboard.

- Have students go outside to expose their prints to sunlight for two minutes.

- Indoors, with lights low, have students remove their objects. Develop the prints by placing them in a tray of plain water for two minutes. Lay flat to dry. As it dries, the print will become darker and more vivid.

OPTIONAL: Quick Activity Students can arrange textured, relatively flat materials on a flat surface. Have them lay a sheet of white paper over the materials and use crayons to make a rubbing.

WRAP-UP

INFORMAL ASSESSMENT

- Look again at pictures A and B. What are some of the reasons artists take photographs? (Possible responses: to show how beautiful certain places are; to show how they feel about certain people; to capture a special moment) ART CRITICISM: SYNTHESIZE

- In what ways did you move items around within the frame of your photogram to make it more interesting? (Responses will vary.) PRODUCTION: PROBLEM SOLVING

LESSON 26: *Is Photography Art?*

CONNECTIONS

ART AND LITERATURE

Think about historical events. Ask students to think about scenes from history up to and including the American Revolution. Call on volunteers to explain how they know about such scenes. (Possible responses: Through television or movies; through reading about them; hearing about them; seeing paintings of the scenes) Then have students read pages 100–101.

Discuss the photograph. Share with students that photography did not become available to the public until the mid-1800s, one hundred years after the scenes depicted in *Spanish Pioneers of the Southwest*. Therefore, Joan Anderson and George Ancona had to use actors, costumes, and settings to re-create the scenes. Ask students to speculate about the settlers' lives based on the photograph. (Possible responses: The people had a hard life; they were poor; they only had what they could make for themselves. The people seem happy together; they have a house for shelter; they have clothing; they have a fireplace for cooking and heating.)

CONNECTIONS ART AND LITERATURE

The Photographic Art of George Ancona

Photographers can open doors to other places and other times.

As a teenager, George Ancona visited the *hacienda*, or ranch, owned by his Mexican relatives. He was fascinated by their way of life. Many years later, George Ancona returned to that area as an award-winning photographer. He and author Joan Anderson worked together to re-create a lost place and time. Through Anderson's story and Ancona's highly detailed photos, they showed what life was like for the earliest European settlers in North America. What can you learn about the settlers' lives from George Ancona's photograph on page 101?

▲ George Ancona

100

SHARE ART HISTORY

A Way of Life

James Van Der Zee opened a studio in 1916 and began to produce a pictorial record of life in Harlem. He photographed social events, such as parades, and he crafted portraits of famous Americans, such as Langston Hughes. His photographs were discovered in 1969, leading to a showing in the Metropolitan Museum of Art. Van Der Zee is now recognized as a master American photographer.

SOCIAL STUDIES

Photo Exhibit

Challenge students to look through magazines to find images of people living their lives—at home, at work, and at play. Have volunteers discuss the center of interest and framing of each photograph. Then encourage students to organize their images on a bulletin board and to give each photo exhibit a title.

UNIT 5: *New Ways to Create*

▲ A scene from *Spanish Pioneers of the Southwest* by Joan Anderson, photographs by George Ancona

WHAT DO YOU THINK?

▶ Do you think George Ancona's photograph looks realistic? Why or why not?

▶ Do you think it is fair to use actors and props to portray real events? Why or why not?

101

WHAT DO YOU THINK?

▶ Do you think George Ancona's photograph looks realistic? Why or why not? (Possible responses: Yes; the details of the clothing and the house seem real; the light seems real, coming only from the doorway and the fireplace.) ART CRITICISM: EVALUATION

▶ Do you think it is fair to use actors and props to portray real events? Why or why not? (Responses will vary. Possible response: Yes, as long as people understand that the photographs are not real.) AESTHETICS: MAKE JUDGMENTS

LANGUAGE ARTS

Painting vs. Photography

Call for two teams of volunteers to debate the topic: *Is a historic scene better depicted in a painting or in a photograph?* Encourage the debaters to think of the possibilities and the limitations of each medium. If possible, have them bring in examples of paintings and photographs to illustrate their points.

IN THE STUDIO

Plan a Tableau

A tableau [tab•LOH] is a living portrait, usually of a historic event. Have students work in groups to plan tableaus.

- The tableau should present a scene from American history.
- It should include major and minor characters in costume of the time.
- The tableau should include props and scenery to indicate what is taking place.

Groups can take turns describing or presenting their tableaus.

CONNECTIONS: *Art and Literature* **101**

LESSON 27

Sculptures Through Time

OBJECTIVES: Understand that over the centuries sculptors have used similar ideas but different materials. Use two different materials to sculpt the same subject.

MOTIVATE

Identify materials used to make sculptures. Encourage students to think of materials sculptors had available long ago, as well as materials they use today.

VIEWING ART

TEACH

Discuss the sculptures. Tell students to read the text and view the sculptures. Ask which sculpture was made in the twentieth century (without reading the captions), and what helped them figure this out. (Possible response: C; the subject and the materials look modern.)

Discuss how sculptors' choices of materials have changed over time. Draw on the board a time line beginning with 1000 B.C. and ending with A.D. 2000. Invite volunteers to draw arrows that show when A, B, and C were made. Ask: Why do you think each sculptor chose the materials he or she did? (Possible response: Each sculptor used materials that were available or popular at the time.)

Critical Thinking Questions

- **Why do you think modern sculptors carve in stone less often than ancient sculptors did?** (Possible responses: Long ago sculptors mostly carved natural materials. Now they also use many different kinds of manufactured materials.) ART HISTORY: HYPOTHESIZE

- **Did learning when A was made affect your opinion of it? Why or why not?** (Possible response: Yes, because it was carved without using any modern tools.) ART CRITICISM: MAKE JUDGMENTS

MEETING INDIVIDUAL NEEDS

CHALLENGE Ask students to research different sculpting techniques such as casting in molds and carving wood or stone.

LESSON 27   SCULPTING WITH TWO MATERIALS

Sculptures Through Time

How have sculptors used similar ideas, but different materials, over the centuries?

Look at sculptures **A**, **B**, and **C**. All three have women as their subjects, but they are different in many ways. Which of these sculptures was made in the twentieth century? What clues did you use to figure this out?

Each sculpture is made of a different material. The oldest one, A, is made of terra-cotta, or clay. B was created out of bronze metal about 2,000 years later. C is made from modern materials.

Long ago, sculptors worked with materials such as clay and stone. Over time, new materials such as metal became available to them. Today sculptors use many different natural and **synthetic**, or human-made, materials. How do you think a sculptor chooses a material?

A Draped, standing woman
Between 776 B.C. and 323 B.C. Terra-cotta.
The Louvre, Paris.

B Queen Mother head
Early sixteenth century. Bronze, 20 in.
National Museum, Lagos, Nigeria.

102

SHARE ART HISTORY

A In the third century B.C., hundreds of terra-cotta statuettes such as sculpture A were shipped to regions around the Mediterranean Sea from the workshops of Tanagra [TAN•ah•grah], Greece. These figurines were originally coated with white paint and then painted in vivid colors.

B The *Queen Mother head* was made in Benin [beh•NEEN] (present-day Nigeria), a large West African kingdom that flourished from the 1400s until the 1800s. Artists made sculptures such as this one to honor kings and queens who had died.

C American sculptor **George Segal** (1924–) is considered a Pop artist. He became famous for making one-color plaster sculptures of ordinary people in ordinary places. Segal began making these sculptures by wrapping live models in plaster-soaked cheesecloth.

102   UNIT 5: *New Ways to Create*

IN THE STUDIO BIG BOOK p.27

C
Blue Girl on Park Bench, George Segal
1980. Painted plaster and painted aluminum, 51 × 78 × 44 in.
Sidney Janis Gallery

IN THE STUDIO

MATERIALS
- small, clean milk carton with top cut off
- mixed plaster of Paris
- plastic knife
- aluminum foil
- scissors

Use two different materials to make sculptures. (Or, choose one of these sculptures to make.)

1. Your teacher will mix plaster of Paris and water. Pour the wet plaster into a milk carton. Wait for the plaster to set, and peel away the milk carton. Draw your object on the plaster. Use the plastic knife to scrape away bits of plaster from the column until you have formed the shape you want.

2. Now make a sculpture from aluminum foil. Crumple the foil loosely to make arms and legs. Bend the arms and legs to show movement.

103

ART ACROSS THE CURRICULUM

LANGUAGE ARTS: WRITING A DESCRIPTION Have students write a detailed description of George Segal's sculpture. Ask them to tell what objects are in the sculpture besides the figure, how big the sculpture is, what materials and colors of paint were used to make it, and what message the sculptor may have been trying to convey when he made it.

HEALTH AND SAFETY: ARTISTS' SAFETY RULES Point out that sculptors sometimes work with dangerous tools and poisonous or hazardous materials. Have the class brainstorm some hazards that sculptors might face. Then ask groups to create lists of safety rules. (Examples: Wear safety goggles; wear gloves when handling hazardous materials; label all poisonous materials; store all tools in a safe place; follow instructions.)

IN THE STUDIO

MATERIALS: small, clean milk cartons with tops cut off, mixed plaster of Paris, plastic knife, heavy-duty aluminum foil, scissors

Sculpting with Two Materials   CREATING ART

- Read the directions on page 103 with students. Ask students to think of an object or person they would like to sculpt using two different materials.

- Have students prepare their plaster casts and then work on their foil sculptures until the plaster is dry.

- For the foil sculpture of a person, students can start with a 12 in. × 14 in. sheet, carefully tear it, and then loosely crumple the foil to form the trunk, limbs, and head.

- When the plaster is dry, demonstrate how to draw the sculpture's shape on the block and cut the block into a rough outline before shaping it more precisely.

- When students are finished with both of their sculptures, ask them how the two sculpting processes differ.

OPTIONAL: Quick Activity Have students create the foil sculpture only. Ask why foil might be a better medium than others for this type of sculpture. (Possible responses: It is light; it holds its form.)

WRAP-UP   INFORMAL ASSESSMENT

- **What did making your own sculptures teach you about problems that the sculptors of A, B, and C might have had to solve?** (Possible response: When you carve a sculpture you must go slowly, because if you cut away too much you cannot replace that part.) PRODUCTION: PROBLEM SOLVING

- **How is sculpting with plaster of Paris similar to subtracting in math?** (Possible response: When you carve plaster of Paris, you take away.) PRODUCTION: ANALYSIS

LESSON 27: *Sculptures Through Time*   103

LESSON 28

The World of Animation

OBJECTIVES: Understand how animators bring still pictures to life. Make a flip book that creates the illusion of movement.

MOTIVATE

Discuss animated films. Ask students to name and discuss animated films or TV cartoons that they have seen. Ask: Are the people who create these films artists? Why or why not?

VIEWING ART

TEACH

Discuss two methods of animation. Ask students to read the paragraphs. Explain that in early animated films such as *Pinocchio,* all the characters and other details were painted by hand and then filmed. To create animated films such as *Toy Story,* animators use computers to produce detailed images.

Compare the two images. Have students tell how images A and B are alike. (Possible responses: Both show children's stories about toys; both are brightly colored.) Ask students which image they think is more interesting or attractive, and why.

Critical Thinking Questions

- From what point of view do you see picture B? (Possible response: I see the scene from the point of view of a moving camera at street level.) ART CRITICISM: ANALYSIS

- Do you think that filmmakers will stop making animated films in the style of *Pinocchio*? Why or why not? (Responses will vary.) ART HISTORY: HYPOTHESIZE

STUDENTS ACQUIRING ENGLISH Clarify the meaning for *frame* taught in this lesson. Draw on the board a strip of film with several frames. Help students understand that the drawings have a slight change in each frame.

LESSON 28 CREATING A FLIP BOOK

The World of Animation

How do artists bring still pictures to life?

Animation is the art of making still pictures seem to move. An animated movie is made up of many still pictures. Each one is slightly different from the one before. These pictures, or **frames**, are shown on a screen very quickly, one after the other. This creates the illusion of movement.

Picture **A** is a frame from the movie *Pinocchio*, made in 1940. This picture was painted by hand. Picture **B** is from the movie *Toy Story*, made in 1995. Artists used computers to create picture B. How are the frames alike?

A Frame from *Pinocchio*
1940. The Walt Disney Company.

104

SHARE ART HISTORY

A Early animation studios employed layout artists, who planned the setting for each scene; background artists, who drew the scenery; and animation artists, who drew the characters, movement by movement. **Walt Disney (1901–1966)** was the first successful producer of animated films. He began by making short cartoons. By 1937 his studio employed hundreds of artists and had produced *Snow White and the Seven Dwarfs*, the world's first feature-length animated film.

B Fifty-five years after the production of *Pinocchio*, Walt Disney Pictures and Pixar co-produced *Toy Story*, the first completely computer-animated feature film. It required so much work that its large crew produced only about 3.5 minutes of film per week. The film is made up of 114,240 frames of computer animation.

IN THE STUDIO BIG BOOK p.28

Artists can create three-dimensional pictures with computer animation. The toys in picture B look like objects you could actually pick up. Picture A looks two-dimensional, like a painting. Yet some people find picture A more interesting. What about you?

B Frame from *Toy Story* 1995. The Walt Disney Company.

IN THE STUDIO

MATERIALS
- 10 or more index cards cut into halves
- colored markers
- stapler

Make a flip book that creates the illusion of movement.

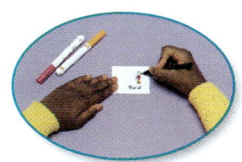

1. Decide what kind of movement you will show. Draw a simple character or object on a card.

2. Copy your drawing onto another card, but change the position slightly. Continue to do this on 15 to 20 more cards.

3. Staple your cards together to make a book. Flip the cards with your thumb and watch your own animation!

105

ART ACROSS THE CURRICULUM

LANGUAGE ARTS: WRITING A FILM SCENARIO Have students read the story of Pinocchio or another children's tale. Then ask them to write a summary of the first scene or two, noting dialogue and changes in setting, as well as physical descriptions of the characters and movements. Explain that this kind of summary could be used to help produce an animated film.

SOCIAL STUDIES: HOLLYWOOD Students may be interested in researching the development of the American film industry. The industry has traditionally been centered in the district of Los Angeles known as Hollywood. Hollywood's first studio was opened in 1911. The area soon attracted many more studios because of its wealth of natural land areas to use as settings.

IN THE STUDIO

MATERIALS: ten or more unlined index cards cut from top to bottom into halves, narrow-tip colored markers, heavy-duty stapler

Creating a Flip Book

CREATING ART

- Read through the directions on page 105 with students. Advise them to draw simple images, leaving a one-inch margin at the top of each card.

- Demonstrate how to trace a picture, changing it slightly, and then trace the new picture, changing that one slightly, so the images together show movement. Students can copy the traced images onto the cards. (If possible, have students trace the images from one card to the next by using a light source or by holding the cards against a windowpane.)

- Encourage students to draw outlines first and then go back and add color.

- Staple students' cards together at the top. Demonstrate how to flip the cards with your thumb.

OPTIONAL: Quick Activity Have students create a shorter version of the flip book described above, using only five cards. They can use very simple images.

WRAP-UP

INFORMAL ASSESSMENT

- **Suppose you were working with a few classmates to create a longer flip book. How would you divide the tasks? Which task would you prefer? Why?** (Possible responses: One person might draw the backgrounds, one might draw figures, and another might add color. Encourage students to explain why they would prefer a certain task.) PRODUCTION: APPLICATION

- **Which would you enjoy more, working on a hand-painted film such as *Pinocchio* or working on a computer-animated film such as *Toy Story*? Why?** (Responses will vary.) AESTHETICS: PERSONAL RESPONSE

LESSON 28: *The World of Animation*

Connections

CAREERS IN ART

Identify favorite toys. Have students name favorite toys they have had and discuss how they played with them. Ask students how they would feel about making those toys actually move and talk. (Responses will vary: Dolls, soldiers, robots; we moved them from place to place, dressed them, talked for them; it would be great to be able to bring them to life.) Have students read pages 106–107.

Discuss 2-D and 3-D animation. Ask students to name 2-D, or hand-drawn, animated movies that they have enjoyed. (Responses will vary.) Explain that 3-D animation involves continually stopping the camera and making adjustments to the characters. Ask volunteers to name 3-D animated shows or commercials they have seen. (Responses will vary.)

Connections CAREERS IN ART

Computer Animator

Karen Kiser *was one of twenty-seven animators who worked on the movie* **Toy Story.** *As a professional animator, Karen has worked in 2-D, in stop-motion, and in computer animation. Here she talks about her career.*

■ "In 2-D, you draw your characters by hand, changing their shapes with each drawing. In stop-motion, you move a puppet in front of a camera and then take a picture of each change. In computer animation, you manipulate a 3-D model that is programmed into a computer."

▼ Karen working stop-motion the *Gumby* series

106

SHARE CAREER INFORMATION

Animators in Training

Share with students that Karen Kiser prepared for her career by attending the California Institute of the Arts, a school founded by Walt Disney. Students at the California Institute of the Arts can pursue traditional "cell animation," as well as experimental forms of animation such as stop-action and claymation.

MATH

Precious Seconds

Share with students that Karen Kiser's work quota during the creation of *Toy Story* was 6 seconds of movie per week. Ask students to try to solve this word problem.

- If motion is detected when 16 images per second flash before the eyes, how many images are seen in a two-hour movie? (16 x 60 seconds x 60 minutes x 2 hours = 115,200 images)

Then encourage discussion about the time involved in creating animation.

106 UNIT 5: *New Ways to Create*

Six lively characters from *Toy Story*

■ "I owe a lot to the toys I played with as a child. Dolls and action figures helped shape my imagination as I played out stories in my mind. Most of the animators I know bring their toy collections with them to work."

■ "As a computer animator, you need to know how to use a computer. However, to make your characters come alive, you need to understand the art of animation. And to make your stories appealing, you need to understand the art of storytelling."

Karen at work at Pixar Studios, the home of *Toy Story*

WHAT DO YOU THINK?

- Which style of animation would you prefer to work in? Why?
- What might be some important qualities for an animator to have?

WHAT DO YOU THINK?

▶ Which style of animation would you prefer to work in? Why? (Responses will vary.) AESTHETICS: COMPARE/CONTRAST

▶ What might be some important qualities for an animator to have? (Responses will vary: humor—to appeal to the audience; patience—because production takes a long time; vision—to see how the different parts of a project fit together) PRODUCTION: APPLICATION

THEATER

Just One Second

Share with students that shortly after photography was invented, photographers began using stop-action to capture movement. Have volunteers demonstrate simple motions that take only a second, such as turning the head. Then have them re-create the same movement, stopping 16 times in the process. Suggest that they try changing expression too. This stop-action technique is still used in experimental animation.

IN THE STUDIO

Describe a Character

COOPERATIVE LEARNING Have pairs take turns as animators and programmers.

- Each animator should think of an original cartoon character and describe the character in great detail.
- Each programmer should draw exactly what the animator says and ask questions about further details.

Have partners share how close each programmer's drawing came to each animator's vision.

CONNECTIONS: *Careers in Art*

LESSON 29

Celebrations in Stone

OBJECTIVES: Understand that buildings express a culture's values. Make a scale drawing of a grand building.

MOTIVATE

Discuss local buildings. Ask students to imagine that a group of tourists from another country is visiting their city or town. Ask what buildings students would show the tourists to help them learn about local life.

VIEWING ART

TEACH

Discuss a visit to building A or B. Invite students to view the buildings and read the paragraphs. Have volunteers tell how they might feel if they were walking up to one of the buildings. (Possible responses: small, amazed, awed, impressed)

Discuss the builders. Guide students to compare and contrast A and B. Ask students what they think each building shows about the people who built it. (Possible responses: They were highly skilled; they valued beauty.) Challenge students to identify each arch, spire, and minaret.

Critical Thinking Questions

- Do you think these buildings are a form of art? Why or why not? (Possible response: Yes, because they are one-of-a-kind buildings designed by people who were trying to create something innovative or beautiful.) ART CRITICISM: MAKE JUDGMENTS

- How do you think people built these buildings without using modern equipment? (Possible response: Maybe they used horses, carts, a lot of workers, and rope pulleys.) ART HISTORY: HYPOTHESIZE

MEETING INDIVIDUAL NEEDS

STUDENTS ACQUIRING ENGLISH Reinforce the terms *arch*, *spire*, and *minaret* by pointing to an example of each in the photographs.

LESSON 29 MAKING A SCALE DRAWING

Celebrations in Stone

How do buildings express a culture's values?

Imagine that you are walking up to a huge stone building such as **A** or **B**. The tall **arch** of the doorway curves over your head. Slender towers point toward the sky. How do you think you would feel?

It took workers hundreds of years to build the Lincoln Cathedral (A). It has thin, pointed towers, called **spires**. A cathedral is a large place of worship for Christians.

Hundreds of years ago, a ruler in India ordered the building in picture B, the Taj Mahal [TAHZH muh•HAHL], built in memory of his wife. It is made of white marble that glows in

A *Lincoln Cathedral*
Completed circa 1400. 271 ft. tall (central tower).
Lincoln, England.

108

SHARE ART HISTORY

A During medieval times, cathedrals served as community centers as well as places of worship. The Lincoln Cathedral was originally built by the Normans. In 1185, earth tremors destroyed much of the cathedral. Reconstruction was not completed until about 1400.

You may want to display **Art Print 10**. Tell students it shows a modern cathedral in Spain. Ask them to compare its style to that of the Lincoln Cathedral.

B The Taj Mahal [TAHZH muh•HAWL] is a famous building in Agra, India. When Emperor Shah Jahan's wife, Mumtaz Mahal, died in 1631, he ordered the Taj Mahal built in her memory. It took 20,000 people about twenty years to complete the gigantic memorial. The walls are decorated with verses from the Muslim holy book, the Koran, and with precious jewels. Today, tourists from around the world visit the Taj Mahal. It is especially spectacular at sunrise.

IN THE STUDIO BIG BOOK p.29

sunlight or moonlight. The area has two mosques [MAHSKS], which are places of worship for Muslims. The four thin towers at its corners are called **minarets**.

Building A is in the western part of the world, and B is in the eastern part. What feelings do both buildings inspire?

B Taj Mahal
Circa 1632–1648. Marble,
186 ft. square, 120 ft. tall.
Agra, India.

IN THE STUDIO

MATERIALS
- large sheets of white paper
- colored pencils
- ruler
- compass

Make a scale drawing of a grand building.

1. Sketch a design for a grand building to celebrate your community.

2. Decide how tall and how long the building will be. Then decide how many feet each inch in your drawing will equal. For instance, 1 inch in your drawing might equal 10 feet in the actual building.

3. You might want to use a ruler and compass to draw your building. Add details with the colored pencils.

109

ART ACROSS THE CURRICULUM

LANGUAGE ARTS: WRITING A TRAVEL BROCHURE Encourage students to write a brochure that would make tourists want to visit the Taj Mahal, the Lincoln Cathedral, or the building students designed themselves when they made their scale drawing. Encourage students to do research to find information that will make their descriptions of the buildings more interesting.

SOCIAL STUDIES: BUILDING ACROSS CULTURES Work with students to develop a list of famous buildings around the world. Encourage each student to choose a building to research. Have students create posters of their buildings. Hold a "Famous Buildings of the World" exhibition, in which students and their families can "visit" each building and receive a guided tour.

IN THE STUDIO

MATERIALS: large sheets of white paper, colored pencils, ruler, compass

Making a Scale Drawing

CREATING ART

- Direct students to read the steps. To introduce the concept of scale, draw a horizontal 10-in. × 4-in. rectangle on the board and tell students it represents the side of a building. Explain that one inch in your drawing stands for 20 feet in real life. Ask how large the building you drew would be in real life. (200 feet long and 80 feet tall)

- Encourage students to think of a design for a grand building in their own community. Students should decide how tall and long the building will be. (For reference, you may want to point out that the dome of the Taj Mahal is 120 feet high.) Direct them to make a key that shows the scale of the drawing.

- Tell students to use a ruler to draw their building to scale. Demonstrate how to use a compass to draw rounded architectural elements such as arches and domes.

- Students can add details with colored pencils.

OPTIONAL: Quick Activity Students can make a freehand drawing of a grand building for their community. Have students label the length and height of the building to show its actual size.

WRAP-UP

INFORMAL ASSESSMENT

- **Is the building you designed anything like the Taj Mahal or the Lincoln Cathedral? Explain how.** (Responses will vary.) ART CRITICISM: COMPARE/CONTRAST

- **What problems did you need to solve in order to make your drawing the right scale?** (Responses will vary. Students may indicate that they had to decide on which small unit would stand for a larger unit.) PRODUCTION: PROBLEM SOLVING

LESSON 29: *Celebrations in Stone*

LESSON 30

Unusual Architecture

OBJECTIVES: Understand that bold modern architecture can be exciting and controversial. Make a foil model of a modern-style building.

MOTIVATE

Discuss local architecture. Discuss with students some modern buildings in your community. Ask students to share their opinions.

VIEWING ART

TEACH

Explain why modern architecture can be controversial. Have students read the text and view the buildings. Ask them to describe the first things they noticed about each. (Possible response: their unusual shapes) Ask students whether these modern buildings look attractive next to the older, traditional buildings. (Responses will vary.)

Discuss innovations in architecture. Explain that the original sections of the Louvre were built in 1200. When a new addition was planned, some people thought a newer style would show the importance of the Louvre today. Discuss whether creating the glass pyramid to add light and space to the museum was a good idea.

Then discuss Frank Lloyd Wright's solution to the problem of creating a space to view artworks. The artworks in the Guggenheim are viewed by walking around the spiral.

Critical Thinking Questions

- **Compare the glass pyramid with the older section of the Louvre.** (Possible response: The pyramid is simple and light; the old building is solid and strong.)
  AESTHETICS: COMPARE/CONTRAST

- **What does the shape of B remind you of?** (Possible responses: a seashell; a corkscrew)
  ART CRITICISM: INTERPRETATION

MEETING INDIVIDUAL NEEDS

CHALLENGE Have interested students research and make a time line of the history of the Louvre.

LESSON 30   MAKING A FOIL MODEL

Unusual Architecture

Should buildings look very different from their surroundings?

In Lesson 29 you looked at two buildings that were built hundreds of years ago. Pictures **A** and **B** show modern buildings. Each is an art museum designed by a famous architect. What was the first thing you noticed about each building?

Some people, including art critics, disliked these buildings. They said their forms were too different from the older buildings nearby. What do you think?

The stone building in picture A is hundreds of years old. It was once a palace. The pyramid in front is part of the roof

A The Grand Louvre, I. M. Pei
Paris, France.

SHARE ART HISTORY

A **I. M. Pei** (1917–) was born in Guangzhou, China. He came to the United States in 1935 to study architecture and today is one of the foremost architects in the world. He has designed art museums, office buildings, apartment complexes, and hotels. Many critics praise his buildings for their simplicity and beauty. However, the glass pyramid at the Louvre has been highly controversial.

B World-famous American architect **Frank Lloyd Wright** (1867–1959) used nature as his guide in designing buildings. Some of the buildings are shaped like snails and seashells; others are like trees with a central trunk and radiating branches. He installed skylights so sunlight could filter into a building as if through the trees of a forest. Like the Grand Louvre, the Guggenheim caused a public uproar when it was completed, in 1959.

UNIT 5: *New Ways to Create*

IN THE STUDIO BIG BOOK p.30

of a new section that was built underground. The architect wanted to give the museum more space and sunlight. Do you think the glass pyramid was a good solution? Why or why not? What do you think of the museum in picture B?

B The Solomon R. Guggenheim Museum, Frank Lloyd Wright
1956–1959. Cast concrete, steel. New York.

In The Studio

Think of an unusual building that you would like to build. Make a model of your building.

MATERIALS
- foam board or cardboard
- aluminum foil
- paper towel rolls, small boxes, or blocks
- balloons or small balls
- tape or wire
- tempera
- paintbrushes

1. Choose at least five shapes and forms to use in your model. Wrap each one in foil. Arrange your foil-covered shapes and forms into a structure that satisfies you. Attach the pieces with tape or wire.

2. Glue your model to a piece of foam board or cardboard. Paint the base to show what is around your building.

111

In The Studio

MATERIALS: foam board or cardboard, aluminum foil, paper towel rolls, small boxes or blocks, balloons or small balls, tape or wire, tempera paints, paintbrushes

Making a Foil Model

CREATING ART

- Ask students to read the steps on page 111. Encourage them to spend some time planning their buildings. Ask them to decide on the building's purpose and location.

- Have students choose one to three large items (such as boxes or balloons) and wrap them in foil. They can use wire and cardboard strips for additional features.

- Remind students to consider what each part of the building will be used for. Ask them to think about the effect of the building on people standing outside.

- When students are satisfied with their arrangements, have them glue the shapes to the foam board or cardboard bases. Have students paint the bases to show their buildings' surroundings.

OPTIONAL: Quick Activity Invite students to draw houses based on natural forms such as trees, shells, snails, or mountains.

WRAP-UP

INFORMAL ASSESSMENT

- **Do you prefer modern architecture or older architecture? Why?** (Responses will vary. Students should support their opinions with reasons.) AESTHETICS: PERSONAL RESPONSE

- **How did you arrive at your building design?** (Possible responses: I moved the shapes until they looked right. I thought about what it would feel like to work in one of the rooms.) PRODUCTION: PROBLEM SOLVING

ART ACROSS THE CURRICULUM

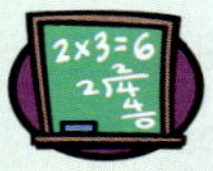

MATHEMATICS: GEOMETRIC DISPLAY
Invite students to create a classroom display of buildings with geometric shapes. The display might include diagrams of geometric forms and photographs of buildings that include pyramids and cylinders in their design. Have students label each geometric shape.

PERFORMING ARTS: THEATER Invite students to plan and stage a debate about architecture. Have students debate the installation of the glass pyramid at the Louvre or a controversial local building project. Groups can prepare a script with facts and opinions, and several students can stage the debate, playing the roles of experts, concerned citizens, and architects.

LESSON 30: *Unusual Architecture*

UNIT 5

REFLECTING AND REVIEWING

Pages 112–113	**Reflect on the unit theme.** Have students read the first paragraph on page 112. Remind students that the artworks in this unit show how artists use technology and adapt to new technologies. **Ask students to discuss the artwork.** Students might describe all the interesting and unusual aspects of the artwork. Ask them whether they think the sculpture is or is not a work of art. Students should discuss the fact that this artwork would not have been possible many years ago because it is based on new technologies.
About the Artist	Nam June Paik (1932–), Korean-born composer and video artist, studied music and art history at Tokyo University. In the 1960s he was known as an electronic composer and producer of "action concerts." In 1964 he moved to New York and began concentrating on video art and TV sculptures.
About the Art	*Electronic Superhighway* is a sculpture that takes neon lights, TV sets, and laser disk images and combines them into one unit. The artwork explores the theme of the enormous changes United States society will soon undergo as information systems become more complex and far-reaching. The artist presents a map of the United States transformed by technology.

112 UNIT 5: *New Ways to Create*

UNIT 5 REFLECTING AND REVIEWING

Artists adapt to new technologies.

Think about some of the artwork you saw in this unit. How did the artists find new uses for technology? The artwork on this page shows a spectacular use of technology. *Electronic Superhighway* is composed of television sets, laser disc images, and neon lights. The artist, Nam June Paik, used these materials, along with techniques such as frame and center of interest, to create this unusual work of art.

Electronic Superhighway, **Nam June Paik**
1995. Installation: multiple television monitors, laser disc images, and neon, 15 ft. X 32 ft.

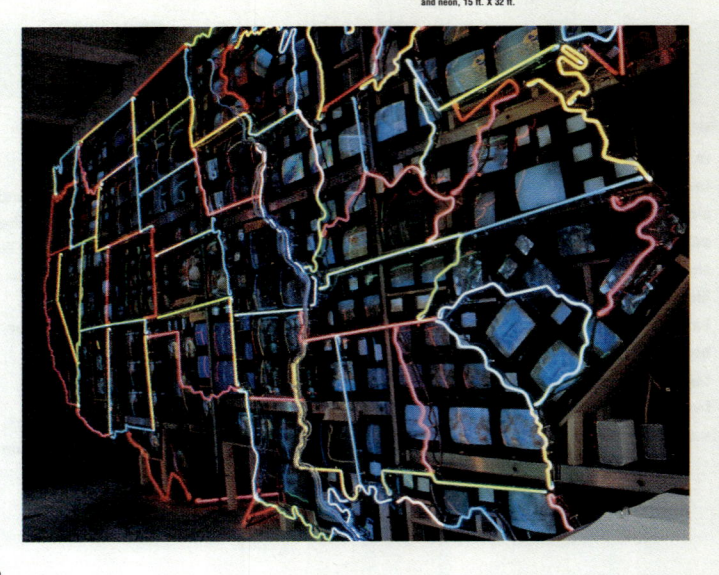

112

ART ACROSS THE CURRICULUM

THEATER: THE OLD SCHOOL Ask small groups of students to imagine that they are going to school seventy years ago. They should brainstorm a list of what has changed between then and the present time: desks, computers, intercoms, digital clocks. Then have each group perform a skit of "The Old School" showing how it might have been to go to school back then. **COOPERATIVE LEARNING**

What Did I Learn?

- **THINK** about the artwork you created in this unit. How did you use a technique or a material in a new way?
- **LOOK** back through the unit. Find examples of frame and center of interest in the art. Compare how different artists used these techniques.
- **FIND** two artworks in this unit that you like. Tell how you think the artists who made these were especially creative.
- **NAME** three kinds of materials used by the artists in this unit. How did the artists find new ways of seeing and doing things with these materials?

113

Just for Fun: CHAIN LINKS

TO ENCOURAGE STUDENTS to take another close look at the artworks in this unit, have them play "Chain Links." Have students choose an artwork from the unit at random. They should choose a detail from the artwork. Then have them look through the other images in the unit and find one that has a detail that is somehow like the detail from the first image. Students should then look for another image that has a detail similar to the detail in the second image. Continue until students have observed details in several of the artworks in the unit.

What Did I Learn?

Encourage students to work in small groups to discuss their answers to these questions that appear on page 113.

- **Think about the artwork you created in this unit. How did you use a technique or a material in a new way?** (Responses will vary.) PRODUCTION: DESCRIPTION

- **Look back through the unit. Find examples of frame and center of interest in the art. Compare how different artists used these techniques.** (Possible response: photographer Carol Guzy, to focus on the smile; the *Toy Story* animators, to focus on the character who is speaking) ART CRITICISM: COMPARE/CONTRAST

- **Find two artworks in this unit that you like. Tell why you think the artists who made these were especially creative.** (Responses will vary.) AESTHETICS: MAKE JUDGMENTS

- **Name three kinds of materials used by the artists in this unit. How did the artists find new ways of seeing and doing things with these materials?** (Responses will vary.) ART CRITICISM: SYNTHESIZE

Students may select images from this unit to add to their portfolios.

Reflecting and Reviewing

UNIT 6

Heritage and Change

Art offers us a means of recording our history and traditions. Artists often create images that represent or build on their culture. Many artists use their talents to tell a people's story. Others try to create artworks that continue a people's tradition.

In this unit, students will look at how artists pay homage to and build upon traditions.

Using the Art Prints

Display and introduce *Art Prints 11* and *12*. (Discussion suggestions appear on the back of each *Art Print*.) Talk with students about the story each image is trying to tell.

RESPONSE CARD OPTION You may also have students use Response Card 3, *Stories in Art*, on page R58 of this *Teacher's Edition* as they view *Art Print 12*.

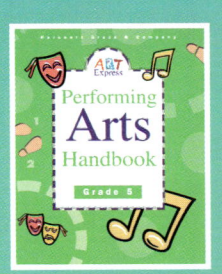

ART PRINT 11 *Zechariah*, detail from Sistine Chapel ceiling by Michelangelo

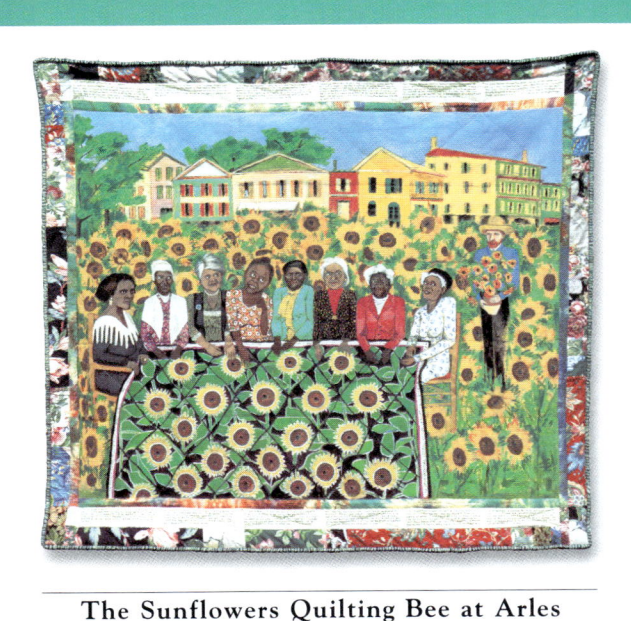

ART PRINT 12 *The Sunflowers Quilting Bee at Arles* by Faith Ringgold

Performing Arts Handbook

Dance, theater, and music activities to extend and enrich students' experiences with these *Art Prints* can be found in the *Performing Arts Handbook*.

UNIT 6: *Heritage and Change*   **114B**

UNIT 6 HERITAGE AND CHANGE

Introducing the Unit pp. 114A–115

LESSON	VIEWING	CREATING	CURRICULUM CONNECTIONS
31 STORIES ON WALLS pp. 116–117 • *Detroit Industry,* North Wall, by Diego Rivera	*Understand murals as wall paintings that tell stories about a culture.* **VOCABULARY:** murals, theme	*Create a mural that tells a story.* **MATERIALS:** tempera paints, paintbrushes, long sheet of butcher paper or white paper	**Social Studies** My Heritage, p. 117 **Performing Arts** Dance: Create a factory worker dance, p. 117
32 CENTURIES IN CLAY pp. 118–119 • White earthenware urn, Tang Dynasty • Porcelain vase, Chinese, circa AD 1300 • Copeland vase, painted by Hürton, 1862	*Understand that potters build upon the materials and methods of the past by innovating.* **VOCABULARY:** slip, porcelain, incised	*Make and decorate a slab pot.* **MATERIALS:** clay, rolling pin, sponges, carving tools (paper clips, toothpicks, plastic knives)	**Language Arts** If Clay Could Speak, p. 119 **Science** How Hot Is Hot? p. 119
CONNECTIONS: ART AND CULTURE	**African Adobe Architecture pp. 120–121**		
33 A TIMELESS ART pp. 122–123 • *Her First Dance* by Pablita Velarde • Iowa sash, Nebraska, circa 1880	*Recognize that some artists continue traditions that are centuries old.* **VOCABULARY:** weaving	*Weave a bookmark out of yarn.* **MATERIALS:** thin yarn in various colors, drinking straws, stirrer straws, scissors	**Reading** Explore Pueblo Culture, p. 123 **Performing Arts** Dance: Learn a traditional dance, p. 123
34 PATCHWORK ART pp. 124–125 • Album Quilt • *Heartland* by Miriam Schapiro	*Understand that some art forms that were developed partly out of necessity continue to thrive today.* **VOCABULARY:** quilts	*Create a patchwork wall hanging using traditional methods and innovation.* **MATERIALS:** scraps of cloth, needles and thread or safety pins, scissors, trim (such as sequins and lace), fabric paint or markers, large sheet of paper	**Language Arts** Life on the American Frontier, p. 125 **Mathematics** Area and Perimeter, p. 125
CONNECTIONS: COMMUNITY ART	**The Artrain pp. 126–127**		
35 ARTWORK TO WEAR pp. 128–129 • Mesopotamian gold necklace • Spanish corsage ornament • Southwestern United States shell and turquoise necklace	*Recognize that artists turn raw materials into traditional and innovative jewelry.* **VOCABULARY:** ornamentation	*Use everyday materials to create beads for a necklace.* **MATERIALS:** wire or string, magazines, glue, scissors, other necklace items such as washers or shells with holes	**Social Studies** Native American Artwork, p. 129 **Science** Diamond Discovery, p. 129
36 FACES FROM FOLK ART pp. 130–131 • Jaguar mask, 20th century • Japanese Nō mask • Iyoba mask, circa 1550	*Learn that for thousands of years folk artists have made masks that help to pass on elements of their cultures.* **VOCABULARY:** folk artists	*Create a mask in the style of one of the masks in this lesson.* **MATERIALS:** tagboard, paper scraps, scissors, glue, raffia, straw, tempera paints, paintbrushes, hole punch, elastic	**Performing Arts** Theater: Design masks for a play, p. 131 **Health and Safety** Masks for Protection, p. 131

Unit 6 Reflecting and Reviewing pp. 132–133

Integrating Your Day

SUGGESTED READING	OPTIONAL VIDEOS/TECHNOLOGY
Diego by Jonah Winter, translated by Amy Price. Knopf, 1991. **EASY** *Murals: Cave, Cathedral, to Street* by Michael Capek. Lerner, 1996. **AVERAGE**	Groups of students can view *The Wall* to learn about walls that pay tribute to important people in American culture.
Children of Clay by Rina Swentzell. Runestone Press, 1993. **AVERAGE** *The Incredible Clay Book* by Sherri Haab and Laura Torres. Klutz Press, 1994. **AVERAGE**	Students can use the *Monstrous Media Kit* to create a time line about the history of clay.
Pueblo Storyteller by Diane Hoyt-Goldsmith. Scholastic, 1995. **AVERAGE** *The Kids' Multicultural Art Book* by Alexandra M. Terzian. Williamson, 1993. **AVERAGE**	Students can use *kidDraw* with *The New Kid Pix* to draw a scene that depicts some aspect of their heritage.
The Patchwork Quilt by Valerie Flournoy. Dial, 1985. **EASY** *The Canada Geese Quilt* by Natalie Kinsey-Warnock. Cobblehill, 1989. **AVERAGE**	Have groups of students view *Tar Beach* written by the well-known story quilt artist Faith Ringgold.
Dazzling! Jewelry of the Ancient World. Runestone Press, 1995. **AVERAGE** *Jewelry: A Practical Guide to Creative Crafts* by Miranda Innes. Dorling Kindersley, 1996. **AVERAGE**	Have students use *HyperStudio* to create a multimedia report about the art of jewelry making.
Masks Tell Stories by Carol Gelber. Millbrook Press, 1993. **AVERAGE** *Paper Animal Masks from Northwest Tribal Tales* by Nancy Lyn Rudolph. Sterling Publishing Co., 1996. **AVERAGE**	Students can use *Crayola Art Studio 2* to design and create a mask that future generations might use to learn about their cultural heritage.

Art Minutes

Present one of these puzzles or activities for students to solve by the end of the week.

- ■ Choose a picture in a magazine. **Write** a story about what happens just before or after the picture. ANALYSIS
- ■ **Identify and describe** a tradition that has been in your family or your school for many years. ANALYSIS
- ■ **Think** of an object from another country. Describe how you can tell it is from that country. ANALYSIS
- ■ **Draw** an asymmetrical mask. Show two different expressions. APPLICATION
- ■ **Look** through your sketchbook. Choose a sketch you like. Make plans to develop it into a finished artwork to give as a gift. APPLICATION
- ■ With a partner, **plan and perform** a pantomime about a fun art project you have done this year. APPLICATION

SCHOOL-HOME CONNECTION

After completing Lesson 34, distribute School-Home Connection 6, found on page R55. Students can work with family members to examine patchwork quilts and create one of their own.

Activities and Resources CD-ROM provides additional teaching materials and interactive student activities for use with Unit 6.

UNIT 6: *Heritage and Change*

UNIT 6

INTRODUCING
THE UNIT

Pages 114–115

Discuss *Moses*. Have students read pages 114 and 115. Invite volunteers to discuss how Michelangelo's works tell the story of his culture's religion. Give students some background information on the Renaissance. Tell them that many art historians feel that Michelangelo brought the art of sculpture to a new level.

Discuss tradition and innovation. Discuss with students the idea that artists in all cultures help preserve their heritage. Point out that artists also tend to be innovators. Their work not only records history but also interprets it. Merely by choosing particular subjects, artists show us what they think is important.

About the Art

Moses is one of Michelangelo's many sculptures and paintings that decorate churches in Italy. The statue is of the Biblical prophet Moses. Have students examine the image closely to help them realize the great detail Michelangelo put into this statue.

Another example of an artwork by Michelangelo can be found on *Art Print 11*.

Moses, Michelangelo
Circa 1513–1515. Marble, approximately 8 ft. 4 in. high.
San Pietro in Vincoli, Rome.

TIME LINE

Have students select two artworks from the unit from different time periods. Suggest that they use the *Time Line* to compare the two periods.

114 UNIT 6: *Heritage and Change*

UNIT 6

Heritage and Change

How do artists preserve the heritage of a culture?

All cultures celebrate their religion and their heritage through art. Michelangelo (my•kuhl•AN•juh•loh) is thought to be one of the greatest artists of the Western world. This statue of Moses is one of his masterpieces. What can you tell about Moses simply by looking at Michelangelo's statue?

Michelangelo's sculptures and paintings can be seen in many great churches in Italy. In his work, Michelangelo not only preserved the stories of the past, he also gave them to future generations.

ABOUT MICHELANGELO

Michelangelo Buonarroti was born in 1475 in Caprese, Italy. At 13, he became an artist's apprentice in Florence and soon earned the support of the rich and art-loving Medici family.

Meet the Artist

Michelangelo Buonarroti (1475–1564) was born in the small village of Caprese near Arezzo, Italy. His father placed him in the workshop of painter Domenico Ghirlandajo when he was just thirteen. Michelangelo produced at least two relief sculptures by the time he was sixteen. After completing some of his most famous sculptures, the artist was commissioned to do his first painting. This eventually led to what is perhaps Michelangelo's best-known work—the frescoes on the Sistine Chapel ceiling in Rome.

Michelangelo's numerous paintings, sculptures, and architectural projects have led to his recognition as one of the most talented and influential artists of the European Renaissance.

LITERATURE CONNECTION

Song of the Chirimia: A Guatemalan Folktale by Jane A. Volkmer. Carolrhoda, 1992.
AVERAGE

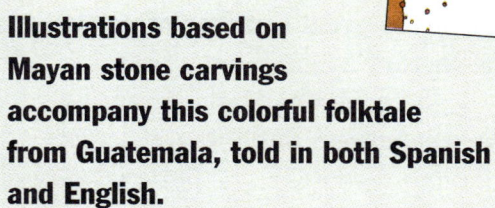

Illustrations based on Mayan stone carvings accompany this colorful folktale from Guatemala, told in both Spanish and English.

CLASSROOM MANAGEMENT

VIEWING: Response Cards If you prefer to have students work independently on one or more lessons in the unit, you may select appropriate Response Cards for them to use as they think about the artworks. For Lesson 36, Faces from Folk Art, for example, you may provide students with Response Card 9, Compare and Contrast. The Response Cards begin on page R56 of this Teacher's Edition.

CREATING: Studio Activity Options If any students have limited time for art activities because of illness, pull-out classes, or other school demands, have them complete the Quick Activity in a lesson to reinforce lesson skills and concepts.

UNIT 6: *Heritage and Change*

LESSON 31 Stories on Walls

OBJECTIVES: Understand murals as wall paintings that tell stories about a culture. Create a mural that tells a story.

MOTIVATE

Talk about how pictures tell stories. Invite students to imagine they have been asked to tell a familiar folktale using one large picture rather than words. Ask students to describe the picture they would create.

VIEWING ART

TEACH

Discuss the mural's theme. Have students read the text and study the art. Explain that the artist painted this mural during the Great Depression, a time when many Americans were unemployed and life was difficult. Ask students what they think this mural is saying about these workers. (Possible responses: Americans are hard workers; we can work together to overcome hardships.) Have students discuss whether Rivera respected these workers. (Possible response: Yes, he painted them to look strong and skillful.)

You may want to display **Art Print 11** and explain that it shows part of a famous fresco, or mural done on wet plaster, by the Italian artist Michelangelo.

Critical Thinking Questions

- **How did Rivera use color to make us aware of the great number of workers in the factory?** (Possible responses: Contrasting colors make the foreground workers stand out; fiery orange draws attention to workers in the background.)
  ART CRITICISM: ANALYSIS

- **Do you think Rivera portrayed the factory setting in a positive way?** (Possible response: Yes. Many people are working together.) AESTHETICS: INTERPRETATION

MEETING INDIVIDUAL NEEDS

CHALLENGE Have students find Rivera murals of scenes in Mexico. Challenge them to discuss how these murals tell stories about Rivera's cultural heritage.

116 UNIT 6: *Heritage and Change*

LESSON 31 PAINTING A MURAL

Stories on Walls

How can artists tell stories with pictures?

Murals are large paintings done on walls. Artists often paint murals to tell stories about people. Like a story in a book, a mural can express a **theme**, or main idea.

Diego Rivera, a Mexican artist, is famous for his murals about Mexican history and culture. Rivera was hired to paint this mural for the city of Detroit, Michigan. It shows workers in one of the many automobile factories. There is so much going on in this noisy place! Everyone seems to be working hard and cooperating. Notice the conveyor belts that snake through the factory. The artist wanted viewers to see the textures and patterns of the machines. He wanted us to feel the rhythm of the men working with machines.

Do you think the artist respected these workers? Why or why not?

SHARE ART HISTORY

Mexican artist **Diego Rivera** [dee•EH•goh ree•VEH•rah] (1886–1957) became famous worldwide for painting murals that portrayed the culture and history of Mexico. Rivera also created murals in the United States, including works at the San Francisco Stock Exchange and the Detroit Institute of Arts. The mural in this lesson is one section of a larger mural at the Detroit Institute of Arts.

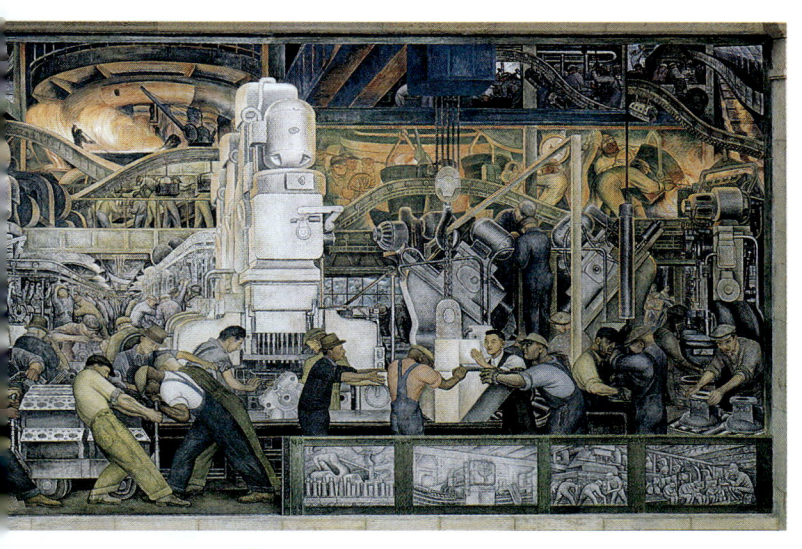

IN THE STUDIO BIG BOOK p.31

Detroit Industry, North Wall (detail), Diego M. Rivera
1932–33. Detroit Institute of Arts, Detroit.

IN THE STUDIO

MATERIALS
- tempera paints
- paintbrushes
- long sheet of butcher paper

Create a mural that tells a story.

With your classmates, plan a mural that tells a story about your school or community. Include a theme in your mural. Begin with a small-scale drawing. Use pencils to sketch your drawing onto butcher paper. Then paint your mural with tempera paints.

117

ART ACROSS THE CURRICULUM

SOCIAL STUDIES: MY HERITAGE Encourage students to research the cultures that make up their own heritage and to bring to class a list of symbols they might use to make a mural celebrating their own cultural background. Students can explain why they chose each symbol.

PERFORMING ARTS: DANCE Factory workers must work at a steady rhythm to keep materials moving smoothly down an assembly line. Have students create a modern dance in which their rhythms symbolize the movements of factory workers. They might accompany the dance with sounds that are similar to the sounds of machines in a factory.

IN THE STUDIO

MATERIALS: tempera paints, paintbrushes, long sheet of butcher paper or white paper

Painting a Mural — CREATING ART

- Direct students to read the steps on page 117. Have them work together to plan a mural that tells about their school or community. Encourage them to brainstorm ideas for the content and layout of the mural.

- When students have chosen the ideas they will use for the mural, suggest that they choose one student to sketch a plan for the whole-class mural on a piece of paper.

- Let the student teams volunteer to paint particular sections of the mural. Make sure that every section is assigned.

- Student teams should paint their sections. As they work, encourage each team to consider the overall effect of the mural and how their area fits into the work as a whole.

OPTIONAL: Quick Activity Have students sketch a plan for a mural about their school or community.

WRAP-UP — INFORMAL ASSESSMENT

- **Compare and contrast your mural with Rivera's mural. Are they alike in any ways? How? How are they different?** (Responses will vary.) ART CRITICISM: COMPARE/CONTRAST

- **How did each team make the different areas of the mural blend together into a unified picture?** (Possible responses: We followed the sketch; we compared as we went along; we compromised.) PRODUCTION: PROBLEM SOLVING

LESSON 31: *Stories on Walls* 117

LESSON 32

Centuries in Clay

OBJECTIVES: Understand that potters build upon the materials and methods of the past by innovating. Make and decorate a slab pot.

MOTIVATE

Discuss the history of pottery. Display **Art Print 2** or another pottery vessel. Tell students that pottery vessels have been made by people the world over for thousands of years. Ask students if they have seen someone make a piece of pottery. Have them describe what they saw.

VIEWING ART

TEACH

View pottery from different ages. Have students read the pages and view the pottery pieces. Ask students to tell which piece they think is most interesting and why.

Compare pottery styles. Ask students to compare the Copeland vase with the two Chinese vases. Encourage them to discuss the pieces' shapes, materials, and decorative details. *(Possible responses: A seems simpler in design; both B and C are made of porcelain; C is very similar in shape to A, but the painting on C is more elaborate.)* Point out that the Chinese produced the first porcelain.

Critical Thinking Questions

- **How can you tell that the creator of C was influenced by Chinese pottery?** *(Possible response: The shapes of the vases are similar.)* ART HISTORY: ANALYSIS

- **How do you think each container was used?** *(Possible responses: A and B were probably used for storing liquids or grains. C looks as if it was made to be displayed, not used.)* ART CRITICISM: HYPOTHESIZE

MEETING INDIVIDUAL NEEDS

CHALLENGE Have students research and create an illustrated flowchart showing the steps in the process of making a particular kind of pottery. The flowchart should begin by describing how the clay was obtained and end with the finished work.

LESSON 32 SCULPTING A SLAB POT

Centuries in Clay

How do artists learn from each other?

The pottery in **A** was made in China about 1,000 years ago. The designs were attached to the pot with **slip**, a mixture of water and clay.

The vase in **B** was also made in China, about 700 years ago. By that time, Chinese potters had learned to use **porcelain**, a hard, pure clay. Some of the designs on B were attached with slip. Others were cut, or **incised**, into the clay.

A White earthenware urn, Tang Dynasty
Circa 600–900. Earthenware, 14 1/2 in.

B Porcelain vase, Chinese
Circa 1300. Porcelain.

SHARE ART HISTORY

A During the Tang Dynasty (618–907) in China, the high-firing technology of bronze making and the development of glazes allowed potters to create earthenware vessels that were impervious to liquids. This piece was used as a funerary urn.

B Porcelain was first made in China during the Sui (581–618) or early Tang Dynasty. This piece is the first documented example of Chinese porcelain in Europe.

Europeans nicknamed porcelain "china," a name that has persisted to this day.

C A formula for English bone china was developed in 1770 by Joshua Spode. The Spode factory produced tableware, vases, and statues. In 1847 William Copeland took charge of the factory. This vase was specially made for a London exhibition in 1862.

UNIT 6: *Heritage and Change*

IN THE STUDIO BIG BOOK p.32

The pottery in **C** was made in England about 140 years ago. The potter who made C had learned from older Chinese vases like A and B. How is C like the Chinese vases? How is it different?

C Copeland Vase, painted by Hürton. 1862. Porcelain, 27 1/2 in.

IN THE STUDIO

MATERIALS
- clay
- rolling pin
- sponge
- tools such as toothpicks and plastic knives

Make a slab pot. Add a design that fits its purpose.

1. Roll out a ball of clay until it is about half an inch thick. Cut out one piece to make the bottom of the pot and four pieces to make the sides.

2. Score, or scratch, the edges, and use slip to stick them together.

3. Use a tool to decorate the outside of the pot. Think about how you will use your pot. Decide what kind of design would fit that purpose.

119

ART ACROSS THE CURRICULUM

LANGUAGE ARTS: IF CLAY COULD SPEAK Have students imagine that one of the pottery pieces pictured in this lesson could tell the story of its existence through the ages. Invite students to write a creative journal entry in which the pot tells about one day of its life.

SCIENCE: HOW HOT IS HOT? Have students learn about the temperatures at which different substances are created, such as hard candy, glass, pottery, and bronze. Ask them to display their findings on a graph.

IN THE STUDIO

MATERIALS: clay, rolling pin, sponges, carving tools (paper clips, toothpicks, plastic knives)

Sculpting a Slab Pot   CREATING ART

- Each student should start with a ball of clay that is about four inches in diameter. Have students knead the clay until it is pliable and easy to work with. They should squeeze out any air bubbles.

- Students should then use a rolling pin to flatten their clay. Make sure the slab of clay they roll out is of even thickness. Students may wish to measure five squares of the same size, using a ruler.

- Demonstrate how to make slip by mixing a small amount of clay with water. Then show students how to score the edges that meet, both at the base of the pot and on the sides, and place a bit of slip on each edge. Students should press each seam together firmly to make sure the slabs adhere.

- Students can use their carving tools to create designs on their pots.

NOTE: If you do not complete this activity in one session, make sure to cover the clay with plastic to prevent it from drying out.

OPTIONAL: Quick Activity Pairs of students can make simple slab pots, using modeling clay.

WRAP-UP   INFORMAL ASSESSMENT

- Look at the designs your classmates created. Do any of these designs resemble the ones on the vases in the lesson? How did your classmates make these designs? *(Responses will vary.)* ART CRITICISM: COMPARE/CONTRAST

- How did you make your slab pot hold together? What would you do differently the next time you make a slab pot? *(Responses will vary. Students probably used scoring and slip to hold their pots together.)* PRODUCTION: PROBLEM SOLVING

LESSON 32: *Centuries in Clay*

LESSON 33

A Timeless Art

OBJECTIVES: Recognize that some artists continue traditions that are centuries old. Weave a bookmark out of yarn.

MOTIVATE

Discuss how traditions are kept alive. Ask students if any of them have a hat, scarf, or other item of clothing that was made by an older relative. Have them discuss how they could help keep the tradition alive.

VIEWING ART

TEACH

View traditional art. Have students read the text and view the images. Ask them to describe what is happening in A. (Possible response: Older women are helping a girl get ready for a dance.) Have them identify items in the scene that might be part of the family's traditional culture, such as the weavings.

Discuss weaving. Ask students how the weavings in A are like the woven belt in B. (Possible responses: Both are woven from yarn; both are traditional crafts.) Help students identify the patterns in the belt. (stripes; repeated geometric shapes)

Critical Thinking Questions

- **What family or cultural traditions are shown in these works?** (Possible responses: A—ceremonial dancing and traditional clothing; the tradition of older people teaching younger people; B—the art of weaving) ART HISTORY: REFLECTION

- **Many different cultures have developed the art of weaving. Why do you think this happened?** (Possible responses: People need clothing. Weaving uses materials that are available everywhere.) ART HISTORY: HYPOTHESIZE

MEETING INDIVIDUAL NEEDS

EXTRA SUPPORT To help students understand what weaving is, point out the loose threads at the bottom of the belt in B and tell students that these individual strands have been woven together to create cloth.

LESSON 33 WEAVING A BOOKMARK

A Timeless Art

How do artists help keep traditions alive?

Have your grandparents or older relatives ever told you stories about their childhoods? Stories of that kind help us learn about earlier times. They can also help us keep important traditions alive.

Pablita Velarde [pab•LEET•uh vel•AHR•day] is a Native American artist. She is a member of the Pueblo culture of the American Southwest. She paints pictures based on her childhood memories and the stories her grandparents told her. Look at the scene in picture **A**. Notice the rugs, blankets, and belts in the room. **Weaving** is the process of

A *Her First Dance,* Pablita Velarde 1953. 16 3/4 in. X 15 in. Denver Art Museum.

122

SHARE ART HISTORY

A **Pablita Velarde** [pab•LEET•uh vel•AHR•day] **Hardin** (1918–) is a Tewa artist born in Santa Clara Pueblo, New Mexico. She broke with Pueblo tradition by deciding to become a painter, an occupation only men were expected to choose. Her paintings depict the traditions of her people. She has drawn from her own experiences living in a Pueblo community, and from stories her grandparents told her. She is also the author of a book of Tewa legends.

B The Iowa Indians, a small Plains tribe, used to live in the state that was named after them. Iowa Indians were farmers and buffalo hunters, and measured their wealth in buffalo hides and carved tobacco pipes. Along with the Oto and Missouri tribes, the Iowa tribe migrated southward from the Great Lakes region. Today, most of the Iowa live in Kansas, Nebraska, and Oklahoma.

122 UNIT 6: *Heritage and Change*

IN THE STUDIO BIG BOOK p.33

turning thread or yarn into cloth. For hundreds of years, weaving has been an important part of the Pueblo heritage.

Look at the woven belt in picture **B**. Native American weavers used wool to make belts such as this one. What patterns can you find in it?

B *Iowa Sash,* Nebraska
Circa 1880. Wool yarn, 79 X 1/4 in.
Museum of the American Indian.

IN THE STUDIO

MATERIALS
- thin yarn, various colors
- straws (5)
- stirrer straws
- scissors

Weave a bookmark. Use analogous colors.

1. Cut five pieces of yarn, each two feet long. Fold the pieces in half. Using a stirrer, push each piece of yarn through a straw. Tie each pair of loose ends together. Thread another piece of yarn through the loops of the folded ends and tie them loosely together.

2. Take another piece of yarn and tie it around one of the outer straws. Weave the yarn over and under each straw to form rows. When you want to change to a different color, tie the new color to the end of the preceding color. Continue weaving.

3. Weave all the way down to the folded end. Then untie the folded ends and pull off the straws. Finish your bookmark by cutting the ends into even lengths of fringe.

123

ART ACROSS THE CURRICULUM

READING: EXPLORE PUEBLO CULTURE

Ask pairs of students to research Pueblo culture in New Mexico. Some students may wish to focus on traditional Pueblo crafts such as pottery, weaving, and jewelry. Other students may wish to focus on the long history of the Pueblo peoples or on adobe architecture. You might suggest that students read *Pueblo Storyteller* by Diane Hoyt-Goldsmith or *The Pueblo* by Charlotte Yue.

PERFORMING ARTS: DANCE Teach students a traditional dance, or invite students or someone in their families to teach a dance to the class. The person teaching may also want to discuss the occasion on which the dance is performed and other customs that are associated with the dance.

IN THE STUDIO

MATERIALS: thin yarn in various colors, drinking straws, stirrer straws, scissors

Weaving a Bookmark   CREATING ART

- Demonstrate cutting and folding the yarn, pushing it through a straw, and tying each end. Also demonstrate tying the five straws together loosely.

- Show students how to tie one end of a sixth piece of yarn to the top straw on the far left. Then demonstrate weaving this long piece of yarn under and over the five pieces of yarn from one side to the other. When you get to the straw on the far right, wrap the yarn around it and begin weaving toward the left.

- Show students how to tie a new color of yarn to the preceding color.

- When the weaving reaches the end of the straws, demonstrate pulling the straws down to create more work space.

- When students' bookmarks are long enough, have them remove the straws and cut the ends.

OPTIONAL: Quick Activity Cut vertical slots in a sheet of construction paper, and have students weave different-colored strips of paper through the slots.

WRAP-UP   INFORMAL ASSESSMENT

- **How is the woven belt similar to other kinds of traditional arts and crafts you have seen?** (Possible responses: They are age-old crafts that are passed from one generation to the next; I have seen similar homemade items at craft shows.) ART CRITICISM: COMPARE/CONTRAST

- **Pablita Velarde Hardin's paintings show traditional Pueblo culture. Why do you think her paintings are important?** (Responses will vary.) ART CRITICISM: MAKE JUDGMENTS

LESSON 33: *A Timeless Art*

LESSON 34

Patchwork Art

OBJECTIVES: Understand that some art forms that were developed partly out of necessity continue to thrive today. Create a patchwork wall hanging using traditional methods and innovation.

MOTIVATE

Discuss making household goods by hand. Brainstorm with students a list of things pioneers made by hand, such as candles, soap, furniture, clothing, and blankets. Ask if any of these items are still being made by hand today.

VIEWING ART

TEACH

Discuss traditional quilts. Ask students to read the paragraphs and view the art. Challenge students to find the individual pieces of cloth that make up the design in one of the quilt panels and find pieces of the same cloth in different parts of the quilt.

View modern-day fabric art. Tell students that the artist who made B drew on the tradition of quilt-making. Ask students to find similarities between the two works. *(Possible responses: flower patterns, repeating shapes, colors)* Have students identify some of the designs in A and B. *(Possible responses: flower shapes, circles, cubes, leaves, birds)* Then ask how B is innovative. *(Possible responses: It is a wall hanging; it is shaped like a heart.)*

Critical Thinking Questions

- **Find an example of symmetrical balance and of asymmetrical balance in A.** *(Possible response: symmetrical balance—the first panel in the top row; asymmetrical balance—the first panel in the fourth row)* ART CRITICISM: APPLICATION

- **What was one way the artist of B created variety in her work?** *(Possible responses: She used many colors, shapes, and patterns; the patches are of various sizes.)* ART CRITICISM: ANALYSIS

STUDENTS ACQUIRING ENGLISH If necessary, clarify who the pioneers were, when they lived, and what their lives were like.

LESSON 34 CREATING A PATCHWORK WALL HANGING

Patchwork Art

How did quilting become an art form?

New blankets were expensive and hard to come by in early America. Pioneer women sewed scraps of cloth together to make **quilts** such as the one in picture **A**. All the work was done by hand. Groups of women gathered at events called quilting bees to help each other sew. A quilt, however, was not just a blanket. It was a work of art.

Patchwork quilting is a form of collage. It combines different materials and designs in one artwork. Today artists use patchwork quilting techniques to make beautiful works of art as shown in picture **B**.

Notice the geometric patterns in quilts A and B. In both quilts, shapes are repeated to create strong designs. Can you identify some of these designs?

Album Quilt, friends and relatives of Mary Brown Turner
Begun in 1846. Appliquéd and quilted cotton, 83 3/8 in. X 85 in.
Metropolitan Museum of Art, New York.

124

SHARE ART HISTORY

A Each panel of the Album Quilt was created by a different person. The panels were given to a woman named Mary Brown Turner as a gift commemorating the upcoming birth of her baby. She never joined the panels. Her daughter completed the quilt some twenty years later. The eagle and flag in the center panel is a motif found on quilts made in Baltimore. Other designs are found in quilts from many parts of early America.

B When artist **Miriam Schapiro** (1923–) created *Heartland*, she drew on the tradition of American quilting. The "baby block" design and the heart-and-flower motif are traditional quilt patterns. Much of Schapiro's work draws its inspiration from the talents of women, who for centuries have expressed their artistic abilities in the form of household arts like quilting. You may want to display *Art Print 12* and discuss the heritage shown in Ringgold's quilt.

---

124 UNIT 6: *Heritage and Change*

IN THE STUDIO BIG BOOK p. 34

B *Heartland*, Miriam Schapiro
1985. Fabric, 85 in. X 94 in.
Orlando Museum of Art, Orlando, FL.

IN THE STUDIO

MATERIALS
- scraps of cloth
- needles and thread or safety pins
- scissors
- trim such as sequins and lace
- fabric paint or markers

Make your own quilt square. With your classmates, make a patchwork wall hanging.

1. Work with your classmates to plan the size, shape, colors, and design of your wall hanging.
2. Decorate your own cloth square with fancy trim and fabric paint.
3. Have a classroom quilting bee! Sew or pin together all of the squares. 

125

ART ACROSS THE CURRICULUM

LANGUAGE ARTS: LIFE ON THE AMERICAN FRONTIER Invite students to learn more about everyday life in the days of the pioneers. Challenge students to find out what people ate, what kinds of clothes they wore, and with what kinds of toys children played. Some students may want to focus on processes such as how log or sod houses were built or how candles were made. Students can share their findings in written reports.

MATH: AREA AND PERIMETER Help students figure out the perimeter and the area of their wall hanging. To find the perimeter, they should add together the lengths of all four sides. To find the area, they should multiply the width of the quilt by its length.

IN THE STUDIO

MATERIALS: scraps of cloth, needles and thread or safety pins, scissors, trim (such as sequins and lace), fabric paint or markers, large sheet of paper

Creating a Patchwork Wall Hanging   CREATING ART

- Have students read the directions on page 125. Help them plan their wall hanging.

- Help students sketch the design on a large sheet of paper. Explain that the wall hanging will include at least one quilt square for each student, but that some students may need to make a second square to make the rows come out even.

- If necessary, assist students in measuring and cutting the squares of cloth. Show them how to thread a needle and use it safely, and demonstrate sewing on sequins and trim. Remind students that they can also color designs on their panel using markers or fabric paint. Students may want to include symbols or images that are important to them.

- To assemble the wall hanging, lay the pieces face up on a flat surface. Help students sew or pin the panels together. Display the finished hanging on a wall.

OPTIONAL: Quick Activity Have students cut paper squares and decorate them with markers. Students can tape the panels together to form a patchwork paper hanging.

WRAP-UP   INFORMAL ASSESSMENT

- **You have learned about pottery making, weaving, and quilting. How are all of these crafts alike?** (Possible responses: All of them have a practical purpose at home; they have often been done by women.) ART HISTORY: GENERALIZE

- **Imagine that you are going to make a quilt square for a special person in your life. For whom would you make it? What designs and colors would you use?** (Responses will vary.) PRODUCTION: APPLICATION

LESSON 34: *Patchwork Art*

CONNECTIONS

EVERYDAY ART

Identify some purposes of museums. Ask students why they think museums exist. Then have students name things they might find in museums. (Responses will vary: Museums are places where works of art can be seen; paintings, statues, clothing, inventions, documents, dolls, coins, cars.) Have students read pages 126–127 to learn about an unusual museum.

Discuss the Artrain. Ask students to look at the designs of the outside and the inside of the Artrain. Ask them why it makes a good museum. (Possible responses: It is large; it has lots of wall space; it seems easy to enter, walk through, and exit. Best of all, *it* comes to *you*.)

CONNECTIONS   COMMUNITY ART

THE ARTRAIN

It's a bird! It's a plane! It's a museum on wheels called the Artrain!

Not every community has a museum people can visit. However, for any community that has railroad tracks, there is a museum that can visit people. In fact, the Artrain has been visiting people all over the United States since 1971. What are some reasons why a train makes a good museum?

▼ The Artrain on the move

SHARE CULTURAL BACKGROUND

Railroad Tracks

An engineer named John Stevens built the first successful railroad track in the United States in 1825, but it ran only in a circle. By 1869, railroad tracks extended across the entire North American continent.

SOCIAL STUDIES

Museum Manners

COOPERATIVE LEARNING Point out to students that objects and paintings in museums are to be handled by museum personnel only. Remind them to appreciate art without touching it and to use their eyes to experience texture and form. Have students work in pairs to practice this skill. Challenge them to describe the textures of objects around the classroom.

126   UNIT 6: *Heritage and Change*

▲ Pointing out a feature

◀ Taking a closer look

WHAT DO YOU THINK?

▶ If you could choose art for the Artrain, what would it be? Why?

▶ Why might it be important for people in different parts of the United States to view the same art?

127

WHAT DO YOU THINK?

▶ If you could choose art for the Artrain, what would it be? Why? (Responses will vary.) AESTHETICS: PERSONAL RESPONSE

▶ Why might it be important for people in different parts of the United States to view the same art? (Possible responses: Having a shared culture helps bring people together; it helps people understand each other.) AESTHETICS: HYPOTHESIZE

MATH

Artrain Poster

Ask students to solve the following math problem and to use the answer to design a poster advertising the Artrain.

- If 15 students enter the Artrain every 10 minutes, how many students can see the art collection from 9:00 A.M. to 4:40 P.M.? ($15 \times 6 = 90$; $90 \times 7 = 630$; $15 \times 4 = 60$; $630 + 60 = 690$)

Have students display their posters on a bulletin board.

IN THE STUDIO

A Moving Museum

COOPERATIVE LEARNING Have students work in groups to design a museum with these requirements:

- The museum must be on a large motor vehicle, such as a bus or a truck.
- The vehicle must be able to move.
- The vehicle must be easy to enter, walk through, and exit.
- The museum must have a name.

Have volunteers share their museum designs and names.

CONNECTIONS: *Community Art* **127**

LESSON 35

Artwork to Wear

OBJECTIVES: Recognize that artists turn raw materials into traditional and innovative jewelry. Use everyday materials to create beads for a necklace.

MOTIVATE

Discuss pieces of jewelry. Invite volunteers to describe interesting pieces of jewelry they have seen.

VIEWING ART

TEACH

Discuss the functions of jewelry. Have students read pages 128 and 129 and look at the jewelry pictured. Ask students to suggest reasons people wear jewelry today. (Possible responses: for fun; to impress people; for its beauty; rings may symbolize marriage or pride in a school)

Discuss the materials jewelry is made of. Encourage students to compare the materials used to create the jewelry shown in the pictures. Ask students why they think each artist used the materials he or she did. (Possible responses: The artists used materials they could easily find or trade for, or that people thought were beautiful and valuable.)

Critical Thinking Questions

- How do you think jewelry making has changed over time? (Possible response: Long ago, jewelers used simple tools. Today, machines have made some types of jewelry making easier.) ART HISTORY: SPECULATE

- How do you think these three pieces of jewelry might have been used? (Possible responses: They were all probably worn on special occasions; the corsage and necklace might have been used in ceremonies. They all seem too valuable for everyday wear.) AESTHETICS: DRAW CONCLUSIONS

MEETING INDIVIDUAL NEEDS

CHALLENGE Invite interested students to make a chart of precious and semiprecious gems, where they are found, and their colors and characteristics.

LESSON 35   MAKING JEWELRY

Artwork to Wear

How do artists turn raw materials into jewelry?

Long ago, people wore jewelry as a sign of power and wealth. Is jewelry worn for the same reasons today? What are some other reasons people wear jewelry?

The gold and gemstone headdress in picture **A** was found in the tomb of an ancient king. It was made by hand more than 4,000 years ago!

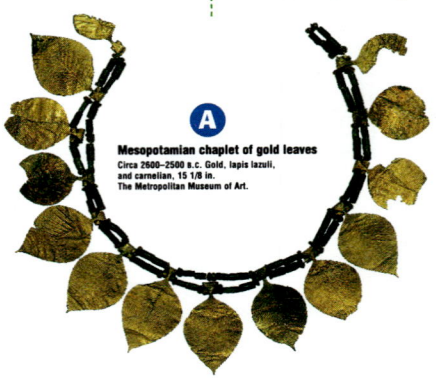

The jewelry in picture **B** was crafted in Spain about 300 years ago. Emeralds, diamonds, enamel, and gold were used to create the delicate **ornamentation**, or decoration. Can you see the repeated flower shapes?

A Mesopotamian chaplet of gold leaves
Circa 2600–2500 B.C. Gold, lapis lazuli, and carnelian, 15 1/8 in.
The Metropolitan Museum of Art.

B Spanish corsage ornament
Beginning of the eighteenth century. Gold, enamel, emeralds, and diamonds.
Victoria & Albert Museum, London.

128

SHARE ART HISTORY

A This wreath of gold beech leaves was discovered in a grave in the Royal Cemetery at Ur, in what is now Iraq. The headdress adorned the forehead of a female attendant. Gold, lapis lazuli, and carnelian, not found in Mesopotamia, imply an elaborate trading network.

B In Europe during the Middle Ages, jewelry was worn exclusively by members of the royal court. By 1400 a wealthy middle class had emerged, and the demand for jewelry increased. By the 1700s, new gem-cutting techniques led to the popularity of diamonds and emeralds.

C Pendants made of turquoise and shells have been important in Native American ceremonies for about a thousand years. Necklaces such as this one were traded along the Gulf of California. This style of jewelry is still made in the American Southwest.

UNIT 6: *Heritage and Change*

A modern Native American artist made the necklace in picture **C** from a shell. He decorated it with turquoise, mother-of-pearl, and black stone. Notice the strong geometric patterns on this necklace. Why do you think each artist used the materials he or she did?

C Southwestern United States shell and turquoise necklace, "Ca Win" Jimmy Calabaza. 1984. Spondylus shell, inlaid with mother-of-pearl, jet, and turquoise.

IN THE STUDIO

MATERIALS
- wire or string
- magazines
- glue
- scissors
- other necklace items such as pasta and washers

Create your own beads. Use them to make a bead necklace.

1. Cut brightly colored magazine pages into 1-inch strips.
2. Spread glue on one strip at a time. Fold one end of the strip around a pencil and gently roll it into a tight tube. Remove the pencil and let the glue dry. Repeat for other strips.
3. String the beads on wire or strong string. Think of creative items to use as spacers as you string the other necklace items in a pattern.

ART ACROSS THE CURRICULUM

SOCIAL STUDIES: NATIVE AMERICAN ARTWORK Encourage students to learn about different styles of Native American jewelry. Point out that although similarities can often be seen among the jewelry styles of different groups, there are also distinct differences. Have students present an informal oral report on their findings.

SCIENCE: DIAMOND DISCOVERY Have interested students learn more about diamonds. You might provide these questions to help them focus their research: What are diamonds made of? In what part of Earth's crust do they form? How long does it take for a diamond to form? How are diamonds used in industry?

IN THE STUDIO

MATERIALS: wire or string, magazines, glue, scissors, other necklace items such as washers or shells with holes

Making Jewelry

CREATING ART

- Direct students to read the instructions on page 129. Have students cut 1-in. strips from brightly colored magazines.

- Demonstrate how to make beads by spreading glue onto a strip of paper, rolling the strip around a pencil, and gently removing the pencil. Encourage students to be creative when choosing their paper from magazines. Allow time for the beads to dry.

- Have students slide their beads onto string or wire in a colorful pattern. (Each string should be 16–24 in. long.)

- Students may wish to add other items such as shells or metal washers to their necklaces. Make sure students leave about an inch of string or wire at each end so they can tie a knot or attach a clasp.

OPTIONAL: Quick Activity Have students use colored pencils or markers to draw a bead necklace that has a repeating pattern.

WRAP-UP

INFORMAL ASSESSMENT

- **Remember that the jewelry in this lesson was probably meant for special occasions. When might you either wear your necklace or give it as a gift?** (Responses will vary.) PRODUCTION: SYNTHESIZE

- **What problems did you encounter while making your necklace? How did you solve them?** (Responses will vary.) PRODUCTION: PROBLEM SOLVING

LESSON 35: *Artwork to Wear*

LESSON 36

Faces from Folk Art

OBJECTIVES: Learn that for thousands of years folk artists have made masks that help to pass on elements of their cultures. Create a mask in the style of one of the masks in this lesson.
MATERIALS: any kind of mask

MOTIVATE

Wear a mask. Ask students how they felt when they first saw you wearing it. Discuss reasons why mask making is popular all around the world.

VIEWING ART

TEACH

Learn about masks and folk artists. Have students read the paragraphs and view the masks. Ask them why people wear masks. (Possible responses: as disguises; to portray characters in shows) Point out that the masks on this page were made by folk artists. Explain that formally trained artists have taken art classes, while folk artists often learn traditional forms and techniques from their elders.

Identify expressions. Ask students what emotion each mask seems to express. (Possible responses: A looks bright; B seems to be laughing; C looks dignified or serious.)

Critical Thinking Questions

- **Each mask is made of different materials. How do you think each artist made each mask?** (Possible response: Masks A and B were probably carved; mask C was probably made in a mold.) PRODUCTION: SPECULATION

- **Which mask do you like best? How do you think people would react to you in this mask?** (Responses will vary.) AESTHETICS: PERSONAL RESPONSE

MEETING INDIVIDUAL NEEDS

STUDENTS ACQUIRING ENGLISH Make sure students know that *elders* are the oldest people in a group, respected for their knowledge and experience.

LESSON 36 CREATING A MIXED-MEDIA MASK

Faces from Folk Art

Why is mask-making popular all around the world?

A Jaguar mask
About 1960. Painted wood, 9 1/2 in. Mexico.

When do people wear masks? Why do they wear them? In some cultures, masks are worn to represent story characters or important people. In many places the tradition of mask-making is passed from one generation of **folk artists** to the next. These artists learn the craft by watching their elders.

Picture **A** shows a jaguar mask from Mexico. It is worn in dances in which the jaguar is a character. In Mexico, the jaguar is a traditional symbol of courage and strength.

Mask **B** was made for an actor in a Japanese play. Masks for these plays have been made for hundreds of years. Every detail follows rules that have been handed down through generations.

B Nō mask of Okina, Ujiharu Nagasawa
Twentieth century. 7 in. tall.

130

SHARE ART HISTORY

A The jaguar mask is worn by dancers and actors impersonating "el tigre," a character popular in southwestern Mexico.

B The Nō mask is worn by an actor while performing a Japanese Nō play known as Okina. The play, which is performed only on special occasions, consists of several dances, and has been performed for over 900 years.

C This mask was worn by a king, or *oba*, on his left hip to symbolize his mother's influence.

IN THE STUDIO BIG BOOK p.36

Mask **C** shows the mother of an African king. The king's mother, called the *iyoba*, had a special place of honor in the African kingdom of Benin.

C

Mask representing an iyoba
Circa 1550. Ivory, iron, copper, 9 3/8 in. tall. Benin.

IN THE STUDIO

MATERIALS
- tagboard, about 7 in. X 11 in.
- paper scraps
- scissors
- glue
- raffia, straw, or other natural fibers
- tempera paints
- paintbrushes
- hole punch
- elastic, 8 in. long X 1/4 in. wide

Create a mask. You may want to work in one of the styles shown in this lesson or in a style that reflects your own heritage.

1. Decide which style of mask you want to make. Draw an outline of your mask on tagboard.

2. Cut out two holes for the eyes and a hole for the mouth. Use paper scraps and other materials to make the ears, nose, hair, and other features. Glue them to the mask.

3. Paint your mask. When it is dry, punch holes on both sides of the face so you can attach an elastic band across the back. Try it on!

131

ART ACROSS THE CURRICULUM

PERFORMING ARTS: THEATER Have students choose a folktale or fairy tale and imagine it is to be performed as a play. Ask students to design a mask for each major character. They might make a sketch of each mask, write a detailed description of it, and list materials that would be needed to create it.

HEALTH AND SAFETY: MASKS FOR PROTECTION Point out that many people wear masks for health and safety reasons. Prompt students to think of different examples of workers who sometimes need to wear protective masks. (Possible responses: welders, doctors and nurses, firefighters, athletes) Have students find out what each kind of mask is made of and the purpose it serves.

IN THE STUDIO

MATERIALS: tagboard, about 7 in. × 11 in.; paper scraps; scissors; glue; raffia, straw, or other natural fibers; tempera paints; paintbrushes; hole punch; elastic, 8 in. × 1/4 in.

Creating a Mixed-Media Mask   CREATING ART

- Invite students to read the steps on page 131. Tell them to choose the style of mask they will create.

- Direct students to draw an outline of a mask as large as, or larger than, their faces on tagboard and cut it out. Have them hold up the masks to their faces. Partners can lightly draw circles where each other's eyes and mouth are. Students can then cut out these holes.

- Encourage students to use stiff paper to add three-dimensional features such as noses and ears. Some students may want to make their masks asymmetrical.

- Have students paint their masks. Allow them to dry overnight. Students might add other decorations after their masks are dry. They can attach an elastic band across the back so that their masks can be worn.

OPTIONAL: Quick Activity Students can draw a design for a mask that they might create at a future date.

WRAP-UP   INFORMAL ASSESSMENT

- **Look at a classmate's mask. How is it similar to the masks in the lesson? How is it different?** (Responses will vary.) ART CRITICISM: COMPARE/CONTRAST

- **Pretend that you are a folk artist living hundreds of years ago near the ocean. If you were making a mask, what materials might you use?** (Possible responses: I might use driftwood and shells.) ART HISTORY: SYNTHESIZE

LESSON 36: *Faces from Folk Art* 131

UNIT 6

REFLECTING AND REVIEWING

Pages 132–133

Reflect on the unit theme. Have students read the paragraph on page 132. Remind them that all the artworks in this unit reflect the cultural traditions and heritage of artists.

Ask students to discuss the dance. Students should explore the artistic possibilities of forms other than painting, drawing, architecture, and sculpture. Ask them to think of some other art forms and discuss how different forms of art are similar.

About the Art

Ballet Folklórico is an art form that combines costume, dance, and music into a performance that celebrates Mexican heritage. The movements are very disciplined and vary with the region of Mexico in which they originated. Members of the group, of which there are hundreds throughout Mexico and the United States, carefully research the traditions of their chosen region in order to interpret the authentic folklore of Mexico.

UNIT 6 REFLECTING AND REVIEWING

Artists preserve and build upon their heritages.

Art is not always the brushstrokes of a painting or the lines of a statue. Art can be the movements of dancers, the playing of musicians, and so on. The artists of Ballet Folklórico (folk dance) celebrate traditional Mexican forms of dance and music. They use them in lively new combinations. How is their creation like a painting?

Ballet Folklórico Dancers from McAllen, Texas, at Texas Folklife Festival in San Antonio.

132

ART ACROSS THE CURRICULUM

MUSIC: MAKE SOME NOISE Ask small groups of students to imagine that they are at a performance of Ballet Folklórico. They should think of what the music might sound like based on the picture of the dancers in action. Have each group list some of the kinds of songs they think might be playing at the performance. The list may include folk, classical, or jazz, or popular music. **COOPERATIVE LEARNING**

What Did I Learn?

- **THE** artistic traditions of many cultures were represented in this unit. Which tradition was the most interesting to you? Explain your choice.
- **IDENTIFY** two artworks in this unit that had cultural themes or that told stories about a culture.
- **YOU** made some traditional artwork of your own in this unit. How did you use theme and storytelling in your artwork?
- **WHICH** artists in this unit wanted to preserve their heritage? Which artists were interested in adding new things to their heritage?

What Did I Learn?

Encourage students to work in small groups to discuss their answers to these questions that appear on page 133.

- **The artistic traditions of many cultures were represented in this unit. Which tradition was the most interesting to you? Explain your choice.** (Responses will vary.) AESTHETICS: PERSONAL RESPONSE

- **Identify two artworks in this unit that had cultural themes or that told stories about a culture.** (Possible responses: *Her First Dance* has a clear cultural theme; *Detroit Industry* tells a story.) ART CRITICISM: ANALYSIS

- **You made some traditional artwork of your own in this unit. How did you use theme and storytelling in your artwork?** (Responses will vary.) PRODUCTION: DESCRIPTION

- **Which artists in this unit wanted to preserve their heritage? Which artists were more interested in adding new things to their heritage?** (Possible response: The mask makers preserved heritage; Miriam Schapiro advanced it.) ART CRITICISM: MAKE JUDGMENTS

Students may select images from this unit to add to their portfolios.

Just for Fun — TREASURE HUNT

TO ENCOURAGE STUDENTS to take another close look at the artworks in this unit, ask them to respond to the following questions and statements:

- Find three or more objects in this unit that are useful as well as beautiful. (Possible responses: the vases, the belt, and the quilt)
- Name two things in the unit that were made long ago.
- Find two images that use repetition, and describe how they use it.
- Think about the places represented in this unit. Which place would you like to visit? Show where it is on a map.

Reflecting and Reviewing

ART SAFETY

Pages 134–135

Read aloud, or have a volunteer read, each safety rule. Ask students to tell why each one is important, and what might happen if they don't follow it. You may wish to display the safety poster and encourage students to review the rules often.

ART SAFETY

Listen carefully when your teacher tells how to use art materials.

Wear a smock to keep your school clothes clean.

Use the kind of markers and inks that will not stain your clothes.

Use tools carefully. Hold sharp objects so that they cannot hurt you or others. **Wear safety glasses** if something could get in your eyes.

Check labels on materials before you use them. Look for the word *nontoxic*, which means "not poisonous."

134

134   ART EXPRESS

Cover your skin if you have a cut or scratch. Some art materials, such as clay, can make cuts sting.

Keep your area clean and neat. Clean up spills right away so no one will fall. Put materials back when you finish with them.

Tell your teacher if you have allergies or breathing problems. Some people are allergic to the kinds of dust in some art materials.

Show respect for other students. Walk carefully around their work. Never touch classmates' work without asking first.

Always wash your hands after using art materials.

Additional Safety Considerations

Art Express recommends materials and techniques that do not pose health or safety risks. Some materials or tools, however, may require close supervision during use. Note the following reminders:

- Nontoxic glue is recommended for use in all activities requiring glue.

- Scissors with rounded tips are recommended for use in the early grades.

- Powdered tempera paint can cause irritation if accidentally inhaled, rubbed, or blown into the eyes.

- Chalk and charcoal produce dust and may aggravate allergies. Chalk may be used safely if it is first dipped in milk or liquid starch. Oil pastels and soft pencils are dust-free substitutes for chalk and charcoal.

- Water-based colored markers are suggested for use in all grades. Permanent felt markers should not be used by students because they contain solvents that can irritate the lungs.

- Both nonwaterproof and permanent inks stain badly. It is a good idea to wear old clothing, a smock, or a bibbed apron when working with these inks.

- When plastic bags are required for sculpture activities, students should be reminded to keep the bags away from their heads and faces.

- If spray fixatives are used, they should be applied with a nonaerosol spray pump by an adult in a well-ventilated area away from the students.

Student Resources

EXPLORING ART TECHNIQUES
R1
This section invites students to experiment with a variety of media and techniques, without necessarily creating final products.

ELEMENTS & PRINCIPLES
R5
A visual "glossary" that illustrates the elements of art and principles of design—the tools that artists use to communicate their ideas.

GALLERY OF ARTISTS
R8
Brief biographies of the artists whose works appear in **Art Express.**

GLOSSARY
R11
Definitions and pronunciations of the art terminology used in the student book.

ARTISTS & ARTWORKS
R13

INDEX
R14

ACKNOWLEDGMENTS
R15

135A   ART EXPRESS

EXPLORING ART TECHNIQUES

Trying Ways to Draw

There are lots of ways to draw. You can draw quickly to show action, or you can draw something very carefully to show just how it looks to you. Try to draw every day. Keep your drawings in your sketchbook so you can see how your drawing changes.

Here are some ideas for drawing. To start, get out your sketchbook or a sheet of paper and some pencils.

GESTURE DRAWING

Gesture drawing is used to show movement or action instead of details. Look at the two pictures of a baseball player. The drawing on the left shows details of the player's uniform, but the gesture drawing catches the feeling of movement as the player swings the bat.

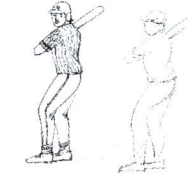

Find some photographs of people or animals in action. Make gesture drawings of them. Draw quickly. Don't try to show details.

Then make some gesture drawings while watching a sporting event. Catch the movement, not the details. Make your sketches quick and lively.

CONTOUR DRAWING

Look closely at the lines and shapes in this photograph. The lines that go around shapes are called contours. Use your finger to trace around the outlines of the objects in this picture. Trace the lines inside the shapes too. In a contour drawing, you draw all the lines, edges, and shapes.

Blind contour drawing is a way to learn to look closely at what you are drawing. Choose a simple object, like a leaf. Draw the object without looking at your paper. Move your pencil as your eyes slowly follow the contours. Don't worry if your drawing doesn't look much like the object. Remember, you are using blind contour drawing to learn how to look at things carefully, the way an artist does.

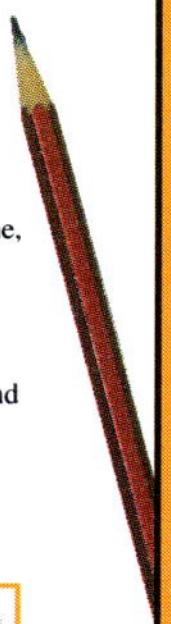

Now try a continuous contour drawing. Draw something simple, like a chair. This time, look back and forth between the object and your paper. Work more quickly. Draw all the edges and shapes without lifting your pencil off the paper. Your drawing will look loose and lively.

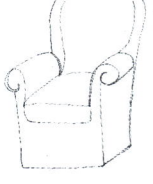

Now try making contour drawings of another object, such as a shoe. Lift your pencil whenever you want to. When you feel ready, try a contour drawing of a person.

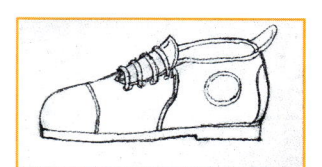

TONAL DRAWING

You can show the shape of something without using contour lines. Look at the photograph of the steps. Notice which areas are dark and which are light. (The darkness or lightness of a color is its **value**.) Now look at the drawing of the steps. It was made with only tones, or **shades**. Even without contour lines, you can tell what the object is.

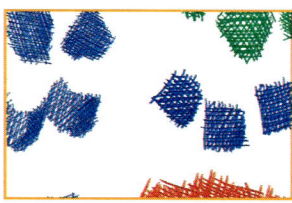

Experiment with your pencils. Try making a series of lines that go from light values to dark values. Try smudging some of the lines together with your fingers. Then use an eraser to lighten some of the smudges. The light areas are called **highlights**. Try this with **cross-hatching** or another small **pattern**.

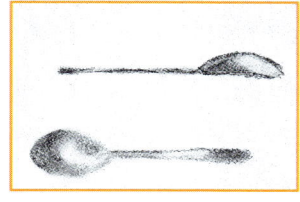

Try a tonal drawing of a simple object like a spoon. Look at the object closely. Use a flashlight to change the lighting on the spoon. Watch what happens to the highlights as you move the flashlight. Now draw what you see. Show the highlights by erasing the shading where the light looks brightest. Move the flashlight to a different position and make another tonal drawing. Can you tell that the light is coming from a different direction in each drawing?

CONTOURS AND TONES

Try combining tonal drawing with contour drawing. Start by making a tonal drawing of something with an interesting shape, like a book bag. Look at it carefully to see the tones of dark and light.

Then look at the object again to see its contours. Add the outline, edges, and other contour lines.

You might prefer to start with a contour drawing. Be sure you draw the outline of each shape and detail. Then add tones with shading or patterns.

DID YOU PREFER to start with shading or with contours? Either way is fine.

ART TECHNIQUES

ART TECHNIQUES

Experimenting with Paint

Working with colors is always fun. Experimenting with paints will help you learn about how artists use color and how you can use it in your artwork.

These are some things you should have when you paint: old newspapers to cover your work area, an old shirt to cover your clothes, tempera paints or watercolors, old dishes or plastic egg cartons for mixing paint, paper, paintbrushes, a jar or bowl of water, and paper towels.

TEMPERA PAINTS

Tempera paints are water-based, so they are easy to clean up. The colors are bright and easy to mix.

● GETTING STARTED

Start experimenting by dipping your paintbrush into one color. Try different kinds of **brushstrokes**. Try painting with lots of paint on the brush and with the brush almost dry. (You can dry the paintbrush by wiping it across a paper towel.) Twist the paintbrush on the paper and roll it, press it, or dab it.

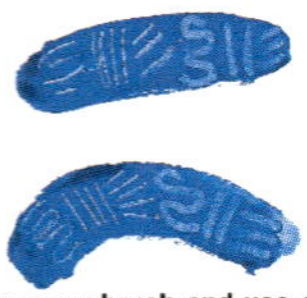

Now clean your brush and use a different color to make a heavy brushstroke. Use a craft stick or another tool to draw a pattern in it.

Make a pattern or a picture on a fresh sheet of paper. Use some of these methods of painting. Try using a different color for each method.

● MIXING COLORS

Even if you have only a few colors of tempera paints, you can mix them to make almost any color you want. An old saucer makes a good palette for mixing paint. You can also use a plastic egg carton. Try using different amounts of the same colors.

To make darker values of colors (shades), add black. Add colors to white to make lighter values (**tints**). See how many shades and tints of a single color you can make. Try starting with a color you have mixed from two colors.

TECHNIQUES TO TRY

Pointillism is a technique that makes the viewer's eyes mix the colors. Start with two colors. Make many small dots of one color very close together. About half an inch away, make many small dots of the other color. In between, make many small dots of each color without letting the dots touch. Stand back from your paper. What happens to the colors as your eyes move across them?

Impasto is a technique that uses a thick mixture of paint and wheat paste. Put some wheat paste in a small bowl. Stir in some paint. Spread some of the mixture on a small piece of cardboard. Experiment with tools such as a toothpick, a plastic fork, or a comb to make textures in the impasto. Then mix more colors. Use them to make an impasto picture or design.

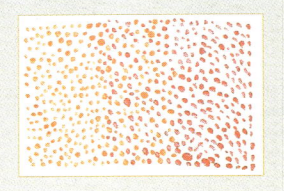

WATERCOLORS

Watercolors usually come in little dry cakes. You have to add the water! So keep a jar of clean water and some paper towels nearby as you paint. Use paper that is made for watercolors.

● GETTING STARTED

First put a few drops of water on each cake of paint. To start experimenting with watercolors, dip your paintbrush in water and then dab it in one of the colors. Try some brushstrokes. Watercolors are transparent. Since you can see through them, the color on your paper will never be as dark as the color of the cake. Use different amounts of water. What happens to the color when you use a lot of water?

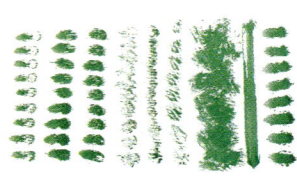

Now rinse your brush in the water and use another color. Try different kinds of brushstrokes—thick and thin, squiggles and waves, dots and blobs. Change colors often.

Try using one color on top of a different color that is already dry. Work quickly to keep the colors clear. If your brushstrokes are too slow, the colors can get muddy. If you want part of your painting to be white, don't paint that part. The white comes from the color of the paper.

● MIXING COLORS

Experiment with mixing watercolors right on your paper. Try painting with a very wet brush over a dry color. Try a wet color on or just touching another wet color. Try three colors together.

You can also mix colors on your paintbrush. Dip your brush into one color and then another before you paint. Try it with green and yellow. Clean your paintbrush and try some other combinations. To clean any paint cakes that you have used for mixing, just wipe them with a paper towel.

TECHNIQUES TO TRY

Try making a wash. Start with a stripe of dark blue. Then clean your paintbrush and get it very wet. Use it to "wash" the color down the page. (You can do this with a wide brush or a sponge, too.) Also try wetting all of one side of the paper. Then brush a stroke of color across it and let the color spread. Try two or three color washes together. For a special effect, sprinkle salt onto a wet wash.

Try using tempera paints and watercolors together. Start with a two-color watercolor wash. Let it dry. Then use several kinds of brushstrokes to paint a design on the wash with one color of tempera. How does the background color change the way the tempera color looks?

Remember these techniques when you paint designs or pictures. Be sure to clean your paintbrushes and work area when you have finished.

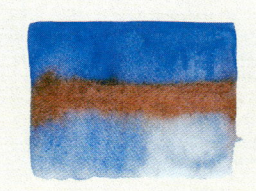

Working with Clay

Clay is a special kind of earth that holds together and is easy to shape when it is mixed with water. Water-based clays can be fired, or heated at a high temperature, or just left in the air to dry until hard.

To make an object with clay, work on a clean, dry surface. (A brown paper bag makes a good work surface.) Have some water handy to work into the clay a few drops at a time if it starts to dry out. When you are not working with it, store clay in a plastic bag to keep it from drying out.

You can use an assortment of tools. To help you shape your clay or to add texture or designs to something you make out of clay, you can use a plastic knife and fork, a rolling pin, keys, a comb, a pencil, a piece of burlap, and other tools.

Start working with a piece of clay by making sure it has no air bubbles in it. Press it down, fold it over, and press it down again. This process is called kneading.

MODELING

Try making different forms with your clay. If one of your forms reminds you of an animal or a person, continue to model, or shape, the form by pinching and pulling the clay.

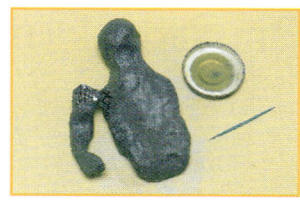

To join shaped pieces, score, or make lines in, the clay surfaces, and wet them. Or you can coat the surfaces with **slip**, which is clay mixed with water until it is like cream. Then press the surfaces together and smooth the seams.

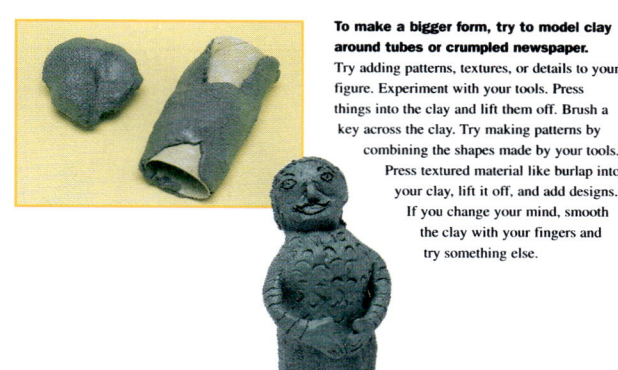

To make a bigger form, try to model clay around tubes or crumpled newspaper. Try adding patterns, textures, or details to your figure. Experiment with your tools. Press things into the clay and lift them off. Brush a key across the clay. Try making patterns by combining the shapes made by your tools. Press textured material like burlap into your clay, lift it off, and add designs. If you change your mind, smooth the clay with your fingers and try something else.

USING SLABS

Roll your clay out flat, between a quarter-inch and a half-inch thick. If it is soft, you can shape it by draping it over something like a bowl or crumpled paper.

To make a slab box, roll your clay out flat. Cut two squares the same size with a plastic knife. One square will be the bottom of your box, and the other will be the top. To make the sides, cut four rectangles the same length as the square. (Later you can try this with other shapes.)

Score the edges and then let the pieces dry until they feel like leather. Join the pieces together with slip. Then smooth the seams with your fingers.

USING COILS

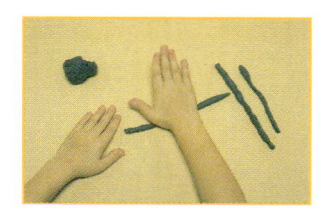

To make a coil pot, roll pieces of clay against a hard surface. Use your whole hand to make long clay ropes.

Make the bottom of your pot by coiling together one or more ropes of clay. Smooth the coils with your fingers. To start the sides, place a rope of clay around the edge of the bottom. Keep attaching ropes and continue the coiling until your pot is as high as you want it. Smooth the inside as you work. You may smooth the outside or let the coils show.

MAKING A CLAY RELIEF

A relief is a sculpture raised from a surface. To make a relief out of clay, start with a slab of any shape. Draw a simple design on the clay, using a brush dipped in slip. Roll some very thin coils. Apply the thin coils to the lines of the design.

You can also make small balls of clay and use slip to add them to the design. Try using some of your other tools to add texture to your design.

ART TECHNIQUES

ART TECHNIQUES

Exploring Printmaking

When you make a print, you transfer color from one object to another. If you have ever left a muddy footprint on a clean floor, you know what a print is. Here are some printmaking ideas to try.

COLLOGRAPH PRINTS

A collograph is a combination of a **collage** and a print. To make a collograph, you will need cardboard, glue, paper, newspapers, a brayer (a roller for printing), printing ink, a flat tray such as an old cookie sheet, and some paper towels or sponges. You will also need some thin objects to include in the collage. Try things like these: old keys, string, lace, paper clips, buttons, shells, and burlap.

Spread glue on the cardboard. Arrange several objects on the cardboard in a pleasing design. Press the objects down firmly. Let the glue dry.

Prepare your ink while the collage is drying. Place a small amount of ink on your cookie sheet. Roll the brayer through the ink until it is evenly coated. Gently run the brayer over the collage. Most of the ink should be on the objects.

Now press a piece of paper onto the inked collage. Gently rub the paper. Peel off the paper and let the ink dry. You've made a collograph!

MULTICOLOR PRINTS

You can use different colors of tempera paint to make a multicolor print with repeated patterns. You will need a plastic foam tray (such as a meat tray), cardboard, scissors, glue, paper, water, tempera paint, and a paintbrush.

First cut out some interesting shapes from the plastic foam tray. Carve or poke holes and lines into the shapes. Arrange the pieces on the cardboard to make an interesting design. Glue down the pieces.

When the glue is dry, paint the pieces with different colors of tempera paint. Try not to get paint on the cardboard.

While the paint is wet, place a sheet of paper on top of your design. Gently rub the paper, and peel it off carefully. Let the paint dry. Wipe the shapes dry, and paint them again with different colors. Print the same paper again, but turn it so that the designs and colors overlap.

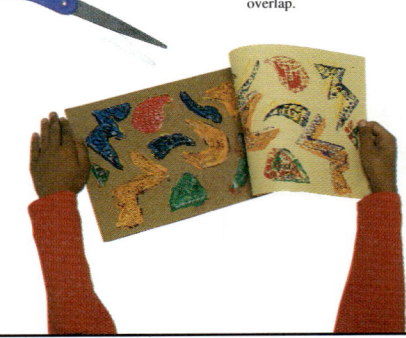

TRY DIFFERENT COLORS, paper, and objects to make prints.

Displaying Your Artwork

Displaying your artwork is a good way to share it. Here are some ways to make your artwork look its best.

DISPLAYING ART PRINTS

Select several pictures that go together well. Line them up along a wall or on the floor. Try grouping the pictures in different ways. Choose an arrangement that you like. Attach a strong string across a wall. Use clothespins or paper clips to hang your pictures on the string.

Frame your picture. Use a piece of cardboard that is longer and wider than the art. Draw a rectangle on the cardboard that is larger than your picture. Have an adult cut out the rectangle. Then decorate your frame. Choose colors and textures that look good with your picture. You can paint the frame or use a stamp print design. You can add texture by gluing on strips of cardboard or rows of buttons.

Mount your picture. Glue the corners to a piece of cardboard the same size as the frame. Measure carefully to be sure you get your picture in the center. Then glue the frame to the mounting. Tape a loop of thread on the back. Hang up your framed work.

DISPLAYING SCULPTURES

To display your clay pieces or sculptures, find a location where your work will be safe from harm. Look for a display area where people won't bump into your exhibit or damage your work.

Select several clay pieces or sculptures that go together well. Try grouping them in different ways. Place some of the smaller objects on boxes. Choose an arrangement that you like. Tape any boxes to the table.

Select a large tablecloth or piece of fabric to drape over the table. Pick a plain cloth that looks good with your artwork. Place your artwork back on the table. Try adding a few interesting folds in the cloth near your pieces.

NOW INVITE your friends and family over to see your work!

R4 ART EXPRESS

ELEMENTS & PRINCIPLES

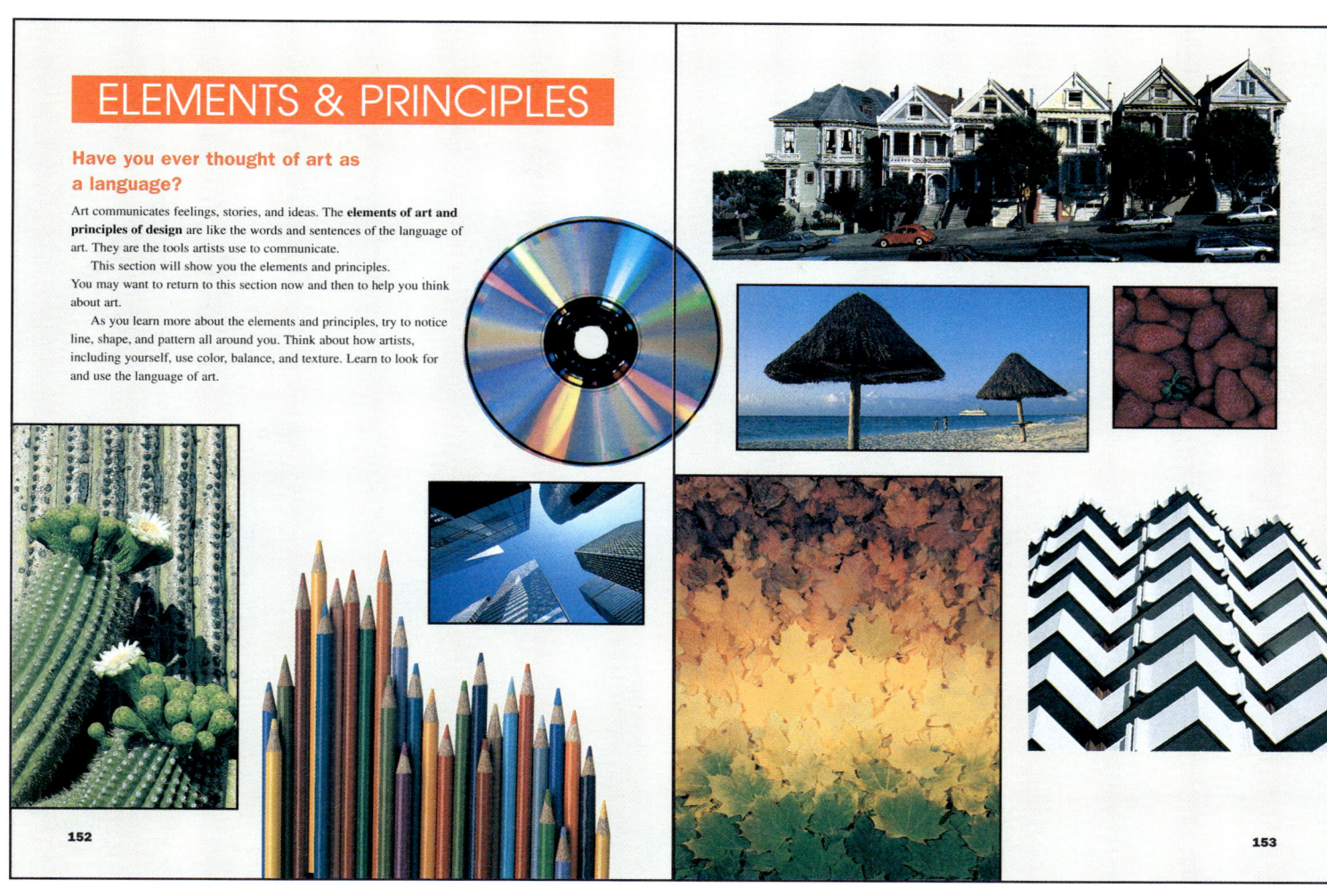

Have you ever thought of art as a language?

Art communicates feelings, stories, and ideas. The **elements of art and principles of design** are like the words and sentences of the language of art. They are the tools artists use to communicate.

This section will show you the elements and principles. You may want to return to this section now and then to help you think about art.

As you learn more about the elements and principles, try to notice line, shape, and pattern all around you. Think about how artists, including yourself, use color, balance, and texture. Learn to look for and use the language of art.

152

153

ELEMENTS & PRINCIPLES

ELEMENTS
Line

- horizontal
- straight
- curved
- diagonal
- zigzag
- vertical
- wavy

154

ELEMENTS
Texture

- silky
- soft
- rough
- smooth
- bumpy

155

ELEMENTS & PRINCIPLES

R5

ELEMENTS & PRINCIPLES

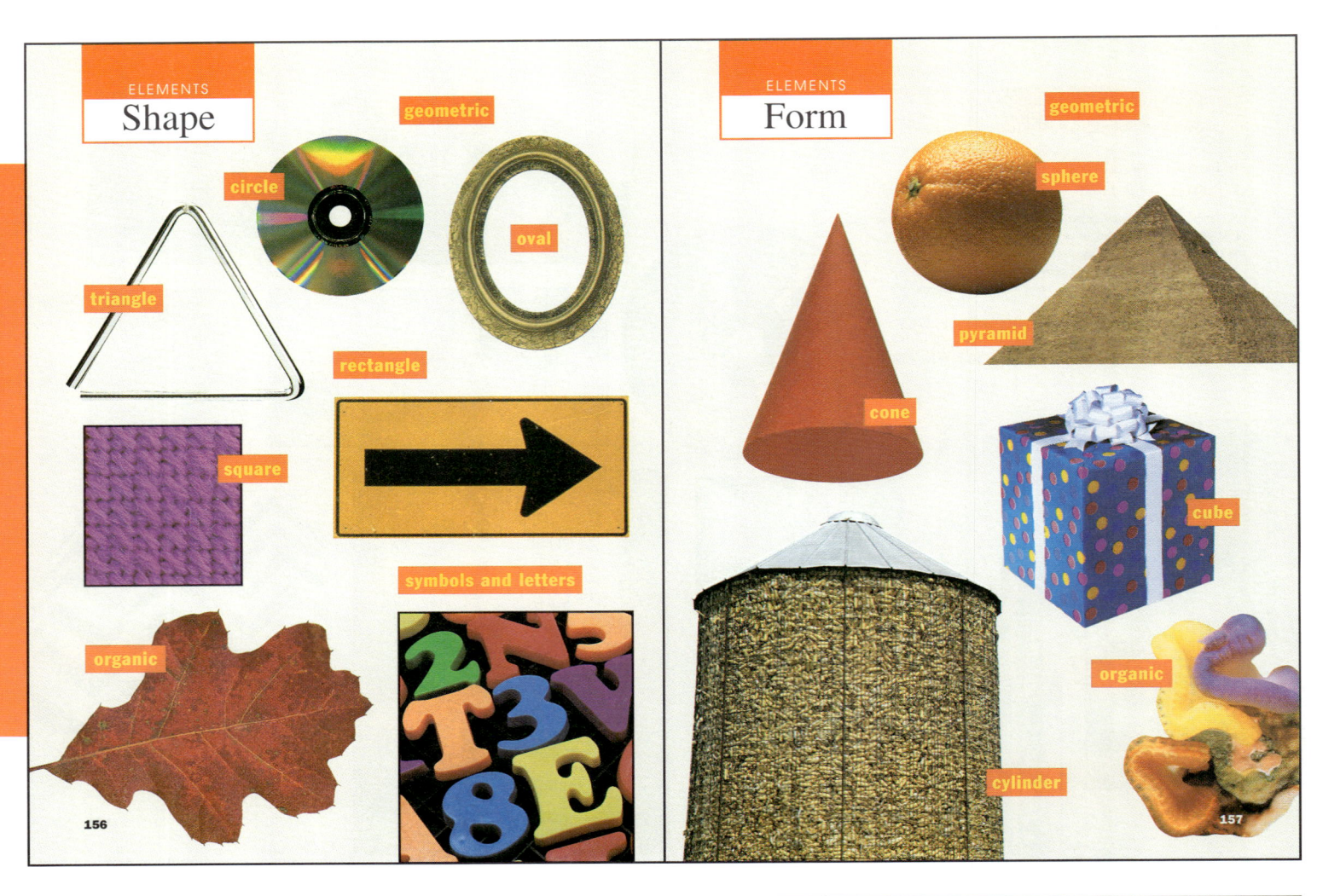

ELEMENTS: Shape

- triangle
- circle
- geometric
- oval
- square
- rectangle
- organic
- symbols and letters

ELEMENTS: Form

- geometric
- sphere
- pyramid
- cone
- cube
- cylinder
- organic

ELEMENTS: Color

- complementary
- warm
- cool
- Primary, Secondary, Intermediate

ELEMENTS: Value

- shadows
- light to dark
- tint
- shade

ELEMENTS: Space

- positive, negative
- background
- middle ground
- foreground
- proportion
- point of view
- eye level
- worm's eye
- bird's eye

R6   ART EXPRESS

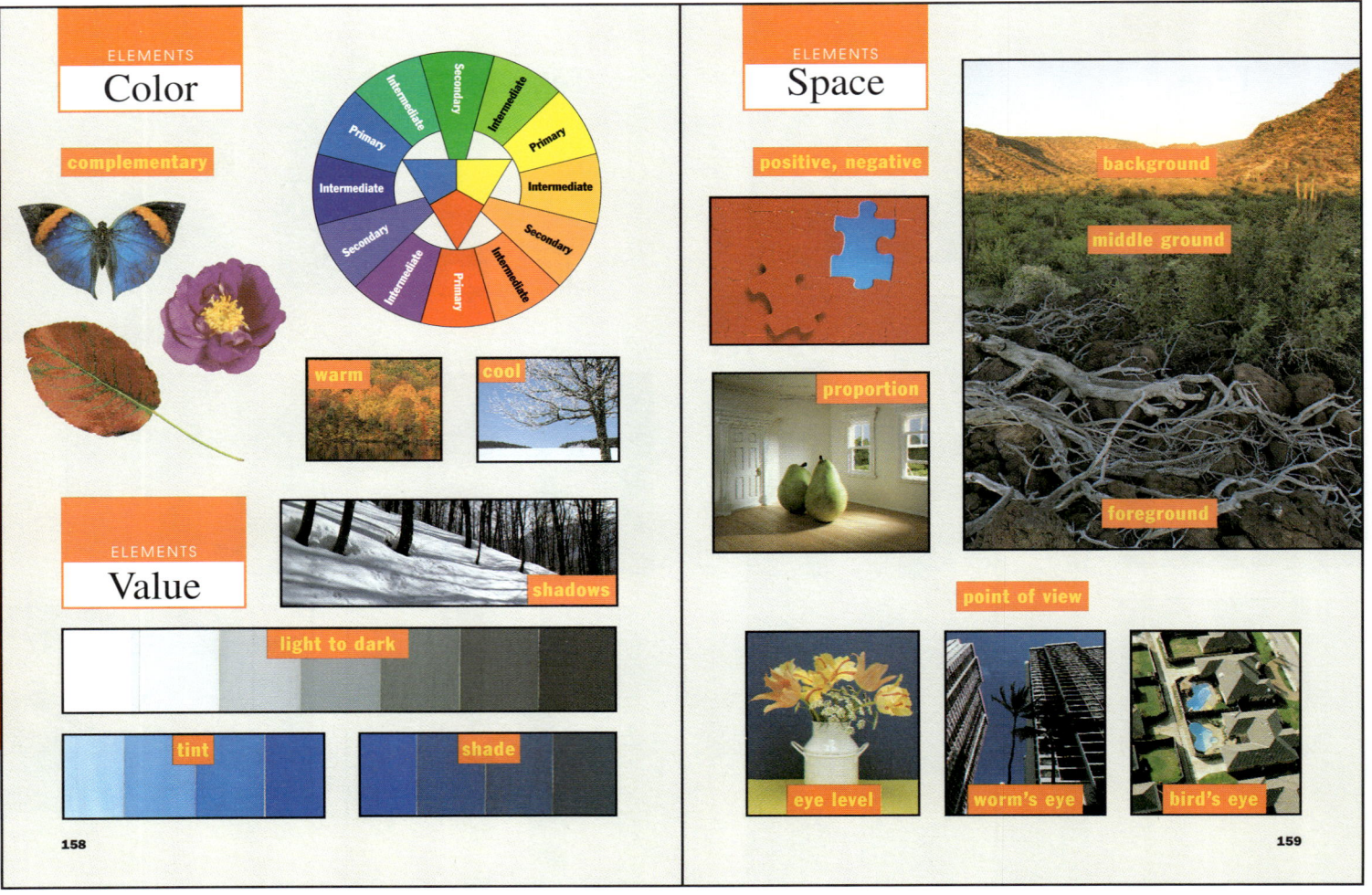

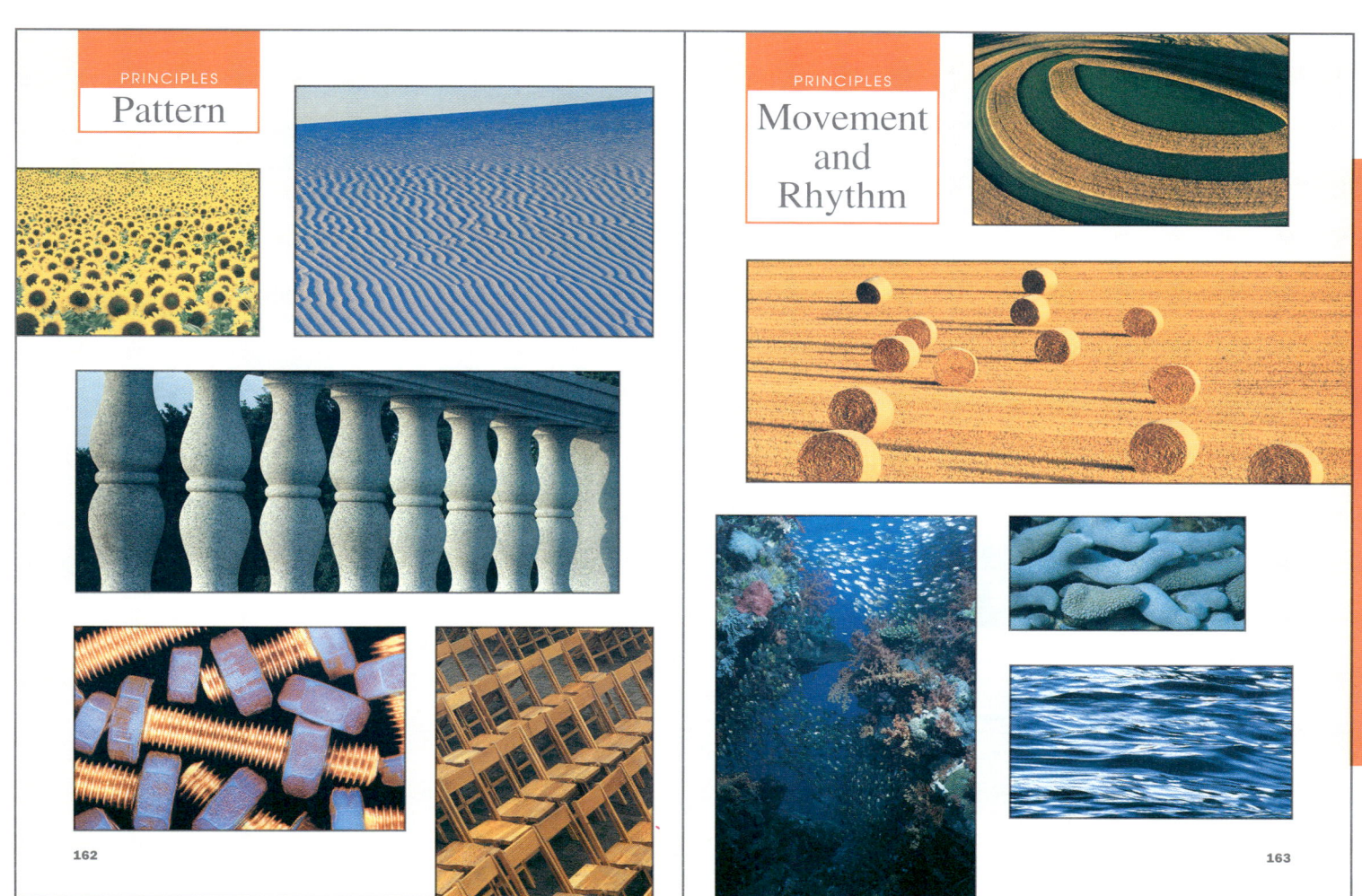

PRINCIPLES
Unity
repeated lines, textures, colors, shapes, forms

PRINCIPLES
Variety
different lines, textures, colors, shapes, forms

PRINCIPLES
Emphasis

PRINCIPLES
Pattern

PRINCIPLES
Movement and Rhythm

ELEMENTS & PRINCIPLES

R7

ELEMENTS & PRINCIPLES

PRINCIPLES
Proportion

PRINCIPLES
Balance

asymmetrical

symmetrical

physical balance

GALLERY OF ARTISTS

George Ancona (1929–) United States, photographer. Ancona was born in Coney Island, New York. After high school, he attended the Academy of San Carlos in Mexico. His work has since been published nationwide in magazines and children's books. **pages 100–101**

Richard Anuszkiewicz [a•nuh•SKAY•vich] (1930–) United States, painter. Anuszkiewicz, whose parents came to the United States from Poland, was born in Erie, Pennsylvania. He was one of the first American painters to create the effect of vibration on a flat surface. He was also a pioneer of using the technique of mixing colors optically. **page 59**

Frédéric-Auguste Bartholdi [bar•TOHL•dee] (1834–1904) France, sculptor. Bartholdi, who designed the Statue of Liberty, may have modeled Liberty's face after his mother's. Bartholdi created many huge patriotic sculptures. His style was influenced by the monuments of ancient Egypt. **page 44**

Barbara Bash United States, illustrator. Bash began her publishing career as an artist specializing in calligraphy and botanical illustration. She is now an award-winning author and illustrator of books about nature for young people. **pages 20–21**

Behzad (c. 1455 – c. 1536) Persia, painter. Behzad was an important Persian painter whose style had a strong influence on Persian Islamic painting. He was an orphan who was raised by the painter Mirak Naqqash. In 1522 he was placed in charge of the royal library and made responsible for producing its illuminated and illustrated manuscripts. **page 97**

Thomas Hart Benton (1889–1975) United States, painter. Benton was born in Missouri and studied at the Art Institute of Chicago as well as in Paris. He painted a number of murals, including those on the walls of the Lounge in the Capitol Building in Washington, D.C. He was thought of as a Regionalist. **page 76**

Selma Burke (1900–1995) United States, sculptor. Burke, one of ten children, was born in Mooresville, North Carolina. She studied to be a nurse but decided to pursue a career in art. She gained national fame in 1945 when she was commissioned to create a plaque of President Franklin Delano Roosevelt. This same image was used on the Roosevelt dime. **page 34**

Alexander Calder (1898–1976) United States, sculptor, painter. Calder was born in Lawnton, Pennsylvania, and studied at the Art Students League in New York. He had his first one-person show at a gallery in New York in 1926. Calder's work is owned by museums around the world. **pages 30, 83**

Mary Cassatt [kuh•SAT] (1844–1926) United States, painter. Cassatt was born in Allegheny City, Pennsylvania, to wealthy parents. She studied at the Pennsylvania Academy of Fine Arts and traveled to Europe often before finally moving there in 1874. She lived in France for the rest of her life. **page 28**

Christo (1935–) Bulgaria, sculptor, painter. Christo studied at the Fine Arts Academy in Sofia, Bulgaria. In 1960, he began wrapping found objects—such as bottles, cans, and even cars—using cloth and plastic and tying them with string. Christo works with his wife, Jeanne-Claude. Their wrapped objects include monuments, bridges, and buildings. **page 72**

Thomas Cole (1801–1848) United States, painter. When Cole was young, he hiked around and sketched the Hudson River valley and areas around the Catskill and Adirondack mountains. He was one of the first artists to capture the spacious feeling of the wilderness, and he had a strong influence on American landscape painting of the 1800s. **page 22**

Salvador Dalí [dah•LEE] (1904–1989) Spain, painter, sculptor. Dalí, a Surrealist, was born in the town of Figueras in the Catalan region of Spain. He had a studio at home when he was growing up. In 1921 he began his studies at the San Fernando Royal Academy of Fine Arts in Madrid. Many of the images in Dalí's work came from dreams. **page 54**

R8 ART EXPRESS

GALLERY OF ARTISTS

Leonardo da Vinci [dah VIN•chee] (1452–1519) Italy, painter, sculptor. Da Vinci was born in the town of Vinci near Florence, Italy. He was apprenticed to Andrea del Verrocchio, a leading painter and sculptor. In 1478 da Vinci went to work on his own. He was hired to do many paintings, and he became one of the greatest artists of the European Renaissance. **page 18**

Sonia Terk Delaunay [SOHN•yuh terk duh•loh•NAY] (1885–1979) Russia, painter. Delaunay was born in the Ukraine and moved to Paris to work among French painters. In 1964 she became the first living woman to have her work shown at the Louvre [LOOV] Museum. She created abstract images in which colors seemed to move rhythmically. **page 88**

Felix de Weldon (1907–) Austria, sculptor. De Weldon is the only artist in the world to have a monumental sculpture on every continent, including Antarctica. He has created more than 2,000 public works, including 33 in Washington, D.C. De Weldon modeled his *Marine Corps Memorial* sculpture on Joseph Rosenthal's famous photo of U.S. Marines raising the flag on Iwo Jima during World War II. **page 45**

David Diaz United States, illustrator. Diaz, of Rancho La Costa, California, has won many awards, including the highest honor in children's book illustration, the Caldecott Medal. His books include *Neighborhood Odes*, *Smoky Night*, and *Going Home*. **pages 80–81**

James Montgomery Flagg (1877–1960) United States, painter, illustrator. Flagg, born in Pelham Manor, New York, was an American illustrator and poster designer. He worked for several magazines, including *St. Nicholas* and the *Saturday Evening Post*. Flagg also drew caricatures of famous people and painted portraits. **page 48**

Flor Garduño (1957–) Mexico, photographer. Garduño studied at the San Carlos School of Fine Arts in Mexico City. She now travels around Mexico seeking subjects for her photographs and creating a photographic record of Mexico's culture and heritage. **page 94**

Liliana Wilson Grez United States, painter. Grez studied printmaking and painting at Southwest Texas State University from 1990 to 1993. She won first prize in the Ninth Annual Juried Women's Art Exhibit in San Antonio, Texas, and has had her work shown in museums that include the Guadalupe Cultural Arts Center in San Antonio. **page 69**

James Gurney (1958–) United States, author, illustrator. Gurney, the youngest of five children, grew up in Palo Alto, California. He was introduced to dinosaurs when he went to visit a San Francisco museum as a child. By the time he was in high school, Gurney knew he would be an artist. Gurney is both the author and the illustrator of the *Dinotopia* series. **pages 62–63**

Nachum Gutman (1898–1981) Russia, mosaic artist. Gutman was born in Russia and moved to Palestine (Israel) with his family when he was seven. His first one-person show was held at the Bezalel National Museum in Jerusalem in 1933. His work has been shown in museums and galleries around the world. **page 42**

Carol Guzy United States, photographer. Guzy is a photographer for the *Washington Post* newspaper. While studying at the Art Institute of Fort Lauderdale in Florida, she worked as an intern at the *Miami Herald*. Guzy went on to win the Pulitzer Prize for her photography. **page 98**

David Hockney (1937–) England, mixed-media artist. Hockney studied at the Bradford College of Art in England. His first exhibit was in 1963, when he was only twenty-six. In addition to painting, Hockney has designed sets and costumes for operas. He now concentrates on photography. **page 78**

Winslow Homer (1836–1910) United States, painter. Homer was born in Boston, Massachusetts. He was apprenticed to a printer when he was eighteen. When he completed this apprenticeship, he became a freelance illustrator and moved to New York. He traveled widely during his lifetime and painted many different scenes. **page 39**

Edward Hopper (1882–1967) United States, painter. Hopper was an American painter who worked mostly in New York. He made three trips to Europe, but they had little effect on his artistic style. From 1913 until 1923 he stopped painting and began to make a living as a commercial illustrator. When he took up painting again, he became famous for the way he showed his view of life in America. **page 18**

Yusaku Kamekura [yoo•SAH•koo kah•meh•KOO•ruh] (1915–) Japan, graphic designer. Kamekura was born in Japan. He has designed many books, magazines, symbols, and neon signs. His most widely known works in the United States have been the emblem and posters for the 1960 Olympic Games in Tokyo. **page 49**

Jacob Lawrence (1917–) United States, painter. Lawrence was born in Atlantic City, New Jersey. At age fifteen he decided to become a painter. One of his most famous works, *The Migration of the Negro*, includes his parents as models. In 1941 Lawrence became the first African American artist represented in the permanent collection of the Museum of Modern Art. **page 44**

René Magritte [ruh•NAY muh•GREET] (1898–1967) Belgium, painter. Magritte studied at the Academe des Beaux-Arts in Brussels, Belgium, where he was exposed to many art movements, such as Cubism, Futurism, and Symbolism. He found his own unique style and is today among the best known of the Surrealist painters. **page 68**

Stanley Marsh 3 United States, sculptor. Marsh, a Texas millionaire Pop artist, created what he called "the world's largest soft pool table" on a farm outside Amarillo, Texas. Marsh offered a piece of land to a group of artists called the Ant Farm, and it is on this land that Cadillac Ranch is built. **page 71**

Homer Dodge Martin (1836–1897) United States, painter. Martin was born in New York and had a lifelong love of nature. Despite (or perhaps because of) being barely able to see, he studied nature constantly, making mental images of natural scenes and painting them. In his final years, he continued to paint even though he was almost completely blind. **page 28**

Henri Matisse [ahn•REE mah•TEES] (1869–1954) France, painter. Matisse was born in the Picardy region of France. He was the leader of the Fauvist movement in painting. He was active as an artist until the end of his life. When he was too weak to stand at an easel, he created papercuts. Many people consider him to be the most important French painter of the twentieth century. **pages 56, 79**

Florence McClung (1896–1992) United States, painter. McClung lived in Dallas from age three until her death. She was married to Rufus McClung, a cotton broker. She began to study art in 1927 and joined the Taos Society of Artists. McClung liked to paint scenes that could only be found in Texas. Her Texas landscapes brought her national attention. **page 77**

Michelangelo Buonarroti [bwoh•nar•RAH•tee] (1475–1564) Italy, painter, sculptor. Michelangelo was born in the small village of Caprese near Arezzo, Italy. His father arranged for him to work and study with the painter Domenico Ghirlandajo when he was just thirteen. By the time he was sixteen years old, Michelangelo had produced at least two relief sculptures. He went on to become one of the greatest artists of the European Renaissance, excelling in painting, sculpture, and architecture. **page 114**

Arthur Mole (1889–1947) United States, photographer. Mole began his career at the age of seventeen when he became the apprentice to a Chicago photographer. Just six months later, Mole started his own photography business. He is best known for his elaborate "living photography" tributes. **page 52**

Piet Mondrian [PEET MOHN•dree•ahn] (1872–1944) Netherlands, painter. Mondrian was born in the Netherlands. Along with several other Dutch artists, he created a style of nonrepresentational art that had a great influence on artists, architects, and designers. In his paintings, Mondrian wanted to show that people can live in harmony with the universe. **page 88**

Michael Naranjo [nah•RAHN•hoh] (1944–) United States, sculptor. Naranjo was born in Santa Clara Pueblo in New Mexico. He dreamed of being a sculptor but was blinded in an accident in the Vietnam War. Despite being blind, Naranjo decided to sculpt. He uses his memory of things he has seen to create figures out of wax or stone. **page 31**

Louise Nevelson (1899–1988) Russia, sculptor. Nevelson was born in Kiev, Russia. When she was six years old, her family moved to the United States. From 1929 to 1930 she studied at the Art Students League in New York. She worked as an assistant to artist Diego Rivera and had her first one-person show in 1941. **page 65**

Claes Oldenburg [KLAHS OHL•den•burg] (1929–) Sweden, sculptor. Oldenburg was born in Stockholm, Sweden, but his family moved to the United States when he was seven. He studied at the Art Institute of Chicago. He is married to artist Coosje van Bruggen, and has worked with her on several large-scale public projects. **page 70**

Gallery of Artists

Diana Ong (1940–) United States, multi-media. Ong studied at the National Academy of Art and the School of Visual Arts. Her work has been exhibited and sold in more than thirty countries and displayed on numerous book jackets. Ong works in several media including watercolor, acrylic, ceramic, and computer art. **page 84**

John Outterbridge (1933–) United States, sculptor. Outterbridge is an assemblage artist who was born in South Carolina. He often makes his sculptures out of the rusted steel and iron that his father collected throughout his lifetime. **page 64**

Nam June Paik (1932–) Korea, composer, video artist. Paik studied music and art history at Tokyo University. In the 1960s he was known as an electronic composer and producer of "action concerts." In 1964 he moved to New York and began making video art and TV sculptures. **page 112**

I. M. Pei (1917–) China, architect. Ieoh Ming Pei was born in Canton, China. He studied at Harvard University and later became an assistant professor at Harvard Graduate School of Design. His works include the Dallas City Hall building, the National Gallery of Art East building, and the Rock 'n' Roll Hall of Fame and Museum. **page 110**

Pablo Picasso (1881–1973) Spain, painter. Picasso was born in Málaga, Spain, and educated in Paris. He was one of the leaders of the twentieth-century art world. His works changed the way people thought about art. Picasso helped start a style of painting called Cubism. He was greatly influenced by African sculpture when he began painting in the Cubist style. **page 92**

Jerry Pinkney (1939–) United States, illustrator. Pinkney grew up in Philadelphia, Pennsylvania, and graduated from the Philadelphia Museum College of Art. His career began in commercial illustration—designing ads and greeting cards. His first book was a collection of West African folktales. Since then, he has won some of the highest awards in children's illustration. **page 12**

Horace Pippin (1888–1946) United States, painter. Pippin left school at the age of fourteen to work on a farm. He had no formal art training, but he began painting seriously after his right arm was partially paralyzed as a result of an injury in World War I. Many of his works show scenes from the Bible or from the daily life of African American families. **page 82**

Frederic Remington (1861–1909) United States, painter, sculptor. Remington was born in his grandmother's house in New York. During his career he produced over three thousand illustrations and paintings and twenty-two sculptures. Remington's work depicts the settling of the West. **page 14**

Betsy Graves Reyneau [ray•NOH] (1888–1964) United States, painter. Reyneau was born in Battle Creek, Michigan. She studied art all over the world including Boston, Paris, and Rome. Some of her portraits were featured in a national exhibition, and two of her works hang in the National Portrait Gallery in Washington, D.C. **page 36**

Bridget Riley (1931–) England, painter. Riley was born in London, England. She studied at Goldsmiths College of Art and at the Royal College of Art. She has traveled widely but continues to live and work in London. **page 58**

Diego Rivera (1886–1957) Mexico, painter. Rivera, a Mexican artist, is famous for his huge murals. Rivera was only ten years old when he began taking art courses at the Academy of San Carlos in Mexico City. He once said, "In my work, I tell the story of my nation, Mexico—its history, its Revolution, its amazing Indian past, and its present-day popular traditions." **pages 116–117**

Miriam Schapiro (1923–) Canada, painter. When Schapiro created *Heartland*, she drew on the tradition of American quilting. Much of her work is inspired by the talents of women, who for hundreds of years have expressed artistic abilities in the form of household crafts such as quilting, embroidering, and sewing. **page 125**

Jane Wooster Scott United States, painter. Scott was born in the small town of Havertown, Pennsylvania. She attended just one semester of college before moving to New York to work in television and movies. After she retired from acting, she began painting as a hobby. She began her professional painting career in 1973. **page 38**

George Segal (1924–) United States, sculptor, painter. Segal was operating a chicken farm when he first began painting. He started to experiment with sculpture in 1958, using wire netting. He has produced several public sculptures, including *The Rush Hour* in London. **page 103**

Gilbert Stuart (1755–1828) United States, painter. Stuart was born in Rhode Island before the United States became a nation. He painted several of our earliest Presidents. Stuart also created a very famous engraving—the relief portrait of George Washington that appears on the one-dollar bill. **page 36**

Robert Summers (1940–) United States, sculptor. Summers was born and raised in Glen Rose, Texas, and has created many sculptures throughout Texas and the United States. Summers is especially interested in depicting the lore of the West, which he enjoyed as a boy and has studied seriously as an adult. **page 32**

Wayne Thiebaud [TEE•boh] (1920–) United States, painter. Thiebaud was born in Mesa, Arizona, and held various art-related jobs in New York and California. He is best known for his texture paintings of ice cream, cakes, and hot dogs. **page 51**

Alma Woodsey Thomas (1891–1978) United States, educator, painter. Thomas was born in Columbus, Georgia. In 1924 she began teaching art at a junior high school. It was not until after she had retired from teaching that she had time to devote to painting. **page 89**

Coosje van Bruggen [KOOS•yeh van BROO•gen] (1942–) Netherlands, sculptor. Van Bruggen was born in Groningen in the Netherlands and earned a degree in art history from the University of Groningen. She began to work with Claes Oldenburg on such projects as *Trowel I* in 1976. She married Oldenburg in 1977. **page 70**

Vincent van Gogh [van GOH] (1853–1890) Netherlands, painter. Van Gogh was born in Zundert, Netherlands. He created about 800 paintings and drawings in only ten years, during which he suffered from severe mental illness. Next to Rembrandt, he is generally considered the greatest Dutch painter. **pages 24, 90**

Pablita Velarde (Hardin) [pah•LEET•uh vel•AHR•day] (1918–) United States, painter. Velarde, a Tewa artist, was born in Santa Clara Pueblo, New Mexico. She broke away from tradition by deciding to become a painter, a career that only men were expected to choose. Her paintings show the traditions of her people. She is also the author of a book of Tewa legends. **page 122**

Andy Warhol (1928–1987) United States, painter. Warhol was born in McKeesport, Pennsylvania. He studied at the Carnegie Technical College and then worked as a commercial illustrator and store window designer in New York. He was one of the leaders of the Pop Art movement. **page 50**

Anna Belle Lee Washington United States, painter. Washington, the oldest of seven children, grew up in Detroit, Michigan. Her first job was as a social services clerk. Many years later, she moved to St. Simons Island, Georgia, to retire. Instead she began a new career, starting by taking drawing and painting lessons at the Coastal Center for the Arts there. **page 23**

Leah Ann Washington United States, photographer. Washington was born in New Orleans, Louisiana, where her mother owned and operated a photographic studio. She attended Brooks Institute of Photography and became the school's first African American woman graduate. Both of her brothers are photographers as well. **page 99**

Frank Lloyd Wright (1867–1959) United States, architect. Wright was born in Wisconsin and created buildings all over the world. He attended the University of Wisconsin. Some of his most famous works include the Guggenheim Museum in New York and the Madison Convention Center in Wisconsin. **page 111**

Andrew Wyeth (1917–) United States, painter. Andrew is the son of N. C. Wyeth, a famous illustrator. Like his father, Andrew developed a love of nature, a sense of romance, and great artistic ability. His work is a combination of abstract style and realistic detail. **page 74**

Lance Wyman (1937–) United States, designer. Wyman was born in Newark, New Jersey. He studied design at the Pratt Institute in Brooklyn, New York. His works include the first postage stamp honoring Dr. Martin Luther King, Jr.; maps for the Washington, D.C., Metro train system; and posters for the World Cup of Soccer, held at Mexico City in 1971. **page 49**

GLOSSARY

The Glossary contains important art terms and their definitions. Each word is respelled as it would be in a dictionary. When you see this mark (´) after a syllable, pronounce that syllable with more force than the other syllables.

add, āce, câre, pälm; end, ēqual; it, īce; odd, ōpen, ôrder; tōōk, pōōl; up, bûrn; yōō as *u* in *fuse*; oil; pout; ə as *a* in *above*, *e* in *sicken*, *i* in *possible*, *o* in *melon*, *u* in *circus*; check; ring; thin; **th**is; zh as in *vision*

A

abstract [ab´strakt] A style of art that does not show a scene in a realistic way. Abstract art uses the elements and principles of design to convey ideas and feelings.

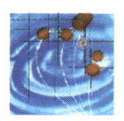

abstract

advance [ad•vans´] To move forward—speaking of a background color that seems to jump outward. (*See also* recede.)

analogous colors [ə•na´lə•gəs kəl´ərz] Colors that are closely related and near each other on the color wheel. Families of analogous colors include the warm colors (reds, oranges, and yellows) and the cool colors (greens, blues, and violets). (*See also* cool colors, warm colors.)

animation [a•nə•mā´shən] The art of making objects, such as drawings of cartoon characters, appear to move; making a motion picture using still drawings or objects. (*See also* frame.)

arbitrary colors [är´bə•trer•ē kəl´ərz] Colors that go beyond what is natural or common in a scene.

arch [ärch] A curved structure over an opening such as a door or window.

assemblage [ə•sem´blij] A piece of art made by combining a collection of three-dimensional objects.

asymmetry, asymmetrical [ā•si´mə•trē, ā•sə•me´tri•kəl] Having a kind of balance in which things on each side of a center line are different, but still look balanced. (*See also* balance, symmetry.)

atmospheric perspective [at•məs•fir´ik pər•spek´tiv] The illusion of depth and distance created by using dull, pale colors and hazy details in the background of a painting. (*See also* perspective.)

B

background [bak´ground] The part of a work of art that appears to be in the back, farthest away from the viewer. (*See also* foreground, middle ground.)

balance [ba´ləns] The arrangement of elements in a work of art; how important the elements in one part are compared to those in other parts. (*See also* asymmetry, symmetry.)

brushstroke [brush´strōk] The application of paint with a paintbrush. Also, the look of paint that has been applied with a paintbrush.

C

center of interest [sen´tər əv in´trest] The most important area in a work of art. All other parts should center around, provide background for, or draw attention to this area.

cityscape [si´tē•skāp] A painting or drawing showing a view of a city.

cityscape

collage [kə•läzh´] A work of art created by gluing bits of paper, fabric, scraps, photographs, or other materials to a flat surface.

collage

color [kəl´ər] The visual sensation produced when different wavelengths of light strike the eye.

complementary colors [kom•plə•men´tə•rē kəl´ərz] Colors that are opposite on the color wheel and that contrast with each other. Pairs of complementary colors include orange/blue and violet/yellow.

composition [kom•pə•zi´shən] The arrangement or design of elements in an artwork.

contrast [kon´trast] A notable difference between two things; for example, light and shadow. (*See also* complementary colors.)

cool colors [kōōl kəl´ərz] The family of related colors ranging from the greens through the violets. (*See also* analogous colors, warm colors.)

D

cross-hatching [krôs´ha•ching] Shading done by drawing closely set parallel lines that cross one another.

daguerreotype [də•ge´rō•tīp] An early form of photography.

depth [depth] The apparent distance from front to back or from near to far in an artwork.

detail [di•tāl´] A small, often less important feature of a person or an object.

diagonal [dī•a´gə•nəl] Slanting between horizontal and vertical. (*See also* line.)

diorama [dī•ə•ra´mə] A scene, usually smaller than in real life, in which three-dimensional models are displayed against a realistic painted background.

diorama

E

emphasis [em´fə•sis] The drawing of attention to important areas or objects in a work of art.

Expressionists [ik•spre´shə•nists] Artists who used a style of art that stresses emotion over realism in proportion, color, and so on.

expressive [ik•spre´siv] Showing feelings or ideas.

F

flip book [flip bōōk] A simple form of animation in which pages of drawings are flipped through by hand to create the illusion of movement. (*See also* animation.)

flip book

focus [fō´kəs] The clearest possible image seen through a camera lens.

folk artists [fōk ärt´ists] People who create traditional art using styles and techniques that have been handed down through generations.

F (cont.)

foreground [fôr´ground] The part of a work of art that appears to be in the front, nearest to the viewer. (*See also* background, middle ground.)

foreshortened [fôr•shôr´tənd] Drawn or painted in a way that shows length or depth. For example, to make an object that is pointing at the viewer seem lifelike, the artist shortens its length. (*See also* perspective.)

form [fôrm] A three-dimensional unit in an artwork, such as a cube.

form

frame [frām] A border that encloses an artwork. Also, one of a set of many still pictures, each slightly different, created for an animated cartoon or movie.

G

geometric [jē•ə•me´trik] Based on simple shapes such as rectangles, triangles, circles, straight lines, or sharp, angled designs.

H

harmony [här´mə•nē] An orderly, pleasing state, such as when colors or objects blend well together in an artwork.

hatching [ha´ching] Shading done by drawing tiny, closely set parallel lines.

highlighting [hī´lī•ting] Using color to draw attention to or to emphasize.

horizon [hə•rī´zən] A level line where water or land seems to end and the sky begins.

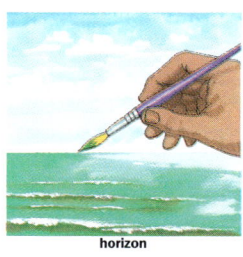

horizon

horizontal symmetry [hôr´ə•zon•təl si´mə•trē] A condition in which the top and the bottom of a picture or object are alike.

GLOSSARY

illuminated pages

illuminated pages [i•lōō′mə•nā•təd pāj′əz] Pages having fancy designs and pictures, often decorated with gold or silver to make them look as if they are lit up.

illusions [i•lōō′zhənz] False impressions, such as those brought about by artistic techniques or by nature.

impasto [im•pas′tō] A technique in which thick paint is applied in layers, creating a heavily textured appearance.

Impressionists [im•pre′shə•nists] Artists of the late 1800s and early 1900s who showed nature in new ways. They often used dots and strokes of bright colors in their paintings. Many Impressionists concentrated on showing the effects of light on people and objects.

incising [in•sī′zing] Cutting or carving a design into clay objects.

incising

intermediate colors [in•tər•mē′dē•ət kəl′ərz] A color created by mixing a primary color with a secondary color. Sometimes called a tertiary color. (*See also* primary colors, secondary colors.)

landscape [land′skāp] A painting or drawing showing a view of a natural scene, such as mountains, rivers, flowers, fields, or forests.

line [līn] A slender, continuous mark moving through space that can vary in length, width, direction, shape, and color.

linear perspective [li′nē•ər pər•spek′tiv] The use of converging lines to show depth and distance in a picture. Lines that are parallel in nature, such as railroad tracks, come together at the vanishing point in a picture. (*See also* perspective.)

material [mə•tir′ē•əl] Basic substance from which other things are made. Clay, plaster of Paris, and wood are examples of art materials.

middle ground [mi′dəl ground] The part of a work of art that lies between the foreground and the background. (*See also* foreground, background.)

minarets

minarets [mi′nə•retz′] Slender towers with one or more balconies, attached to a mosque.

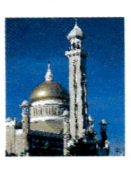

minarets

mixed-media [mikst•mē′dē•ə] A term used to describe an artwork that uses two or more media, such as painting and collage.

mobile [mō′bēl] A type of sculpture in which objects are suspended and balanced so that they move with currents of air.

mood [mōōd] An overall feeling or emotion.

mosaics [mō•zā′iks] Artworks made by fitting small pieces of colored paper, glass, tile, stone, or other similar materials, called *tesserae*, onto a background.

movement [mōōv′mənt] The arrangement of elements in an artwork to create a sense of motion.

mural [myōōr′əl] A very large painting done on a wall.

mural

negative space [ne′gə•tiv spās] The empty space surrounding shapes or forms in a work of art. (*See also* positive space, space.)

nonrepresentational [non•re•pri•zen•tā′shə•nəl] A style of art that does not show recognizable objects.

Op Art [op ärt] An abstract style of art, based on visual illusions, that was popular in the 1960s.

optical illusion [op′ti•kəl i•lōō′zhən] A vision, human-made or natural, that tricks the eye and the brain.

organic [ôr•ga′nik] Having a quality that resembles living things. Also, having a flowing, rounded shape.

ornamentation [ôr•nə•men•tā′shən] The use of details or items such as jewelry to create a beautiful appearance.

overlapping [ō′vər•lap•ing] A technique in which one shape in a painting covers up some part of another. Since partly covered objects appear to be farther away, this technique is used to show distance.

180 / 181

papier-mâché

papier-mâché [pā•pər•mə•shā′] An art material made of paper torn into strips or made into pulp and mixed with paste.

pattern [pa′tərn] The repetition of shapes, lines, or colors in a design.

perspective [pər•spek′tiv] The art of drawing three-dimensional objects on a two-dimensional surface. Perspective is achieved by creating the illusion of depth and distance. Two types of perspective are *atmospheric* and *linear*.

photogram [fō′tə•gram] A technique for producing an image by placing an object on light-sensitive paper and exposing the paper to light. Sometimes called a sun print.

photomontage [fō•tə•mon•täzh′] Photographs that are arranged into one picture expressing a single theme.

photomontage

Pop Art [pop ärt] A style of art—based on popular foods, fads, and brand names—made famous in New York in the 1950s.

porcelain [pôr′sə•lən] A fine-grained, hard type of clay used to make dishes, vases, and small statues.

portrait [pôr′trət] A painting, photograph, or other work of art showing a person. Portraits usually show only the face but can include part or all of the body as well.

portrait

pose [pōz] The position of a subject for a portrait or photograph. (*See also* portrait.)

positive space [pä′zə•tiv spās] The solid shape of an object in a work of art. (*See also* negative space, space.)

primary colors [prī′mer•ē kəl′ərz] The colors—red, yellow, and blue—that in different combinations produce all other colors except white. (*See also* intermediate colors, secondary colors.)

proportions [prə•pôr′shənz] The relationships of placement and size among objects in a composition.

quilts [kwilts] Bedcovers made by sewing scraps of cloth together.

recede

recede [ri•sēd′] To move backward—speaking of foreground colors that seem to move back. (*See also* advance.)

relative size [re′lə•tiv sīz] The size of an object when compared to the objects around it.

rhythm [ri′thəm] The regular repetition of lines, shapes, colors, or patterns in a work of art.

scale [skāl] The size of an object in an artwork compared to its original size. If a picture is drawn *to scale*, all of its parts are equally smaller or larger than the original.

score [skôr] To mark by scratching or cutting.

sculpture [skulp′chər] A carving, model, or other three-dimensional piece of art.

secondary colors [se′kən•der•ē kəl′ərz] The colors—orange, green, and violet—created by combining two of the three primary colors. Orange is a mixture of red and yellow. Green is a mixture of blue and yellow. Violet is a mixture of red and blue. (*See also* intermediate colors, primary colors.)

shades [shādz] Darker variations of a color made by mixing black with the color. For example, black added to red makes a darker *shade* of red. (*See also* tints.)

shape [shāp] A two-dimensional unit in an artwork, such as a square.

sketch [skech] A simple, quick drawing done to catch the chief features and a general impression of an object or a scene.

sketch

slab method [slab me′thəd] A method of making pottery in which a thick, flat plate or slice of clay is cut into shapes that are then joined together to form an object.

slip [slip] A creamy mixture of clay and water or vinegar used to cement together two pieces of clay, such as a handle on a cup.

space [spās] The distance, area, or depth shown in a work of art. Also, the open areas between or inside shapes.

spires [spīrz] Pointed tops of towers or church steeples.

spires

182 / 183

R12 ART EXPRESS

Glossary

statues [sta´chooz] Free-standing carved, modeled, or sculpted three-dimensional figures, especially of a person or an animal.

storytelling [stôr´ē•tel•ing] The technique of adding a narrative to a work of art such as a mural or a quilt.

Surrealism [sə•rē´ə•li•zəm] An art movement, beginning in the 1920s, that emphasized images from the unconscious mind, such as from dreams. Surrealists mixed and matched real objects in unusual or impossible combinations, but painted objects in a realistic way.

symbols [sim´bəlz] Things that stand for other things, such as a dove that represents peace.

symmetry, symmetrical [si´mə•trē, sə•me´tri•kəl] Having a kind of balance in which things on each side of a center line or around a central point appear the same. (See also asymmetry, balance.)

synthetic [sin•the´tik] A human-made material. Something that is not created naturally, such as plastic and steel.

tempera [tem´pə•rə] Water-soluble paint that does not allow light to pass through. Also called poster paint.

tesserae [te´sə•rē] The individual pieces used to make a mosaic. (See also mosaics.)

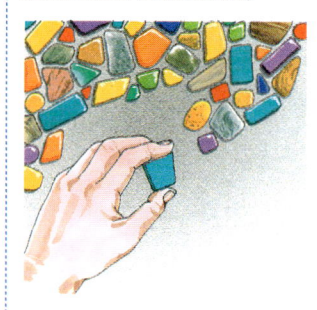

tesserae

texture [teks´chər] The way a surface looks or feels—rough, smooth, silky, shiny, or dull.

theme [thēm] The subject or main idea in an artistic work.

three-dimensional [thrē•də•men´shə•nəl] Having length, width, and depth. A sculpture is three-dimensional, but a drawing is two-dimensional. (See also two-dimensional.)

tints [tints] Lighter variations of a color made by adding white to the color. For example, white added to blue makes a lighter blue *tint*. (See also shades.)

trompe l'oeil [trômp•loi´] An image that appears to be real rather than painted. *Trompe l'oeil* is French for "tricks the eye."

two-dimensional [too•də•men´shə•nəl] Having length and width, but not depth; flat. Paintings and drawings are examples of two-dimensional art forms. (See also three-dimensional.)

type [tīp] A style of printing.

unity [yoo´nə•tē] A quality of oneness, or a pleasing sense, achieved by connecting all the different elements in an artwork.

value [val´yoo] The lightness or darkness of colors. For example, white and yellow have a light value; black and purple have a dark value.

vanishing point [va´ni•shing point] In linear perspective, the place on the horizon where parallel lines appear to meet or converge. The part of the art that looks farthest away. (See also perspective.)

variety [və•rī´ə•tē] An assortment of lines, colors, forms, shapes, textures, or other elements in a work of art.

vertical symmetry [vər´ti•kəl si´mə•trē] A condition in which the left and right sides of a picture or an object are matched.

warm colors [wärm kəl´ərz] The family of related colors ranging from the reds through the browns. (See also analogous colors, cool colors.)

watercolor [wô´tər•kəl•ər] A transparent paint made by mixing powdered colors with a binding material, such as glue, and water. The term also refers to a painting done with watercolors.

weaving [wē´ving] The process of turning thread or yarn into cloth. Artwork created by lacing together fibers—such as threads or yarn—on a loom.

weaving

Artists & Artworks

George Ancona	from *Spanish Pioneers of the Southwest* 101
Richard Anuszkiewicz	*Plus Reversed* 59
Frédéric-Auguste Bartholdi	*Liberty Enlightening the World* 44
Barbara Bash	from *Tree of Life: The World of the African Baobab* 21
Behzad	*Old Man and Youth in Landscape* 97
Thomas Hart Benton	*Trail Riders* 76
Selma Burke	*Franklin Delano Roosevelt* 34
Alexander Calder	*Horse and Rider* 30, *Untitled* 83
Mary Cassatt	*Summertime* 28
Christo and Jeanne-Claude	*Surrounded Islands, Biscayne Bay* 72
Thomas Cole	*The Oxbow* 22
Salvador Dali	*Clothed Automobile* 54
Leonardo da Vinci	*A Spray of a Plant* 18
Sonia Terk Delaunay	*Rhythme Colore* 88
Felix W. de Weldon	*The Marine Corps Memorial* 45
David Diaz	from "*La Bamba*" 80-81
James Montgomery Flagg	*Uncle Sam Wants You* 48
Flor Garduño	*Basket of Light* 94
Liliana Wilson Grez	*Niña con su pescado rojo* 69
James Gurney	from *Dinotopia* 62-63
Nachum Gutman	*Shalom Mayer Tower* 42
Carol Guzy	*A Child's Brilliant Smile* 98
David Hockney	*Nichols Canyon* 78
Winslow Homer	*The Country School* 39
Edward Hopper	*The Lighthouse at Two Lights* 18
Yusaku Kamekura	*Tokyo Olympic Games* 49
Jacob Lawrence	from *The Migration Series* 44
René Magritte	*The Castle in the Pyrenees* 68
Stanley Marsh	*Cadillac Ranch* 71
Homer Dodge Martin	*Harp of the Winds: View of the Seine* 28
Henri Matisse	*The Swimmer in the Pool* 56, *The Toboggan* 79
Florence McClung	*Squaw Creek Valley* 77
Michelangelo	*Moses* 114
Arthur Mole	*The Living American Flag* 52
Piet Mondrian	*Broadway Boogie Woogie* 88
Michael Naranjo	*Skyward, My Friend* 31
Louise Nevelson	*Royal Tide IV* 65
Claes Oldenburg	*Spoonbridge and Cherry* 70
Diana Ong	*Confusion of Shapes* 84
John Outterbridge	*California Crosswalk* 64
Nam June Paik	*Electronic Superhighway* 112
Charles Willson Peale	*Staircase Group* 60
I. M. Pei	*The Grand Louvre* 110
Pablo Picasso	*Three Musicians* 92
Jerry Pinkney	from *In for Winter, Out for Spring* 12
Horace Pippin	*Victorian Interior* 82
Frederic Remington	*The Fall of the Cowboy* 14
Betsy Graves Reyneau	*Mary McLeod Bethune* 36
Bridget Riley	*Suspension* 58
Diego Rivera	*Detroit Industry* 116-117
Miriam Schapiro	*Heartland* 125
Jane Wooster Scott	*A Really Swell Parade Down Main Street* 38
George Segal	*Blue Girl on Park Bench* 103
Gilbert Stuart	*George Washington* 36
Robert Summers	*Pioneer Plaza* 32
Wayne Thiebaud	*Untitled* 51
Alma Woodsey Thomas	*Atmospheric Effects II* 89
Coosje van Bruggen	*Spoonbridge and Cherry* 70
Vincent van Gogh	*Avenue of the Alyscamps* 24, *The Starry Night* 90
Pablita Velarde (Hardin)	*Her First Dance* 122
Andy Warhol	*Peach Halves* 50
Anna Belle Lee Washington	*Gould's Inlet* 23
Leah Washington	*Point Lobos, at Carmel, California* 99
Frank Lloyd Wright	*The Solomon R. Guggenheim Museum* 111
Andrew Wyeth	*Faraway* 74
Lance Wyman	*Mexico City Olympic Games* 49

INDEX

A
Abstract, 42-43, 176
Activities
  See Production activities.
Adobe, 120-121
Analogous colors, 76-77, 81, 176
Animation, 104-105, 106-107, 176
Arbitrary colors, 85, 176
Arch, 108, 176
Architecture, 108-109, 110-111, 120-121
Art and Culture
  African Adobe Architecture, 120-121
  Magazine Art, 40-41
Art and Literature
  The Lively Art of David Diaz, 80-81
  The Natural Art of Barbara Bash, 20-21
  The Photographic Art of George Ancona, 100-101
Artists
  See Gallery of Artists, Index of Artists and Artworks.
Artworks
  See Index of Artists and Artworks.
Assemblage, 64-65, 176
Asymmetrical balance, 82, 176
Atmospheric perspective, 22, 176

B
Background, 22-23, 177
Balance, 82-83, 93, 165, 177
Book design
  The Book of Lindisfarne, 96
  illuminated page from the *Haggadah,* 96
Brushstroke, 28-29, 177

C
Careers in Art
  Computer Animator, 106-107
  Set Designer, 26-27
Celebration Art
  Tournament of Roses Parade, 86-87
Center of interest, 98-99, 113, 177
Ceramics
  porcelain, 118, 182
  slip, 118-119, 183
Cityscape, 91, 177
Clay, 119, 144-147
  Making a clay relief, 147
  Modeling, 145
  Using coils, 147
  Using slabs, 146
Collage, 57, 85, 124, 177
Color, 158, 177
  advancing, 78, 176
  analogous, 76, 176
  arbitrary, 85, 176
  complementary, 59, 79, 177
  contrast, 78-79, 177
  intermediate, 180
  primary, 182
  receding, 78, 183
  secondary, 183
  shades, 77, 183
  tints, 77, 184
  value, 19, 158, 185
  warm/cool, 39, 62, 177, 185
Community Art
  The Artrain, 126-127
  Heroic Statues, 46-47
  The Power of Art, 66-67
Complementary colors, 59, 79, 177
Computers, 104-105, 106-107
Constructing and Modeling Three-Dimensional Forms, 31, 63, 65, 71, 83, 103, 111, 119, 131
  See also Production activities.
Contrast, 78-79, 177
Cool colors, 39, 177
Cross-hatching, 178

D
Dance
  Ballet Folklórico, 132-133
Depth, 178
  See also Perspective.
Diagonal lines, 30, 178
Diorama, 63, 178
Displaying, 150-151
  Art prints, 150
  Sculptures, 151
Distance, 22-23
Drawing, 17, 19, 25, 37, 79, 109, 136-139
  Contour drawing, 137
  Contours and tones, 139
  Gesture drawing, 136
  Tonal drawing, 138
  See also Production activities.

E
Elements of Art
  Color, 19, 39, 59, 62, 76-79, 84-85, 158, 177
  Form, 18-19, 110-111, 157, 179
  Line, 16-17, 30, 79, 90-91, 154, 180
  Shape, 56-57, 76-77, 124, 156, 183
  Space, 56-57, 159, 183
   See also Perspective.
  Texture, 16, 50-51, 155, 184
  Value, 19, 158, 185
Emphasis, 36, 161, 178
Evaluating Art, 10-11, 32-33, 52-53, 72-73, 92-93, 112-113, 132-133
Everyday Art
  Can You Believe Your Eyes?, 60-61
Exploring Art Techniques, 136-151
Expressionists, 91, 178
Expressive, 91, 178

F
Flip book, 105, 178
Focus, 98, 178
Folk artists, 130-131, 178
Foreground, 22-23, 179
Foreshortened, 48, 179
Form, 18, 110, 157, 179
Frame, 98-99, 113, 179
Frames, 104-105

G
Gallery of Artists, 166-175
Geometric shapes, 16-17, 179
Glossary, 176-185

H
Harmony, 74-75, 76-77, 93, 179
Hatching, 18-19, 179
Highlighting, 19, 179
Home and community design, 43, 49, 125
  Community Art, 46-47, 66-67, 126-127
  See also Production activities.
Horizon, 25, 179
Horizontal symmetry, 29, 179

I
Illuminated pages, 96-97, 180
Illusions, 22-23, 32-33, 58-59, 60-61, 180
Impasto painting, 50-51, 180
Impressionists, 28-29, 180
Incising, 118-119, 180
Index of Artists and Artworks, 186-187
In the Studio
  See Production activities.

J
Jewelry, 128-129

K
Keeping a Sketchbook, 12-13

L
Landscape, 91, 180
Line, 16-17, 30, 79, 90-91, 154, 180
Linear perspective, 25, 180
Literature
  "La Bamba," by Gary Soto, illustrated by David Diaz, 80-81
  Spanish Pioneers of the Southwest, by Joan Anderson, photographed by George Ancona, 100-101
  Tree of Life: The World of the African Baobab, by Barbara Bash, 20-21
Looking at Art, 10-11

M
Magazine art, 40-41
Manipulating Fibers, 123, 125
  See also Production activities.
Masks, 130-131
Material, 70, 102-103, 180
Middle ground, 22-23, 180
Minarets, 109, 181
Mixed-Media, 131, 181
Mobile, 82-83, 181
Model, 37, 111
Mood, 38, 181
Mosaics, 42-43, 181
Movement, 30-31, 33, 78-79, 80-81, 163, 181
Mural, 42, 60-61, 66-67, 116-117, 181

N
Negative space, 56-57, 181
Nonrepresentational art, 42-43, 88-89, 181

O
Op Art, 58, 181
Optical illusion, 58-59, 181
Organic shape, 16-17, 181
Ornamentation, 128, 181
Overlapping, 23, 181

P
Painting, 29, 39, 51, 69, 77, 91, 117, 140-143
  Tempera, 140-141, 184
  Watercolor, 142-143, 185
  See also Production activities.
Papier mâché, 71, 182
Patchwork, 124-125
Pattern, 88-89, 93, 162, 182
  geometric, 125
Perspective, 22-23, 25, 182
Photogram, 99, 182
  See also Production activities.
Photography, 45, 52-53, 98-99, 100-101
Photomontage, 45, 182
Pop Art, 50-51, 182
Porcelain, 118, 182
Portraits, 36-37, 182
Pose, 36-37, 182
Positive space, 56-57, 182
Posters, 48-49
Primary colors, 182
Principles of design
  Balance, 82-83, 93, 165, 177
  Emphasis, 36, 161, 178
  Movement and Rhythm, 30-31, 33, 78-81, 88-89, 93, 163, 181, 183
  Pattern, 88-89, 93, 162, 182
  Proportion, 37, 68, 164, 182
  Unity, 50, 64, 160, 185
  Variety, 50, 160, 185
Printmaking, 89, 148-149
  Collograph prints, 148
  Multicolor prints, 149
  See also Production activities.
Production activities
  Creating an Assemblage, 65
  Creating a Flip Book, 105
  Creating an Impasto Painting, 51
  Creating a Mixed-Media Mask, 131
  Creating a Mobile, 83
  Creating a Patchwork Wall Hanging, 125
  Designing a Book Cover, 97
  Designing a Persuasive Poster, 49
  Drawing Everyday Forms, 19
  Drawing Organic and Geometric Shapes, 17
  Drawing a Portrait, 37
  Experimenting with Colors, 59
  Making a Collage, 85
  Making a Diorama, 63
  Making a Foil Model, 111
  Making Impossible Paintings, 69
  Making Jewelry, 129
  Making a Mosaic, 43
  Making a Papier-Mâché Model, 71
  Making a Photogram, 99
  Making a Photomontage, 45
  Making a Print with Visual Rhythm, 89
  Making a Scale Drawing, 109
  Making a Wire Sculpture, 31
  Painting a Landscape, 91
  Painting a Mural, 117
  Painting the Past, 39
  Painting a Reflection, 29
  Painting with Watercolors, 77
  Sculpting a Slab Pot, 119
  Sculpting with Two Materials, 103
  Showing Contrast and Movement, 79
  Showing Depth, 23
  Using Linear Perspective, 25
  Using Positive and Negative Space, 57
  Weaving a Bookmark, 123
Proportion, 37, 68, 164, 182

Q
Quilts, 124-125, 182

R
Review, 32-33, 52-53, 72-73, 92-93, 112-113, 132-133
Rhythm, 88-89, 93, 163, 183

S
Safety, 134-135
Scale, 45, 70, 183
Scale drawing, 108-109
Sculpture, 16-17, 30-31, 32-33, 44-47, 64-65, 70-71, 102-103, 114-115, 183
Secondary colors, 183
Shades, 77, 183
Shadows, 18-19
Shape, 16-17, 76-77, 125, 156, 183
Sketch, 12-13, 183
Slab method, 119, 183
Slip, 118-119, 183
Space, 56-57, 159, 183
  See also Perspective.
Spire, 108, 183
Statues, 44-45, 46-47, 184
Storytelling, 42, 107, 116-117, 184
Surrealism, 68-69, 184
Symbols, 36, 44, 53, 184
Symmetry, 29, 82-83, 97, 179, 184

T
Techniques, 136-151
  See also Production activities.
Tempera, 140-141, 184
Tesserae, 42-43, 184
Texture, 16, 50-51, 155, 184
Theater, 26-27
Theme, 116, 184
Three-dimensional, 18-19, 184
  See also Perspective, Sculpture.
Tints, 77, 184
Two-dimensional, 18-19, 185
Type, 48, 185

U
Unity, 50, 64, 160, 185

V
Value, 19, 185
Vanishing point, 24-25, 185
Variety, 50, 160, 185

W
Warm colors, 39, 62, 185
Watercolor, 77, 142-143, 185
Weaving, 122-123, 185

ACKNOWLEDGMENTS

PHOTO CREDITS

Cover
Superstock

Table of Contents:
Harcourt Brace & Company
6, Weronica Ankarorn; 7, Weronica Ankarorn.

Other
5(l), Steve Helbert/AP/Wide World Photos; 5(r), Corbis-Bettmann; 8(l), Michael Holford; 8(r), Reunion des Musees Nationaux; 9, Scala/Art Resource, NY.

Front Matter:
11,Richard Nowitz; 12-13, From In for Winter, Out for Spring by Arnold Adoff, illustrated by Jerry Pinkney. Harcourt Brace & Company. Sketch courtesy of Jerry Pinkney;

Unit 1:
Harcourt Brace & Company
17(c)&(b),Weronica Ankarorn; 19(b), Weronica Ankarorn; 23(c)&(b), Weronica Ankarorn; 25(t)&(b), Weronica Ankarorn; 29(ct&b)(b), Weronica Ankarorn; 31(ct&b)(b), Weronica Ankarorn; 33, Weronica Ankarorn.

Other
14, Frederic S. Remington, The Fall of the Cowboy, 1895, oil on canvas, 1961.230. Copyright Amon Carter Museum, Fort Worth, Texas; 16, Giraudon/Art Resource, NY; 17(t), Catalogue No. 234314, Department of Anthropology, Smithsonian Institution; 18(t), The Royal Collection (c) Her Majesty Queen Elizabeth II; 18(b), The Metropolitan Museum of Art, Hugo Kastor Fund, 1962. (62.95); 20, Courtesy, Barbara Bash; 21, From Tree of Life: The World of the African Baobab by Barbara Bash. Little, Brown & Company; 22, The Metropolitan Museum of Art, Gift of Mrs. Russell Sage, 1908. (08.228); 23(t), Superstock; 24, Christie's Images/ Superstock; 26, courtesy, Bob Phillips; 27(all), courtesy, Bob Phillips; 28(t) The Armand Hammer Collection, UCLA at the Armand Hammer Museum of Art and Cultural Center, Los Angeles, CA; 28(b), The Metropolitan Museum of Art, Gift of Several Gentlemen, 1897. (97.32); 29(t), Courtesy, Ping Wang; 30 Photo Galerie Maeght, Paris; 31(t), Mark Nohl; 32, Jeff Shaw/Mercury Pictures.

Unit 2:
Harcourt Brace & Company
37(all), Weronica Ankarorn; 40, Weronica Ankarorn; 41(both), Weronica Ankarorn; 45(b), Weronica Ankarorn; 49(b), Weronica Ankarorn; 51(b), Weronica Ankarorn; 53, Weronica Ankarorn.

Other
34, Wide World Photos; 35, FDR Library; 36(l), White House Historical Association; 36(r), National Portrait Gallery, Gift of the Harmon Foundation, Smithsonian Institution/Art Resource, NY; 38, Collection of Mr. and Mrs. Ernest Borgnine/Superstock; 39, The Saint Louis Art Museum; 42, Eddie Gerald/Documentary Photography; 43, Scala/Art Resource,NY; 44(l), Robert Rathe/Folio; 44(r), Jacob Lawrence, "The Migrants Arrived in Great Numbers" Panel 40 from the Migration Series. Photograph © 1998 The Museum of Modern Art, New York; 45(t), Peter Gridley/FPG; 46, Philip & Karen Smith/Tony Stone Images; 47(l), Chris Kleponis/Woodfin Camp & Associates; 47(r), Steve Helbert/AP/Wide World Photos; 48, Corbis-Bettmann; 49(tl), ©IOC/Olympic Museum Collection; 49(tr), ©IOC/Olympic Museum Collections; 50, Staadsgalerie, Stuttgart; 51(t), Wayne Thiebaud; 52, Mole & Thomas photograph, negative #ICHi-16299/Chicago Historical Society.

Unit 3:
Harcourt Brace & Company
57(all), Weronica Ankarorn; 63(b), Weronica Ankarorn; 65(b), Weronica Ankarorn;
71(c)&(b), Weronica Ankarorn.

Other
54, photo © DESCHARNES & DESCHARNES; 55, UPI/Corbis-Bettmann; 56, The Museum of Modern Art, New York. The Louis E. Stern Collection. Photograph © 1998 The Museum of Modern Art, New York; 58, Collection Walker Art Center, Minneapolis. Gift of Mr. and Mrs. Julius E. Davis, 1981; 59, Archer M. Huntington Art Gallery, The University of Texas at Austin, Gift of Mari and James A. Michener, 1991. Photo by George Holmes. © 1988 Richard Anuszkiewicz/Licensed by VAGA, New York, NY; 60, Philadelphia Museum of Art, George W. Elkins Collection; 61, Travelpix/FPG International; 62-63, ©1998 James Gurney. All Rights Reserved. Published by Arrangement with Turner Publishing, Inc.; 64, California Afro-American Museum Foundation; 65(t), Museum Ludwig © Rheinisches Bildarchiv, Museen der Stadt Köln; 66(both), Courtesy of Lily Yeh; 67, Courtesy of Lily Yeh; 68, Hersovici/Art Resource, NY; 69, Courtesy, Women & Their Work, Austin, Texas; 70, Collection Walker Art Center, Minneapolis, Gift of Frederick R. Weisman in honor of his parents, William & Mary Weisman; 71, McSpadden Photography; 72, Al Messerschmidt/Folio.

Unit 4:
Harcourt Brace & Company
77(c)(b), Weronica Ankarorn; 83(b), Weronica Ankarorn; 85, Weronica Ankarorn; 89(c)&(b), Weronica Ankarorn; 91, Weronica Ankarorn.

Other
74, Faraway, drybrush,1952, Copyright 1997 Andrew Wyeth. Photograph Courtesy of Wyeth Collection; 75, Richard Schulman/Gamma Liaison; 76, Trail Riders, Gift of the Artist © 1998 Board of Trustees, National Gallery Of Art, Washington. 1975.42.1(2678)/PA. © 1998Thomas H. Benton & Rita P. Benton Testamentary Trusts/Licensed by VAGA, New York, NY; 77(t), Dallas Museum of Art, gift of Florence E. McClung; 78, David Hockney, "Nichols Canyon", 1980, acrylic, 84" X 60". © David Hockney; 79, The Louis E. Stern Collection, The Museum of Modern Art. Photograph ©1998 The Museum of Modern Art, New York; 80(t), Cecelia Diaz Zieba; 80(b), David Diaz; 81(t) & (b), David Diaz; 82, The Metropolitan Museum of Art, Arthur Hoppock Hearn Fund, 1958. (58.26); 83(t), Untitled, 1976, National Gallery of Art, Washington, Gift of the Collectors Committee. 1977.76.1.(SC) A-17994. Photo by Philip A. Charles.; 84, Superstock; 86, AP/Wide World Photos; 87, AP/Wide World Photos; 88(t), Piet Mondrian, "Broadway Boogie Woogie". 1942-43. Oil on canvas, 50 x 50" (127x127 cm) The Museum of Modern Art, New York. Given anonymously. Photograph © 1998 The Museum of Modern Art, New York; 88(b), Christie's Images/Superstock; 89(t)National Museum of American Art, Washington, D.C./Art Resource,New York; 90, Vincent van Gogh. The Starry Night.(1989). Oil on canvas, 29x36 1/4" (73.3 x 92.1 cm). The Museum of Modern Art, New York. Acquired through the Lillie P. Bliss Request. Photograph ©1998 The Museum of Modern Art.; 92, Pablo Picasso, Three Musicians, Fontainebleau, summer, 1921, oil on canvas, 6'7" x 7' 3 3/4". The Museum of Modern Art, New York. Mrs. Simon Guggenheim Fund. Photograph © 1998 The Museum of Modern Art, New York.

Unit 5:
Harcourt Brace & Company
99(c)&(b), Weronica Ankarorn; 103(c)&(b), Weronica Ankarorn; 105(ct&b)(b), Weronica Ankarorn; 109(c)&(b), Weronica Ankarorn; 111 (c)&(b), Weronica Ankarorn.

Other
94, Flor Garduño; 95, Vilma Slomp; 96(l), Bridgeman/Art Resource,NY; 96(r) , Moshe Caine/The Israel Museum, Jerusalem; 97, Freer Gallery of Art, Smithsonian Institution;98, 1994 Washington Post Photo by Carol Guzy. Reprinted with permission; 99(t), Leah A. Washington; 100, Marina Ancona; 101, George Ancona; 102(l), Michael Holford; 102, (r)Reunion des Musees Nationaux; 103(t), Sidney Janis Gallery ©1998 George Segal/Licensed by VAGA, New York, NY; 104, Motion Picture & TV Photo Archive; 105 (t), Motion Picture & TV Photo Archive; 106, Courtesy of Karen Kiser; 107(t), Motion Picture & TV Photo Archive; 107(b), Courtesy of Karen Kiser; 108, Luiz C. Marigo/Peter Arnold, Inc.; 109 (t), The Granger Collection, New York; 110, Stephen Johnson/ Tony Stone Images; 111(t), Bernard Boutrit/Woodfin Camp & Associates; 112, Courtesy of the artist and Holly Solomon Gallery, New York.

Unit 6:
Harcourt Brace & Company
119(ct&b)(b), Weronica Ankarorn; 123(c)&(b), Weronica Ankarorn; 125(c)&(b), Weronica Ankarorn; 129(c)&(b), Weronica Ankarorn; 131(c)&(b), Weronica Ankarorn; 133, Weronica Ankarorn.

Other
114, The Granger Collection, New York; 115, Scala/Art Resource, NY; 116-117, Photograph © 1997 The Detroit Institute of Arts, Gift of Edsel B. Ford; 118(l), National Museum of Ireland; 118(r), Ann Ronan Picture Library; 119(t), Spode Museum Trust; 120, Carollee Pelos, from Spectacular Vernacular; N.Y.:Aperture, 1996; 121, Carollee Pelos, from Spectacular Vernacular; N.Y.:Aperture, 1996; 122, Denver Art Museum collection ; 123(t), Photograph © 1997 The Detroit Institute of the Arts Founders Society Purchase # 81.425; 124, The Metropolitan Museum of Art, Bequest of Margaret Brown Potvin, 1987. (1988.134); 125(t), Gift of the Women for Special Acquisitions and Council of 101/Orlando Museum of Art; 126, Kelly Culpepper; 127(both), Kelly Culpepper;

128(t), The Metropolitan Museum of Art, Dodge Fund, 1933. (33.35.3); 128(b), Courtesy of the Trustees of the Victoria & Albert Museum; 129 (t), JJ Foxx/NYC; 130, K. Kitamura; 131, Planet Art; 132, Bob Daemmrich Photography.

Art Safety:
134- 135 Harcourt Brace and Company/Terry Sinclair.

Exploring Art Techniques:
138(t), Susan McCartney/Photo Researchers; 140-151, Weronica Ankarorn/Harcourt Brace & Company.

Elements and Principles:
152-153 (t), Damien Lovegrove/SPL/Photo Researchers;152 (bl), Paul McCormick/The Image Bank; 152 (bc), Peggy & Ronald Barnett/The Stock Market; 152 (br), Gabe Palmer/The Stock Market; 153 (t), Harald Sund/The Image Bank; 153 (cl), Will & Deni McIntyre/Photo Researchers; 153 (cr), Jim Corwin/Photo Researchers; 153 (bl), John Gillmoure/The Stock Market; 153 (br), F. Tetefolle/Explorer/Photo Researchers; 154 (tl), Renee Lynn/Photo Researchers; 154 (tr), Nuridsany et Perennou/Photo Researchers; 154 (cl), Alan Carruthers/Photo Researchers; 154 (cr), Frank P. Rossotto/The Stock Market; 154 (bl), Grafton Marshall Smith/The Stock Market; 154 (br), Tom Bean/The Stock Market; 155 (tl), Stephen Marks/The Image Bank; 155 (tc), Charles D. Winters/Photo Researchers; 155 (tr), Lee F. Snyder/Photo Researchers; 155 (c), Doug Plummer/Photo Researchers; 155 (bl), Phil Jude/SPL/Photo Researchers; 155 (br), James Carmichael/The Image Bank; 156 (tl), Ed Bock/The Stock Market; 156 (tc), David Parker/SPL/Photo Researchers; 156 (cl), Adrienne Hart-Davis/SPL/Photo Researchers; 156 (cr), Chromosohm/Sohm/Photo Researchers; 156 (br), Murray Alcosser/The Image Bank; 157 (tc), Arthur Beck/The Stock Market; 157 (tr), Raga/The Stock Market; 157 (c), Chris Collins/The Stock Market; 157 (bl), B. Seitz/Photo Researchers; 157 (br), Zefa Germany/The Stock Market; 158 (tl), Michael Lustbader/Photo Researchers; 158 (tr), Alan & Linda Detrick/Photo Researchers; 158 (c), Brownie Harris/The Stock Market; 158 (cl), Bryan F. Peterson/The Stock Market ; 159 (tl), Stuart Dee/The Image Bank; 159 (tcl), Wm. Whitehurst/The Stock Market; 159 (tr), Patricio Robles Gil/Bruce Coleman, Inc.; 159 (bl), Sonya Jacobs/The Stock Market; 159 (bc), Bob Abraham/The Stock Market; 159 (br), David Sailors/The Stock Market; 160 (tl), Farlely Lewis/Photo Researchers; 160 (tr), P. Saloutos/The Stock Market; 160 (cl), Art Wolfe/Tony Stone Images; 160 (c), Michal Heron/The Stock Market; 160 (cr), Dan McCoy/The Stock Market; 160 (b), Aaron Rezny/The Stock Market; 160 (bc), Jeff Hunter/The Image Bank; 161 (tl), Zefa Germany/The Stock Market; 161 (tr), Bryan Peterson/The Stock Market; 161 (c), Charles Krebs/The Stock Market; 161 (bl), Viviane Moos/The Stock Market; 161 (br), Jack Baker/The Image Bank; 162 (tl), Zefa Germany/The Stock Market; 162 (tr), Richard J. Green/Photo Researchers; 162 (c), Art Stein/Photo Researchers; 162 (bl), Dr. Jeremy Burgess/SPL/Photo Researchers; 162 (br), Joseph Nettis/Photo Researchers; 163 (t), Kevin Horan/Tony Stone Images; 163 (c), Geoff Dore/Tony Stone Images; 163 (bl), David Hall/Photo Researchers; 163 (br), Jeff Spielman/The Image Bank; 163 (bc), David Sailors/The Stock Market; 164 (tl), Zefa Germany/The Stock Market; 164 (c), Zefa Germany/The Stock Market; 164 (bl), Johnny Johnson/Animals Animals; 164 (br), Anup & Manoj Shah/Animals Animals; 165 (t), Kjell B. Sandved/Photo Researchers; 165 (tl), Will & Deni McIntyre/Photo Researchers; 165 (tr), Mickey Gibson/Animals Animals; 165 (bl), Russell D. Curtis/Photo Researchers; 165 (bc), Grafton Marshall Smith/The Stock Market.

Gallery of Artists (pg. 166-175) by artist's last name:
Anuszkiewicz, Arnold Newman; Bartholdi, Culver Pictures, Inc.; Benton, Corbis-Bettmann; Burke, FDR Library; Calder, Inge Morath/Magnum Photos; Christo, Arnold Newman; Cole, National Portrait Gallery, Smithsonian Institution/Art Resource, NY; DaVinci, Art Resource, NY; Degas, National Portrait Gallery, Smithsonian Institution/Art Resource, NY; Diaz, Cecelia Diaz Zieba; Flagg, Corbis-Bettmann; Garduño, Vilma Stomp; Gaudi, The Granger Collection; Grez, Liliana Wilson Grez; Gurney, Mark Ferri; Guzy, Carol Guzy; Hockney, Woodfin Camp & Associates; Homer, Corbis-Bettmann; Hopper, Pach/Corbis-Bettmann; Lawrence, Eden Arts; Lee, The Glynn Art Association; Magritte, Giraudon/Art Resource, NY; Marsh, Courtesy of Stanley Marsh 3; Martin, The Granger Collection, New York; Matisse, Cartier-Bresson/Magnum Photos; McClung, courtesy Florence McClung; Michelangelo, Superstock; Mole, Chicago Historical Society, ICHi-18716, photographer unknown; Mondrian, Arnold Newman; Naranjo, Mark Nohl; Nevelson, Charles Moore/Black Star; Oldenberg, Charles Moore/Black Star; Ong, Superstock; Outterbridge, California Afro-American Museum Foundation, Willie Robert Middlebrook; Paik, Novovitch/Liaison; Pei, Corbis-Bettmann; Picasso, Giraudon/Art Resource, NY; Pinkney, Alan Orling/Black Star; Pippin, Albright-Knox Art Gallery Buffalo, New York; Riley, Arnold Newman; Rivera, UPI/Corbis-Bettmann; Scott, Scott Art Graphics; Segal, Barbara Pfeffer; Stuart, National Portrait Gallery, Smithsonian Institution/Art Resource, NY; Summer, Ron Kunzman; Thomas, National Museum of American Art, Washington DC, Art Resource, NY; van Bruggen, Thomas Hoepker/Magnum Photos; van Gogh, Erich Lessing/Art Resource; Velarde, US Department of the Interior, Indian Arts and Crafts Board; Warhol, Bernard Gotfryd/Woodfin Camp & Associates; Washington, Leah Washington; Wyeth, Richard Schulman/Gamma Liaison; Wyman, Steve Allen.

Glossary:
Arch, Doug Armand/Tony Stone Images; City Scape, Superstock; Minaret, Superstock; Mural, Richard Blake/Tony Stone Images; Portrait, Corbis-Bettmann; Portrait, The Granger Collection, New York; Spire, Superstock; Weaving, National Museum of the American Indian; Found Objects, Weronica Ankarorn/Harcourt Brace & Company;

Teacher Resources

MEDIA AND TECHNIQUES R17
Descriptions of art media and techniques, accompanied by photographs and illustrations, provide guidance for helping students create their own artworks.

ASSESSMENT R26
Reproducible checklists for the teacher, for individual students, and for groups guide the evaluation of art processes and artworks.

MEETING INDIVIDUAL NEEDS R32
Suggestions for customizing instruction to meet special needs ensure successful experiences for all students in viewing and creating art.

SEASONAL ACTIVITIES R38
These engaging activities can be used at appropriate times of the year to reinforce the concepts taught in **Art Express.**

COPYING MASTERS
  Home Letters R44
  Reproducible letters, available in English and Spanish, foster communication with family members about the art program.

  School-Home Connections R50
  Students and family members can work together at home on simple but satisfying production activities.

  Response Cards R56
  Reproducible cards may be used independently by individual students or groups to guide their viewing of and response to artworks.

MATERIALS R66

FOR YOUR INFORMATION R69

ACROSS-THE-CURRICULUM CHARTS AND CORRELATIONS R74

SCOPE AND SEQUENCE R84

INDEX R88

MEDIA & TECHNIQUES

Creating art is an exhilarating process of self-expression.

CHILDREN WHO ARE EXPERIENCED in the basic techniques have the confidence to take risks and try new approaches, with surprisingly original pieces of artwork often resulting. Here are some brief descriptions of media and techniques suitable for students in elementary school.

● TYPES OF PAPER

Butcher Paper
Available in wide rolls and several colors, this paper is useful for murals and other large art projects, and for projects that require a hard-surfaced paper.

Construction Paper
Available in different colors, this paper is useful for tempera painting, collage, and paper sculpture.

Drawing and Painting Paper
This slightly rough paper is useful for drawing and painting projects, especially at the elementary level.

Newsprint Paper
This thin paper, used for printing newspapers, is inexpensive and easily torn. It is good for sketching, printmaking, and making papier-mâché.

Tissue Paper
Thin, strong, and available in bright colors, tissue paper is especially useful for making collages and for projects that require transparent color. Although it is expensive, it lends itself to small-scale projects that don't require a lot of paper.

Photographic Paper
Available through catalogs and art-supply or camera stores, this chemically coated paper is used to create photograms.

● USING PAPER

Folding
Bend the paper. Smooth the paper until it creases, then press the crease between finger and thumb.

Tearing
Paper may be torn apart freehand, causing the edges to look ragged or fuzzy, or it may be folded, creased, and then torn along the creased fold, which gives a neater edge.

Cutting
To cut a small piece of paper from a large sheet, cut from the edge, not from the center.

Piercing
For such tasks as cutting out eyeholes in paper masks or making symmetrical stencils, students can use pointed scissors to pierce and then cut into the paper, removing unwanted center parts. Primary-grade students can fold the paper and cut through the fold, instead of piercing it.

Safety Tip: Closely supervise students when they are using hard or pointed instruments. When students are using the piercing technique described above, caution them not to put their fingers underneath the paper, where the scissors come through.

GLUE, STARCH, AND PASTE

White Glue
This nontoxic, creamy liquid comes in plastic squeeze bottles and in larger containers. It is recommended for use with cardboard, wood, cloth, plastic foam, and pottery. White glue causes wrinkling when used with paper, especially when too much is used.

Powdered Art Paste or Starch
Mixed to a thin, watery consistency, this material is recommended for use in making tissue-paper collages.

School Paste (Library Paste)
Although this substance is nontoxic, young children like its smell and may be tempted to eat it. This paste is available in small jars and is good for pasting pieces of paper flat on other pieces of paper or on cardboard. Demonstrate for students how to apply it evenly on just one surface to avoid loosening when dry. Paste is not recommended for more elaborate projects because it may not hold the materials together.

Using Glue or Paste
1. Spread out sheets of newspaper.
2. Place the artwork to be glued facedown. Spread the glue or paste evenly from the center, using a finger or a piece of cardboard. Be sure the edges and corners of the paper are covered.
3. Lift the paper and carefully lay it in the desired position on the surface to which it will be affixed. Place a sheet of clean paper over the artwork and smooth it with the palm of the hand.

Tip: Use the smallest amount of glue possible. Too much glue will spoil the appearance of the artwork.

DRAWING TOOLS AND TECHNIQUES

Pencils
Many different effects can be created with an art pencil, depending on how it is held and how much pressure is exerted. Such pencil lead varies from 6B, which makes the darkest, softest mark, to 9H, which makes the lightest, hardest mark. Very soft lead breaks and smears easily. Several pencils of different hardness can be used in one drawing if desired. Pencils used in the primary grades should be large, with a broad lead surface that makes a strong drawing point.

Details are made with medium-range, hard pencil leads, such as regular number 2 or 2-1/2 pencils. Shading, or making light and dark values to produce the effect of shadows and a feeling of solidity and depth, can be produced with the flat side of a soft-leaded pencil.

Colored pencils are most effectively used by first making light strokes, then building up the color to develop darker areas.

Crayons
Made of hard wax, crayons are available in a variety of colors. When applied with heavy pressure, they produce rich, vivid colors. Always save crayon stubs; allow students to peel or unwrap them so that they can experiment with using the side of the crayon rather than the tip.

Crayon etching is a technique in which layers of light-colored crayon are built up on shiny, nonabsorbent paper. They are covered with black crayon or black tempera paint that has been mixed with a small amount of liquid soap. Students must press hard with all the crayons so that enough wax is on the paper. With a toothpick, fingernail, or other pointed tool, students etch, or scratch away, the black paint to expose the colors or the white paper underneath. **(Figure 1)**

Figure 1. Crayon etching

Oil Pastels

Softer than wax crayons and similar to chalk, oil pastels produce bright, glowing color effects. Pressing an oil pastel hard on the paper creates rich, vibrant color; less pressure produces a softer color. Oil pastels smudge more easily than crayons. As with crayons, drawing can be done with the points or with the unwrapped sides, and students may wish to break their oil pastels in half. Encourage students to take command of their art tools; this will help them build self-confidence in their artistic abilities.

Colors can be mixed by adding one over another or by placing dots of different colors side by side and blending them by rubbing. Neither crayons nor oil pastels mix with water, so a wash that is brushed over a drawing creates a **crayon or oil-pastel resist.**

Colored Markers

Nonpermanent felt- or plastic-tipped markers are safe and easy to use, and they are available in a wide range of colors and sizes. They are useful for outdoor sketching, for making contour drawings, and for other art assignments. Since markers dry out easily, caps should be kept on the tips when the markers are not in use.

● PAINTING TOOLS AND TECHNIQUES

Tempera

Tempera paint works best when it has the consistency of thick cream. It is available in powder or, more commonly, liquid. Tempera is opaque—the paper beneath cannot be seen through paint of normal consistency.

Tempera powder is available in cans or boxes, and it should be mixed in small amounts. Mix water and powder to the desired consistency and amount. Dried tempera paint should not be used again.

Tempera may be mixed with wheat paste to make a very thick paint for **impasto** painting.

> **Safety Tip**
> Liquid tempera is recommended because powdered tempera can irritate eyes and nasal passages. If you prefer to use powdered tempera, mix it ahead of time.

Liquid tempera is available in jars or plastic containers and is ready to use. Shake the container well each time the paint is to be used. Keep a lid on the paint when it is not being used, and keep paint cleaned out of the cap to prevent sticking. Stuck bottle caps often loosen in warm water.

Some manufacturers supply helpful pouring spouts. If you use them, put a galvanized nail in the spout openings when not in use to keep them from stopping up.

Watercolors

Available in hinged boxes, watercolors must always be used with a wet brush. Students may use the top of the open box to mix colors. Small, soft-bristle brushes are used with watercolors to achieve the transparent, fluid quality of the medium.

Interesting effects with watercolors include

- making a watercolor wash by painting a line and then smudging the line with a wet brush.
- blotting watercolors with crumpled paper.
- sprinkling salt on a watercolor picture.
- painting on wet paper.

Brushes

Choose well-made brushes with metal ferrules (the metal ring around the paintbrush shaft near the bristles) that are tightly bonded to the wooden handles so the bristles will not come off. Poorly made brushes are frustrating to students, since the bristles often come off onto their paintings.

Dozens of sizes and varieties of brushes are available, from nylon-bristle brushes to fairly expensive sable brushes. Students should have access to a wide variety of brushes—round and flat, thick and thin, square-ended and oval-tipped. Brushes should be cleaned after each art session in a warm solution of mild detergent and water. Other kinds of painting tools may be kept on hand for students to experiment with, such as toothbrushes, eye-makeup brushes, various kinds of sponges and sponge applicators, cotton swabs, and bristled cleaning brushes. With these unusual painting tools, students can create interesting and varied effects.

Paint Containers

Mixing trays or paint palettes can be made from many free or inexpensive materials, such as pie pans, muffin tins, plastic trays from frozen foods, and paper plates. Egg cartons made of plastic foam make especially good mixing trays, as they provide plenty of room for color mixing, and they can be closed, labeled with the student's name, and stored for later use.

When storing tempera paint in a mixing tray for later use, add a little water to keep the paint from drying out overnight. You can use a water-spray bottle for indoor plants.

Always provide students with containers of water for cleaning their brushes while painting. Use plastic margarine containers, coffee cans, or clean, empty milk cartons. Demonstrate for students how to rinse the brush in the container of water before dipping it into a new color. Students can dry the brush as needed by stroking it across a folded paper towel.

> **Tip:** Make your own portable paint dispenser by putting four colors of paint in containers with pouring spouts. Carry the containers in cardboard drink carriers available from fast-food outlets.

Color-Mixing Techniques

- Begin with light colors; then add darker colors. For example, when mixing tints, start with white and gradually add small amounts of color to make the desired tint. When mixing shades, start with a color and gradually add small amounts of black to form the desired shade.
- Tempera paint that has become too dark cannot be lightened.
- To make gray, add small amounts of black tempera to white.
- To make green, add small amounts of blue to yellow.
- To make orange, add small amounts of red to yellow.
- To make violet, add small amounts of blue to red.
- To make brown, use one of these color combinations (each will make a variation of brown):
  a. red and green
  b. red, yellow, and black
  c. red and black

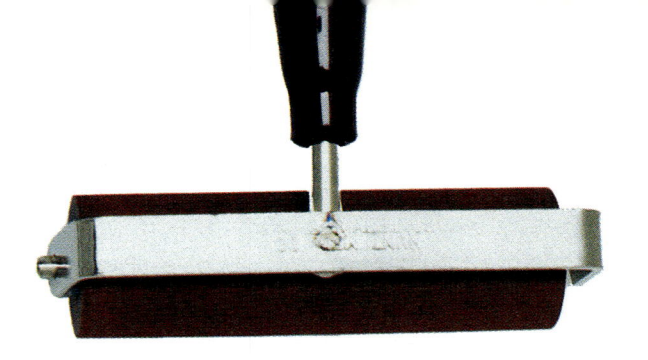

PRINTMAKING TOOLS AND TECHNIQUES

Prints can be made from a wide variety of materials, including plastic foam meat trays, glue lines on cardboard, and cut or torn pieces of paper or tagboard pasted to cardboard. Almost any variation on an otherwise flat surface will be enough to create a relief print.

The following technique may be used for printmaking:

1. Pour printing ink or liquid tempera paint on a flat surface, such as a metal or plastic tray, a pan, or a cookie sheet.
2. Roll the brayer over the ink or paint to spread it so the brayer can pick up an even coat.
3. Roll the coated brayer over the printing surface until it is evenly covered. Roll first in one direction, then in another at right angles.
4. Place the paper on top of the surface. Press it down gently with the palm of the hand. Rub the back of the paper with the fingertips or the back of a spoon. Be sure to cover all areas, including the edges, being careful not to move the paper.
5. Pull the paper away from the surface. This is called "pulling the print." The print is ready to dry.

Inks

In elementary school, printing ink should be water-based, since it dries quickly and cleans easily. It needs to be thinned often.

> **Safety Tip:** Even water-based ink stains clothing. Have students wear smocks or old shirts when they are making prints.

Printmaking Paper

Recommended paper for printing includes newsprint, construction paper, and tissue paper. Avoid using paper with a hard, slick finish because it absorbs ink and paint poorly.

> **Tip**
> To use paint while making a relief print, mix several drops of glycerine (available in drugstores) with one tablespoon of thick tempera paint. If brayers are not available, have students apply the ink or the paint with a brush.

Cleanup

Drop a folded piece of newspaper into the pan filled with ink. Roll the brayer on the newspaper. This removes a lot of the ink from both the pan and the brayer. Unfold the newspaper and refold it with the inked side inside. Crumple and throw away the newspaper. Repeat. Once most of the ink is out of the pan, it is easy to rinse the pan and the brayer at the sink.

● ASSEMBLAGE

An assemblage is a piece of art made by combining a collection of three-dimensional objects into a whole. It can be either free-standing or mounted on a panel, and it is usually made from "found" materials—scraps, junk, and objects from nature. Students can help you collect and sort objects, such as

- carpet, fabric, foil, leather, paper, and wallpaper scraps.
- boxes in all sizes, film cans, spools, corks, jar lids.
- packing materials such as foam peanuts and cardboard.
- wire, rope, twine, string, yarn, ribbon.

● SCULPTURE TOOLS AND TECHNIQUES

Sculpture is three-dimensional art. It is usually made by carving, modeling, casting, or assembling. Sculptures can be created by adding to (additive) or taking away from (subtractive) a block of material.

Materials recommended for additive sculpture include clay, papier-mâché, wood, and almost any material that can be joined together.

Materials appropriate for subtractive sculpture in school include clay, chalk, soap, wax, soft salt blocks, and artificial sandstone. Synthetic modeling materials are also available.

In the primary grades, salt dough may be substituted for clay in some art activities. Combine 2 cups of flour with 1 cup of salt. Add 1 cup of water and mix thoroughly. Press the mixture into a ball and then knead for several minutes on a board.

Foil offers interesting possibilities for sculpture and embossing. Heavy aluminum foil works best. Besides making three-dimensional forms with foil, students can also smooth it over shapes to make a relief sculpture or jewelry. **(Figure 2)**

Wire, including pipe cleaners, telephone wire, and floral wire, is easily shaped and reshaped. When using long wires, tape the ends to prevent injury. Students should wear safety goggles and sit a safe distance from each other.

Figure 2. Foil sculpture

Paper Sculpture

Stiff paper or tagboard, cut in a variety of shapes and sizes, yields colorful and inventive three-dimensional forms, especially when shaped with simple tools. For best results, students should always use glue, not paste, when assembling a paper sculpture. They can use a paper clip or piece of tape to hold parts together and stationary while the glue is drying.

Clay

Clay comes from the ground and usually has a gray or reddish hue. It is mixed with other materials so that it is flexible, yet able to hold a shape.

Oil-based clay is mixed with oil, usually linseed, and cannot be fired or glazed. It softens when it is molded with warm hands. As it becomes old and loses oil, it becomes difficult to mold and will eventually break apart. Oil-based clay is available in a variety of colors.

Water-based or wet clay comes in a variety of textures and can be fired to become permanent. It should be kept in a plastic sack to keep it moist until it is used. If a piece begins to dry out, dampen it with a fine spray of water. If it has not been fired, dried water-based clay can be recycled by soaking it in water.

Before firing, or baking clay in a kiln, there are two important considerations:

- Read and carefully follow the instructions for operating the kiln.
- Be certain that the clay has been kneaded before being molded to prevent air pockets that can explode during firing.

Preparing Clay

If clay is reused or made from a powder mix, remove air pockets before it is molded. Clay that has air pockets can explode during firing. To get rid of air pockets:

- Take a large chunk of clay and form it into a ball. Then use a wedging wire to cut the ball in half. Put one chunk on a hard surface and slam the other half down on top of it.
- Take a large chunk of clay and press it down with the palms of both hands against a hard surface. Turn clay around, and press hard again. Keep turning and pressing in this manner until the clay has a smooth, even texture.

Figure 3. Pinch method

Methods for Molding Clay

Clay can be molded and formed using the pinch, slab, and coil methods or a combination of these.

- To make a pot using the pinch method (**Figure 3**), mold a chunk of clay into a ball. Holding the ball in one hand, press the thumb in and carefully squeeze the clay between thumb and forefinger. Begin at the bottom, and gradually work upward and out. Continually turn the ball of clay while pinching it.
- To make a slab, use a rolling pin to flatten a chunk of clay to between a quarter of an inch and half an inch thick. Shapes cut from the slab can be draped over bowls or crumpled newspapers and left to dry. Shapes cut from the slab can also be joined together to form containers or sculptures. (**Figure 4**) The shapes should be scored around the edges and dried until they feel like leather before they are joined.

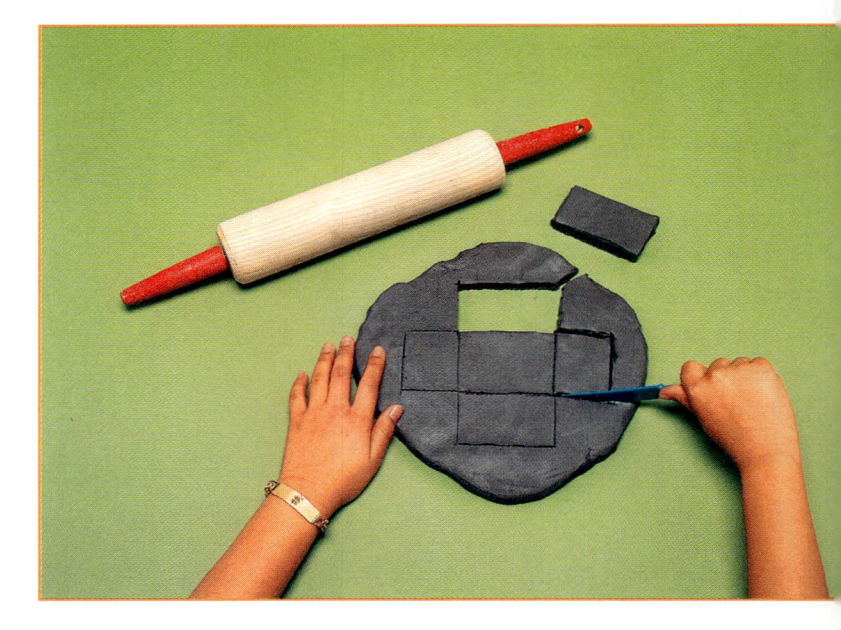

Figure 4. Slab method

- To create a coil, use the whole hand to roll a chunk of clay against a hard surface until it forms a rope of clay of even thickness. **(Figure 5)** Coils can be attached to each other and built into a shape, or they can be added to a slab base and smoothed out.
- Textures can be created by pressing found objects, such as combs, coins, bolts, burlap, buckles, keys, chains, utensils, sticks, shells, straws, toothpicks, pencils, buttons, bottle caps, old jewelry, and other interesting objects into the clay. Designs can also be etched with tools such as pencil points, paper clips, and toothpicks.

Figure 5. Coil method

Carving

Use a sturdy plastic knife to cut away unwanted clay.

Tip
Canvas and duck cloth are work surfaces that are reusable and easy to store. The cloth will not absorb the moisture from the clay. If cloth is unavailable, substitute brown paper sacks.

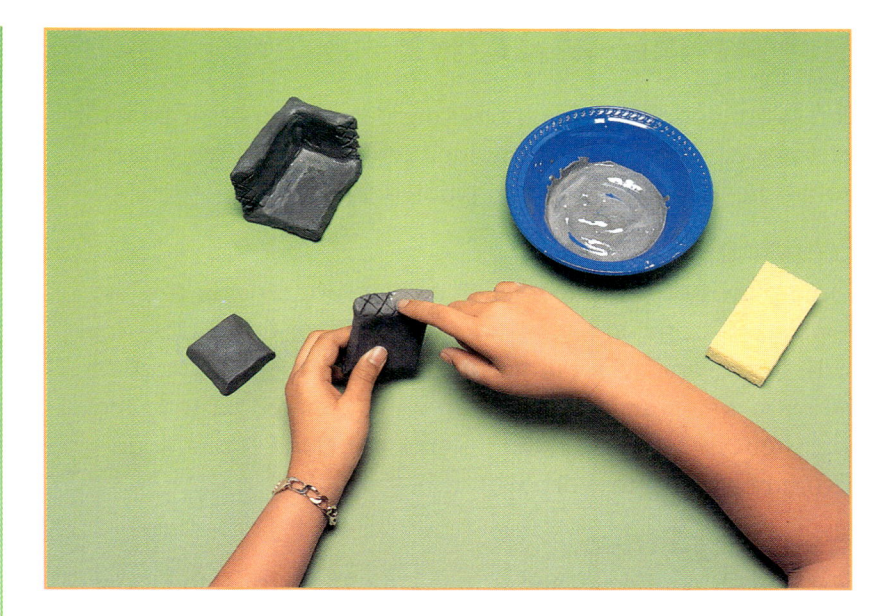

Figure 6. Joining clay pieces

Joining Clay Together

Oil-based clay can be pressed together and blended with the fingertips.

Water-based clay pieces should be joined by rubbing the surface of the parts with a toothbrush dipped in water. The wet toothbrush will automatically score the clay and create a watery mixture on the parts to be joined. An alternative is to score the adjoining pieces with the tip of a toothpick, adding slip, or water-thinned clay, to make the two pieces adhere. **(Figure 6)**

Safety Tip
Pour the water used for dipping the toothbrush into a disposable container and throw it away. Any form of clay can block pipes and drains.

PAPIER-MÂCHÉ

This art material is made by mixing paper pulp or strips with art paste or glue. It can be molded into various three-dimensional shapes when wet, then painted when dry.

Preparing Pulp

Shred pieces of soft paper, such as newsprint, paper towels, newspaper, or facial tissue, into small bits or thin strips. Soak them for several hours in water, then drain them, squeeze out the extra water, and mix the pulp with prepared paste to the consistency of soft clay. Let the mixture stand for an hour before beginning to work with it.

Preparing Strips

Tear newspaper or newsprint into long, thin strips about one-half inch wide. Dip the strips into art paste or a white-glue mixture, and put down a layer of wet strips over the shape to be covered. Allow the piece to dry after every two layers of applications. Continue putting strips on the form until there are five or six layers. This thickness is strong enough to support most papier-mâché projects.

Foundations

Good forms that can be used as foundations for papier-mâché include rolled newspapers secured with string, tape, or thin wire; inflated balloons; plastic bottles; paper sacks stuffed with newspapers and tied with string; wire or wooden armatures shaped into skeletal forms.

Safety Tip: Do not use pages of newspaper that may contain toxic pigments in colored printing inks.

FABRIC ARTS

Batik

The traditional batik method of dyeing fabric involves first covering patterned areas with wax. After the fabric has been dyed, the wax is removed and the pattern emerges. In an acrylic batik, white tempera paint, rather than wax, is applied to the patterned areas of the fabric. The fabric is then dyed or brushed with a paint wash. After it has dried, the fabric must be soaked in water and the white paint scratched off to reveal the pattern. **(Figure 7)**

Figure 7. Simple batik

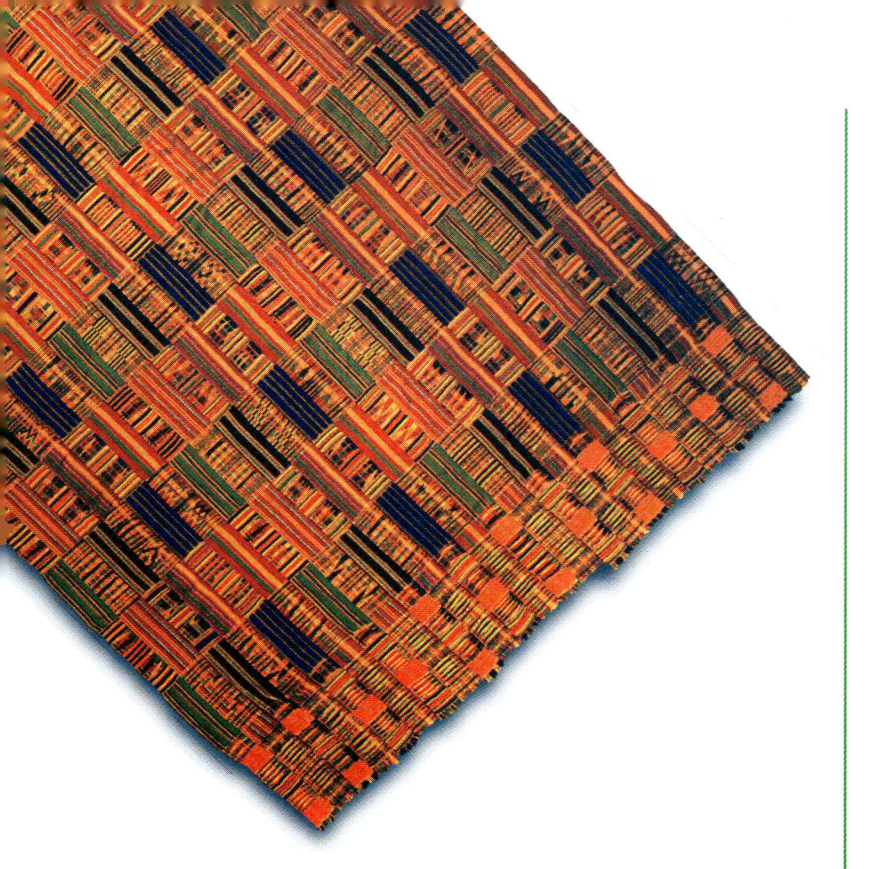

Weaving

Weaving is artwork created on a loom by lacing together or interlocking fibers, such as strands of thread, yarn, or other materials, to create a piece of fabric or a decorative work. Various kinds of looms may be purchased through art supply houses or made using readily available materials. Simple square looms can be made by stretching thick rubber bands across stiff cardboard. Circular weavings are made on looms formed from wire hangers bent into a circle. Parent volunteers can construct more permanent looms using wood frames, nails, and string. Students can weave a variety of materials through the loom, including ribbon, yarn, lengths of beads, twine, and fabric strips. **(Figure 8)**

Figure 8. Weaving

● FRAMING ARTWORK

Frames usually improve the appearance of artwork, and they make attractive displays.

Mounting

The simplest kind of frame is a mount. It is made by putting a small dab of paste at each corner of an artwork. The artwork is then placed in the center of a sheet of construction paper or cardboard that is at least an inch larger than the work on all sides. For a well-balanced appearance, make the border slightly narrower at the top and slightly wider at the bottom.

Matting

A mat is a frame with a cutout center. A picture is taped in place behind it, with the mat forming a border. Students can make mats out of black or colored construction paper. Professional-style mats made from matboard should be done only by the teacher. You may wish to do this if you are preparing drawings or paintings for an art show.

To make a mat, take a piece of medium-thick cardboard or matboard that extends two or three inches beyond the picture on all sides. Measure the picture to be matted. Then, on the back of the matboard, mark the position where the art is to be placed. (The mat will look balanced if the bottom margin is a little larger than the other sides.) Then measure one-fourth inch in from the outer edge, and mark it all around the frame. This will make the picture overlap the cutout window on all sides.

Use a mat knife to cut along the inside measurements. Cut very carefully when a corner is reached so the matboard is not cut beyond the mark. When all four sides have been cut, the center will come out. Fasten the artwork to the back with tape, and the mat is complete.

Safety Tip: Work carefully when using a mat knife. Keep the blade pointed away from you, and retract the blade or return the knife to its container when not in use. Keep the knife edge sharp so that the cardboard edges do not ravel.

MEDIA & TECHNIQUES

ASSESSMENT

The focus of assessment in *Art Express* is on process rather than product. Tools the teacher may choose to use to track students' growth and development include portfolios, sketchbooks, observation checklists, and student self-assessment checklists that encourage reflection.

Two types of art **portfolios** may be kept by students for assessment purposes. A *show portfolio* might contain only finished artworks that students have selected for display. A *working portfolio* might include sketches, works-in-progress, notes, and self-assessment checklists. Both provide opportunities for periodic discussions, revealing a student's development and interests.

In a **sketchbook,** students may record ideas and track art experiences and their own observations, opinions, and judgments about what they have seen and done.

Observation checklists provide a tool for the teacher to focus on and track behaviors that promote growth and development.

Self-assessment checklists, used periodically, help students reflect on artworks they have seen and art they have produced. These checklists actively involve students in their own development as artists and critical viewers.

Duplicate and use the following pages to record observations of a student's behaviors during art viewing and production activities, and to promote student self-assessment of viewing and creating art.

OBSERVATION CHECKLIST — Viewing and Discussing, R27
Use this page periodically to help assess a student's growth and development.

OBSERVATION CHECKLIST — Studio Activities, R28
Use this page periodically to help assess a student's growth and development.

STUDENT SELF-ASSESSMENT — Reflecting on the Unit, R29
Use this page at the end of the unit to help students reflect on their art experiences and to gain information regarding a student's interests and attitudes about art.

STUDENT SELF-ASSESSMENT — Working in a Group, R30
Use this page periodically to help students reflect on their art experiences and to gain information regarding a student's interests and attitudes about art.

Student _____ Teacher _____ Date _____

Observation Checklist
VIEWING AND DISCUSSING

The student	Observed Regularly	Observed Occasionally	Not Observed
participates thoughtfully in discussions.			
uses basic art vocabulary appropriately in discussions.			
identifies art elements and principles in natural and human-made environments.			
compares and contrasts artworks from different cultures and historical periods.			
analyzes artworks by major artists, self, classmates, and other students.			
demonstrates respect for others' artworks.			
respects differences in opinions about artworks.			
understands the difference between judging an artwork and expressing a personal preference.			
uses the critical process to clarify the meaning of art and to share discoveries about art.			
relates information about an artist's work to an artist's life and times.			
demonstrates awareness of the relationship between history and culture and the visual arts.			
makes connections between visual and performing arts, and between visual arts and other content areas.			
recognizes that art can contribute to the quality of daily life.			
explores art careers and identifies the role of the visual arts in business, in industry, and in architectural and commercial design.			

COMMENTS AND GOALS:

ASSESSMENT R27

Student _____ Teacher _____ Date _____

Observation Checklist
STUDIO ACTIVITIES

The student	Observed Regularly	Observed Occasionally	Not Observed
follows directions.			
follows art safety rules and procedures.			
uses materials and tools in a safe and responsible manner.			
works well independently.			
works effectively in small and cooperative groups.			
produces artwork to meet the requirements of the studio experience.			
selects and combines media and materials to solve problems and interpret ideas.			
experiments with new ideas, elements, principles, forms, media, and materials.			
demonstrates creative thinking, imagination, and problem-solving skills when creating artwork.			
expresses visually individual ideas, feelings, and thoughts.			
creates original and imaginative artworks in two and three dimensions.			
creates compositions using specific placement or organization of elements, symbols, and images.			
produces art that reflects a knowledge of cultural influences.			
displays pride in his/her finished products.			
establishes criteria and selects artworks for display.			
uses a sketchbook regularly.			

COMMENTS AND GOALS:

Harcourt Brace School Publishers

Name _____ Date _____

Reflecting on the Unit

Art and Artists

1. My favorite work of art from this unit is _____ because _____ .

   This work of art is about _____ .

   The artist created it using tools and materials such as _____ _____ .

2. My favorite artist from this unit is _____ because _____ _____ .

3. The most interesting thing I learned from this unit is _____ _____ .

4. I would like to see more artwork like _____ .

Studio Activities

1. My favorite studio experience was _____ because _____ .

2. The most interesting problem I had to solve was _____ _____ .

3. I would like to try _____ again because _____ _____ .

4. I chose to put _____ in my portfolio because _____ _____ .

5. I am becoming a better artist because _____ _____ .

ASSESSMENT **R29**

Name _____ Date _____

Working in a Group

	Did a Great Job	Did a Fair Job	Could Have Done Better
1. I shared my ideas with the group.			
2. Each member shared his or her ideas.			
3. We listened carefully to each other's ideas.			
4. We divided the group's work fairly.			
5. Everyone did his or her share.			
6. We completed the project on time.			
7. We presented, or shared, the project.			

8. Some things I contributed:

9. Some things I could do better next time:

10. Some things the group could do better next time:

Strategies for Success

Professionals often analyze their own behaviors and objectives.
Reflect on your use of the following strategies.

VIEWING

Provide appropriate background information (personal, cultural, historical, or social context) to students about an artist or an artwork

Provide sufficient viewing and discussion time and encourage multiple interpretations of an artwork

Suggest a variety of strategies to help students better "see" an artwork, such as:

- look away, then look back
- vary the viewing distance
- focus on an element, object, shape, color, etc.

Encourage active involvement of students

Help students understand that the critical process is exploratory, not argumentative

Help students make connections between their daily lives and art

Help students learn about the practical applications of art, including information about art careers

Provide opportunities for students to make connections between art, music, dance, and the other disciplines

Notes

CREATING

Respect each student's unique efforts and insights about art

Provide opportunities for students to explore and to experiment with art media, tools, techniques, and processes

Simplify directions, and model techniques as necessary

Provide opportunities for sensory learning

Encourage the creation of original artwork

Notes

INFORMAL ASSESSMENT

- **Encourage** students to establish and maintain their sketchbooks and/or portfolios
- **Meet** periodically with students to discuss their progress and growth

MEETING INDIVIDUAL NEEDS

Art can be an enjoyable experience for all students because it enables them to explore new ideas, media, and techniques.

CLASSROOM TEACHERS AND ART SPECIALISTS often have students of varying abilities within a single classroom. Usually, with only a few adjustments and a good understanding of the four stages of artistic development, they can help all students have fulfilling art experiences.

▲ Primary Stage

STAGES OF ARTISTIC DEVELOPMENT

Since students' skills and interests develop at different rates, teachers are likely to find a large range of artistic abilities within an age group. Because of these differences, it is important for teachers to be aware of the four stages of students' artistic development and to adapt instruction to meet the needs of individual students.

Scribbling Stage (USUALLY PRE-K TO GRADE 1)

The first stage that all children go through is the scribbling stage, which occurs through about age five. Children begin drawing disorganized scribbles, progress to more controlled scribbling, and then advance to named scribbling, in which they begin to name the shapes they create. By the time they reach first grade, they have usually advanced to the Primary Stage.

Primary Stage (USUALLY GRADES K–2)

In this stage, children often portray themselves as the dominant figure in their art, with figures floating in space. Children tend to include only the parts of themselves that they consider important, and there are few correct proportions. However, children at this stage also like to use their imagination and are open to discovery. Teachers can provide ample opportunities for exploration and discovery in a variety of ways:

Introduce simple subjects which have outlines that children may have attempted previously, such as animals, people, and buildings.

Encourage children to keep a sketchbook, which can serve as a record of ideas, enabling children to refer to a developing record of how to represent things.

Provide experiences and practice to enable children to learn to use tools and techniques.

Enable children to perceive or discover things through their senses. Remember that at this stage every experience is a new one.

Respect all artwork completed by children. Encourage and praise children's attempts while their skills and abilities develop.

Intermediate Stage (USUALLY GRADES 1–3)

Students in this stage are moving away from a preoccupation with themselves and are developing an interest in others. They are more open to ideas and are refining their techniques. At this stage, students begin to develop composition techniques, to present objects in proportion, and to pay attention to the arrangement of objects on a page. Students use lines to represent the ground or sky and place objects on lines or along the bottom edge of the paper. Teachers can help students develop their skills in the following ways:

Involve students in discussion-and-sharing sessions so that they can talk about their ideas and techniques with each other.

Encourage students to explore further aspects of color, such as tints and shades, and of line, such as direction and movement.

Provide opportunities for students to see how artists use various media by visiting artists' studios, galleries, and museums, and then discuss what students discovered.

▲ Intermediate Stage

Upper Intermediate Stage (USUALLY GRADES 3–6)

Students become more independent at this stage, and their understanding of art matures. Students pay greater attention to detail and often try to mirror reality in their artwork. By this stage, students have a working art vocabulary and a good understanding of techniques and ideas. They also have a good background for analyzing, discussing, and criticizing different artworks. Teachers can best help students at this stage in these ways:

Develop more fully the concepts dealing with spatial visualization, such as perspective, vanishing points, and both realistic and abstract variations on space.

Provide opportunities for students to extend their understanding of techniques and concepts so that students can make choices about the best way to communicate their ideas to others.

Emphasize originality in developing ideas and in working with media.

Help students experiment with new materials if they are developing a keen interest in three-dimensional work.

▼ Upper Intermediate Stage

Look for

CHALLENGE notes

GIFTED AND TALENTED STUDENTS

Gifted and talented students work or respond at extraordinarily high levels. When these students produce art, they

- frequently draw or sketch.
- create and collect large amounts of artwork.
- frequently show originality.
- use art freely to express ideas and feelings.
- use art materials and tools with ease.
- show keen interest in other people's artwork.
- experiment willingly with new techniques and media.

Challenging Students

Enhance opportunities for gifted students and accelerate their artistic growth in these ways:

Provide opportunities for students to participate in long-term art activities. Enable them to study an area of interest in depth, such as the work or style of a particular artist or a special technique.

Plan for additional outlets and audiences for students' work—in the community as well as at school.

Enable students to observe and interact with professional artists. Arrange for students to attend exhibitions and visit artists' studios.

Individualize activities so that students can follow their own inclinations.

Arrange for additional art opportunities, such as noon "drop-in" classes or after-school classes.

KEEP IN MIND

Gifted students

- may be gifted in one area of study and not in another.
- may not be the highest achievers.
- may not be the most socially mature.
- may not be the most intellectually advanced.

STUDENTS ACQUIRING ENGLISH

Because the art classroom typically provides an abundance of visual images and hands-on experiences, students acquiring English can benefit greatly from peer interaction and can quickly build self-esteem as well as language ability. You can help second-language learners gain the most from art experiences in various ways:

- Have students work in small groups or pairs whenever possible to increase their comfort level and to share language.

- Model art activities as you give clear step-by-step instructions. Repeat instructions, giving them differently each time.

- Invite students' family members to share examples of art or techniques from their culture.

- Use physical movement and gestures, realia, and visuals to make language comprehensible and to encourage oral language development.

Developing Oral Language

To help students develop oral language:

Introduce concepts and words using rhymes and poetry. At Grades 1 and 2, you will find poems in the unit openers as well as in some Teacher's Edition lessons.

Discuss ideas and concepts using *Art Express Big Books* and *Art Prints*.

Display artworks, pointing to examples of concepts as you discuss them. Encourage volunteers to provide answers to the best of their level of language acquisition.

Encourage students to speak, but never force them to do so. All responses should be voluntary.

Avoid correcting students when they make errors in pronunciation, grammar, or syntax.

Allow spoken fluency and grammatical accuracy to emerge gradually over time as the student progresses.

Give a simple command such as "Pinch the clay" to students after you demonstrate the action.

Using the First Language

If you or a student knows the child's first language, give background information in that language before providing it in English. Use the *Spanish Translation "In the Studio" Activities* to help children with activity directions. Also, display posters or charts of the elements of art and principles of design in the first language. *Posters of Elements, Principles, and Safety* are available in Spanish and English.

Look for

STUDENTS ACQUIRING ENGLISH *notes*

Look for

EXTRA SUPPORT notes
MEETING INDIVIDUAL NEEDS

EXTRA SUPPORT

Students who need extra support may have learning disabilities that affect the way they receive and process information. They may also be at risk due to insufficient background experiences or home support. Students who need extra support may have difficulty in these areas:

- following directions
- organizing work
- completing tasks
- expressing speech and language
- maintaining attention

Providing Support

To help students who need extra support:

Maintain a consistent art program schedule.

Model an art activity before you have students try it.

Modify art instruction to meet students' learning styles so that all students may be successful.

Provide several concrete examples of elements and principles to help students retain new concepts and vocabulary.

Review weekly what students have done or learned previously.

Give positive feedback when students show real effort to participate in discussions or complete production activities.

Talk to students about their specific interests and adjust activities to build on those interests.

SPECIAL-NEEDS STUDENTS

Special-needs students may be visually impaired, hearing impaired, physically disabled, or multiply disabled. These students are usually capable of participating with other students in art experiences despite their disabilities. Art experiences can provide these students with unique opportunities to express their ideas and feelings and to improve their self-esteem and independence. For some of these students, sharing a completed artwork with the class may provide them with significant pride in their accomplishments.

Strategies for Success

Use these strategies to help these students achieve success in their art experiences:

Provide opportunities for additional repetition of skills, such as making brushstrokes or mixing colors.

Set up an uncluttered work environment that is visually stimulating and well organized.

Break down all complex skills and tasks into small steps.

Expect students to participate in all class art activities with other students.

Use multisensory approaches, such as having students see and touch as well as listen to and discuss information about textures and artwork.

Encourage individual choices and self-expression to help empower students. Would they like to use a paintbrush or finger painting to express what they feel? Would they rather use red or blue?

VISUALLY IMPAIRED STUDENTS

- **Have students explore different kinds of lines by working with string or yarn.**
- **Provide a magnifying glass to allow better viewing of details.**
- **Have students use their other senses, such as touch, to examine artworks and explore concepts.**

HEARING-IMPAIRED STUDENTS

- **Provide as many visual models and pictures as possible.**
- **If you or a student in the class knows signing, provide this assistance.**

PHYSICALLY CHALLENGED STUDENTS

- **Have students participate in group projects, such as murals, that do not limit freedom of motion.**
- **Use an adaptive device that will enable these students to use a crayon or paintbrush independently. You can order these devices from medical equipment suppliers.**
- **Suggestions for working with disabled students can be found in *Beyond the Limits*, a publication available through the Museum of Fine Arts, Houston; P.O. Box 68265; Houston, TX 77265.**

SEASONAL ACTIVITIES

Fall

Crayon Etching: Fall Tree

MATERIALS: drawing paper
crayons or oil pastels
pencil, paper clip for scratching
newspaper

1. Show students pictures of trees in autumn with leaves turning various colors. Tell them they will create their own tree with autumn colors.

2. Give each student a padding of newspaper to place under their drawing paper. Have them choose bright autumn colors and cover the entire drawing paper with solid patches of color. Tell them to press hard with the crayon or pastel. Ask them not to use black or brown.

3. Instruct students to cover all of their colors with a thick layer of black crayon.

4. Give each student a pencil or opened paper clip to draw a tree or many trees in autumn by scratching away the black to reveal the color underneath. Encourage students to use various lines, textures, and patterns. Remind them to leave some areas untouched.

Students can glue their trees onto construction paper and display them in the classroom.

Fall

Favorite Foods

MATERIALS: modeling clay and tools such as paper clips, plastic knives and forks
rollers
paper plates
paintbrushes
tempera paint

1. Discuss with students traditional meals during the fall season. Ask them to think of a favorite food that they might re-create in clay.

2. Have students mold the clay into their favorite foods. Some may wish to create an entire Thanksgiving meal, from turkey leg and baked potato to pumpkin pie with ice cream.

3. Allow the clay to dry or fire it, according to the directions that come with the clay you use. Then have students paint their foods with tempera paint.

Have students arrange their clay foods on paper plates. You may want to display them together on a table as a harvest or Thanksgiving feast.

Fall

Eggshell Mosaics

MATERIALS: clean, empty eggshells
tempera paint or food dye
pencils
glue
paintbrushes
tagboard or cardboard

1. Give students tagboard or cardboard to draw a design, fall scene, or holiday picture lightly in pencil. Suggest that they keep their art simple. Explain that they will be using broken eggshells to make mosaics of their drawings. You may need to explain that mosaics are pictures made from small pieces of tile, stone, or glass set in plaster or glue.

2. Have students think about the colors they want in each section of their mosaics. Help them paint or dye the clean eggshells in the colors they need. Allow time for the paint to dry.

3. Have students break the eggshells into small pieces. Tell them to paint glue onto one section of their drawings at a time. Instruct them to place the pieces of eggshell on the glued areas.

Students can display their art in the classroom for the holidays.

Winter

Greeting Cards

MATERIALS: index cards
watercolors
paintbrushes
construction paper
glue

1. Show students examples of nonrepresentational art by Jackson Pollock, Helen Frankenthaler, or another artist.

2. Encourage them to paint their own colorful designs on index cards. Students can use line, color, and shape to express their feelings about a holiday or about the winter season.

3. After the paintings dry, students can glue them to folded construction paper. Instruct them to put the glue on the index card and mount it carefully.

Students can make as many cards as they wish, write holiday greetings inside, and give them to friends and family.

New Year's Paper Cuts

MATERIALS: colored paper or construction paper
glue
scissors

1. Explain to students that paper cuts are an important part of some New Year's celebrations. Flowers are used to decorate windows as reminders that spring will soon be coming.

2. Have students fold colored paper in half and draw, from the fold, half a flower shape, including stem and leaves if desired. Encourage them to draw crescent shapes in the center of their flowers. Later, they will cut them out.

3. To hold the two sides of the paper in position as students cut, tell them to add drops of glue at the outer edge of their folded papers. When the glue dries, have students cut out their flowers, cutting the designs in the center of their flowers first. Instruct them to try to cut the curves as smoothly as they can. Caution them to be careful not to cut through narrow places such as stems.

Students can glue their unfolded flowers to paper of contrasting color and tape them in a window at school or at home.

Soft Sculpture President Puppet

MATERIALS: old stocking or pantyhose
scissors
glue
needle and thread
tempera paint mixed with a little glue
buttons, yarn, and scrap fabric

1. Tell students to each choose a president and to find a picture of him for a model.

2. Direct them to cut a stocking at the knee and the ankle. Have them tie a knot in one end and turn the stocking inside out. This is the puppet's head.

3. Tell students to stuff the head with old newspaper or scraps of fabric, stocking, or pantyhose and to tie a knot at the open end.

4. Have them glue or sew on a button nose. Tell them to add yarn for hair, eyebrows, mustache, and beard. They can paint eyes, ears, and other features for the face.

5. Students can glue or sew scrap fabric to the neck for the puppet's body. Suggest that they add details such as a hat or tie to make their puppets look like their pictures.

Have students interview their puppets for the class. They should prepare by finding out what was happening at the time of each puppet's presidency. Students might also have all of the president puppets discuss among themselves how our country is different today than during their times in office.

Spring

Carp Windsock

MATERIALS: brown wrapping paper or coated butcher paper
scissors
tempera paint or colored markers
thin but sturdy wire
strong tape
gummed cloth hole-punch reinforcements
string

1. Have students draw a fish shape about 24 inches long and 8 inches wide on their paper. The fish mouth should be open. Have them cut out the shape.

2. Direct students to trace the shape on another piece of paper and cut out the second shape. Tell them to decorate their fish with eyes, scales, and fins. Remind them that the two sides of their fish should be symmetrical.

3. Have students glue their fish together at the top and bottom inside edge. The mouth and tail are not glued, to allow the wind to flow through.

4. Help students make wire circles to tape in place in the mouths of their carps. (Safety goggles are needed.)

5. Have students make small holes on each side of the carp mouth and stick on gummed reinforcements inside and outside.

Students should thread a 20-inch loop of string through the holes and knot the ends. They can fly their carps from poles, or hang them in the classroom from clothesline or a suspended hoop.

Spring

Dreamhouses for Birds

MATERIALS: drawing paper
cardboard or tagboard
pencil
crayons or colored markers

1. Ask students to discuss the importance of birds and their need for nesting places.

2. Have each student fold a piece of drawing paper in thirds like a business letter. The middle section will be the front of the bird dreamhouse.

3. Have students sketch on their folded drawing paper the front and two sides of a birdhouse for any bird of their choice. They can make them as fanciful as they wish as long as they keep the needs of the bird in mind. Encourage students to research their bird to find out nesting habits and to learn information such as size of door openings to allow the bird in but not an enemy.

4. You might then have students draw their dreamhouses on cardboard. Encourage them to draw textural details such as stones or logs and architectural details such as gingerbread trim or front porch railings. They can use crayons or markers to add color. Have them score and fold the cardboard in thirds so that the houses can stand.

Students might display their dreamhouses with a card to explain what type of bird might call it home.

Spring

Painted Birds

MATERIALS: self-hardening clay
1½-inch plastic foam balls or small round rocks
tempera paint
paintbrushes

1. Have students mold the clay around the balls or rocks into the shape of a bird body with wings at its sides. Tell them to form small balls of clay into heads, necks, and beaks, scoring and smoothing the clay to attach the head to the body.

2. Encourage students to make the bird's body smooth and to check for cracks in the clay. Allow the clay to dry before students begin to paint.

3. Have students paint their birds with a base of white paint. When the birds are dry, students can add colorful designs, flowers, and details to their birds.

Students might bring their painted birds home to use as part of a centerpiece display at the dinner table.

Summer

Ocean Sunsets

MATERIALS: drawing paper
tempera paints in primary colors
paintbrushes
cardboard
black construction paper
scissors
glue

1. Show students pictures of sunsets over the ocean, and have them discuss the colors surrounding the setting sun. Encourage them to describe how to make those colors using only primary colors.

2. Direct students to draw on their paper a horizon line and a semicircle for the sun somewhere on that horizon. Have them paint the sun yellow.

3. Instruct students to wet their paper above and around the sun. The water will allow the colors to bleed or run into each other.

4. Have students mix colors for their sunsets on the cardboard. Direct them to keep the paint thinned with water. Tell them to paint their sunsets starting near the sun, moving from orange to red to violet-red to purple to deep blue.

5. Below the sun and sky is water. Tell students to imagine that the sun and sunset colors are reflected in the water and to paint what they see in their minds.

6. On the black construction paper, students can draw a sailboat, a palm tree on an island, or anything they wish to silhouette on their ocean sunsets. Direct them to cut out their silhouettes and glue them on their dry paintings.

Students might mount their paintings on black background paper to display at home or in the classroom.

Summer

3-D Shoe Designs

MATERIALS: tempera paints in primary colors
paintbrushes
construction paper
scissors
glue or stapler
newspaper

1. Have students fold a sheet of construction paper in half the long way and place one foot on the paper next to the fold. Direct them to trace around the toes and part of the way down the side to the ankle. Have them then make a right-angle line to the edge of the paper to form a boot shape. See the diagram below.

2. Tell them to cut out the boot shape.

3. Have students lay their paper shoes flat and draw symmetrical designs on both sides. Encourage them to think about adding holes and laces or drawing zippers. They might draw socks at the ankle opening.

4. Have students glue or staple their shoes together at the edges, leaving the ankles open at the top. Have them stuff their shoes with newspaper.

Pin the new summer shoe designs to the classroom bulletin board.

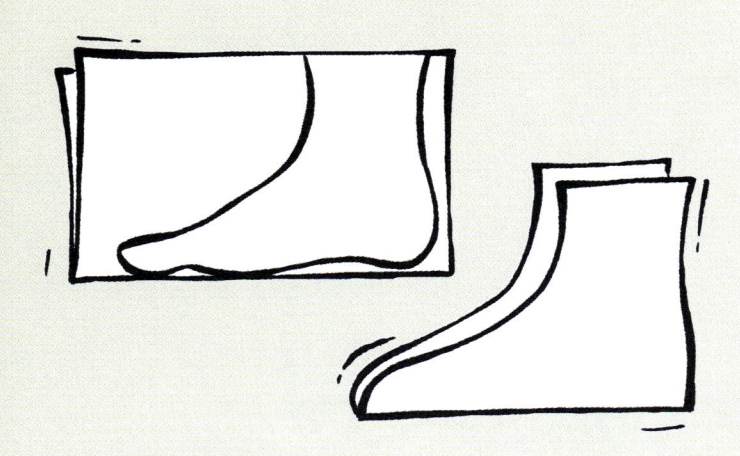

Summer

Freedom Art

MATERIALS: chalk
drawing paper
pencils

1. For safety information about using chalk, please see page 135 in this *Teacher's Edition*.

2. Discuss with students the Emancipation Proclamation and the fact that it helped to free people who had been enslaved. Explain that students will be drawing sidewalk art in chalk with the theme of freedom. Have them brainstorm ideas that they associate with this theme for their art.

3. Ask students to sketch ideas related to the theme that they would like to draw on a sidewalk. (This temporary art could also be drawn in a safe area of the school parking lot.) After they finish their sketches, discuss in what order they will draw the scenes depicted in their art on the chosen sidewalk (especially if chronological order is important).

4. Allow a full art period to give students time outdoors to complete their art.

Inform the rest of the school when the art is ready for viewing. Though rain will soon wash away students' chalk art, the collaborative art experience will be remembered.

SEASONAL ACTIVITIES

_____
(Date)

Dear Family,

Our children see an amazing number of images every day. Just look around. Our world is a very *visual* place. We are surrounded by images, whether they are on television, in videos, in magazines and newspapers, on billboards, or in textbooks. Children need to know how to read, judge, and act on the information they receive from these images.

This school year the children in my class will discover how to think critically about what they see. Exploring art from various cultures will help children analyze, explain, and judge art images. They will also have the opportunity to produce art, allowing them to share their ideas with others.

You can help to make your child's art experiences rich and fulfilling. If you or someone you know has an artistic talent or skill to share with us, call me to arrange a convenient time for a visit. If you know of public displays of art that the class might visit, please let me know so that I might arrange a field trip.

Another way you can help is by sending in materials to use in the children's artwork. Contributions of any of the following materials would be appreciated:

- beads
- newspapers and magazines
- buttons and fabric scraps
- cardboard tubes
- broken costume jewelry
- ribbons, lace
- foam trays and egg cartons
- sponges
- paper clips, plastic utensils
- yarn, thread, spools
- clean socks, stockings

I'm looking forward to a wonderful year exploring art with your child. I am confident that we will share many rewarding experiences.

Sincerely,

Carta a los padres

_____
(Fecha)

Estimados padres,

Nuestros niños ven un número increíble de imágenes todos los días. Miren a su alrededor y se darán cuenta. Nuestro mundo es muy visual. Estamos rodeados de imágenes que vemos en televisión, vídeos, revistas y periódicos, anuncios o en libros de texto. Los niños necesitan saber cómo leer, juzgar y actuar con la información que reciben de esas imágenes.

En este año escolar los niños de mi clase descubrirán cómo pensar con criterio sobre lo que ven. Explorar el arte de diversas culturas los ayudará a analizar, explicar y juzgar imágenes artísticas. También tendrán la oportunidad de producir arte y se les permitirá compartir sus ideas con otros.

Ustedes pueden ayudar a enriquecer las experiencias artísticas de su hijo. Si ustedes o alguien que conozcan tienen talento y habilidades para el arte y las quieren compartir con nosotros, llámenme para arreglar el tiempo conveniente para una visita. Si conocen de exhibiciones públicas de arte que nuestra clase pueda visitar, por favor háganme saber para planear un viaje al lugar.

Nos pueden ayudar mandándonos materiales para usar en las labores artísticas de los niños. También aceptamos contribuciones de cualquiera de los siguientes materiales:

- cuentas de collar
- periódicos y revistas
- botones y retazos de tela
- tubos de cartulina
- joyas de fantasía
- cintas, encaje
- espuma de estireno y cartones para huevos
- esponjas
- presillas, utensilios plásticos
- hilo, estambre, carretes
- calcetines limpios, medias

Espero con ilusión que éste sea un año lleno de maravillas en la exploración del arte con su niño. Confío en que compartiremos muchas experiencias provechosas.

Atentamente,

Home Letter

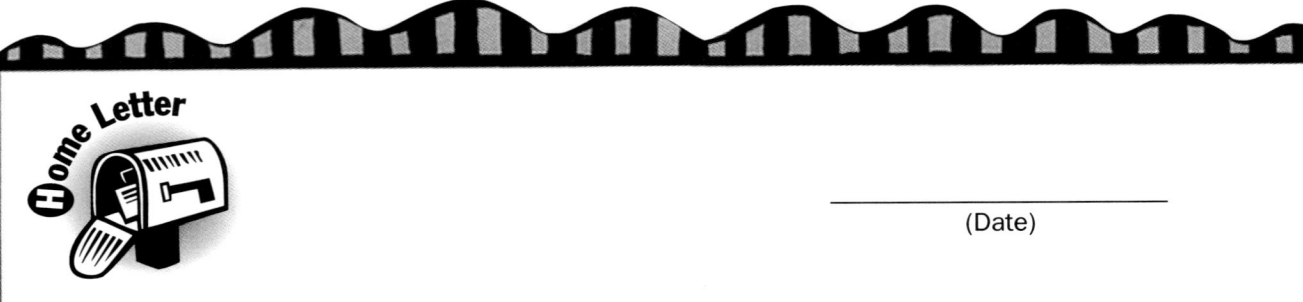

_____
(Date)

Dear Family,

We will be doing an art project in the near future and are in need of some materials to complete it. If possible, please collect and send in with your child any of the materials listed below. We need the materials

by _____.

_____

_____

_____

_____

_____

_____

Your interest in your child's experiences in school encourages success. Thank you for your time.

Sincerely,

Carta a los padres

(Fecha)

Estimados padres,

Próximamente estaremos haciendo un proyecto de arte y necesitamos algunos materiales para su culminación. Si es posible, por favor, envíennos algunos de los que listamos a continuación con su niño.

Necesitamos los materiales para el día _____.

_____

_____

_____

_____

_____

_____

Su interés en las experiencias de su niño en la escuela nos ayuda a triunfar. Gracias por su tiempo.

Atentamente,

Home Letter

_____
(Date)

YOU ARE INVITED!

Come to our

ART SHOW!

We have worked on paintings, sculptures, weavings, prints, and much more. Please visit this special exhibit of our favorite artworks.

DATE: _____

TIME: _____

PLACE: _____

GIVEN BY: _____

Carta a los padres

_____
(Fecha)

¡USTED ESTÁ INVITADO!

¡Venga a nuestra

EXHIBICIÓN DE ARTE!

Hemos trabajado en pinturas, esculturas, impresiones, tejedurías y mucho más. Por favor visite esta exhibición especial de nuestros trabajos artísticos favoritos.

FECHA: _____

HORA: _____

LUGAR: _____

DADO POR: _____

Harcourt Brace School Publishers

Name _____

Landscape Drawing

Draw a landscape that includes organic and geometric shapes.

MATERIALS
• drawing paper • pencil • crayons, colored pencils, or markers • magazines and newspapers

1 **Ask** someone in your family to help you collect magazines and newspapers. Together, look for a photograph of a scene that includes such forms as trees, clouds, and buildings.

2 **Lightly** draw the scene on a sheet of drawing paper. You can add objects that were not in the original scene or leave things out. Remember to use perspective to show depth.

3 **Think** about your setting and the time of day. Add color and shading to your drawing. Add texture to show rough and smooth objects.

4 **Talk** about your drawing with your family. Explain what you did to show depth. Point out how you used color and shading to show time of day. Decide where to display your drawing so that visitors can see it.

R50 ART EXPRESS

SCHOOL-HOME CONNECTION

Name _____

Magazine Covers for Heroes

MATERIALS
- pencil
- crayons, colored pencils, or markers

Draw a portrait of a hero for a magazine cover.

1 **Magazines** often honor people who have done special things. Work with a family member to make a list of people you both admire. They can be well-known people or people in your neighborhood or town. Decide whom you would honor on a magazine cover.

2 **Sketch** the person's portrait below. Then add color and details. After you have completed the portrait, add symbols of the person's achievements. For instance, if the person is a police officer, you might show a badge. After you have completed your portrait, think of a name for the magazine. Share your cover design with others and explain your choice of hero.

Harcourt Brace School Publishers

SCHOOL-HOME CONNECTIONS   **R51**

Name _____

Part Photograph, Part Drawing

Create a scene that is part photograph and part drawing.

MATERIALS
• old magazines
• scissors
• thick paper
• crayons or colored markers
• glue

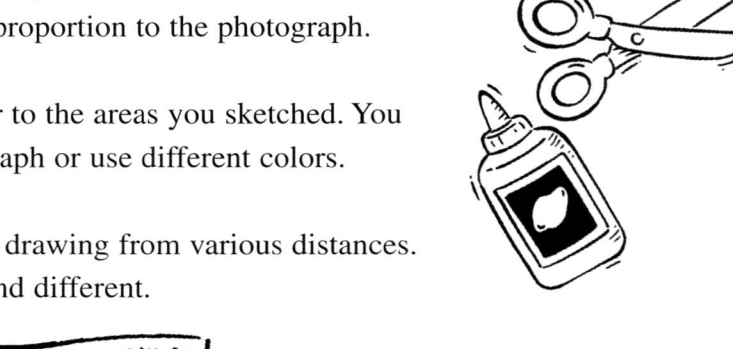

1 **Ask** an older family member to work with you. He or she can help you find a photograph in a magazine. This will be the object or scene that you recreate. Decide which sections of the scene to cut out. Glue them on the paper. Be sure you place the sections in the proper place on the paper.

2 **Sketch** pencil lines connecting the separate sections of the photograph. Keep your drawing lines in proportion to the photograph.

3 **With** markers or crayons, add color to the areas you sketched. You can match the colors in the photograph or use different colors.

4 **Ask** family members to look at the drawing from various distances. Discuss how the parts are similar and different.

R52 ART EXPRESS

Name _____

Printmaking

Make two prints with a variety of shapes. Use colors that show harmony and conflict.

1 **Ask** a family member to help you collect almost-flat objects. Try to find objects with interesting shapes.

2 **Arrange** the objects on the cardboard. Try to create a design that shows balance. Remember that a large object on one side can balance a few small ones on the other.

3 **Glue** or tape down the objects. (Use tape, not glue, on anything that someone needs.)

4 **Lay** the paper over the design. Rub the crayon over the paper to create a print. (Use the side of the crayon, not the tip.)

5 **Ask** a family member whether he or she can tell what objects you used in your design.

MATERIALS
- objects and shapes that are almost flat, such as string, scraps of cardboard, leaves, paper clips, and coins
- smooth cardboard
- white drawing paper
- crayon
- glue
- tape

Name _____

Collage of Art Forms

Make a collage of different art forms.

MATERIALS
• old magazines and newspapers
• scissors
• cardboard
• glue

Work with someone in your family to look through old magazines and newspapers. Clip pictures of as many art forms as you can. You can clip pictures of book covers, movie advertisements, interesting photographs, pictures of unusual or famous buildings, and pictures of paintings, sculptures, and pottery. As you find examples, point out the art forms that you have tried so far this year. Create a collage of your choices. Share your collage with your family.

SCHOOL-HOME CONNECTION

Name _____

A Paper Quilt

Make a patchwork quilt out of construction paper.

MATERIALS
• construction paper in various colors
• tape
• crayons or markers
• ruler
• scissors

1 **Work** with someone in your family. If you can, look at patchwork quilts you may have at home, or visit the library to look at some pictures in books. Discuss how the designs and colors are put together to make one work of art.

2 **Decide** what designs and colors you want in your patchwork quilt. Also, decide how large to make it.

3 **Cut** out identical squares, approximately six inches by six inches, from the colored construction paper. Then use crayons or markers to draw designs on the squares.

4 **Tape** the squares together at their back edges. Ask someone to hold the pieces flat as you do this. Then you can hang up your quilt to display it in your home.

SCHOOL-HOME CONNECTIONS **R55**

RESPONSE CARD 1

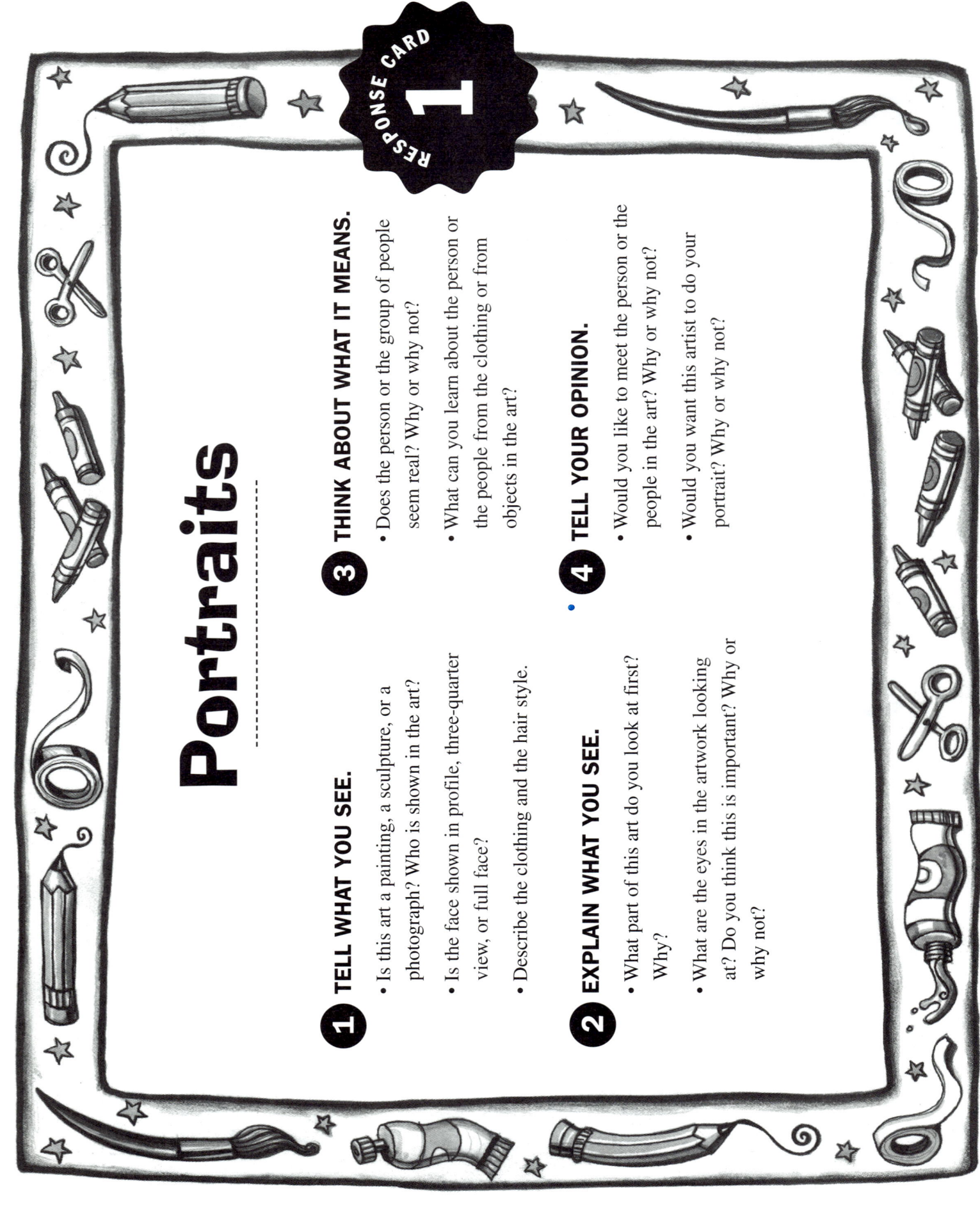

Portraits

1. TELL WHAT YOU SEE.
- Is this art a painting, a sculpture, or a photograph? Who is shown in the art?
- Is the face shown in profile, three-quarter view, or full face?
- Describe the clothing and the hair style.

2. EXPLAIN WHAT YOU SEE.
- What part of this art do you look at first? Why?
- What are the eyes in the artwork looking at? Do you think this is important? Why or why not?

3. THINK ABOUT WHAT IT MEANS.
- Does the person or the group of people seem real? Why or why not?
- What can you learn about the person or the people from the clothing or from objects in the art?

4. TELL YOUR OPINION.
- Would you like to meet the person or the people in the art? Why or why not?
- Would you want this artist to do your portrait? Why or why not?

Everyday Life

1 TELL WHAT YOU SEE.
- What is happening in the art?
- What lines, shapes, and colors did the artist use?

2 EXPLAIN WHAT YOU SEE.
- Did the artist repeat lines, shapes, or colors? If so, why do you think he or she did so?
- How do your eyes move around the art? What is the center of interest? Explain your answer.

3 THINK ABOUT WHAT IT MEANS.
- What can you tell about everyday life at the time shown in this art?
- Why do you think the artist recorded this scene?

4 TELL YOUR OPINION.
- What do you find most interesting in this art? Explain your answer.
- Where do you think this art should be displayed? Why?

RESPONSE CARD 2

RESPONSE CARD 3

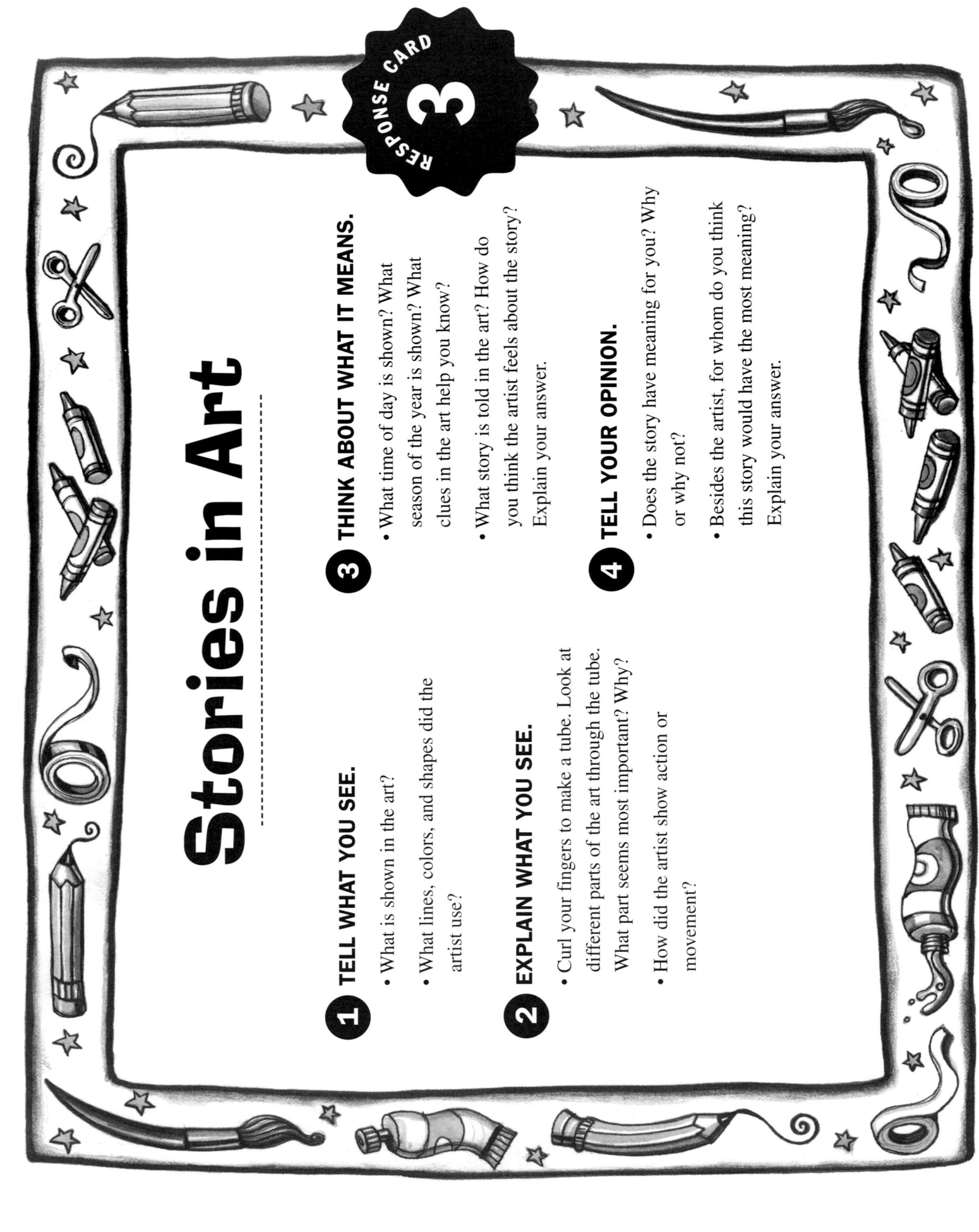

Stories in Art

1 TELL WHAT YOU SEE.
- What is shown in the art?
- What lines, colors, and shapes did the artist use?

2 EXPLAIN WHAT YOU SEE.
- Curl your fingers to make a tube. Look at different parts of the art through the tube. What part seems most important? Why?
- How did the artist show action or movement?

3 THINK ABOUT WHAT IT MEANS.
- What time of day is shown? What season of the year is shown? What clues in the art help you know?
- What story is told in the art? How do you think the artist feels about the story? Explain your answer.

4 TELL YOUR OPINION.
- Does the story have meaning for you? Why or why not?
- Besides the artist, for whom do you think this story would have the most meaning? Explain your answer.

Still Lifes and Objects in Nature

1 TELL WHAT YOU SEE.
- What objects do you see in the artwork?
- What lines, shapes, and textures did the artist use?

2 EXPLAIN WHAT YOU SEE.
- How did the artist arrange the objects in the art? Do the objects overlap? Are they repeated?
- How did the artist balance the objects in the art?

3 THINK ABOUT WHAT IT MEANS.
- Which of your five senses does the artwork appeal to?
- Are symbols used in the art? If so, what do you think they stand for?

4 TELL YOUR OPINION.
- Do you think this artwork is important or valuable? Why or why not?
- If you owned this artwork, where would you display it? Why?

RESPONSE CARD 4

RESPONSE CARD 5

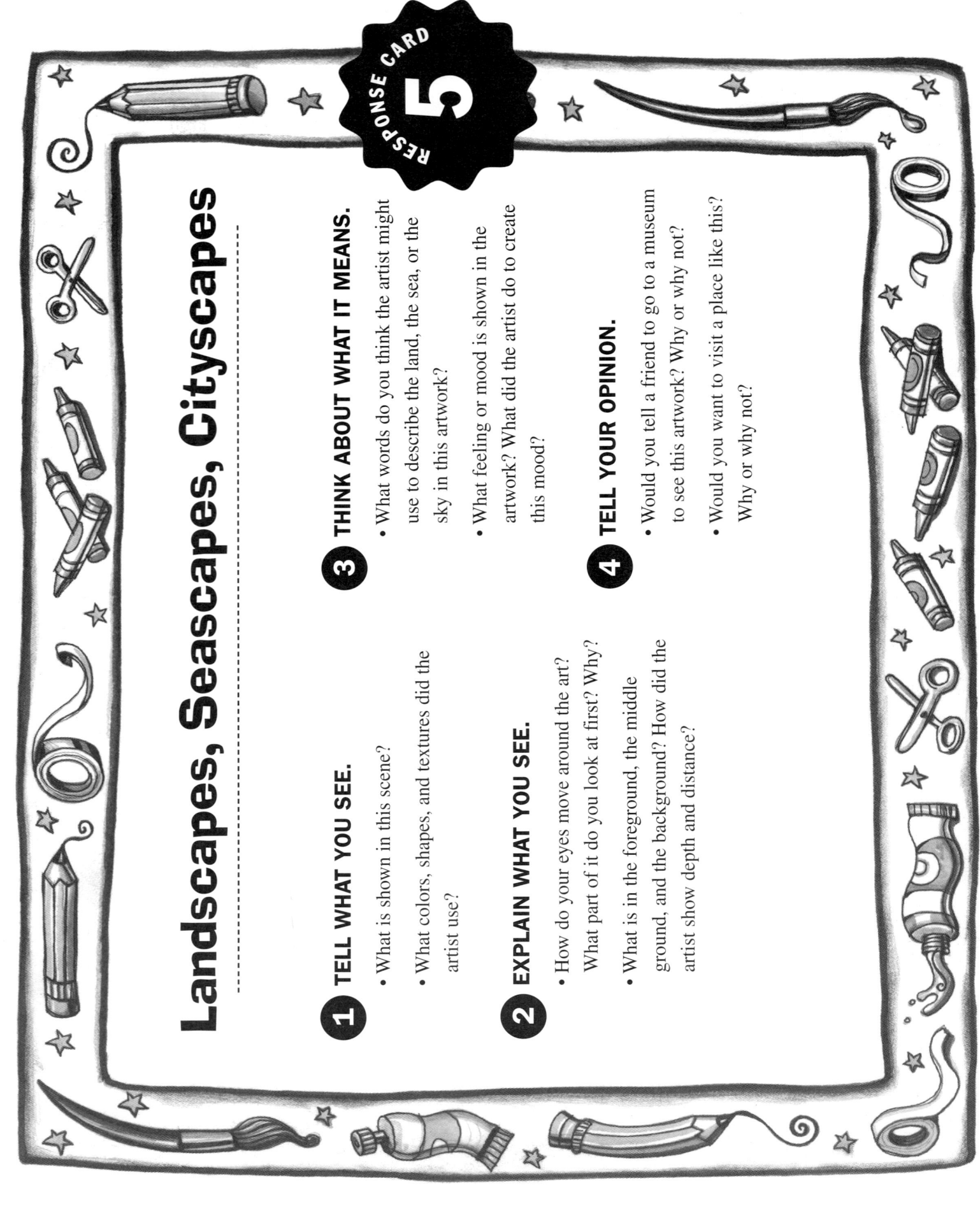

Landscapes, Seascapes, Cityscapes

① TELL WHAT YOU SEE.
- What is shown in this scene?
- What colors, shapes, and textures did the artist use?

② EXPLAIN WHAT YOU SEE.
- How do your eyes move around the art? What part of it do you look at first? Why?
- What is in the foreground, the middle ground, and the background? How did the artist show depth and distance?

③ THINK ABOUT WHAT IT MEANS.
- What words do you think the artist might use to describe the land, the sea, or the sky in this artwork?
- What feeling or mood is shown in the artwork? What did the artist do to create this mood?

④ TELL YOUR OPINION.
- Would you tell a friend to go to a museum to see this artwork? Why or why not?
- Would you want to visit a place like this? Why or why not?

Nonrepresentational Art

1 TELL WHAT YOU SEE.
- Describe the artwork. How is it unusual?
- What materials is it made of?

2 EXPLAIN WHAT YOU SEE.
- How do you think the artist created this art?
- How do your eyes move around the artwork?

3 THINK ABOUT WHAT IT MEANS.
- How do the colors and lines show a feeling or mood in this art?
- What do you think this artwork means?

4 TELL YOUR OPINION.
- What interests you most about this art? Explain your answer.
- Did this artwork surprise you? Why or why not?

RESPONSE CARD 6

RESPONSE CARDS R61

RESPONSE CARD 7

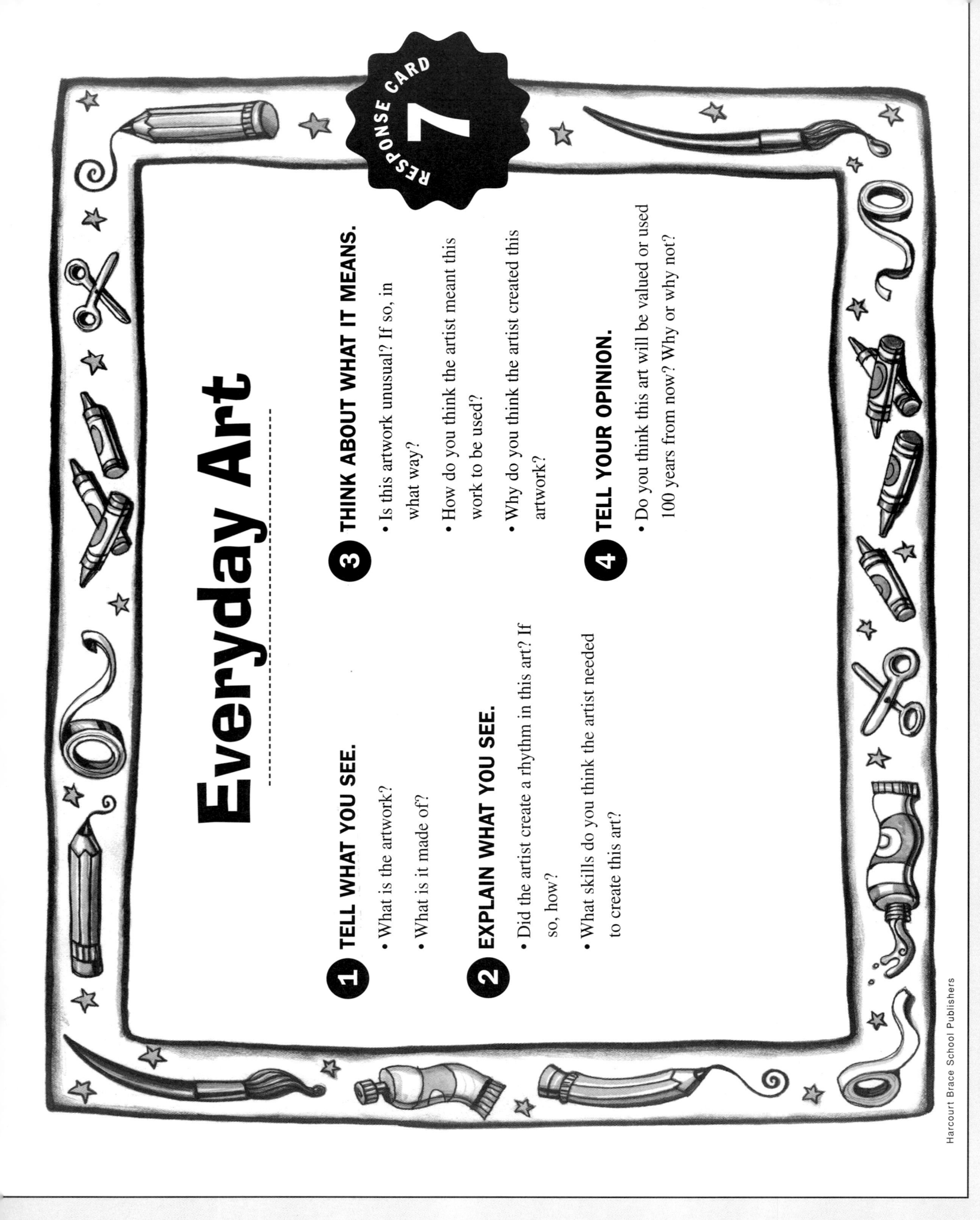

Everyday Art

① TELL WHAT YOU SEE.
- What is the artwork?
- What is it made of?

② EXPLAIN WHAT YOU SEE.
- Did the artist create a rhythm in this art? If so, how?
- What skills do you think the artist needed to create this art?

③ THINK ABOUT WHAT IT MEANS.
- Is this artwork unusual? If so, in what way?
- How do you think the artist meant this work to be used?
- Why do you think the artist created this artwork?

④ TELL YOUR OPINION.
- Do you think this art will be valued or used 100 years from now? Why or why not?

Art Critics' Circle

As a member of an Art Critics' Circle, you will discuss one or more artworks. Here's what to do:

1 Look carefully at the artwork that you will discuss.

2 Keep the Response Card handy to guide the discussion.

3 Read each question on the Response Card. Write notes that might help you discuss the artwork.

4 Decide with your group when you are ready to discuss the artwork.

5 Be sure that every member of the group can see the artwork during the discussion.

6 Be courteous. Allow each member of the group time to respond to each question. Accept all viewpoints.

7 If members of the group think of more questions, allow time to discuss them.

RESPONSE CARD 8

RESPONSE CARDS R63

RESPONSE CARD 9

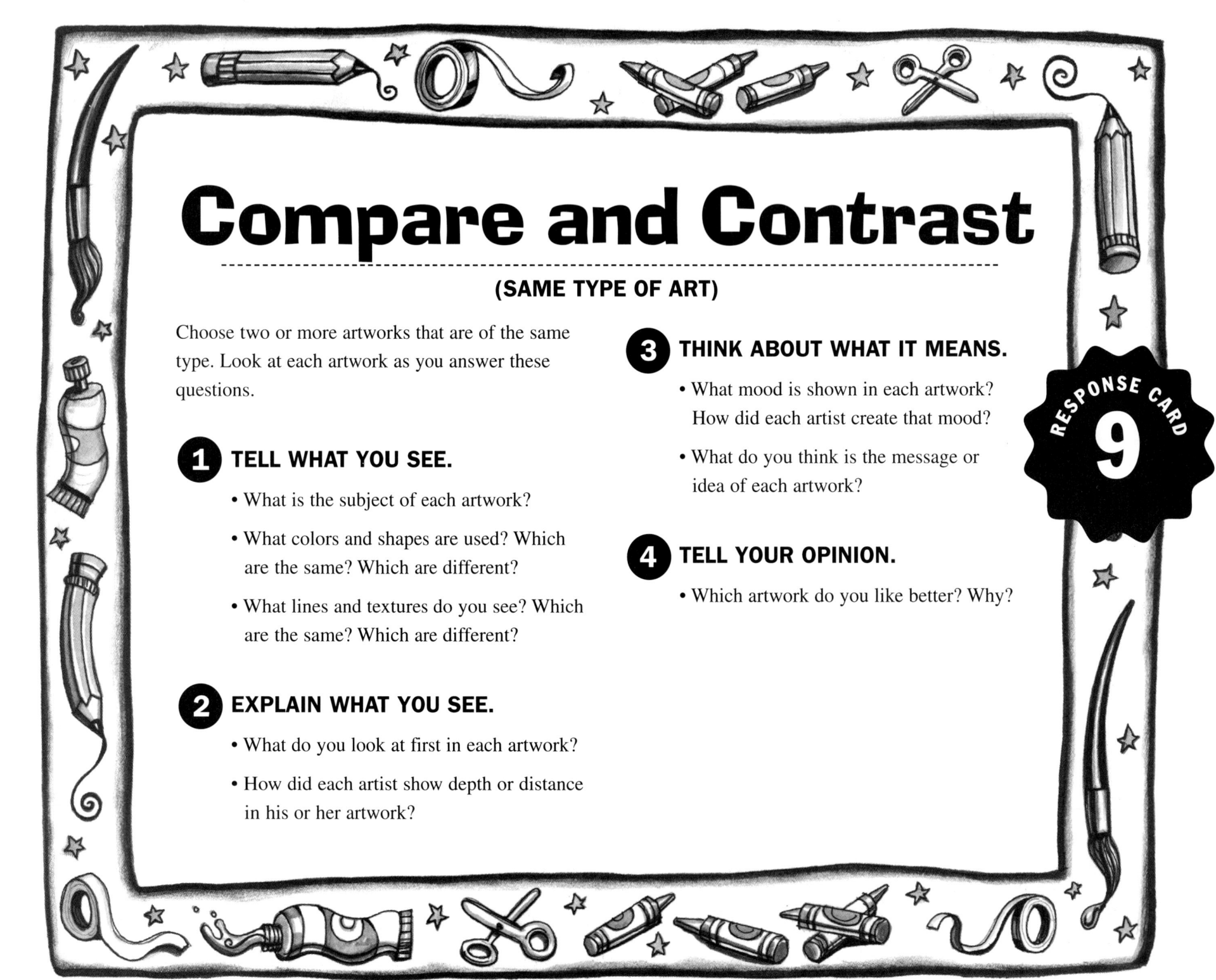

Compare and Contrast
(SAME TYPE OF ART)

Choose two or more artworks that are of the same type. Look at each artwork as you answer these questions.

① TELL WHAT YOU SEE.
- What is the subject of each artwork?
- What colors and shapes are used? Which are the same? Which are different?
- What lines and textures do you see? Which are the same? Which are different?

② EXPLAIN WHAT YOU SEE.
- What do you look at first in each artwork?
- How did each artist show depth or distance in his or her artwork?

③ THINK ABOUT WHAT IT MEANS.
- What mood is shown in each artwork? How did each artist create that mood?
- What do you think is the message or idea of each artwork?

④ TELL YOUR OPINION.
- Which artwork do you like better? Why?

Harcourt Brace School Publishers

Compare and Contrast

(ART BY SAME ARTIST)

Choose two or more artworks by the same artist. Look at each artwork as you answer these questions.

1 TELL WHAT YOU SEE.
- What is shown in each artwork?
- What colors and shapes can you find? Which are the same? Which are different?
- What lines and textures did the artist use? Which are the same? Which are different?

2 EXPLAIN WHAT YOU SEE.
- What part of each artwork do you look at first? How did the artist draw your attention to that part?
- Is the art balanced in each artwork? If so, explain how the artist did that.

3 THINK ABOUT WHAT IT MEANS.
- What is the mood of each artwork? How did the artist create the mood?
- What clues tell you that these artworks were made by the same artist?

4 TELL YOUR OPINION.
- If you could choose one of these artworks to display in your school, which would you choose? Why?

RESPONSE CARD 10

MATERIALS LIST

	Unit 1	Unit 2	Unit 3	Unit 4	Unit 5	Unit 6
PAPER						
Butcher paper, 10–12 ft. per class						•
Cardboard, 3–4 large pieces per student		•	•		•	
Fadeless paper, all colors, 18–24 sheets per student	•	•	•	•		
Construction paper, all colors, 10 sheets per student		•	•			
Manila paper, 1–2 large sheets per student	•					
Newsprint, 1–2 sheets per student			•			
Oak tagboard, 3–4 sheets per student	•			•		•
Paper scraps in assorted sizes						•
Poster board, 4–5 pieces per student		•	•			
Watercolor paper, 1–2 sheets per student		•				
Wax paper, 1–2 sheets per student	•					
White paper (large, 10–16 sheets per student; small, 10–15 sheets per student; heavy, 1–2 sheets per student)	•	•	•	•	•	•
PAINTING, DRAWING, AND PRINTMAKING						
Colored pencils, assorted colors, 1 box per student	•				•	
Crayons, assorted colors, 1 box per student	•	•		•		
Dry sponges, 1–2 per student				•		
Fabric paint or markers, assorted colors, 1 box per class						•
Liquid tempera, assorted colors, 1 or 2 pints each per class	•	•	•	•	•	•
Markers (narrow-tip colored, water-based), 1 box per student			•	•	•	•
Paintbrushes, 1 small and 1 medium per student; various sizes, 2–4 per class	•	•	•	•	•	•
Pastels (oil or chalk), assorted colors, 1 box per student	•	•				
Soft pencils, 1 or 2 each per student	•	•		•		
Watercolor paints, assorted colors, 1 package per student	•	•		•		
CLAY						
Carving tools (paper clips, toothpicks, plastic knives)						•
Ceramic clay in 25 lb. bag						
Modeling clay			•			
Rolling pin						•

	UNIT					
MATERIALS USED LESS FREQUENTLY	1	2	3	4	5	6
Aluminum foil, 1–2 rolls per class					•	
Balloons, balls (rubber, foam)	•			•	•	
Books and magazines					•	•
Boxes (assorted sizes)				•		
Twigs, leaves, rocks, ferns, feathers, wood chips	•			•	•	
Cardboard boxes (shoe box or larger), 1 per student			•			
Craft sticks, 2 per student		•				•
Dry wheat paste		•				
Fabric, scraps of cloth, netting					•	•
Foam board			•		•	
Index cards (unlined), 10–20 per student					•	
Milk cartons, paper-towel rolls, blocks					•	
Objects with interesting textures	•					
Photogram kits or sun print paper, 1–2 sheets per student					•	
Pipe cleaners, 5 per student	•					
Plaster of paris, 10–15 packages					•	
Raffia, straw, or other natural fibers						•
Safety glasses, 1 per student	•					
Stones (colored), shells		•		•		•
Straw						•
Straws (drinking, 5 per student; stirrer, 1–2 per student)						•
String, fishing line, thread and needles				•	•	•
Trim or lace, beads		•				•
Washers						•
Wire, 5–6 feet per student, wire cutter	•				•	•
Yarn (various colors)						•

General Classroom Materials: glue (white), hole punch, liquid detergent, paper towels, newspapers, rulers, compass, scissors, soft pencils, stapler (heavy-duty), staples, tape (cellophane and masking), tapes of harmonious and rhythmic/percussive music, tape player, towels and/or rags, water, sponges

FREE AND INEXPENSIVE MATERIALS

General Classroom Materials	Where to Find Them
Art samples	Art materials manufacturers
Books, cards, catalogs, magazines (damaged, outdated)	Book shops, department stores, newsstands, seed companies, stationers, library book sales
Building materials (dowels, scrap lumber, wood shavings, furniture parts, bricks, screws, nuts, bolts)	Contractors, builders, lumberyards
Clothing trim, buttons, thread spools	Fabric/garment manufacturers, fabric shops
Fabric/carpet remnants, leather scraps	Carpet manufacturers and shops, fabric/garment manufacturers, fabric shops, shoe manufacturers and repair shops
Paper (scrap, wrapping, samples)	Copy shops, department stores, paper manufacturers, printers, newspapers, stationers
Styrofoam™	Department stores, florists, supermarkets
Tile (damaged, samples, seconds)	Hardware/paint stores, plumbers, tile manufacturers
Wire, wire spools	Florists, hardware stores, plumbers, telephone/power companies

Printed Informational Resources	Where to Find Them
• "Beyond the 3 Rs: Transforming Education with the Arts" • The "ArtsEdNet Offline" Newsletter • "Educating for the Workplace Through the Arts: A *Business Week* Insert"	Getty Education Institute for the Arts 1200 Getty Center Drive Suite 600 Los Angeles, CA 90049-1683 (800) 223-3431
• "The Theater and Your Child" • "Your Child and the Visual Arts"	Consumer Information Center P.O. Box 100 Pueblo, CO 81002

Technology Resources	Where to Find Them
Activities that support the concepts taught in **Art Express**	The Learning Site http://www.hbschool.com/art
Curriculum frameworks and materials, art education news, interactive areas for students, a searchable database of art education information	ArtsEdge http://artsedge.kennedy-center.org/
Lesson plans, curriculum ideas, access to images	ArtsEdNet http://www.ArtsEdNet.getty.edu/
Shareware, software samples, links to other useful sites	The Incredible Art Department http://www.in.net/~kenroar/artstuff.html
Newsletters, curriculum resources, information about staff development and museum collaboration programs	North Texas Institute for Educators on the Visual Arts http://www.art.unt.edu/ntieva/
Activities, lesson plans, art techniques, information about products	Crayola http://www.crayola.com/

FOR YOUR INFORMATION

BOOKS AND ARTICLES

Alejandro, Ann. "Like Happy Dreams: Integrating Visual Arts, Writing, and Reading." *Language Arts,* January 1994.

Armstrong, Carmen L. *Designing Assessment in Art,* National Art Education Association, 1994.

Armstrong, Carmen L. "Stages of Inquiry in Producing Art: Model, Rationale and Application to a Teacher Questioning Strategy." *Studies in Art Education,* September 1986.

Armstrong, Carmen L.; Armstrong, Nolan A. "Art Teacher Questioning Strategy." *Studies in Art Education,* 1977.

Atkins, Robert. *Artspoke: A Guide to Modern Ideas, Movements, and Buzzwords.* Abbeville, 1993.

Baker, David W. "'Git Real': On Art Education and Community Needs." *Art Education,* November 1990.

Barber, Wendy; Hinchcliffe, John. *Ceramic Style: Making and Decorating Patterned Ceramic Ware.* New York: Sterling, 1996.

Battin, Margaret P. "Cases for Kids: Using Puzzles to Teach Aesthetics to Children." *Journal of Aesthetic Education,* September 1994.

Battin, Margaret P.; Fisher, John; Moore, Ronald; Silvers, Anita. *Puzzles About Art: An Aesthetics Casebook.* New York: St. Martin's Press, 1989.

Berk, Ellyn; Ross, Jerrold. *A Framework for Multicultural Arts Education.* New York: The National Arts Education Research Center at New York University, 1989.

Blandy, Douglas; Hoffman, Elizabeth. "Toward an Art Education of Place." *Studies in Art Education,* 1993.

Blizzard, Gladys S. *Animals in Art.* Charlottesville, VA: Thomasson-Grant, 1992.

Blizzard, Gladys S. *Enjoying Art with Children.* Charlottesville, VA: Thomasson-Grant, 1993.

Bolin, Paul. "We Are What We Ask." *Art Education,* September 1996.

Bolognese, Don. *Mastering the Computer for Design and Illustration.* New York: Watson-Guptill, 1988.

Bresler, Liora. "Imitative, Complementary, and Expansive: Three Roles of Visual Arts Curricula." *Studies in Art Education,* December 1994.

Brookes, Mona. *Drawing with Children* (tenth edition). New York: G.P. Putnam's Sons, 1996.

Brown, Rachel. *The Weaving, Spinning, and Dyeing Book.* New York: Knopf, 1983.

Clarkin, Maura A. *National Gallery of Art Activity Book.* Bergenfield, NJ: Harry N. Abrams, in association with the National Gallery of Art, 1994.

Cole, Bruce; Gealt, Adelheid. *Art of the Western World: From Ancient Greece to Post-Modernism.* New York: Simon and Schuster, 1989.

Cowan, Marilee Mansfield; Clover, Faith M. "Enhancement of Self-Concept Through Discipline-Based Art Education." *Art Education,* March 1991.

Cullinan, Bernice E.; Galda, Lee. *Literature and the Child* (third edition). Fort Worth, TX: Harcourt Brace College Publishers, 1994.

Cummings, Pat. *Talking with Artists.* New York: Macmillan, 1992.

Cummings, Pat. *Talking with Artists, Two.* New York: Macmillan, 1995.

Daniel, Vesta A. H. "The Artist as Professional: An Ethnic-Cultural Perspective." *Journal of Career Education,* March 1982.

Daniel, Vesta A. H.; Daniel, Philip T. K. "Multicultural Strategies for Teaching Art." *School Arts,* October 1979.

Daniel, Vesta A. H.; Delacruz, Elizabeth Manley. "Editorial: Art Education as Multicultural Education: The Underpinnings of Reform." *Visual Arts Research,* Fall 1993.

Davidson, Rosemary. *Take a Look: An Introduction to the Experience of Art.* New York: Viking, 1993.

DiBlasio, Margaret K. "Reflections on the Theory of Discipline-Based Art Education." *Studies in Art Education.* Summer 1987.

Dorn, Charles M. *Thinking in Art: A Philosophical Approach to Art Education.* Reston, VA: National Art Education Association, 1994.

Dunnahoo, Dan E. "Rethinking Creativity: A Discipline-Based Perspective." *Art Education,* July 1993.

Edwards, Betty. *Drawing on the Right Side of the Brain.* New York: J. P. Tarcher, 1979.

Edwards, Ruby J. *Aesthetics and Art Criticism: Questioning Strategies for Elementary Children.* Dayton, OH: University of Dayton Press, December 1991.

Eisner, Elliot W. "The Emergence of New Paradigms for Educational Research." *Art Education,* November 1993.

Eisner, Elliot W. *The Misunderstood Role of the Arts in Human Development.* Bloomington, IN: Phi Delta Kappan, April 1992.

Eisner, Elliot W. "What Artistically Crafted Research Can Help Us to Understand About Schools." *Educational Theory,* December 1995.

Eisner, Elliot W. "What the Arts Taught Me About Education." *Art Education,* September 1991.

Elsen, Albert E. *Purposes of Art* (fourth edition). CBS College Publishing, 1981.

Feldman, Edmund Burke. "The Teacher as Model Critic." *Journal of Aesthetic Education,* January 1973.

Feldman, Edmund Burke. *Thinking About Art.* Englewood Cliffs, NJ: Prentice Hall, 1985.

Feldman, Edmund Burke. "Visual Literacy." *Journal of Aesthetic Education,* July 1976.

Freedman, Kerry. "Interpreting Gender and Visual Culture in Art Classrooms." *Studies in Art Education,* Spring 1994.

Greenberg, Jan; Jordan, Sandra. *The American Eye: Eleven Artists of the Twentieth Century.* New York: Delacorte, 1995.

Greenberg, Jan; Jordan, Sandra. *The Painter's Eye: Learning to Look at Contemporary Art.* New York: Delacorte, 1991.

Greenberg, Jan; Jordan, Sandra. *The Sculptor's Eye: Looking at Contemporary American Art.* New York: Delacorte, 1993.

Hamblen, Karen A. "An Art Criticism Questioning Strategy within the Framework of Bloom's Taxonomy." *Studies in Art Education,* September 1984.

Hanson, Lee. *Learning Through Visual Art.* Los Angeles, CA: Performing Tree, 1985.

Hickman, Richard. "A Student Centered Approach for Understanding Art." *Art Education,* September 1994.

Innes, Miranda. *Jewelry: A Practical Guide to Creative Crafts.* New York: Dorling Kindersley, 1996.

Isaacson, Philip M. *A Short Walk Around the Pyramids and Through the World of Art.* New York: Knopf, 1993.

Kellogg, Rhoda. *Analyzing Children's Art.* Bethesda, MD: National Press Books, 1970.

Kleiner, Fred S.; Tansey, Richard G. *Gardner's Art Through the Ages* (tenth edition). Fort Worth, TX: Harcourt Brace College Publishers, 1996.

Krull, Kathleen. *Lives of the Artists: Masterpieces, Messes (and What the Neighbors Thought).* San Diego: Harcourt Brace, 1995.

Lasky, Lila; Mukerji-Bergeson, Rose. *Art: Basic for Young Children.* Washington, D.C.: National Association for the Education of Young Children, 1995.

Laver, David A. *Design Basics.* Austin, TX: Holt, Rinehart and Winston, 1979.

Lazear, David. *Seven Pathways of Learning: Teaching Students and Parents About Multiple Intelligences.* New York: Zephyr Press, 1994.

Lewis, Samella. *African American Art and Artists.* Berkeley, CA: University of California Press, 1990.

Lowenfeld, Viktor; Brittain, W. Lambert. *Creative and Mental Growth* (eighth edition). Englewood Cliffs, NJ: Prentice Hall, 1987.

Mayer, Ralph. *Art Terms and Techniques.* New York: HarperCollins, 1991.

McElroy, Guy C.; Powell, Richard J.; Patton, Sharon F. *African-American Artists 1880–1987: Selections from the Evans-Tibbs Collection.* Washington, DC: Smithsonian Institution Traveling Exhibition Service, 1989.

Mims, Sandra Kay; Lankford, E. Louis. "Time, Money, and the New Art Education: A Nationwide Investigation." *Studies in Art Education,* Winter 1995.

Monteverde, Susana. "Art Museum Education and Creative Drama: Facilitating Individual Interpretations of Art." (Thesis) Austin, TX: University of Texas, 1997.

Moore, Juliet. "Post-Modernism and DBAE: A Contextual Analysis." *Art Education,* November 1991.

Moore, Ronald M. (editor). *Aesthetics for Young People.* Reston, VA: National Art Education Association, 1995.

National Art Education Association. *Safety in the Artroom.* Reston, VA: NAEA, 1986.

National Art Education Association, NAEA Visual Standards Task Force (Jeanne Rollins, Chair). *National Visual Art Standards.* Reston, VA: NAEA, 1994.

Parsons, Michael J.; Blocker, Gene H. *Aesthetics and Education.* Champaign, IL: University of Illinois Press, 1993.

Roalf, Peggy. *Looking at Paintings* (series). New York: Hyperion, 1992–1994.

Seefeldt, Carol. "Art: A Serious Work." *Young Children,* March 1995.

Simpson, Alan; Smith, Ralph A. (editors). *Aesthetics and Arts Education.* Champaign, IL: University of Illinois Press, 1991.

Smith, Peter. "Art and Irrelevance." *Studies in Art Education,* Winter 1995.

Stankiewicz, Mary Ann. "Art Education Reform and New Technologies," *Art Education,* November 1996.

Sullivan, Charles (editor). *Children of Promise: African American Literature and Art for Young People.* Bergenfield, NJ: Harry N. Abrams, 1991.

Sullivan, Charles (editor). *Here Is My Kingdom: Hispanic American Literature and Art for Young People.* Bergenfield, NJ: Harry N. Abrams, 1994.

Sullivan, Graeme. "Art-Based Art Education: Learning That Is Meaningful, Authentic, Critical and Pluralistic." *Studies in Art Education,* September 1993.

Texas Education Agency. *Art Education: Planning for Teaching and Learning.* Austin, TX: TEA, 1989.

Thompson, Christine (editor). *The Visual Arts and Early Childhood Learning.* Reston, VA: National Art Education Association, 1995.

Toale, Bernard. *Basic Printmaking Techniques.* Worcester, MA: Davis, 1993.

Topal, Catherine. *Children and Painting.* Worcester, MA: Davis, 1992.

Turner, Robyn Montana. *Texas Traditions: The Culture of the Lone Star State.* Boston: Little, Brown, 1996.

Walker, Sydney Roberts. "Designing Studio Instruction: Why Have Students Make Artwork?" *Art Education,* September 1996.

Whipple, Laura (editor). *Celebrating America: A Collection of Poems and Images of the American Spirit.* New York: Philomel Books, in association with the Art Institute of Chicago, 1994.

Williams, Doug. *Teaching Mathematics Through Children's Art.* Portsmouth, NH: Heinemann, 1990.

Zurmuehlen, Marilyn. *Studio Art: Praxis, Symbol, Presence.* Reston, VA: National Art Education Association, 1990.

TECHNOLOGY AND VIDEO RESOURCES

INTERNET http://www.hbschool.com

Increasingly, teachers and students have access at home or at school to the Internet, a worldwide communication system that is often called the information superhighway. The World Wide Web is the most user-friendly and fastest growing part of the Internet.

Harcourt Brace School Publishers has established *The Learning Site* on the World Wide Web to extend, enrich, and enhance Harcourt Brace publications. You can visit *The Learning Site* at **http://www.hbschool.com.**

Various units in *Art Express* are correlated to specially designed interactive art activities on the Internet. For correlations to these activities, visit *The Learning Site* or refer to the unit lesson-planner pages.

DISTRIBUTORS OF HARDWARE AND SOFTWARE FOR STUDENT USE

These are the distributors of products listed on the unit lesson-planner pages.

HARDWARE

KidBoard
6545 France Avenue South, Suite 376, Edina, MN 55435
(800) 926-3066 FAX: (800) 926-3066

KidDraw™ is a computer drawing tablet and stylus kit made for children. It can be used for tracing, drawing, and sketching. It is packaged with Adobe® software and is compatible with most popular software packages.

SOFTWARE

Bannister Productions
1155 Park Ave. #8E, New York, NY 10128
(212) 289-5450

Look What I See!—This CD-ROM grew out of popular workshops conducted by Muriel Silberstein-Storfer at the Metropolitan Museum of Art. The program explores some of the key elements of art, such as color and shape, as seen in the world around us and in many works of art from the museum's collections.

Crayola/MicroGrafx
1303 East Arapaho Road, Richardson, TX 75081
(214) 234-1769 FAX: (214) 994-6227

Crayola Art Studio 2™—This coloring program provides many exciting creative activities. Tools include a picture-show maker, a badge and certificate maker, a talking keyboard, a paint program, fill patterns, an art gallery, audio guides, animation, and stickers.

CyberPuppy Software
2248 Park Boulevard, Palo Alto, CA 94306
(716) 326-2449

Monstrous Media Kit™—This storytelling software makes it easy for children to create their own stories using text, sound, realistic images, color, and special effects. Works can be presented as full-screen slide shows, as movies, or in print.

Harcourt Brace School Publishers
6277 Sea Harbor Drive, Orlando, FL 32887
(800) 225-5425 (ordering) FAX: (800) 874-6418

Imagination Express, Destination: Castle

Imagination Express, Destination: Pyramids

Imagination Express, Destination: Time Trip, USA

Imagination Express™ is a storybook maker that gives students the tools to create their own interactive electronic books. Three "destinations" provide a variety of settings and characters that students can size.

The New Kid Pix®—This multimedia program includes hundreds of rubber stamps, paintbrushes, and a slide show feature. Students can create productions combining video, special effects, photos, and music.

Thinkin' Things™ *Collection 1*—Students can create kinetic art and discover spatial relationships, using BLOX-Flying Shapes. They can blend music, art, and science as they experiment with motion and the illusion of depth to create unique visual effects with BLOX-Flying Spheres.

Thinkin' Things Collection 2—Students can create dynamic visual effects that separate pictures into foreground and background layers with Snake BLOX. They can create pictures, map them onto three-dimensional shapes, and experiment with positive and negative space, using 2-3D BLOX.

Roger Wagner Publishing, Inc.
1050 Pioneer Way, Suite P, El Cajon, CA 92020
(619) 442-0522 FAX: (619) 442-0525

HyperStudio®—This multimedia authoring tool allows users to bring together text, sound, graphics, and video. HyperStudio also provides ways to access data on the Internet and to create and edit QuickTime® movies. It has a built-in image capture camera.

DISTRIBUTORS OF SOFTWARE FOR TEACHER USE

Corbis
15395 SE 30th Place, Suite 300, Bellevue, WA 98007
(800) 246-2065

A Passion for Art: Renoir, Cezanne, Matisse, and Dr. Barnes—This cinematic multimedia CD-ROM presents one of the world's greatest, most controversial, and long-hidden private collections of Post-Impressionist paintings. It includes masterpieces by Renoir, Cezanne, Matisse, and others in a virtual gallery that shows the paintings in beautiful detail.

The Learning Company
6160 Summit Drive North, Minneapolis, MN 55430
(612) 569-1500

ArtRageous—With this 3-D interactive software, viewers learn about artists, their different styles and techniques, and the theories that inspired them. The software includes a comprehensive database of biographical information on the artists and their paintings, as well as a reference section that explains art terms and movements.

Microsoft Corporation
One Microsoft Way, Redmond, WA 98057-6399
(206) 882-8080

Microsoft Art Gallery—Experience more than 2,000 masterpieces in detail from the National Gallery of Art in London.

Philips Media
10960 Wilshire Blvd., 7th Floor, Los Angeles, CA 90024
(800) 883-3767

Masterpiece Mansion—*Masterpiece Mansion* combines art appreciation with interactive gaming elements. The interactive CD-ROM centers around 150 famous works of art and 45 artists representing a variety of periods and movements, including ancient Greek art, ancient Roman art, Renaissance art, Dutch Realism, Impressionism, and twentieth-century art.

The Voyager Company
578 Broadway, Suite 406, New York, NY 10012
(212) 431-5199

With Open Eyes—Experience more than 200 works of art from the collection of Chicago's Art Institute. Images are accompanied by games and audio clips that make viewers look closer, laugh, or think twice about what they're looking at.

DISTRIBUTORS OF VIDEOCASSETTES

First Run/Icarus Films
153 Waverly Place, 6th Floor, New York, NY 10014
(212) 727-1711

Linnea in Monet's Garden—A unique blend of imagination and art appreciation, this award-winning video teaches children about the art and life of Monet. Beautiful animation is combined with views of Monet's garden, home, studio, and subjects, as well as his famous paintings.

Harcourt Brace School Publishers
6277 Sea Harbor Drive, Orlando, FL 32887
(800) 225-5425 (ordering) FAX: (800) 874-6418
Get to Know an Author series:

Get to Know Keith Baker—The author-illustrator tells how he finds inspiration for his books, and he demonstrates his creative process.

Get to Know Gerald McDermott—The Caldecott Medalist tells how he created his trickster characters, Coyote, Zoma, and Raven.

Reading Rainbow® videos: Each episode promotes visual and written literacy as children make connections between the story and their own lives. The series is hosted by LeVar Burton.

- *Stay Away from the Junkyard!*—In *Stay Away from the Junkyard!* by Tricia Tusa, Theodora wanders into the forbidden junkyard. There she discovers that, although some things may appear old and useless at first glance, there are creative ways to give them purpose. Viewers of this video meet an artist who collects objects that some people may consider junk. The artist then transforms these everyday objects into beautiful artwork.

- *Tar Beach*—Faith Ringgold's *Tar Beach*, read by Ruby Dee in the video, takes viewers up on the roof to a "tar beach," an urban oasis in the sky. Viewers experience a celebration of life above the city and a soaring tribute to the George Washington Bridge.

- *The Wall*—Inspired by the moving book *The Wall* by Eve Bunting, LeVar visits the Vietnam Veterans Memorial in Washington, D.C. Viewers meet Maya Lin, the talented young architect who designed this amazing monument. A look at Mount Rushmore and a mural dedicated to Louis Armstrong expand the concept of a wall as a way to pay tribute to those who have gone before.

L & S Video, Inc.
45 Stornowaye, Chappaqua, NY 10514
(914) 238-9366

Jacob Lawrence: The Glory of Expression—This superb documentary about the life and work of a great American artist focuses on the epic narratives he painted to show the struggles of the African American people.

Public Media Home Video
5547 N. Ravenswood Ave., Chicago, IL 60640-1199
(800) 826-3456

Winslow Homer: The Nature of the Artist—This program guides viewers through Homer's accomplishments, from Civil War illustrations to powerful images of nature.

Louise Nevelson in Process—Nevelson creates two new sculptures on camera, providing a rare opportunity to share in the unfolding of her unique sculptural process.

ACROSS THE CURRICULUM

SOCIAL STUDIES

Example Artworks and Production Activities from *Art Express*, Grade 5

GEOGRAPHY

• understanding location	Showing Depth, p. 23 Using Linear Perspective, p. 25	Painting a Landscape, p. 91
• understanding place	*Gould's Inlet*, p. 23 *Harp of the Winds: View of the Seine*, p. 28 *A Really Swell Parade Down Main Street*, p. 38	*Squaw Creek Valley*, p. 77 Painting a Reflection, p. 29 Painting a Landscape, p. 91
• understanding human-environment interactions	*The Fall of the Cowboy*, pp. 14–15 Water Jar with Deer, p. 17 *Two Bison*, p. 16 *Summertime*, p. 28 Art Print 7: *The Wreck of the "Covenant"*	*Faraway*, pp. 74–75 *Trail Riders*, p. 76 Making a Diorama, p. 63 Painting a Landscape, p. 91
• understanding movement	*Skyward, My Friend*, p. 31 *The Marine Corps Memorial*, p. 45 *The Migration Series*, p. 44 *The Toboggan*, p. 79	*Nichols Canyon*, p. 78 *The Starry Night*, p. 90 Making a Wire Sculpture, p. 31 Showing Contrast and Movement, p. 79
• understanding regions	*The Lighthouse at Two Lights*, p. 18 *The Oxbow*, p. 22	Art Print 4: *Good Neighbors* *Her First Dance*, p. 122

HISTORY

• understanding time patterns and relationships among events	*Art Express Time Line*	
• identifying and using historical evidence	Art Print 2: *Whistling Jar* Water Jar with Deer, p. 17 *Two Bison*, p. 16 White earthenware urn, p. 118	Porcelain vase, p. 118 Copeland vase, p. 119 Painting the Past, p. 39 Sculpting a Slab Pot, p. 119
• understanding the importance of individuals and groups across time and place	*Franklin Delano Roosevelt*, pp. 34–35 Art Print 3: *Martin Luther King, Jr.* Portrait of George Washington, p. 36 Portrait of Mary McLeod Bethune, p. 36	*Liberty Enlightening the World*, p. 44 *The Marine Corps Memorial*, p. 45 Statues of American Heroes, pp. 46–47 *Spanish Pioneers of the Southwest*, pp. 100–101
• understanding the importance of events across time and place	Detail from Shalom Mayer Tower, p. 43 *Liberty Enlightening the World*, p. 44 *Tokyo Olympic Games*, p. 49	*Mexico City Olympic Games*, p. 49 Painting the Past, p. 39 Making a Photomontage, p. 45
• understanding the times in which people lived	*The Fall of the Cowboy*, pp. 14–15 *The Country School*, p. 39 *The Migration Series*, p. 44	*Spanish Pioneers of the Southwest*, pp. 100–101 Painting the Past, p. 39

• understanding origins, spread, and influence	Lincoln Cathedral, p. 109 White earthenware urn, p. 118	African Adobe Architecture, pp. 120–121 *Album Quilt*, p. 124
• understanding past and present	*Album Quilt*, p. 124 *Pioneer Plaza*, pp. 32–33 *The Country School*, p. 39	*The Migration Series*, p. 44 Painting the Past, p. 39 *St. Nicholas Magazine*, pp. 40–41
• comparing past and present	*Pioneer Plaza*, pp. 32–33 *The Country School*, p. 39	Painting the Past, p. 39 *St. Nicholas Magazine*, pp. 40–41

CIVICS AND GOVERNMENT

• understanding patriotic identity	*A Really Swell Parade Down Main Street*, p. 38 *Liberty Enlightening the World*, p. 44	*Uncle Sam Wants You*, p. 48 *The Living American Flag*, pp. 52–53
• understanding civic values	*Detroit Industry*, pp. 116–117	
• understanding democratic principles	*Liberty Enlightening the World*, p. 44	
• understanding rights and freedoms of citizens	*Art Print 3: Martin Luther King, Jr.*	*Liberty Enlightening the World*, p. 44
• understanding the responsibilities of citizens	*The Marine Corps Memorial*, p. 45	Lily Yeh, Philadelphia Project, pp. 66–67
• understanding types of government (democracy, monarchy, dictatorship)	*Franklin Delano Roosevelt*, pp. 34–35	Queen Mother head, p. 102

ECONOMICS

• understanding scarcity and economic choice	Two Bison, p. 16	*The Migration Series*, p. 44
• understanding markets and prices	*Peach Halves*, p. 50 *Chisholm Trail* facade, pp. 60–61	*Cadillac Ranch*, p. 71
• understanding productivity and economic growth	*California Crosswalk*, p. 64	*Electronic Superhighway*, pp. 112–113

CULTURE

• understanding ideas of shared humanity and unique identity	*Art Print 12: The Sunflowers Quilting Bee at Arles* African Adobe Architecture, pp. 120–121 *Her First Dance*, p. 122	Mask images, pp. 130–131 *Ballet folklórico*, pp. 132–133 Creating a Mixed-Media Mask, p. 131
• understanding social organizations and institutions	*The Country School*, p. 39 Tournament of Roses Parade, pp. 86–87	*Art Print 10: Sagrada Familia* Lincoln Cathedral, p. 108
• understanding means of thought and expression	*The Starry Night*, p. 90 Mask images, pp. 130–131	*Ballet folklórico*, pp. 132–133 Creating a Mixed-Media Mask, p. 131
• understanding human relationships	*Old Man and Youth in Landscape*, p. 97 *Art Print 4: Good Neighbors*	*Art Print 12: The Sunflowers Quilting Bee at Arles*

READING

READING THEMES — Example Artworks and Production Activities from *Art Express*, Grade 5

Theme		
Life Stories	*Art Print 4: Good Neighbors* *Art Print 12: The Sunflowers Quilting Bee at Arles*	*Her First Dance*, p. 122 Painting a Mural, p. 117
Homes and Shelter	*Victorian Interior*, p. 82 African Adobe Architecture, pp. 120–121	Making a Scale Drawing, p. 109 Making a Foil Model, p. 111
Interpreting the Past	*Art Print 2: Whistling Jar* Water Jar with Deer, p. 17	*Two Bison*, p. 16 Painting the Past, p. 39
Day/Night	*The Lighthouse at Two Lights*, p. 18	*The Starry Night*, p. 90
Tools	*Art Print 2: Whistling Jar* California Crosswalk, p. 64	Creating an Assemblage, p. 65 Sculpting with Two Materials, p. 103
Pioneers	*The Fall of the Cowboy*, pp. 14–15 Pioneer Plaza, pp. 32–33	*Spanish Pioneers of the Southwest*, pp. 100–101
Adventures	from *Dinotopia*, pp. 62–63	*Art Print 7: The Wreck of the "Covenant"*
Ecology	*Tree of Life*, pp. 20–21 *The Oxbow*, p. 22	*Trail Riders*, p. 76 *Squaw Creek Valley*, p. 77
Physical Fitness	*Tokyo Olympic Games*, p. 49 *Mexico City Olympic Games*, p. 49	*Ballet folklórico*, pp. 132–133
Environment	*Tree of Life*, pp. 20–21 *The Oxbow*, p. 22	*Trail Riders*, p. 76 *Squaw Creek Valley*, p. 77
Learning About Others	*Art Print 12: The Sunflowers Quilting Bee at Arles* *Detroit Industry*, pp. 116–117	*Album Quilt*, p. 124 Painting a Mural, p. 117
Coming Together	*Art Print 4: Good Neighbors* *Liberty Enlightening the World*, p. 44	*The Migration Series*, p. 44 Tournament of Roses Parade, pp. 86–87
Working Hands	*Art Print 12: The Sunflowers Quilting Bee at Arles*	*Detroit Industry*, pp. 116–117
Poetry	*Rhythme Colore*, pp. 88–89	*Broadway Boogie Woogie*, p. 88
Music for a Purpose	*Art Print 8: Instruments of Dixieland*	*Three Musicians*, pp. 92–93
Technology	*Toy Story*, p. 105 *Electronic Superhighway*, pp. 112–113	Making a Photogram, p. 99 Creating a Flip Book, p. 105
Dare to Dream	from *Dinotopia*, pp. 62–63	*Faraway*, pp. 74–75
Time	from *Dinotopia*, pp. 62–63	Painting the Past, p. 39
Measurement	*Spoonbridge and Cherry*, p. 70	Making a Scale Drawing, p. 29
Courage	*Franklin Delano Roosevelt*, pp. 34–35 *Art Print 3: Martin Luther King, Jr.* Portrait of Mary McLeod Bethune, p. 36	*The Marine Corps Memorial*, p. 45 *The Migration Series*, p. 44 Statues of American Heroes, pp. 46–47

Air, Weather, Climate	*Summertime,* p. 28	*Art Print 7: The Wreck of the "Covenant"*
Origins	Water Jar with Deer, p. 17 Two Bison, p. 16	Detail from Shalom Mayer Tower, p. 43 Weaving a Bookmark, p. 123
Families	*Her First Dance,* p. 122	*Album Quilt,* p. 124
Travel	Artrain, pp. 126–127	
Forces of Nature	*Art Print 7: The Wreck of the "Covenant"*	*The Starry Night,* p. 90
World Corners	Detail from Shalom Mayer Tower, p. 43 Lincoln Cathedral, p. 109	Taj Mahal, p. 108 The Grande Louvre, p. 110
Growing and Changing	*Electronic Superhighway,* pp. 112–113	Making a Foil Model, p. 111
Improving the World	*Art Print 4: Martin Luther King, Jr.* Portrait of Mary McLeod Bethune, p. 36	*Liberty Enlightening the World,* p. 44 Statues of American Heroes, pp. 46–47
Folk Art	Iowa sash, p. 123 *Album Quilt,* p. 124 Mask images, pp. 130–131 *Ballet folklórico,* pp. 132–133	Weaving a Bookmark, p. 123 Creating a Patchwork Wall Hanging, p. 125 Making Jewelry, p. 129 Creating a Mixed-Media Mask, p. 131
Conflict and Resolution	*The Marine Corps Memorial,* p. 45	*Confusion of Shapes,* p. 85

SCIENCE

SCIENCE CONCEPTS	Example Artworks and Production Activities from *Art Express,* Grade 5	
▶ **LIFE SCIENCE** **Interaction of Living Things**	*Tree of Life,* pp. 20–21 Horse and Rider, p. 30 *Skyward, My Friend,* p. 31	*Pioneer Plaza,* pp. 32–33 *Trail Riders,* p. 76 *Squaw Creek Valley,* p. 77
Humans Affect the Environment	*The Fall of the Cowboy,* pp. 14–15 Gould's Inlet, p. 23 *Pioneer Plaza,* pp. 32–33	*Surrounded Islands,* pp. 72–73 *Trail Riders,* p. 76
Inside the Natural World	*A Spray of a Plant,* p. 18	
▶ **EARTH/SPACE SCIENCE** **Seasons**	*Tree of Life,* pp. 20–21 *Summertime,* p. 28	*Art Print 7: The Wreck of the "Covenant"* Painting a Reflection, p. 29
Celestial Objects	*The Starry Night,* p. 90	
▶ **PHYSICAL SCIENCE** **Motion, Movement and Direction**	Horse and Rider, p. 30 *Skyward, My Friend,* p. 31 *Pioneer Plaza,* pp. 32–33 *The Marine Corps Memorial,* p. 45	*The Migration Series,* p. 44 *The Starry Night,* p. 90 *Ballet folklórico,* pp. 132–133

ELEMENTS AND PRINCIPLES

ELEMENTS	IMAGES	PRODUCTION ACTIVITIES
Line	Two Bison, p. 16 *Horse and Rider*, p. 30 *Skyward, My Friend*, p. 31 *The Migration Series*, p. 44 *Broadway Boogie Woogie*, p. 88 *The Starry Night*, p. 90	Making a Photomontage, p. 45 Painting a Landscape, p. 91
Shape	Water Jar with Deer, p. 17 Two Bison, p. 16 *A Spray of a Plant*, p. 18 *The Lighthouse at Two Lights*, p. 18 *Trail Riders*, p. 76 *Squaw Creek Valley*, p. 77 *Album Quilt*, p. 124 *Heartland*, p. 125	Drawing Organic and Geometric Shapes, p. 17 Drawing Everyday Forms, p. 19 Painting with Watercolors, p. 77 Making a Print with Visual Rhythm, p. 89 Create a Patchwork Wall Hanging, p. 125
Texture	Water Jar with Deer, p. 17 Two Bison, p. 16 *Untitled* (Thiebaud), p. 51 *Trail Riders*, p. 76 *Squaw Creek Valley*, p. 77 *Detroit Industry*, pp. 116–117	Drawing Organic and Geometric Shapes, p. 17 Creating an Impasto Painting, p. 51 Painting with Watercolors, p. 77 Painting a Mural, p. 117
Color	*A Really Swell Parade Down Main Street*, p. 38 *The Country School*, p. 39 *Plus Reversed*, p. 59 *Trail Riders*, p. 76 *Squaw Creek Valley*, p. 77 *Nichols Canyon*, p. 78 Student art, p. 84	Painting the Past, p. 39 Making a Photomontage, p. 45 Experimenting with Colors, p. 59 Painting with Watercolors, p. 77 Showing Contrast and Movement, p. 79 Making a Collage, p. 85 Making a Print with Visual Rhythm, p. 89
Value	*A Spray of a Plant*, p. 18 *The Lighthouse at Two Lights*, p. 18 Student artwork, p. 85	Drawing Everyday Forms, p. 19 Painting with Watercolors, p. 77 Making a Collage, p. 85 Making a Print with Visual Rhythm, p. 89
Form	*A Spray of a Plant*, p. 18 Student artwork, p. 19 The Grande Louvre, p. 110 The Solomon R. Guggenheim Museum, p. 111	Drawing Everyday Forms, p. 19 Making a Wire Sculpture, p. 31 Making a Foil Model, p. 111
Space	*The Oxbow*, p. 22 *Gould's Inlet*, p. 23 *Avenue of the Alyscamps*, p. 24 *Harp of the Winds: View of the Seine*, p. 28 *The Swimmer in the Pool*, p. 56 *Suspension*, p. 58 *Plus Reversed*, p. 59	Showing Depth, p. 23 Using Linear Perspective, p. 25 Painting a Reflection, p. 29 Drawing a Portrait, p. 37 Using Positive and Negative Space, p. 57

ELEMENTS AND PRINCIPLES

PRINCIPLES	IMAGES	PRODUCTION ACTIVITIES
Unity	*Untitled* (Thiebaud), p. 51 *Squaw Creek Valley*, p. 77 *Point Lobos, at Carmel, California*, p. 99 *A Child's Brilliant Smile*, p. 98 *Detroit Industry*, pp. 116–117	Making a Print with Visual Rhythm, p. 89 Making a Photogram, p. 99 Painting a Mural, p. 117 Weaving a Bookmark, p. 123
Emphasis	Portrait of George Washington, p. 36 Portrait of Mary McLeod Bethune, p. 36 *Uncle Sam Wants You*, p. 48	Drawing a Portrait, p. 37 Designing a Persuasive Poster, p. 49 Experimenting with Colors, p. 59 Creating a Mobile, p. 83
Balance	*Harp of the Winds: View of the Seine*, p. 28 *Victorian Interior*, p. 82 *Untitled* (Calder), p. 83	Painting a Reflection, p. 29 Creating a Mobile, p. 83
Variety	*Untitled* (Thiebaud), p. 51 Iowa sash, p. 123	
Pattern	*Rhythme Colore*, p. 88 *Broadway Boogie Woogie*, p. 88 Iowa sash, p. 123 Spanish corsage ornament, p. 128	Painting a Reflection, p. 29 Creating a Flip Book, p. 105 Weaving a Bookmark, p. 123 Making Jewelry, p. 129
Proportion	Portrait of George Washington, p. 36 Portrait of Mary McLeod Bethune, p. 36 *The Castle in the Pyrenees*, p. 68 *Niña con su pescado rojo*, p. 69	Showing Depth, p. 23 Drawing a Portrait, p. 37
Movement	*Horse and Rider*, p. 30 *Skyward, My Friend*, p. 31 *The Marine Corps Memorial*, p. 45 *The Migration Series*, p. 44 *The Swimmer in the Pool*, p. 56 *Pinocchio*, p. 104 *Toy Story*, p. 105	Making a Wire Sculpture, p. 31 Showing Contrast and Movement, p. 79 Creating a Flip Book, p. 105
Rhythm	*Rhythme Colore*, p. 88 *Broadway Boogie Woogie*, p. 88 *Atmospheric Effects II*, p. 89	Making a Print with Visual Rhythm, p. 89

ART MEDIA AND PROCESSES

MEDIA	IMAGES	
Sculpture	Art Print 2: *Whistling Jar* *Two Bison*, p. 16 *Horse and Rider*, p. 30 *Skyward, My Friend*, p. 31 *Pioneer Plaza*, pp. 32–33 *Franklin Delano Roosevelt*, pp. 34–35 Art Print 3: *Martin Luther King, Jr.*	*Liberty Enlightening the World*, p. 44 *The Marine Corps Memorial*, p. 45 Statues of American Heroes, pp. 46–47 *Spoonbridge and Cherry*, p. 70 Queen Mother head, p. 102 *Electronic Superhighway*, pp. 112–113 *Moses*, pp. 114–115
Painting	*The Fall of the Cowboy*, pp. 14–15 *The Lighthouse at Two Lights*, p. 18 *The Oxbow*, p. 22 *Gould's Inlet*, p. 23 *Avenue of the Alyscamps*, p. 24 *Harp of the Winds: View of the Seine*, p. 28 *Summertime*, p. 28 Art Print 4: *Good Neighbors* Portrait of George Washington, p. 36 Portrait of Mary McLeod Bethune, p. 36 *A Really Swell Parade Down Main Street*, p. 38 *The Country School*, p. 39 *The Migration Series*, p. 44 *Peach Halves*, p. 50 *Untitled* (Thiebaud), p. 51 *Clothed Automobile*, pp. 54–55 Art Print 5: *The Elephants* *Suspension*, p. 58	*Plus Reversed*, p. 59 from *Dinotopia*, pp. 62–63 *The Castle in the Pyrenees*, p. 68 *Niña con su pescado roja*, p. 69 Art Print 7: *The Wreck of the "Covenant"* *Faraway*, p. 74 Art Print 8: *Instruments of Dixieland* *Trail Riders*, p. 76 *Squaw Creek Valley*, p. 77 *Nichols Canyon*, p. 78 *Victorian Interior*, p. 82 *Confusion of Shapes*, p. 85 *Rhythme Colore*, p. 88 *Broadway Boogie Woogie*, p. 88 *Atmospheric Effects II*, p. 89 *The Starry Night*, p. 90 *Three Musicians*, pp. 92–93
Photography	*The Living American Flag*, pp. 52–53 *Basket of Light*, pp. 94–95 Art Print 9: *Eagle Knight*	*Point Lobos, at Carmel, California*, p. 99 *A Child's Brilliant Smile*, p. 98 *Spanish Pioneers of the Southwest*, pp. 100–101
Mixed-Media	*California Crosswalk*, p. 64 *Royal Tide IV*, p. 65 *Cadillac Ranch*, p. 71 Art Print 10: *Watts Towers* *Heartland*, p. 125	Mesopotamian chaplet of gold leaves, p. 128 Southwestern U.S. shell and turquoise necklace, p. 129 Spanish corsage ornament, p. 128 Mask images, pp. 130–131
Architecture	Art Print 10: *Sagrada Familia* Lincoln Cathedral, p. 108 Taj Mahal, p. 109	The Grande Louvre, p. 110 The Solomon R. Guggenheim Museum, p. 111 African Adobe Architecture, pp. 120–121
Animation	*Pinocchio*, p. 104	*Toy Story*, p. 105
Performing Arts	*Ballet folklórico*, pp. 132–133	

ART MEDIA AND PROCESSES

PROCESSES	PRODUCTION ACTIVITIES	
Drawing	Drawing Organic and Geometric Shapes, p. 17 Drawing Everyday Forms, p. 19 Using Linear Perspective, p. 25 Drawing a Portrait, p. 37	Showing Contrast and Movement, p. 79 Designing a Book Cover, p. 97 Creating a Flip Book, p. 105 Making a Scale Drawing, p. 109
Painting	Painting a Reflection, p. 29 Painting the Past, p. 39 Creating an Impasto Painting, p. 51 Making Impossible Paintings, p. 69	Painting with Watercolors, p. 77 Painting a Landscape, p. 91 Painting a Mural, p. 117
Printmaking	Making a Print with Visual Rhythm, p. 89	Making a Photogram, p. 99
Constructing and Modeling (3-D Forms, Sculpture)	Making a Wire Sculpture, p. 31 Making a Diorama, p. 63 Creating an Assemblage, p. 65 Making a Papier-Mâché Model, p. 71	Creating a Mobile, p. 83 Sculpting with Two Materials, p. 103 Making a Foil Model, p. 111 Sculpting a Slab Pot, p. 119
Manipulating Fibers	Weaving a Bookmark, p. 123	Creating a Patchwork Wall Hanging, p. 125
Mixed-Media	Making a Mosaic, p. 43 Making a Photomontage, p. 45 Making a Collage, p. 85	Making Jewelry, p. 129 Creating a Mixed-Media Mask, p. 131
Photography	Making a Photogram, p. 99	

ART PRINTS AND TRANSPARENCIES

- **Display the artworks,** and use them to introduce a particular type of art (for example, landscapes) before students begin a lesson on it.

- **Have students** point out in the artworks elements of art or principles of design that have just been discussed.

- **Discuss the theme** of an artwork as it relates to the theme of an image from the student book or the unit theme.

LESSONS	ART PRINTS	FINE ART TRANSPARENCIES
1 Images of Nature	Art Print 2: Whistling Jar	*Lion Resting, Turned to the Left* (theme, line) *Penning the Flock* (theme, shadows) *Ecuadorian Rain Forest* (theme)
2 Light and Shadow	Art Print 9: Eagle Knight	*Vesuvius in Eruption* (theme, highlighting) *Threshing Wheat* (theme, repetition)
3 The Illusion of Distance	Art Print 4: Good Neighbors	*Waiting for Dad* (theme, portrait) *Waterhole Northern Kenya* (theme, shape) *Threshing Wheat* (theme, perspective)
4 Into the Scene		*Belvedere* (theme, vanishing point)
5 Impressions of Light	Art Print 9: Eagle Knight	*Penning the Flock* (theme, shadows) *Waterhole Northern Kenya* (theme) *Threshing Wheat* (theme, horizontal symmetry)
6 Showing Movement	Art Print 1: The Stampede Art Print 3: Martin Luther King, Jr. Art Print 4: Good Neighbors Art Print 8: Instruments of Dixieland	*Song of Unity* (theme, storytelling) *Creation of North Mountain* (theme, storytelling) *Belvedere* (theme, lines) *Threshing Wheat* (theme, repetition)
7 Portraits	Art Print 3: Martin Luther King, Jr.	*The Last of England* (theme) *Beauty Rearranging Her Hair* (theme) *A colonial tobacco wharf* (theme)
8 Colors and Feelings	Art Print 4: Good Neighbors	*Creation of North Mountain* (theme)
9 Mosaics		
10 Images That Inspire	Art Print 3: Martin Luther King, Jr.	*Creation of North Mountain* (theme, symbols)
11 The Power of the Poster		
12 Pop Art		
13 Experimenting with Space		*Belvedere* (theme)
14 The Art of Illusion		*Song of Unity* (theme, mural) *Belvedere* (theme, line)
15 Imaginary Worlds	Art Print 5: The Elephants	*Belvedere* (theme)

ART PRINTS AND TRANSPARENCIES

LESSONS	ART PRINTS	FINE ART TRANSPARENCIES
16 Assembled Art	Art Print 6: Watts Towers	
17 Double Takes	Art Print 5: The Elephants	
18 Outdoor Spectacles	Art Print 6: Watts Towers	
19 Feelings of Harmony	Art Print 7: The Wreck of the "Covenant"	*Waiting for Dad* (theme) *Penning the Flock* (theme, repetition) *Threshing Wheat* (theme, repetition)
20 A Sense of Excitement	Art Print 8: Instruments of Dixieland	*Song of Unity* (theme) *Vesuvius in Eruption* (theme)
21 In Balance		*Creation of North Mountain* (theme) *Waterhole Northern Kenya* (theme)
22 Colors in Conflict		
23 Visual Rhythms	Art Print 8: Instruments of Dixieland	
24 Lines of Expression		*The Last of England* (theme, portrait) *Vesuvius in Eruption* (theme)
25 Book Art		
26 Is Photography Art?	Art Print 9: Eagle Knight	
27 Sculptures Through Time	Art Print 3: Martin Luther King, Jr.	
28 The World of Animation		
29 Celebrations in Stone	Art Print 10: Sagrada Familia	*The Russian Museum* (theme) *Safed, Israel* (theme)
30 Unusual Architecture	Art Print 10: Sagrada Familia	*The Russian Museum* (theme) *Safed, Israel* (theme)
31 Stories on Walls	Art Print 11: Zechariah	*Song of Unity* (theme, mural) *Beauty Rearranging Her Hair* (theme, movement)
32 Centuries in Clay	Art Print 2: Whistling Jar	
33 A Timeless Art	Art Print 12: The Sunflowers Quilting Bee at Arles	*Beauty Rearranging Her Hair* (theme)
34 Patchwork Art	Art Print 12: The Sunflowers Quilting Bee at Arles	
35 Artwork to Wear		
36 Faces from Folk Art		

ACROSS THE CURRICULUM R83

SCOPE & SEQUENCE

Awareness and sensitivity to natural and human-made environments

	GR 1	GR 2	GR 3	GR 4	GR 5
Art Elements					
Line					
Discover and identify line as an element of art	■	■	■	■	■
Examine and explore line in art	■	■	■	■	■
curved, straight; vertical, horizontal	■	■	■	■	■
outline; expressive		■	■	■	■
continuous; diagonal		■	■	■	■
action; implied; contour			■	■	■
hatch, crosshatch; sketched; mechanical; gesture				■	■
Shape					
Discover and identify shape as an element of art	■	■	■	■	■
Recognize shape as two-dimensional	■	■	■	■	■
Examine and explore shape in art	■	■	■	■	■
geometric; organic; abstract; repeated; symbols/letters	■	■	■	■	■
symmetrical, asymmetrical		■	■	■	■
Color					
Discover and identify color as an element of art	■	■	■	■	■
Mix primary colors to achieve secondary colors	■	■	■	■	■
Examine and explore color in art	■	■	■	■	■
primary, secondary; warm, cool; value; shades, tints	■	■	■	■	■
intermediate		■	■	■	■
monochromatic			■		■
complementary; analogous; natural; arbitrary; harmonious			■	■	■
Space					
Discover and identify space as an element of art	■	■	■	■	■
Examine and explore space in art	■	■	■	■	■
foreground, background; relative size	■	■	■	■	■
two-dimensional; overlapping; proportion		■	■	■	■
illusion of depth			■	■	■
middle ground; points of view				■	■
positive, negative; three-dimensional; atmospheric perspective; linear perspective; vanishing point				■	■
Value					
Discover and identify value as an element of art	■	■	■	■	■
Examine and explore value in art	■	■	■	■	■
dark, light	■	■	■	■	■
brightness		■	■	■	■
shadows; value scales; color gradations; shades, tints		■	■	■	■
contrast				■	■
Texture					
Discover and identify texture as an element of art	■	■	■	■	■
Recognize texture as the look (visual-sight or simulated) and feel (tactile) of a surface and distinguish between visual and tactile textures	■	■	■	■	■
Examine and explore texture in art	■	■	■	■	■
visual, tactile; repeated lines, shapes, and spaces	■	■	■	■	■

■ Modeling/Instruction/Application

ART EXPRESS

	GR 1	GR 2	GR 3	GR 4	GR 5
Form					
Discover and identify form as an element of art	■	■	■	■	■
Recognize form as three-dimensional	■	■	■	■	■
Examine and explore form in art (geometric; organic; abstract)	■	■	■	■	■
Design Principles (Formal Structure)					
Balance					
Understand balance as a principle of design	■	■	■	■	■
Understand balance as an arrangement that achieves equilibrium in the eyes of the viewer		■	■	■	■
Examine and explore balance in art		■	■	■	■
symmetrical, asymmetrical; midline		■	■	■	■
physical symmetry; visual symmetry		■	■	■	■
radial symmetry		■		■	■
horizontal symmetry		■	■	■	■
Movement					
Understand movement as a principle of design		■	■	■	■
Examine and explore movement on two-dimensional surface		■	■	■	■
Examine and explore movement in three-dimensional space				■	■
Pattern/Repetition					
Understand pattern as a principle of design	■	■	■	■	■
Recognize art element or unit being repeated to create pattern	■	■	■	■	■
Examine and explore pattern in art	■	■	■	■	■
Rhythm					
Understand rhythm as a principle of design		■	■	■	■
Understand that rhythm is achieved by repeating elements in artwork		■	■	■	■
Examine and explore rhythm in art (repetition; movement)		■	■	■	■
Variety and Unity					
Understand variety and unity as principles of design	■	■	■	■	■
Examine and explore variety in art (variety in line, color, texture, shape)	■	■	■	■	■
Examine and explore unity in art (organization of details; use of repetition)	■	■	■	■	■
Recognize the difference between variety and unity	■	■	■	■	■
Emphasis					
Understand emphasis as a principle of design	■	■	■	■	■
Identify emphasis by indicating what parts of an artwork are most important (where the accent or stress is placed)	■	■	■	■	■
Examine and explore emphasis in art (center of interest; details; color)	■	■	■	■	■
Proportion					
Understand proportion as a principle of design		■	■	■	■
Understand proportion as the size relationship between parts of a composition to each other and to the whole		■	■	■	■
Recognize that proportion can indicate distance (large shapes are close-up; small shapes are far away)		■	■	■	■
Examine and explore proportion in art		■	■	■	■
proportion of the human face and figure				■	■
foreshortening					■

■ Modeling/Instruction/Application

	GR 1	GR 2	GR 3	GR 4	GR 5
Creative expression and visual communication					
Safety in Art Process					
Display an awareness of and respect for art tools and materials	■	■	■	■	■
Demonstrate the proper care for and use of tools, materials, and art area	■	■	■	■	■
Follow art safety rules and procedures	■	■	■	■	■
Develop and Apply Art Skills and Concepts					
Apply elements (line, shape, color, space, value, texture, form) in artwork using a variety of art tools, materials, and techniques	■	■	■	■	■
Apply design principles, or formal structure, (balance, movement, emphasis, pattern/repetition, proportion, rhythm, unity and variety) to artwork using a variety of art tools, materials, and techniques	■	■	■	■	■
Display a variety of expressive qualities or moods, meanings, symbols, and themes in artworks	■	■	■	■	■
Develop technical skill with various tools, materials, media, processes, and techniques when creating artwork	■	■	■	■	■
Produce art that reflects knowledge of a variety of cultures	■	■	■	■	■
Explore making art forms that serve a function in daily life	■	■	■	■	■
Use creative thinking and problem-solving skills when creating original art	■	■	■	■	■
Use imagination skills when creating original art	■	■	■	■	■
Use observation and memory skills when creating original art	■	■	■	■	■
Use various media, techniques, tools, materials, and processes to communicate and express ideas, experiences, stories, feelings, and values	■	■	■	■	■
Understanding and appreciation of self and others through historical and cultural heritage					
Understanding the Visual Arts in Relation to History and Cultures					
Historical Background					
Understand that art reflects values, beliefs, expressions, or experiences in a historical context	■	■	■	■	■
Evaluate critically art from various historical eras	■	■	■	■	■
Recognize a variety of artworks as being from various historical eras		■	■	■	■
Recognize that art reflects values	■	■	■	■	■
Investigate major themes in historical/contemporary eras			■	■	■
Recognize or describe art as a visual record of humankind	■	■	■	■	■
Recognize that media, tools, materials, and processes available to artists have changed through history	■	■	■	■	■
Cultural Influences					
Understand that art reflects values, beliefs, expressions, or experiences in a cultural context	■	■	■	■	■
Evaluate critically art from various cultures	■	■	■	■	■
Recognize a variety of artworks as being from various cultures	■	■	■	■	■
Identify the characteristics of art from other cultures, and value the images, symbols, and themes distinguishing a specific culture	■	■	■	■	■
Determine ways in which artworks reflect or express cultural themes	■	■	■	■	■
Acknowledge and appreciate the artistic contributions of various ethnic groups in our culture	■	■	■	■	■
Relate visual arts to theater, music, and dance and to history, society, and culture	■	■	■	■	■
Artists and Artistic Styles					
Identify and discuss the artworks of a particular artist	■	■	■	■	■
Value the diverse contributions of artists	■	■	■	■	■
Recognize various artistic styles	■	■	■	■	■
Recognize artists' roles in history and society (to inform, define, interpret, enlighten, entertain; to raise questions and cause reflection; to provide a visual record of humankind; to communicate values, beliefs, feelings; to reveal social and political customs)	■	■	■	■	■
Recognize that artists are influenced by artists of the past	■	■	■	■	■
Learn that art is universal, made by people in all cultures throughout history	■	■	■	■	■

▓ Modeling/Instruction/Application

	GR 1	GR 2	GR 3	GR 4	GR 5
Understanding the Visual Arts in Relation to the Environment and Everyday Lives					
Art in the Environment					
Develop an awareness of art in natural and human-made environments	■	■	■	■	■
Respond to art elements and design principles (formal structure) found in natural and human-made environments	■	■	■	■	■
Identify art that reflects, celebrates, or communicates sensitivity to natural and human-made environments	■	■	■	■	■
Art in the Community					
Recognize art as an important part of daily life	■	■	■	■	■
Recognize that art can contribute to the quality of daily life	■	■	■	■	■
Recognize the function of visual arts in the family, the neighborhood, and the community	■	■	■	■	■
Develop awareness of the historical relationship between art and daily life	■	■	■	■	■
Recognize the importance of the visual arts in the workplace and explore associated art careers	■	■	■	■	■
Visual discrimination and judgment					
Know about the process of making informed judgments about art	■	■	■	■	■
Analyze art elements (sensory qualities) in art	■	■	■	■	■
Analyze media, processes, techniques (technical qualities) in art	■	■	■	■	■
Analyze design principles (formal structure) in art	■	■	■	■	■
Analyze and interpret moods, meanings, symbolism, themes (expressive qualities) in art	■	■	■	■	■
View and respond to original art and reproductions	■	■	■	■	■
View and respond to art by self and other students	■	■	■	■	■
Express personal preferences	■	■	■	■	■
Use art vocabulary in discussions	■	■	■	■	■
Recognize characteristics that make artworks similar, different	■	■	■	■	■
Distinguish characteristics of style in art	■	■	■	■	■
Respond to evidence of skill and craftsmanship found in art	■	■	■	■	■
Respect the differences in others' responses to and perceptions of art	■	■	■	■	■
Understand the difference between judging a work and expressing a personal preference			■	■	■
Recognize that the aim of criticism is to clarify the meaning of and to share discoveries about art			■	■	■
Connections between and among the arts and other content areas					
Discover and identify connections between the visual arts and dance, music, theater, and other disciplines	■	■	■	■	■
Analyze and interpret similarities and differences between characteristics of the visual arts and other art disciplines	■	■	■	■	■
Develop concepts about self, human relationships, and the environment using elements of visual arts, dance, music, and theater	■	■	■	■	■
Examine a central theme, issue, problem, topic, or experience through the visual and performing arts	■	■	■	■	■
Construct meaning and express ideas, feelings, experiences, and responses through connections to the other arts disciplines as well as other core subjects	■	■	■	■	■
Apply arts disciplines, techniques, and processes to communicate an original or interpretative work	■	■	■	■	■
Analyze, make informed judgments, and pursue meaning in the arts	■	■	■	■	■

▨ Modeling/Instruction/Application

INDEX

A

Abstract, 42–43
Across the Curriculum
  health, 40, 49, 103, 131
  language arts, 17, 21, 25, 29, 31, 37, 43, 45, 49, 51, 65, 69, 85, 91, 97, 99, 101, 103, 105, 109, 119, 125
  mathematics, 23, 25, 43, 59, 83, 106, 111, 125, 127
  performing arts
    dance, 52, 57, 81, 92, 117, 123
    music, 27, 32, 39, 67, 77, 79, 89, 132
    theater, 19, 23, 41, 47, 61, 72, 107, 111, 112, 131
  physical education, 79
  reading, 63, 71, 83, 87, 121, 123, R76
  science, 17, 19, 20, 29, 31, 46, 59, 63, 80, 85, 86, 89, 91, 119, 129, R77
  social studies, 26, 37, 39, 45, 51, 57, 60, 65, 66, 69, 71, 77, 97, 99, 100, 105, 109, 117, 120, 126, 129, R74–R75
Activities
  See Production activities.
Adobe, 120–121
Aesthetics
  analysis, 41, 73, 77
  compare/contrast, 77, 81, 107, 110, 121
  description, 87
  draw conclusions, 16, 98, 128
  evaluation, 47, 64
  hypothesize, 58, 88, 127
  interpretation, 22, 30, 81, 116
  make judgments, 50, 73, 101, 113
  make predictions, 71
  personal response, 24, 28, 36, 57, 62, 69, 70, 76, 82, 105, 111, 127, 130, 133
  reflection, 58
  speculate, 61
  synthesize, 27, 51
Analogous colors, 76, 77, 81, 123

Ancona, George, 100–101
Animation, 104–105, 106–107
Anuskiewicz, Richard
  about, 58
  Plus Reversed, 59
Arbitrary colors, 84–85
Arch, 108
Architecture, 108–109, 110–111, 120–121
Art criticism
  analysis, 16, 24, 33, 38, 39, 44, 47, 48, 53, 63, 67, 79, 85, 96, 98, 104, 116, 124, 133
  application, 25, 78, 93, 124
  compare/contrast, 19, 23, 29, 33, 36, 43, 45, 56, 62, 68, 83, 84, 87, 93, 109, 113, 117, 119, 123, 131
  description, 19, 28, 30, 48, 64, 78, 84, 89
  draw conclusions, 53, 59, 76, 90, 121
  evaluation, 33, 49, 93, 101
  hypothesize, 91, 118
  interpretation, 21, 37, 82, 110
  make judgments, 22, 41, 102, 108, 123, 133
  make predictions, 67
  problem solving, 56
  summarize, 17
  synthesize, 18, 25, 65, 88, 99, 113
Art and Culture
  African Adobe Architecture, 120–121
  Magazine Art, 40–41
Art history
  analysis, 53, 118
  compare/contrast, 70
  draw conclusions, 96, 97
  generalize, 39, 125
  hypothesize, 68, 102, 104, 108, 122
  interpretation, 44
  reflection, 50, 122
  speculate, 128
  synthesize, 131
  See also Share Art History

Art and Literature
  The Lively Art of David Diaz, 80–81
  The Natural Art of Barbara Bash, 20–21
  The Photographic Art of George Ancona, 100–101
Art Prints, 14B, 34B, 54B, 74B, 94B, 114B, R82, R83
Artrain, 126–127
Art styles and movements
  abstract, 42–43
  Cubism, 92
  Expressionism, 90
  Impressionism, 28–29
  Op Art, 58
  Pop Art, 50–51
Assemblage, 64–65, R21
Assessment, R26–R31
  checklists, R27–R28
  informal assessment, 17, 19, 23, 25, 29, 31, 37, 39, 43, 45, 49, 51, 57, 59, 63, 65, 69, 71, 77, 79, 83, 85, 89, 91, 97, 99, 103, 105, 109, 111, 117, 119, 123, 125, 129, 131
  portfolios, 33, 53, 73, 93, 113, 133
  student self-assessment, R29–R30
  See also Review.
Asymmetrical balance, 82
Atmospheric perspective, 22

B

Background, 22–23
Balance, 82–83
Ballet folklórico, 132–133
Bartholdi, Frédéric-Auguste
  about, 44
  Liberty Enlightening the World, 44
Bash, Barbara
  about, 20
  The Tree of Life: The World of the

African Baobab, 20–21
Benton, Thomas Hart
   about, 76
   Trail Riders, 76
Bibliography, R69–R73
Book design, 96
   The Book of Lindisfarne, 96
   illuminated page from the *Haggadah,* 96
Brushstroke, 28–29
Buonarroti, Michelangelo
   See Michelangelo.
Burke, Selma
   about, 35
   Franklin Delano Roosevelt, 34–35

C

Calder, Alexander
   about, 30, 82
   Horse and Rider, 30
   Untitled, 83
Careers in Art
   Computer Animator, 106–107
   Set Designer, 26–27
Cassatt, Mary
   about, 28
   Summertime, 28
Celebration Art
   Tournament of Roses Parade, 86–87
Center of interest, 98–99, 113
Ceramics
   porcelain, 118
   slip, 118–119
Challenge, 30, 36, 42, 58, 68, 102, 110, 116, 118, 128, R34
Christo and Jeanne-Claude
   about, 72
   Surrounded Islands, 72–73
Cityscape, 91
Clay, 119
Cole, Thomas
   about, 22
   The Oxbow, 22
Collage, 56–57, 84–85

Color
   advancing, 78
   analogous, 76
   arbitrary, 84
   complementary, 58, 78–79
   contrast, 78
   intermediate, 58
   primary, 58
   receding, 78
   secondary, 58
   shades, 77
   tints, 77
   value, 18
   warm/cool, 38–39, 62
Community Art
   The Artrain, 126–127
   Heroic Statues, 46–47
   The Power of Art, 66–67
Complementary colors, 58, 78–79
Computers, 104–105, 106–107
Constructing and modeling three-dimensional forms, 31, 63, 65, 71, 83, 103, 111, 119, 131
Contrast, 78–79
Cool colors, 38–39
Cooperative learning, 26–27, 32, 41, 47, 52, 61, 67, 72, 86, 87, 92, 107, 112, 120, 121, 126, 127, 132
Cross-Curricular
   See Across the Curriculum.
Cubism, 92

D

Dalí, Salvador
   about, 55
   Clothed Automobile, 54–55
Dance, 52, 57, 81, 92, 117, 123, 132–133
Da Vinci, Leonardo
   about, 18
   A Spray of a Plant, 18
Delaunay, Sonia Terk
   about, 88
   Rhythme Colore, 88

Depth, 22–23
   See also Perspective.
Designing, 49, 97
De Weldon, Felix W.
   about, *44*
   The Marine Corps Memorial, 45
Diagonal lines, 30
Diaz, David, 80–81
Diorama, 63
Distance, illusion of, 22–23
Drama
   See Theater.
Drawing, 17, 19, 25, 37, 79, 109, R18–R19
   See also Production activities.

E

Elements of art
   color, 19, 40–41, 58–59, 62, 77–79, 84–85
   form, 18
   line, 16–17, 30–31, 79, 90–91
   shape, 16–17, 76–77, 124
   space, 56–57
   texture, 16, 50–51
   value, 19
   See also Perspective.
Elements and principles
   See Elements of art, Principles of design.
Emphasis, 36
English as a Second Language
   See Students Acquiring English.
Evaluating art, 10–11, 32–33, 52–53, 72–73, 92–93, 112–113, 132–133
Everyday Art
   Can You Believe Your Eyes? 60–61
Expressive, 91
Extra Support, 16, 18, 22, 24, 48, 56, 62, 64, 70, 76, 84, 88, 90, 96, 98, 122, R36

F

Flagg, James Montgomery
   about, 48
   Uncle Sam Wants You, 48
Flip book, 105
Focus, 98

Folk artists, 130–131
Foreground, 22–23
Foreshortened, 48
Form, 18, 110
Frame, 98–99
Frames, 104–105

G

Galla Placidia, 42
Games, 33, 53, 73, 93, 113, 133
Garduño, Flor
    about, 95
    Basket of Light, 94–95
Geometric shapes, 16–17
Gifted and talented students, 30, 36, 42, 58, 68, 102, 110, 116, 118, 128, R34
Grez, Lilliana Wilson
    about, 68
    Niña con su pescado rojo, 69
Gurney, James
    about, 62
    Dinotopia, 62
Gutman, Nachum
    about, 42
    mural in Shalom Mayer Tower, Israel, 42
Guzy, Carol
    about, 98
    A Child's Brilliant Smile, 98

H

Harmony, 74–75, 76–77, 93
Hatching, 18–19
Health
    See Across the Curriculum.
Highlighting, 19
Hockney, David
    about, 78
    Nichols Canyon, 78
Home and community design, 43, 49, 125
    Community Art, 46–47, 66–67, 126–127
    See also Production activities.

Home connection
    See Letters to Families, School-Home Connection.
Homer, Winslow
    about, 38
    The Country School, 39
Hopper, Edward
    about, 18
    The Lighthouse at Two Lights, 18
Horizon, 24–25
Horizontal symmetry, 29

I

Illuminated pages, 96–97
Illusions, 22–23, 32–33, 58–59, 60–61
Impasto painting, 50–51
Impressionists, 28–29
Incising, 118–119
Informal assessment
    See Assessment.
Internet research, 14D, 34D, 54D, 74D, 94D, 114D, R68
In the Studio
    See Production activities.

J

Jewelry, 128–129
Just for Fun, 33, 53, 73, 93, 113, 133

K

Keeping a Sketchbook, 12–13
Kamekura, Yusaku
    about, 48
    Tokyo Olympic Games, 49

L

Landscape, 90–91
Lawrence, Jacob
    about, 44
    The Migration Series, 44
Letters to Families, R44–R49
Line, 16–17, 30–31, 78–79, 90–91
Linear perspective, 24–25
Literature
    Art and Literature, 20–21, 80–81, 100–101
    Keeping a Sketchbook, 12–13
    Literature Connection, 15, 35, 55, 75, 95, 115
    Suggested Reading, 14D, 34D, 54D, 74D, 94D, 114D
Looking at Art, 10–11

M

Magazine art, 40–41
Magritte, René
    about, 68
    The Castle in the Pyrenees, 68
Manipulating fibers, 123, 125
    See also Production activities.
Marsh 3, Stanley, and the Ant Farm
    about, 70
    Cadillac Ranch, 71
Martin, Homer Dodge
    about, 28
    Harp of the Winds: View of the Seine, 28
Masks, 130–131
Material, 70–71, 102–103
Materials List, R66–R68
Mathematics
    See Across the Curriculum.
Matisse, Henri
    about, 56, 78
    The Swimmer in the Pool, 56
    The Toboggan, 79
McClung, Florence
    about, 76
    Squaw Creek Valley, 77

Meeting Individual Needs
  challenge, 30, 36, 42, 58, 68, 102, 110, 116, 118, 128, R34
  extra support, 16, 18, 22, 24, 48, 56, 62, 64, 70, 76, 84, 88, 90, 96, 98, 122, R36
  special-needs students, R37
  stages of artistic development, R32–R33
  students acquiring English, 28, 38, 44, 50, 78, 82, 104, 108, 124, 130, R35
Michelangelo
  about, 115
  Moses, 114–115
Middle ground, 22–23
Minarets, 109
Mixed-media, 131
Mobile, 82–83
Model, 37, 71, 111
Mole, Arthur
  about, 52
  The Living American Flag, 52–53
Mondrian, Piet
  about, 82, 88
  Broadway Boogie Woogie, 88
Mood, 38
Mosaics, 42–43
Movement, 30–31, 33, 78–79, 80–81
Mural, 42, 60–61, 66–67, 116–117
Music, 32, 39, 77, 79, 89, 133

N

Naranjo, Michael
  about, 30
  Skyward, My Friend, 31
Negative space, 56–57
Nevelson, Louise
  about, 64
  Royal Tide IV, 65
Nonrepresentational art, 42–43, 88–89

O

Oldenburg, Claes
  about, 70
  Spoonbridge and Cherry, 70
Ong, Diana
  about, 84
  Confusion of Shapes, 84
Op Art, 58
Optical illusion, 58–59, 60–61
Organic shape, 16–17
Ornamentation, 128
Outterbridge, John
  about, 64
  California Crosswalk, 64
Overlapping, 23

P

Paik, Nam June
  about, 112
  Electronic Superhighway, 112–113
Painting, 29, 39, 51, 69, 77, 91, 117, R19–R20
  See also Techniques.
Papier-mâché, 71, R24
Patchwork, 124–125
Pattern, 88–89, 93, 124–125
  geometric, 124–125
Peale, Charles Willson
  Staircase Group, 60–61
Pei, I. M., 110
Performing arts
  See Dance, Music, Theater.
Performing Arts Handbook, using, 14B, 34B, 54B, 74B, 94B, 114B
Perspective, 22–23, 24–25
Photogram, 99
Photography, 45, 52–53, 98–99, 100–101
Photomontage, 45
Picasso, Pablo
  about, 92
  Three Musicians, 92–93
Pinkney, Jerry, 12

Pippin, Horace
  about, 82
  Victorian Interior, 82
Pop Art, 50–51
Porcelain, 118
Portfolios, 33, 53, 73, 93, 113, 133
Portraits, 36–37
Pose, 36–37
Positive space, 56–57
Posters, 48–49
Principles of design
  balance, 82–83, 93
  emphasis, 36
  movement and rhythm, 30–31, 33, 78–81, 88–89, 93, 117
  pattern, 88–89, 93
  proportion, 37, 68
  unity, 50, 64
  variety, 50
Printmaking, 88–89, R20–R21
Production
  analysis, 21, 27, 57, 61, 90, 103
  application, 18, 31, 37, 38, 59, 71, 79, 85, 105, 107, 125
  compare/contrast, 42, 89
  description, 33, 42, 53, 73, 93, 113, 133
  evaluation, 29
  generate alternatives, 23
  problem solving, 17, 31, 43, 49, 51, 63, 83, 91, 97, 99, 103, 109, 111, 117, 119, 129
  reflection, 45, 65, 69
  speculation, 130
  synthesize, 129
Production activities
  Creating a Flip Book, 105
  Creating a Mixed-Media Mask, 131
  Creating a Mobile, 83
  Creating an Assemblage, 65
  Creating an Impasto Painting, 51
  Creating a Patchwork Wall Hanging, 125
  Designing a Book Cover, 97
  Designing a Persuasive Poster, 49
  Drawing a Portrait, 37
  Drawing Everyday Forms, 19

Drawing Organic and Geometric Shapes, 17
Experimenting with Colors, 59
Making a Collage, 85
Making a Diorama, 63
Making a Foil Model, 111
Making a Mosaic, 43
Making a Papier-Mâché Model, 71
Making a Photogram, 99
Making a Photomontage, 45
Making a Print with Visual Rhythm, 89
Making a Scale Drawing, 109
Making a Wire Sculpture, 31
Making Impossible Paintings, 69
Making Jewelry, 129
Painting a Landscape, 91
Painting a Mural, 117
Painting a Reflection, 29
Painting the Past, 39
Painting with Watercolors, 77
Sculpting a Slab Pot, 119
Sculpting with Two Materials, 103
Showing Contrast and Movement, 79
Showing Depth, 23
Using Linear Perspective, 25
Using Positive and Negative Space, 57
Weaving a Bookmark, 123
Proportion, 37, 68

Q

Quick activities, 15, 17, 19, 23, 25, 29, 31, 35, 37, 39, 43, 45, 49, 51, 55, 57, 59, 63, 65, 69, 71, 75, 77, 79, 83, 85, 89, 91, 95, 97, 99, 103, 105, 109, 111, 115, 117, 119, 123, 125, 129, 131
Quilts, 124–125

R

Reading
See Across the Curriculum, Literature.
Ream, Vinnie, 46

Remington, Frederic
about, 15
The Fall of the Cowboy, 14–15
Research activities, 31, 37, 45, 49, 79, 85, 89, 91, 97, 99, 105, 109, 117, 119, 123, 125, 129, 131
Response Cards, R56–R65
using, 14B, 34B, 54B, 74B, 94B, 114B
Review, 32–33, 52–53, 72–73, 92–93, 112–113, 132–133
Reyneau, Betsy Graves
about, 36
Mary McLeod Bethune, 36
Rhythm, 88–89, 92–93, 117
Riley, Bridget
about, 58
Suspension, 58
Rivera, Diego
about, 116
Detroit Industry, 116–117

S

Safety, 134–135
Scale, 45, 70
Scale drawing, 108–109
Schapiro, Miriam
about, 124
Heartland, 125
School-Home Connections, R50–R55
using, 14D, 34D, 54D, 74D, 94D, 114D
Science
See Across the Curriculum.
Scott, Jane Wooster
about, 38
A Really Swell Parade Down Main Street, 38
Sculpture, 16–17, 30–31, 32–33, 44–47, 64–65, 70–71, 102–103, 114–115, R21–R23
Seasonal activities, R38–R43
Shades, 77
Shadows, 18–19
Shape, 16–17, 76–77

Share Art History, 16, 18, 20, 22, 24, 28, 30, 36, 38, 40, 42, 44, 46, 48, 50, 56, 58, 60, 62, 64, 68, 70, 76, 78, 80, 82, 84, 88, 90, 96, 98, 100, 102, 108, 110, 116, 118, 122, 124, 128, 130
Share Career Information, 26, 106
Share Cultural Background, 66, 86, 120, 126
Sketch, 12–13
Slab method, 119
Slip, 118–119
Social studies
See Across the Curriculum.
Space, 56–57
See also Perspective.
Spire, 108
Statues, 44–45, 46–47
Stevens, John, 126
Storytelling, 42, 107, 116–117
Stuart, Gilbert
about, 36
George Washington, 36
Students Acquiring English, 28, 38, 44, 50, 78, 82, 104, 108, 124, 130, R35
Summers, Robert
about, 32
Pioneer Plaza, 32–33
Surrealism, 68–69
Symbols, 36, 44, 53
Symmetry, 29, 82–83, 97

T

Techniques, R17–R25
See also Production activities.
Tesserae, 42–43
Texture, 16, 50–51
Theater, 19, 23, 26–27, 111, 131
Theme, 116
Thiebaud, Wayne
about, 50
Untitled, 51
Thomas, Alma Woodsey
about, 88
Atmospheric Effects II, 89

Three-dimensional, 18–19
   See also Perspective, Sculpture.
Time Line, 14, 34, 54, 74, 94, 114
Tints, 77
Trompe l'oeil, 60
Two-dimensional, 18–19
Type, 48

U

Unit planning charts, 14C–14D, 34C–34D, 54C–54D, 74C–74D, 94C–94D, 114C–114D
Unity, 50, 64

V

Value, 18–19
van Bruggen, Coosje
   about, 70
   Spoonbridge and Cherry, 70
Van Der Zee, James, 100
Van Gogh, Vincent
   about, 24, 90
   Avenue of the Alyscamps, 24
   The Starry Night, 90

Vanishing point, 24–25
Variety, 50
Velarde, Pablita
   about, 122
   Her First Dance, 122
Visual rhythm, 88

W

Warhol, Andy
   about, 50
   Peach Halves, 50
Warm colors, 38–39, 62
Washington, Anna Belle Lee
   about, 22
   Gould's Inlet, 23
Washington, Leah
   about, 98
   Point Lobos, at Carmel, California, 99
Watercolor, 77
Weaving, 122–123, R25
Wright, Frank Lloyd, 110
Wyeth, Andrew
   about, 75
   Faraway, 74, 75

Wyman, Lance
   about, 48
   Mexico City Olympic Games, 49

Y

Yeh, Lily
   about, 66
   Tree of Life mural, 66–67